THE OTHER SIDE OF THE LANTERN

THE GARDEN OF THE UNFORGOTTEN.

THE OTHER SIDE OF THE LANTERN

AN ACCOUNT OF A COMMONPLACE TOUR ROUND THE WORLD

FREDERICK TREVES

ILLUSTRATED

GYAN

Published by

Gyan Publishing House
5, Ansari Road
Daryaganj, New Delhi-110002
Phone: 011-47034999, 9811692060
E-mail: books@gyanbooks.com

Distribution Network
gyanbooks.com
India, USA, Canada, UK, Australia, France

ISBN : 978-81-212-3865-6 (PB)

2nd Impression 2020

Printed at: Gyan Press, Delhi.

The Other Side of the Lantern
Author: Frederick Treves

THE OTHER SIDE OF THE LANTERN

AN ACCOUNT OF A COMMONPLACE TOUR ROUND THE WORLD

BY

SIR FREDERICK TREVES, BART.

G.C.V.O., C.B., LL.D.

Sergeant-Surgeon to H.M. the King. Surgeon-in-Ordinary to H.R.H. the Prince of Wales
Author of "The Tale of a Field Hospital"

WITH FORTY ILLUSTRATIONS FROM
PHOTOGRAPHS BY THE AUTHOR

POPULAR EDITION

CASSELL AND COMPANY, LIMITED
LONDON, PARIS, NEW YORK, TORONTO AND MELBOURNE. MCMVIII

The half-tone blocks in this work were made by
Messrs. André and Sleigh, Limited, of
Bushey, Herts.

First Edition *January 1905.*
Reprinted January, Feb. 1 and 20, March, May and October 1905, 1906.
Popular Edition, *July 1906. Reprinted November 1906, 1907, 1908.*

DEDICATED

BY SPECIAL PERMISSION

TO

HIS MOST GRACIOUS MAJESTY

KING EDWARD VII

PREFACE

A PAPER lantern, round and red, hangs under a cloud of cherry blossom in a Japanese village. There is a very familiar flower symbol painted upon one side of it. Some children have crossed the green to see what is on the other side of the lantern. A like curiosity has led to the writing of this trivial book.

6, *Wimpole Street, London, W.*

October, 1904.

CONTENTS

Part I.—THE MEDITERRANEAN AND THE RED SEA

Part II.—INDIA

CONTENTS.

LIST OF ILLUSTRATIONS

THE OTHER SIDE OF THE LANTERN

Part I

THE MEDITERRANEAN AND THE RED SEA

I.

THE STARTING FROM TILBURY.

TILBURY on the Thames is quite a fitting place from which to take ship for a journey to the Radiant East, especially when the time is November and when the river is shut in by a freezing fog. The spot is benumbing and without sentiment, but it has some interest by contrast. It is the grey curtain hanging before the brilliant scenes of the play.

The voyager, leaving his native island, who would follow entailed impressions, should start from a sunny cove in Devonshire and put off in a boat. He should hear the keel of the galley slide down the pebbled beach to the tread of heavy boots, and should take the splashing sea suddenly. Ruddy men should row him and his luggage to the ship, while those who wave handkerchiefs on the shore should have behind them a green coomb full of comfortable shadows, and above them gorse-covered downs. There should be no sounds but the rumble and swish of the oars, the babbling of the water against the boat's bow, and the cry of the disturbed seagull.

This, however, is not, in modern view, the *embarquement de luxe.* Those "who go down to the sea in ships" go down in a too-animated train filled with restless and disordered folk and their disorderly belongings. Labels, parcels, fragments of refreshments, messages of farewell, unopened letters, and a variable ruin of flowers hang about these people. From the strange assortment of things they clutch some of them might be escaping from a modern Pompeii. They have for the most part adopted that ill-formulated clothing which an undecided public considers to be "suited for the sea"—steamer hats, steamer cloaks, steamer boots. There are women made repulsive by the headgear of men and sober elders garbed like Captain Kettle. There is such a medley of wardrobes that the most dull of men may appear as compounded of a ship's steward and a deer-stalker, while his wife may have the head of a golf caddie on the body of a cook.

They talk or laugh or weep in gusts. They exhibit unaccountable impulses and alarms. A man springs up in the carriage with set lips and glaring eyes and pats himself all over in search of a wallet he has already locked in a trunk. A woman, with a glance of terror, plunges into a bag by her side, and claws up its contents as a terrier digs up earth, in a quest as futile as that of the Philosopher's Stone.

As the train nears the docks it puffs gingerly across many lines of rail, dodging rows of sheds, ramparts of boxes, or barricades of timber. It hesitates many times, going, as it were, step by step and feeling its way. When the damp quay side is reached, the people drop from the train with such hurry that it might be about to sink into the tide. There is surely not a moment to be lost! They stumble and reel along the dock, dragging bags and rugs, children and trunks, over ropes and chains, round Gargantuan posts, and under appalling cranes. Their hurry and anxiety are such that the train might have come from Sodom or Gomorrah.

When the ship is gained they still find no peace. They skurry over the deck, up and down the staircases, and along the corridors, like ants in a disturbed ant-heap, and still dragging things. It would appear that there is scarcely a person who has not lost something—a child, or a bundle, or the site of a cabin. The ship is to them a maze with many ends, where all ends are alike. They perceive folk going down a stair, so they press after them. They see food laid out in a saloon, so they hasten to eat it—but absently, with their loins girded and a sense that at any moment they may be compelled to jump up to commence again the blind tramp of the ship.

Whistles and bells cause shocks which, on every recurrence, galvanise the lethargic into movement. The great underlying passion throughout the vessel is a primary one—to make for the utmost comfort and to miss nothing that the gods (or the shipping company) may provide. As an arena for the display of the resources of selfishness a departing ship has great advantage.

At last there come three ghostly blasts from a whistle. The moment is here when the "friends" are to leave the ship, and the deck becomes dotted with groups of individuals simultaneously bidding one another farewell. It would seem as if at once they had become emotional by signal. A great spasm of feeling has seized the little companies on deck, and if a ship could feel, its beams would be thrilled by all the misery and forlornness which lie in the hollow of two clasped hands.

The "friends" leave the ship like a funeral procession, line up on the quay—a phalanx of blank wretchedness, spurious hilarity, and lack of invention in the matter of facial expression and of utterance. It is obvious that many are at their wits' end to fill the great gaps of silence by appropriate speech. They are, however, promptly driven, like offending sheep, into the waiting train by porters who regard displays of emotion as means merely of making trains late, and who invade the silence of grief by the hearty clanging of bells.

The "friends" at last are off, but not the ship. In due course, however, with infinite slowness and apparent reluctance, the great vessel is coaxed out of the dock into the Thames as one would lead some large suspicious beast into a pool.

The Tilbury of a November day opens into view. This spot then is the starting point, the Cape Farewell, the white headland of home which, according to all traditions, should be gazed at until it fades from the sight. Owing to the mist Tilbury has an aptitude for fading, but no other suitable quality. As a landscape it is a fitting background for any conception of human dreariness, so that those on the ship who are most bereft must feel that the place is quite in accord with their miseries. It is certainly a scene which can claim to be appropriate to "all those who are anyways afflicted or distressed in mind, body, or estate."

Such happy possessions as this spot may have owned in ancient days, or under the summer sun, have been torn from it, and so complete has been the sack that little is left but the mist, the rank flat, some untidy lumber, and the mud.

The Thames creeps from under the fog, as if it came forth from a tunnel. Here at Tilbury it is a villainous tramp of a river. Dirty, sullen, and strong, it lurches down to the sea. It seems to revel in its dirtiness, for every eddy it turns up brings from the depths fresh realisations of a deeper dirt. It rubs its muddy shoulders along the shrinking banks, so that they are soiled by its touch. Mud and mist replace the glories of stream and sky. Where there may have been fields trodden by leisurely folk, with stiles for them to rest at and hedgerows for them to make love among, there are gullies and dykes of slime, a village of dismal sheds, and a spinney of cranes and derricks. The very grass, struggling up among ashes and rusting iron, looks lean and dissipated.

All this is the outcome of man's enterprise and industry. The huge, beery ogre of labour, dirty and sweating from his work, has thrown himself down in the lady's garden, and the lilies and roses are crushed and sullied by his inconsiderate form.

In the background towards London there rises in the mist, beyond a palisade of masts, a forest of chimneys with foliage of smoke. Ships seem to be standing on dry land, and factories to be floating on the river. Spars and rigging, which have hummed with the bright wind of the Indies, hang over rows of callous houses. Here and there is a puff of red flame from a furnace door—a will o' the wisp in a mist of soot.

The stream would appear to come from a Purgatorio of labour, from some spectral workshop in which there is no rest from the dulness of eternal toil. Yet there is something about the place characteristic of England, of the obstinate energy of the race, and of its brutal disregard of all obstacles physical, moral, or æsthetic when work is to be done or money is to be made.

The steamer swings at last towards the sea, and her long journey is begun. The chilled dock quay is deserted save for a few men who are languidly dragging in wet ropes, and a few others who are absorbed in what Stevenson calls that "richest form of idleness—hanging about harbour sides."

Half crouching behind a pile of rusty boiler plates one solitary sobbing woman is trying to hide herself and yet keep her eyes on the ship. She is the only one of the "friends" who has deliberately failed to catch the special train. She alone of the host has remained to see the vessel start on its way. She is a middle-aged widow of lamentable aspect, who has come to see her only son off to India. As she watches, she mops her eyes with a handkerchief rolled up into an anguished ball. She hides because her dear son would be vexed if she had not returned by the train as he had ordered her. The dear son at the moment is drinking whiskey and water in the second-class saloon with unrestrained delight. He has already confided to the acquaintance of an hour how much money "he has screwed out of the old mater."

It is the "old mater" alone who watches the ship glide away and be lost in the mist.

II.

THE MEDITERRANEAN.

As to the actual leaving of England very little lingers in the memory. The afternoon is passed drifting down a dun river in a faint flat country. The river seems to wander where it likes through an unresisting swamp. The banks become more distant and less definite, but no one notes where the river ends and the sea begins. The steamer drifts into the ocean and on into the night. A row of yellow dots against the utter darkness is Dover; a longer and a larger row is Brighton, and that is the last that the ordinary passenger sees of the delectable island.

By the following morning the pilot has been dropped, the steamer is well away down the Channel, and on the next day is in the Bay of Biscay. This bay has been so much abused that the dread of it is apparently constitutional. Yet in the experience of many it is more often smooth than rough. On this particular voyage the sea was as calm as a village mill pond the whole way from London to Port Said. On every day there was fine weather from dawn to sundown. As soon as the Thames was left behind and the night in the Channel was passed the ship sailed into summer.

On the third day the *Burlengas* came into view early in the morning. Afar off these little islands look like half-molten icebergs resting on the sea. As they were approached gaunt yellow cliffs stood up. Above them were quiet downs, and it was a matter of wonder if any just awakened islander was watching the ship glide by from some hidden cove. At the foot of the cliffs, waves were tumbling languidly among the rocks, while within the black shadow among the crags one could fancy

"the blind wave feeling round his long sea-hall."

Beyond the islands came a phantom coast with white specks and patches for houses and towns and strips of fawn-coloured sand for beaches. Between the land and the ship a few white fishing vessels stood out into the bay, and ahead of the little fleet porpoises rollicked along with the streaming tide.

On the morning of the next day the steamer came to *Gibraltar*.

The first impression of this famous colony is one of aggrieved disappointment. It is so unlike the photographs and pictures which have been familiar from youth. Of that grim precipice which rises sheer from the sea of the pictures there is no trace. There is nothing terrible or menacing or even soldier-like about Gibraltar as seen from the western sea. It does not suggest a tunnelled rock nor a lurking ambush full of guns, nor could any place look less like an impregnable fortress.

Where are the walls, the trenches, the frowning ramparts, the glacis, and the bastions?

All that one sees is a steep hillside bare enough towards the sky, but full of the harmless shadow of trees about its foot. There is a harbour, around which crowds a homely, shrinking town, with a glimpse here and there of gardens and nursemaidenly walks. On the summit of the hillside is a look-out, from which women might watch for the home-coming of fishing boats as the sun went down.

There are certain features, however, in the landscape which are anomalous. The harbour is evidently something more than a haven for fishing-boats, for between the green slope and the sea are many grey and monstrous ships of war, which are like anything but ships. One, indeed, looks like a half-submerged gasometer with the skeleton of an iron foundry erected on its sullen dome.

Ashore bugles are to be heard from time to time, and lines of white helmets in steady march show that there is a heart to the colony which it does not wear on its sleeve. A little acquaintance with the place, and it comes to be understood why it is called "the rock." A further knowledge discovers that the familiar precipice—the Lion's Face—rises from low ground and not from the sea, and that it looks ever towards Spain.

The interests of this small Mediterranean settlement are bound up solely with battle, murder, and sudden death. The commodity it cultivates and professes to supply is sudden death. Its wealth is represented by weapons of destruction, its treasure-houses are stored with shot and shell, its vaults with dynamite and gunpowder. The highest aspiration of the little sea town is to kill, and its pious hope is to develop its powers for destroying life to wide limits. It is the further aim and object of the colony to effect these ends with the least amount of personal risk to itself. There is about Gibraltar, therefore, something of the whited sepulchre, something of the vineyard that grows about the slumbering volcano. An enemy so ignorant as to mistake it for a Mediterranean seaside resort would be convinced of error with some suddenness, while the unfriendly who would ask for bread at Gibraltar would receive a scorpion.

Few places are more interesting to Englishmen than is the fortress of Gibraltar, and so long as the galleries which tunnel the rock exist there is no need for any monument to British spirit and endurance in this part of the world. There are few chapters in the history of British arms more electric than is the story of the four years' siege of the rock. It is good to see the gullies and holes in which the besieged lived, and the burrows they dug inch by inch out of the stubborn cliff. Although months dragged on into years, they were never outwitted and never daunted. Although shells rained on them like stones from a crater, they still clung to the rock, till they reached victory in the end.

Those who hurry ashore from the ship see little but one narrow crowded street filled with a suburban type of shop of the kind which is assumed to minister to the needs of tourists. A few reach the base of the great precipice which frowns towards Spain, while still fewer find the odd little hamlet of Catalan Bay, which lies on the eastern side of the mighty crag like a mouse between a lion's paws.

Between Gibraltar and *Marseilles* is a passage of some forty-eight hours.

The approach to Marseilles is picturesque, and the busy town looks well from the sea. It is indeed one of that great series of towns which appear at their best only at a distance. Marseilles stands pleasantly. The sea at its foot is blue. Romantic islands of bare rock hide the entrance to its harbour, while beyond its confines is a line of dignified hills. On a mound above the shining roofs of the town is the Church of Notre Dame de la Garde, with the great golden image of the Virgin erect on its tower.

On a nearer approach to the harbour mouth, the picturesqueness of the town disappears little by little as its details are gradually laid bare. Out of pleasant shadows come factories and gas works. A line of bright colour, that charmed when afar off, changes into a row of sordid sheds. A patch of gold turns out to be a warehouse wall, covered with glaring advertisements, upon which the sun chances to fall. The town which, when seen from the sea, might be an enchanted city, is found to be a place with railway stations, tram lines, jails, barracks, and the usual trailing rags of mean streets.

The morning after the arrival at Marseilles is a morning of restless excitement. The overland contingent is expected. In due course the special train from London crawls down to the quay as if utterly exhausted. The passengers it brings are scanned with suspicious interest as they stumble up the gangway to the ship. They are, for the most part, pallid, have the sickly and crumpled aspect peculiar to a night in the train, wear the clothes of cities, and step on the ship with puzzled diffidence. Any woman on the gangway who awakes to the fact that she is being stared at, at once claps her hands to the back of her head, possessed by the idea that her hair, "done" in the train, is coming down.

The steamer is to sail as soon as the overlanders are on board, and the drama of departure, as acted on the quay and as viewed from the hurricane deck, is stirring enough. The great vessel is close to the dock, where it towers, like a black street side, above the roof of the embarkation shed. The shed is long, low, cavernous. Within its shadows are ramparts of sacks, luggage in helpless clumps, sentry-box-like offices, deck chairs in lines. Among these move cabs, wheelbarrows, passengers, pedlars, lascars, loafers, and gendarmes. Everybody is in a hurry, and when the warning whistle blows this haste degenerates into a mêlée.

Between the shed and the vessel the edge of the quay is glaring in the sun. The ground is black with coal dust. Oranges and lemons in open baskets make a great splash of yellow on the black, and the vendor who screams over them screams from under a scarlet shawl. Behind the fruit baskets a restless cluster of purple air balloons made united efforts to fly away. On the bare stones are displayed those lace scarves and gaudy handkerchiefs which are on sale at every port in the world, and are assumed to be the product of local industry.

A clown with a whitened and unshaven face, in the garb of a pierrot, grins up at the ship. Two sour-looking acrobats in green tights go through languid contortions on a dirty carpet. A boy, in what was once a black evening dress coat, shrieks out the "Marseillaise." Three groups of dejected men, with harp and viol, play three different tunes simultaneously, and a widow grinds "God Save the King" obstinately from an organ. This hubbub is almost drowned by the rattle of incessant hand-barrows over the cobble stones of the quay.

The eyes of the crowd are all turned up to the ship, all brows are wrinkled and dirty, all mouths are open and yelling for money, while any gaps on the black flags are filled by capless urchins, who bawl out of simple lightheartedness.

The steamer is at last dragged away by tugs from this noisome mob, and the filthy water of the dock, dotted as it is by scraps of paper, orange peel, and miscellaneous refuse, is soon changed for the clean sea.

On one evening *Stromboli* was sighted. The volcano chanced to be active. When it first came into view it appeared as a small red dot on the horizon which could not be distinguished from the port light of a ship. In time the dot grew until a kind of fiery tail could be seen to trail down from it. The dot was the crater, and the tail was a stream of glowing lava on the mountain side. On a still nearer approach, the strange light came to look like a wondrous firefly skimming the black sea, and as it grew and grew it changed to a blazing column against the dark—just such a pillar of fire as led the night marches of the Israelites. As the island was passed lurid puffs of flame and smoke could be seen to well forth from the crater, while a cloud of red steam hung like a fiery baldachino over the cascade of red-hot lava. The mountain stood out black against the glare in the sky as if it were a peak of the nether world.

A day passed and the vessel came upon *Crete.* It was about an hour after sunrise that the ship was steaming along the coast of the island, and the view of it was delicate and wonderful. The cliffs that rose from the sea were lean and dim, but the mountains far inland were lit by the rising sun, so that every dome and pinnacle stood out in freshest outline. The whole range was covered with snow, and long shadows, falling across the great snow-fields, deepened the brilliancy of the bare heights and the gloom of the ravines. Above the many peaks towered Mount Ida, a dome of white springing out of the snowdrifts and still tinted by the rising sun with the faint colour of the pink carnation. This dainty vision of Mount Ida was the most beautiful spectacle that had presented itself since the journey began.

III.

THE STAGE VILLAIN'S TOWN.

On the afternoon of the eleventh day the steamer entered the harbour of *Port Said*. The approach to Egypt is in some degree mysterious. As the land is neared the sea becomes duller and deader. To the right there appear on the horizon a skeleton lighthouse, some isolated patches of black, which prove to be houses, some palms, and a minaret. This is Damietta. There is not the faintest sign of land, there is no suggestion of a coast, much less of a continent. The lighthouse, the palms, the two or three houses, and the minaret rise abruptly from the sea. The sea appears to flow between them and around them. If this be Egypt, then the country is buried by an inundation.

It is more a matter of mystery that after Damietta is passed still no land appears, although the vessel steams ever nearer and nearer to port. The few little points standing out of the sea which represent Damietta go by, and then the horizon again shows nothing but a line of unbroken ocean. This strange appearance depends upon the fact that in the north of the Delta the land of Egypt is a dead flat, and Port Said lies in the bend of a wide bay. Thus Damietta looks like a detached fragment of land which is drifting quietly away to sea.

Many miles are traversed, after this segment of a country has floated out of sight, before Port Said comes into view. Its appearance also is peculiar. One becomes aware of a row of houses on the horizon, which spring out of the sea and appear to be lapped by the water on all sides. The row of houses, moreover, presents no unfamiliar appearance. They arouse no suggestion of the brilliant East. If one can imagine a detached street of lodging houses from Southend or an isolated row of middle class premises from a Lancashire town drifting about in the Mediterranean in company with a lighthouse, then there is a conception of Port Said from the sea. Of land there is no hint; there is no coast line, no cliff, none of the appurtenances of a seaside town. The objects that come next into view are two steam dredgers and a statue. Finally, the town reveals itself and the fact that the houses that look seawards have no more architectural character when seen near at hand than they possess when afar off. A minaret or two are noticed, a row of lubeck trees comes into sight, then a line of camels crossing the now visible sand, and finally boats full of strange people bawling in strange tongues.

The steamer moors in the opening of the canal, close to the town, and opposite to its principal street. Those who go ashore go in boats ferried by men who never cease to wrangle in yells. The town lies upon a flat which is raised but little above the level of the sea. If the houses were less shanty-like one might imagine that the steamer had anchored in the Grand Canal of some third-rate Venice.

Port Said owes its interest to its reputation for wickedness and general depravity. Iniquity is, by repute, the chief commodity of the place. The villain of many romances has come from Port Said, and he is always a ruffian of an acrid type. One thinks to find at this town on the mud flat a colony of scoundrels such as Bret Harte loved to depict, swarthy men with long black hair and heavy moustaches, inclined to sombreros and the wearing of scarves for belts, men who carry knives, who play cards on barrel heads, and who talk a language compounded of Spanish oaths and the *patois* of Whitechapel. On going ashore the visitor looks for that lurid form of drinking saloon made familiar by romance, which is a maelstrom for the virtuous and a shooting gallery for the wicked. He expects to find a dead man lying under a tree with a revolver wound in his head, or to meet the dark-eyed Italian lady whose footsteps lead to the pit and whose acquaintance is merely an introduction to the mortuary.

All those who are filled with expectations of this kind will be disappointed. Port Said may be as wicked as even Paris or London, but it does not carry the caste mark upon its face. Its criminality—even if it flourished like the green bay tree—is well concealed. The town would hardly be selected as a place for the education of youth, but then it does not profess to be an academy for morals any more than it pretends to be a health resort. Port Said is, without doubt, physically dirty, and it is probable that its morality is about as neglected as its streets, but—in justice to the claims of other Levantine towns—its pretence to especial eminence in the matter of depravity cannot be allowed.

The principal street of Port Said is made up of a series of houses and shops which are little above the dignity of shanties. The thoroughfare gives the visitor the impression of being some sort of "native street" in a London exhibition. Everybody lives in the road, and the crowd the tourist struggles through is made up of Arabs, Egyptians, Bedouins, Greeks, Turks, Maltese, French, Spanish, and English, of donkey boys, postcard sellers, beggars, native policemen, Nile boatmen, British sailors, coal coolies, and tavern touts.

The people of Port Said live largely on the tourist; they regard him as prey; they look upon him as game; they hunt him; they rob him; they give him an effusive welcome but no peace. When the first boat lands the whole street rises and swoops down with yells upon those who step ashore; and with the host come their dogs, their donkeys, their blind, their halt, and their lame.

The boys dance round each new-comer with delight. They address him as "Mr. Gladstone" and his wife as "Mrs. Langtry." They protest that they know him or that they carried his bag when last he landed. They offer to do all things for him, and never for one moment, while he walks the unsavoury streets of the town, do they leave him. He is invited to buy postcards, sun helmets, Japanese carvings, bananas, Maltese lace, and live mice in a box. He is implored to allow himself to be led to the station, to the custom house, to the post office, to a dancing saloon, or to the English cemetery. It is a relief to return to the quiet of the boat, even though the boat is coaling. All night long noise of some sort continues. Port Said neither slumbers nor sleeps. Indeed, the chief music-hall of the town announces, as the greatest of its joys, that it is "open all night."

It is said of Port Said that it is the spot where the East meets the West. If so, the meeting is not happy for the East. The man from the desert, as he draws near to western civilisation, may expect to be led by benevolent hands to some Palace of Delight. In reality he is taken by the scruff of the neck and is pushed into a Slough of Despond. What is ill in the man is made more evil; what is good in him is trampled out. The blessings of civilisation come to him in the guise of tinned meat, gin, and coal carrying, and he obtains doubtful advantage from these means of grace. He finds himself as much out of place as is a palm in a drinking bar, and by the time he is admitted into the beneficent bosom of the West he has become as dirty in mind and body as are the streets of this outpost of the greater world.

Port Said affords a display of the West at its worst and of the East spoiled. Yet at the time of sunset, a glory of the East can even make beautiful this mongrel city, with its reeking taverns, its slop shops, and its gambling halls. At this time the squalid house-tops become turrets and battlements of gold. The sky is the colour of the yellow rose, the clouds are tinted with lilac, the shadows in the street are purple and long. Picking her way across the dirty quay is an English girl in a white dress, and as the light which the East alone has seen falls upon her dainty face and makes a halo of her fair hair it is possible to realise how at Port Said the East and the West may meet

IV.

COALING AT PORT SAID.

The miseries of coaling have often enough been dwelt upon. They are depressing in their coarseness and gloom. The ship is rendered desolate. Everyone escapes from it who can. Even the familiar deck chairs go. They pile themselves in a heap on the front deck, where they are covered with tarpaulins so that the whole mass of them looks like a hurriedly constructed bier. There is indeed some suggestion that the ship has become a house of mourning. All the port holes are closed, whereby the cabins are rendered suffocating. Deck rooms are locked as a comment upon the habits of ship loafers generally, and the owners of these rooms are rendered homeless. The stairs, the corridors, and the music-room are covered with rough canvas. Furniture is muffled up. The smoking-room is made a waste. The ship looks like a house which has been made ready for an auction, or has been taken in hand for the purposes of spring cleaning, or has been "packed up" preparatory to evacuation at the end of the season.

Clouds of coal-dust envelop the poor vessel and penetrate into every part of it. The deck becomes as ash drift. Whatever the hand finds to touch it finds to be black. Coal-dust becomes the breath of the nostrils, coal-dust settles upon the face, powders the neck, and creeps among the hair. Moreover, in no part of the ship is there any escape from the husky din which accompanies the ritual of coaling.

Coaling at Port Said by daylight is a pageant which could be of interest only to a dust contractor. Coaling at Port Said at night is one of the sights of the world, and would have fired the heart of Dante.

The ship lies at her moorings in the middle of the still canal.

The passengers have gone ashore, and a strange quiet has fallen upon the vessel. The clang of the ship's bell, marking the hour, and the splash in the water of an empty bottle, thrown out of a scuttle, may be the only sounds to be heard. The night is dark; the few lights visible are those that flicker on the quay and about the restless street, or that stream from the port-holes of a ship near by in regular dots of light which seem to pour from the interior of a ponderous flute.

Without the least warning the stillness of the gloom is broken by a far-away noise, by a sound which at first is like to the humming of millions of eager insects pouring out of the desert. As the sound draws nearer it inclines to the wailing of beasts, and then to the murmuring of a countless host of men.

Any on deck who run to the ship's side and look into the dark see, bearing down on the vessel, two enormous black rafts, which might be the rafts of Charon drifting from the banks of the Styx. High aloft on each raft are cressets blazing with fire. The flames and the smoke from the iron baskets twist and eddy over the rafts, and by the wavering glare they cast it is seen that the decks are swarming with a horde of men. They are sending up through the murk horrible yells and shouts mingled with a still more loathsome babble of unhuman talk.

As the rafts glide nearer, propelled by some unseen force, the red glow from the cressets falls upon the mob. It falls upon them as a fluttering light which now blazes forth and now is buried in smoke. Half of the wild crew will be furnace-red, half will be invisible.

The raft is a raft of coal, and on its black plateau are hundreds of men, vague as the shadows they crowd among. Their garments flutter in the wind, showing bare arms and legs, grinning faces and white teeth, with here and there a dun turban or the shred of a blue scarf. Their clothing consists of long and scanty gowns, so that many of the awful gang look like old women or bony witches in tattered skirts. Around the edge of the raft, wherever there is room to sit, these men, with so horrible a semblance to old women, crouch, with their heads wrapt up in rags like harridans with aching jaws.

When the floating cauldrons of smoke and men reach the ship it becomes apparent that they are no crafts of Inferno sailing hither from the pit, but a commonplace gang of coolies who have come to do the coaling.

The rafts are made fast to the great vessel, planks are run up to the coal bunkers, and then there begins an unceasing procession of gaunt folk carrying yellow baskets full of coal up one plank and returning with them empty along another. As they pass up and down their rags dance in the wind, clouds of coal-dust and smoke circle round them, while the light from the cressets flashes fitfully upon the file, making their sweating limbs glow as with a fervent heat. The stream of basket carriers might be coming out from the crater of a volcano, and it is a matter of wonder that they are neither charred nor smothered. They are all so much alike that the procession on the plank may be made up of one toiling man multiplied a hundred times. The figures on the slope and the figures grubbing among the black caverns of the coal never cease to give forth a discordant chant as if they were moaning the phrases of some dismal litany.

Hour after hour the dry tramp of feet along the plank continues, hour after hour the same hoarse dirge is screamed forth from a hundred creaking throats, hour after hour the spades are at work and the baskets come and go. Then the scuffle of feet ceases, the scrape of the shovels dies away, the fire in the cressets flutters out, the barges are empty, and to the same weird chant they glide away and are lost in the gloom.

V.

THE SUEZ CANAL.

On the morning of the day after Port Said was reached the steamer from Brindisi arrived with mails and passengers. Some two hours were occupied in the transference of the mails, and as soon as the last bag was on board the Brindisi steamer slipped away, and we were free to start on our journey. The ship almost directly entered the Suez Canal. The canal, it is needless to say, extends from Port Said to Suez, and is nearly one hundred miles in length. The larger proportion of this distance is represented by an artificially made canal, and the rest by a channel through the Bitter Lakes and Lake Timsah. The vessel, in the charge of a pilot, proceeds at the rate of five or six knots an hour. The passage of the canal, therefore, may occupy some twenty hours, allowing for stoppages.

The journey is remarkable, and is one of the strangest which can be made in an ocean-going liner. The canal is narrow and straight, while from sea to sea it traverses the desert. From the deck of the ship the wandering plain lies stretched out on either side, an arid wilderness of yellow sand. Through this dead and barren waste the little canal makes its way like a stream of life.

The landscape is the most rudimentary that the mind could imagine. It is almost in a monotone. The biscuit-coloured desert extends wherever the eye can follow, the sky is cloudless. Here and there are patches of starving bush or a rocky hillock half hidden in a sand drift. There are a line of telegraph posts, a distant mud dredger with a few natives at work on the bank, and that is all except the stream of green water. The landscape is wearisome, the scene is repeated over and over again—ever the sand, the sun, and the small stream. If one stretched out a large sheet of dust-coloured paper and made a crease along it from one margin to the other and let a little water trickle along the crease, it would show to a child the Suez Canal in the desert. The very loneliness of this scorched wilderness is terrible, its monotony and its lack of limit are oppressive.

It is just such a landscape as might have been found upon the primitive earth when it was still almost without form and void, when its surface was still heated, cracked, and stifling, and when as yet no form of life had crept out into the air. It looks so very lifeless and so old. The wrinkles of a million years are upon its shrivelled face. It may be that since the world came into being this part of its surface has never changed, so that looking over the waste one can gaze still upon the first dry land that rose out of the abyss, and upon which fell the first light of the dawning sun. Through these sands, which may have drifted and eddied under primeval winds, the tiny stream runs straight from ocean to ocean. There is so little that looks artificial about the canal that it might be a living river, and possibly the first stream which trickled across the still warm earth was like unto this.

The steamer moves at so slow a pace that the pulsations of the engines cannot be felt, and the vessel seems to be blown along by the light wind. For some time after leaving Port Said the railway to Cairo runs by the side of the canal, while between the railroad and the waterway is the sweet water canal. A few villages are passed and many "stations" of the canal company. These trim settlements are real oases in the sand, pleasant to look at.

The great Bitter Lake is a beautiful expanse of water, and the passage across it is an agreeable relief after the somewhat too formal canal. We anchored in the lake to allow three other steamers to pass. It was just at sunset, when the daring colours in the sky are such as can be seen only in Egypt.

This peculiarly picturesque scene had a great fascination for the many who, leaning over the ship's rail, looked across the plum-coloured waters of the lake and had their faces lit by the strange glow from the west.

On entering the canal again it was already so dark that an electric searchlight was fixed to the ship's prow. This white light produced a quite extraordinary illusion. The water of the canal became the deepest indigo, and its banks an intense white. The ship seemed to be afloat in arctic regions, and to be slowly creeping along a crack or open way between two ice floes. Any boulder or hillock on the bank threw a long, black shadow across the snow, the sea seemed to be freezing, and there was a chilly-looking mist in the air. Beyond the area illuminated by the searchlight there was nothing but the blackest night.

At *Suez* the steamer remained one hour. It was in the middle of the night. The noise with which the business of that port is conducted was quite astounding. If there be any proportion between the amount of business done and the clamour with which it is attended, Suez must be a flourishing seaport.

Lying in the dark in a deck cabin, one might have imagined that the vessel was being boarded by pirates. Much of this noise proceeded from a fussy tug. As the steamer, to the relief of all, began to steam away from Suez, the tug again came into being, and, following the ship, apparently tried to cling to her side. This manœuvre was attended by a series of fearful screams from the tug, which far surpassed anything that the port had up to that time produced. Lascars, not to be outdone, shrieked at the tug from the ship's decks, and an abusive quartermaster, who spoke in the English tongue, could at least claim that in the matter of personal invective he omitted nothing. The tug still pounded after the steamer, while the yells that came from those on board were finally raised to a pitch of the most acute agony. At last out of the awful clamour from the persistent craft it was possible to isolate the sentence, "Men a boat," which utterance was repeated with such rapidity that it might have been fired from a Maxim gun. No reviling from the steamer could stay or drown this cry, but as the smaller vessel was falling astern from sheer weakness, it was discovered that the native owner, by repeating the words "Men a boat," wished it to be known that one of his crew had been left on board the liner. This information he endeavoured to communicate by one hundred dying gasps. The steamer was stopped, the panting tug came once more alongside under another hail of abuse and the lost man was restored with appropriate curses to his hoarse and now speechless friends. After this we passed into the quiet of the open sea, and were able to appreciate what Kipling calls "her excellent loneliness."

During the morning of the next day the ship was steaming down the *Gulf of Suez*, and in the afternoon of that day entered the Red Sea. The weather was fine, the sea profoundly blue, the wind astern and strong enough to bring a white crest upon each wave. The land on either side was still barren and waterless, without trace of life of any kind. There were nothing but scorching rock and sand, yellow beaches with scarred cliffs standing bare in the sun, so that such shadows as fell seemed hot and red.

The whole coast was a mockery. Where there should have been green downs upon the cliffs there was only dust; where a cool valley should have opened to the sea there was nothing but a rift in the rock, hoarse with burning winds; where a stream should have dropped to the beach from a ledge of wet fern there was merely a cascade of sand. Sand dunes took the place of living hills, and sand drifts of grassy slopes. The country looked as if it were made up of the output of a furnace where the soil was ash and the rocks calcined stône.

Yet at night in this ship, on its way through a land of drought and utter emptiness, some few hundred folk would be merry over a dinner furnished with food from all parts of the world, drinking the wines of France and Spain, and eating salads and fruits from English gardens.

Some way down the coast, lying dead on the shore, was the wreck of a small "tramp" steamer. One can only wonder what happened to the crew. Had they all been drowned, or had they landed upon this blistering beach to be mocked by the memory of kindly beaches at home? Had they climbed the charred cliff and from the summit found nothing but a waste stretching away hopelessly to the horizon, or had they wandered about, tricked by dark hollows in the rocks or by shadowed places where water should have been, until they died of thirst?

The poor wreck lying on the beach—the only sign the foul country afforded of anything that had lived—was like a skeleton of white bones by the side of a track in a desert.

VI.

THE RED SEA.

The passage of the Red Sea occupies about three and a half days. Between Suez and Aden certain barren islands are met with, which are of little interest beyond that they provide an excellent scenic effect when it chances that the sun sets directly behind them.

The island of Perim is passed some six hours before Aden is entered. It is probably the most melancholy of the possessions of Great Britain. The island stands well out of the sea, and is one and a half miles long. At a distance it appears to be composed solely of brown, dried earth. There is apparently not a blade of grass nor of anything green in the colony, and it is as dull to contemplate as a dust-heap. A toy settlement can be seen close to the sea, made up of houses so white and prim that they might be built of cardboard. At the south of the island is a sandy beach, and on the headland above it, a lighthouse. Between the beach and the lighthouse a sorry path extends across the drab hillside. There is a fascination about this path on account of its supernatural dreariness. It is a matter of wonder that anyone should find occasion to follow this narrow way to the beach unless it be to seek death in the water.

Apart from Perim, some glimpses of other islands, and the exploits of flying fish, the sole interest in the Red Sea is the weather. This sea is famous for the peculiar type of climate it provides. It is assumed that there is no heat of so uncommon a kind as that of the Red Sea. Thus it is that this waterway is one of the few places on the globe where the weather is an ever sincere subject of conversation.

Arrangements are made for dealing with the eccentricities of temperature as soon as Suez is left. Sun screens are put up on each side of the vessel so as to keep the deck in shade; wind scoops are thrust into the scuttles of the cabins; electric fans are set buzzing, and punkahs swing over every table of the dining saloon. The officers, the crew, and the stewards appear in white dresses. The sofas in the music saloon and the settees in the smoking room are covered with white linen.

The weather becomes hot by subtle degrees, but the discomfort it leads to is not to be measured by any thermometer. The temperature—as taken on deck at noon—was 70° F. on the first day in the Red Sea. It rose to 82° on the second day, and 88° on the third and fourth days. On these days the temperature in the lower cabins was over 90°. It was considered to be a cool passage, for there was a head wind nearly all the way, while a benevolent thunderstorm with heavy rain came out of the sky one morning. Notwithstanding these blessings the heat was trying. In the words of the German manager of an Egyptian hotel, the weather was, in fact, "enormous 'ot."

It was a moist heat, like that of a rich man's greenhouse. It made everyone limp, sticky, and irritable. The nights were little better than the days. Children declined to sleep and were very fretful while some of the ladies were moved to tears.

There was a disposition to do nothing but foster the art of lying about. After lunch every chair on the shady side of the ship was occupied by sleeping passengers or by people at least with closed eyes and dropped books. The long row of recumbent figures made the deck look like a hospital ward filled with anæsthetised patients.

It was the ambition of everyone to lie or sit in what is called a "complete draught," so that wherever any wind could be found there would be little groups gathered together drinking it in. In England there is a desire to get out of a draught, in the Red Sea to get into one; and at night the most fortunate were those who slept in such a blast as made their scanty garments flutter like a flag.

Many of the passengers slept on deck—a few ladies in the music saloon, a few men in the smoking-room, but the greater number of both sexes in the open. It was necessary only to have a mattress and a pillow placed on the floor, and the sleeping arrangements were complete. The ladies took possession of the forward deck, where they built themselves a kind of zareba out of deck chairs and other loose barricades. They did not, however, diffuse around themselves either the blessing of peace or the charm of repose. They talked more or less all night, and, according to the impressions of some, the zareba might have enclosed a parrot house.

On one morning, about 4 a.m., the occupants of the ladies' laager had fallen upon sleep, to the joy of all. But at that hour a thunder-storm arose, and on the first flash of lightning the more timid burst out of the corral, and, trampling on the bodies of prostrate men, rushed screaming down the companion.

After this, the suburbs of the ladies' quarter were regarded as unsafe to sleep in.

At 6 a.m. each morning the ladies went below, and then for one hour the deck was given up to the men, who paraded luxuriantly in pyjamas. Military officers, learned judges, and responsible merchants were brought down to one level—that of pyjamas. In these simple garments they walked the ship, while the decks were being washed down with that lavish use of water and noise which is peculiar to the mariner.

Gasping and damp women who had spent a night of steamy misery below were early to appear on deck. Some, who were led up by stewardesses, looked like imprisoned miners, just rescued, and brought to the pit's mouth.

Among these was a nurse who was in charge of a popular baby. The baby was a boy, aged about twelve months. According to the smoking-room account it was given a sleeping draught in the train between Paris and Marseilles to keep it quiet, and was brought on board at Marseilles still comatose. It caused some alarm by declining to wake the whole of the next day, and became at once famous as the child with the "sleeping sickness." Early one Red Sea morning the nurse, who was rendered flabby by heat, crawled up on deck with the baby. She soon became "that ill" that she had to stumble below, leaving the infant with a pyjama-clad officer of dragoons, who offered to take it. The child was not sleeping on this occasion, and indeed, as soon as the nurse had fled, it began to howl dismally. The dragoon was much alarmed by this change in the habits of the infant. He was himself suffering at the time from prickly heat, and it struck him that the baby's unhappiness might be due also to the same cause. So, with the assistance and advice of a mining expert, who was smoking in pyjamas in the next chair, the baby was entirely undressed, and rubbed with a tobacco pouch. This treatment, although not in accord with the usages of the nursery, was immediately effectual, for when the still limp nurse returned to the deck the baby was naked, but neither ashamed nor complaining.

VII.

THE IDLER AT SEA.

It was dark when Aden was reached, so of this isolated sunburnt settlement nothing could be seen but the broken row of lights which dotted the shore and the hillside. The run of four days from Aden to Bombay was uneventful, but it was occupied by those incongruous amusements which are a phenomenon of all long sea voyages, and which are accepted as among the wonders of the deep. On the evening of the first day out from Aden there was a fancy dress ball, and on the succeeding days there followed "sports" peculiar to ocean life.

The promenade deck in this particular vessel was covered in by a boat deck, so that viewed from either end the former looked like a long tunnel open on one side of its length to the sea. That deck which faced the sun was always an avenue of lights and shadows, and the ripple of the sea was reflected on the white beams which formed the roof of the covered way. All along this avenue was a disjointed row of deck chairs, the occupants of which, in bright summer costumes, were writing, sleeping, reading, or playing cards.

The promenade was narrowed to the space between the line of chairs and the ship's rail. Here some would be strolling, some playing "buckets" or deck quoits, while others watched the children who crawled about the deck promiscuously. The children's toys were not necessarily appropriate to the sea. One small boy had, as a means of relaxation, a live dormouse in a box, while another dragged a motor-car along, to which was attached a Noah's Ark. The small girls devoted most of their time to putting dolls to bed or to making imagined tea.

On a still and warm day the deck suggested a verandah overlooking the sea, or a miniature promenade at some place which was fashionable, idle, and sunny. The young man and the maiden would lean over the rail as they would loll over the balustrade by the Casino Garden at Monte Carlo, but they looked seawards, so that the words they whispered were lost in the babble of the ship's wake. They would lean there to watch the sun go down, and their figures would stand out as black silhouettes against the crimson sky. After the sun had set they would go to the forecastle to look for the Southern Cross. This search always involved some time, for the forecastle was apt to be deserted, so there was no one to instruct them, and as the light of the early moon fell upon this part of the deck it often appeared as if the young man was looking for the Southern Cross in the maiden's eyes.

Many on the ship watched this companionship with kindly interest, wondering if it would last till the end of a voyage which was longer than this, and if in years to come the sound of the sea would bring back to these two a memory of ineffable delight.

Every day and all day long there was something to see, and the sight was one that never fretted the spirit of warm laziness which drugged the loungers on the deck. There was always the "stark-barrelled swell" of the sea, with now and then a misty cape, and now and then a ship on its way homewards. There were the porpoises who tumbled in the vessel's course, shooting out of and in the glazed water as if they were black, glutinous drops thrown up from some fountain under the ocean. There was the timid fringe of phosphorescent light which hung about the wave from the ship's bows, and there was the pathway made by the moon across the indigo plain of waters at night.

When all lights were out and the decks were deserted there was still the swish of the sea along the side, the ship's bell marking the hour, the deep pulse of the engines, and the mysterious creaking of innumerable bulkheads.

Part II

INDIA

I.

THE COMING TO INDIA.

ON the morning of the 21st day after leaving Tilbury, *Bombay* was sighted. It was a fine sunny morning—as all had been—but ahead was a haze along the horizon which hid the land. There were sea birds in the air, and on the water a boat with a white lateen sail. The life seemed to have gone out of the sea, for the waves had become dull and of a sluggish green. Every eye was turned in the direction of the ship's bow, and soon there emerged from the mist a low hill, alone like an island, grey and indistinct. This was India.

As the ship drew near, other high ground came into view, rising above a ghostly coast. In due course a lighthouse, gaudy in stripes of red, white, and black, appeared. Behind the lighthouse were a narrow spit of land with soft rounded trees on it and the tower of a disused pharos. Here, too, were white houses with red roofs, dotting the green, and below them a sandy beach by a fortified wall.

Beyond this narrow spur of land—called, as I came to know, Colaba—was the city of Bombay, shrouded by the mist. Through the haze it was possible to make out the steeples and towers, the domes and pinnacles of a great city.

The approach is stately, for the harbour is magnificent, but there is no particular character about the scene. One is conscious of entering a wide sound and of a city on a bright inlet; but the sound might be in Italy and the city in England. This is not the India one has dreamed about. There is no suggestion of

"India's coral strand," no hot beach peopled by turbaned heathen, no line of cocoanut palms by the water's edge. One looks in vain for buildings that follow in some way the architecture of the "willow pattern plate," and, above all, one looks for elephants with howdahs on their backs.

There is, in place of the palms, a line of factory chimneys; while a quite common row of quays meets the sea in place of the coral strand. There are no heathen recognisable as such, and certainly none in the act of bowing down to stocks and stones. There are people in turbans, but they are evidently mere loungers about harbour sides, and the buildings appear, at the distance, to differ but little from those at Limehouse. Of elephants there are none.

A launch, illumined by a chuprassie, or messenger, in scarlet robes, landed us on the quay at about the time of high noon.

On stepping into the street it was evident enough, in spite of any previous impressions, that we were in a strange country. There were all the elements of the life of a large city, but every one of these factors was in some way made curious by unexpected details, foreign to a standard founded upon accustomed towns. There were roads and houses, cabs and tram cars, as well as a continuous crowd of passers-by, but both the place and the people were strange. The very stones were strange, the roads were covered by a peculiarly smelling dust, the houses were unusual in design, being prominent in the matter of roofs and balconies, in verandahs, and in lack of orthodox windows. The cabs were a type of victoria, which were driven by lounging men in turbans or tarbooshes. The tram cars were skeletons of tram cars, and the horses that drew them had solar topees on their heads.

The passers-by were as unexpected as if they had just strolled out of a comic opera house the stage of which was cumbered by unavoidable dirt, and the wardrobe of which was composed of reproductions of Joseph's coat of many colours. The crowd, although large enough, had neither the bustle of London nor the vivacity of Paris.

There were slouching dogs, too, of unfamiliar breed hanging about entries, and on the housetops the cosmopolitan sparrow was ousted by crows with grey heads, or by kites who whistled with an affected tremolo when they sailed languidly over the town. There were uncouth carts drawn by bullocks and filled with unwonted wares, while often there lolled through the crowd a dusty buffalo, a blue bare beast who may once have had both intelligence and hair, but who, on the loss of both, remained a dejected embodiment of the ugliness of stupidity and of the beastliness of life.

Bombay is what is called a fine city, but its interest to the visitor goes little beyond the statement presented in the guide books to the effect that it is situated in Lat. 18° 53′ 45″ and on an island (which is not apparent), that it has over 820,000 inhabitants, that it is happy in possessing an "impressive line of Government buildings," that much of its excellence clings about "public offices and educational institutions," and that it is peculiarly rich in cemeteries. Beyond these attractions the charm of Bombay to those who land for the first time upon its "spacious quays" is bound up in the fact that it is one of the cities of India, that the soil and the people are Indian, and that it is part of that continent which has entered with so much romance into the history of the world.

There is interest in everything that one sees, in the railway trains, the shops, the boats on the beach, the policemen, the street sweepers, the unfamiliar trees and shrubs, and the fragmentary demonstrations of how the people live. Kites and crows, vultures and squirrels are all elements new to city life; while the first time that a parrakeet is sighted, perched on a house top, there arises the conviction that it must have escaped from a cage.

Beyond all this it may be claimed that the chief things, which in tourist language will "well repay a visit" in Bombay, are the native quarter and the Malabar Hill.

The Malabar Hill is a modest mound behind the city, brave with gardens and bright villas, from whose summit is to be obtained a view of the sea and of the gleaming harbour. It is a matter of interest that all large bays, viewed from a height, are supposed to resemble the Bay of Naples. The harbour of Bombay comes into this classification of bays, and is therefore regarded as a local Bay of Naples; but the very stones on Malabar Hill must turn when each inspired tourist after another discovers and reveals this stale resemblance, for the sweeping Sound of Bombay shows scarcely a feature which has any parallel in the great Italian inlet.

It may be well to notice here also another experience of new-comers. If any complaint be made of the climate of a place, the visitor is assured that the weather (strangely enough) is quite exceptional for the time of the year. The Riviera, for instance, is supposed to enjoy a winter climate of everlasting sunshine and clear skies, and when the chilled visitor to the Mediterranean finds —as he often does—a drab and depressing heaven, filled with the wind of an English November, he, at the same time, finds that the circumstance is so uncommon that he may be proud of it, for the weather he has come upon is practically unheard of during the Mediterranean winter.

So in Bombay. The climate was unpleasantly hot, steamy, and enervating; but then came the assurance that this experience was so rare that it might be cherished in the memory, as it would be, no doubt, in that of the oldest inhabitant.

II.

AN IMPRESSION OF INDIA.

An impression of India, based upon a sojourn in the country of little more than two months, must of necessity be imperfect. Although in my journeyings in India I travelled between three and four thousand miles, I scarcely went beyond that great plain which occupies the central part of the continent, and which stretches from the Himalayas in the north to the tableland of the Deccan in the south. Moreover the season was the winter, when little or no rain falls, when the land is dried up and the hillsides are brown, when the great rivers have shrunk into sluggish streams, sulking through a gully of sand and stones, and when most of the flowers have gone. It was possible only to picture the land as it would be in the summer. Then the rivers would be bustling tides swinging to the sea, the bare wastes would be green, while rivulets would be dripping from a thousand hills.

Still, the country as it was was wonderful enough, with its forests of unfamiliar trees, its fields strange with a curious husbandry, its villages which had so little to suggest that they were abodes of men. Although the face of the land changes as the seasons pass, the inhabitants are still the same, and it is they who give to the country its most impressive interest.

Unchanged also by the rise and waning of the heat, or by the rains, are the crowded towns with their bazaars, their temples, and their maze of streets.

Possibly the first impression of India, which succeeds the realisation of the strangeness of all things, is an impression of *teeming life*—of the unwonted number of living beings, human and animal, who crowd the land. The country would seem to be overrun by a multitude of men, women, and children all of about the same degree, a little below the most meagre comfort, and a little above the nearest reach of starvation. They crowd everywhere over the length and breadth of the Peninsula, for they number two hundred and ninety millions.

In the towns they hustle one another as they trample along in the dust, so that each narrow street is full to its walls. The driver of a donkey has to yell himself hoarse to make a way for his beast, and the bullock reaches the lane's end by ploughing his shoulders through the crowd as through a field of maize. From the tower of any walled city a many-coloured stream can be seen moving out of each gate across the plain. The streams are made up of brown-faced men, tramping away to be lost on the horizon, tramping in to be lost in the town. From sunrise to sundown the muffled sound of their steps never ceases, and at night there is no dark alley without the sleeping figure of the homeless man.

Beyond the confines of the cities the dry road that leads from town to town is alive with the same wandering folk. They are busy in a hundred fields; they huddle against the mud walls of the villages, and even in the open plain or in the jungle one will not long miss a man's white turban or a woman's blue hood.

These are some of the great hordes who provide in their lean bodies victims for the yearly sacrifice to cholera, famine, and plague. Plague will slay 20,000 in a week, cholera will destroy ten times that number in a year, and the famine of one well-remembered time accounted for five-and-a-quarter millions of dead people. Yet the numbers of the living seem ever the same. There may be, now and then, a freer passage through the bazaars, less colour in the stream from the city gate, less bustle on the highway, but the living column wavers not, for the host that can give up one hundred thousand on one fell march can move on as a great host still.

It may interest the curious to know that the density of the population of British India is such that there are—on an average—279 people to the square mile. "How thick this population is," writes Sir William Hunter,* "may be realised from the fact that, in 1886, France had only 187 people to the square mile."

This ever-pressing crowd is not limited to human beings.

* "A History of the Indian Peoples." Oxford, 1897.

Animal life seems to swarm everywhere in proportionate degree. Wherever the traveller goes he will see always

> "kites sailing circles in the golden air."

Vultures perch on high gates or ruined turrets about the outskirts of the city. The grey-headed Indian crow is everywhere, on the walls, in the alleys, in the temple courts. Always alert and impudent, he pries into everything, watching, wrangling, and thieving with unquenchable energy.

The cheery mina birds are scarcely outnumbered by the crows. They are less noisy, less vulgar, but they are present in their thousands. The plumage of the mina is a little dingy, but there is some white hidden in the wing which flashes forth like a dainty, unintended display of white linen when the bird flutters coquettishly away. Green parrakeets are as common as rooks in a cathedral town. Flocks of pigeons, disturbed from some scene of pillage, are constantly fluttering over the houses; while sparrows, hoopoes, peacocks, cranes, and birds of less well-known types fill up the ranks in the great company of winged things.

In the pinched streets of the bazaar there are nearly as many animals as men. Camels stalk along indifferently as if they were alone in the desert, donkeys with packs patter on their way in companies of twenty, while with them are bullocks drawing carts, cows coming in from the fields, or buffaloes carrying bundles of indefinite garbage.

A Brahmani bull will be lying asleep in front of a temple. Sheep will be dodging in and out of the crowd in search of a living, and to every empty cart or to any convenient awning pole a calf is likely to be tied. A rat or two will now and then run across the little lane; while the disreputable, snarling Pariah dog with the mark of the starving rogue upon his brow, will be skulking wherever a shadow will hide him from the fate of Cain.

It may be that the impression of a host of animals in the street is due to their unwonted admixture with the traffic. This would be understood by imagining the Bond Street of Delhi transferred to the Bond Street of London. One could then see camels striding down the road with supercilious disregard of the police, a train of donkeys winding among the hansoms, and goats picking their way between the carriages. A fat grey bull would be dozing on the step of a hatter's shop, a couple of sheep would be nosing among the trifles on a milliner's counter, while a buffalo, laden with a pile of straw, would hustle the frock-coated lounger from the pavement.

Another animal who helps to make up the crowd of living things in India is the monkey. He assumes many sizes and shapes, and appears particularly to favour the haunts of men. The first time the traveller sees him grinning from a house-top or stealing along a verandah a momentary impression arises that he must have escaped from some organ-grinder's "outfit."

In a street of shops, in the native quarter of Agra, I had the good fortune to see a considerable mêlée among a company of monkeys. Some thirty baboons, large and small, were engaged in this disturbance. It may have been a family quarrel, a phase of a vendetta, or a mere vulgar riot. Anyhow, it was serious. The fighting took place on the house-tops, along balconies, on shop awnings, and in the street. The noise was amazing, for those monkeys who were actually unable to attempt feats of arms were encouraging spectators, who chattered and screamed without ceasing. The whole place seemed alive with devil-possessed baboons. There was a general haze of disorder, violence, and outrage illumined by horrible spasms of fighting in many quarters. Two monkeys locked in a shrieking embrace—a hairy, electrified bundle of wriggling arms, tails, and feet, grinning teeth and gibbering mouths—would drop from a parapet on to a shop awning to the terror of the shopkeeper beneath. The crowd in the street stood still to gaze at the spectacle until some buffaloes, crawling along with smug unconcern, strolled into them as if they had been invisible. The battle ended as abruptly as it had commenced.

Lastly there is everywhere the little grey-striped squirrel. He suggests an alert, impressionable lizard rather than a squirrel, for he moves always in ecstatic jumps. If he is not neurotic, he simulates that fashionable disorder admirably. He is as much at home on the top of a palace as in the gutter, and apparently only uses a tree as a place of refuge. He will be found in every town, as well as in every street in the town and on all high roads. When his nerves are very tried he makes a curious clicking noise which suggests the winding up of a clockwork top.

Next to the impression of this all-pervading host comes the realisation that India is *a country of intense colour.* The atmosphere is bright, contrasts in shade are extreme, and colours are brilliant, crude, and lavish. All the plains and the hillsides at this season of the year are brown with dried-up grass, while the roads that lead into the towns are grey with powdered earth. In contrast with these great monotonous tints the patches of cultivated ground—the cotton fields, the winter wheat, and other crops—stand out as slashes of daring green. Among these tracts of grey, green, and brown are the towns with white walls, flashing minarets or domes, and shaded lanes. In these lanes will be found the people who give the great mass of colour to the country by their many-tinted costumes. In any bazaar are to be seen all the colours of the spectrum dotted about a background of chequered light, and tempered by the comfortable browns and umbers of mere dirt.

If one could recall any picture of India which would convey these two impressions of the living crowd and the crowd of colours, it would come to the memory in some such scene as this:—

A hard, azure sky against which stands out, keenly out, some cocoanut palms and a slate-coloured dome. The dome rises above a white wall which ends below in a dusty road. It is ever in India the white wall with the sun on it. In the wall are shops—square recesses where men squat as mere patches of red and yellow, white and blue. An awning of brown matting, propped up by bamboos, takes a little from the bareness of the wall and shades the spots where the plaster has fallen away from the bricks. Crows glistening like beetles look down from the wall.

The road is full of moving figures, lean and black-haired. The gaunt garments that are wrapped about them are of every colour in the world. A purple hood for the head and a scarlet gown, a bright green turban with an amber cloak, an orange-tinted tunic and a yellow scarf, a naked brown boy, and a man clothed all in white make up the ever-changing eddies of colour in the street.

The light that beats upon all this is blinding, while the shadows by the walls are lit up with the gleam of brass vessels and the silver bangles on the women's feet.

A further impression which soon possesses the traveller in India is that of the *melancholy* which hangs over both the land and its people. The country in the first place is not beautiful. So far as it can be seen during a journey of some few thousand miles it is monotonous and often dreary. Its boundless extent is oppressive, since for league after league the face of the land may remain the same.

It looks homeless. The villages are piteous clusters of mud walls, daubed around the sides of a thick pond in the bare earth. Where there should be a village green there is a patch of stained dust covered with rubbish and peopled by fowls and dogs, by naked children and bony cattle. Cultivation is carried out in despairing patches snatched from the waste, and the labour of the husbandman seems infinite. Every drop of water for these sorry fields has to be drawn from a well in a bucket of cow-hide. Masses of parched cactus make a poor substitute for the hedge of English hawthorn or wild rose, and an unsteady tract of dust through the jungle takes the place of the turnpike road of the old country.

As a town is approached the land becomes, as a rule, less desolate. There are wider roads, with trees by the side of them, ampler fields, greener crops, and possibly the park-like expanse of a cantonement. Some parts of the country, where the water supply is good, are as green as the land in England, but there is never about it the comfortable look of Dorset or Devon. The best patch of green wheat suggests such a crop as a lonely man, wrecked on a desert island, may have produced after many seasons of labour and of grubbing with his hands.

India leaves on the mind an impression of poorness and melancholy, even if in certain districts cultivation is luxuriant, and if, after the rains, the country is brilliant with blossoms which no meadow in England can produce.

The great continent, moreover, is a country of grim extremes. It has a range of mountains, and those mountains are the loftiest in the world. It has plains, and they extend in a dead flat for endless thousands of square miles. There are months of absolute drought followed by months of unceasing rain; so that the cactus hedge may only exchange its covering of brown earth to be half swept away by the flood. There is nothing in the land that is temperate, and it is seldom at peace from some climatic plague or another.

Sadder than the country are the common people of it. They are lean and weary-looking, their clothing is scanty, they all seem poor, and "toiling for leave to live." They talk little and laugh less. Indeed, a smile, except on the face of a child, is uncommon. They tramp along in the dust with little apparent object other than to tramp. Whither they go, Heaven knows, for they look like men who have been wandering for a century. Their meagre figures are found against the light of the dawn, and move across the great red sun as it sets in the west, and one wonders if they still tramp on through the night.

There are many who squat on the ground in little groups in the street or with their backs against walls. They seem to be waiting for some end, and to be weary of the watching, although there is about them the air of most pitiable patience. Vivacious they are not; energetic they are not; nor are they either hearty or brisk. They appear feeble and depressed, and to have cultivated with extraordinary finish the features of utter boredom.

They are a religious people, but their religion is gloomy. They have changed the bright deities of the Veda—the God of the Clear Blue Sky and the Goddess of the Dawn—for less kindly objects of worship. They are terrified by demons, or are haunted by the burden of sins which they have committed in a previous state of existence. Every misfortune is a punishment, and their priests can offer them little comfort other than to warn them to avert worse troubles to come by suitable offerings. Their Heaven is hard to reach, for, even if the way be straight, it is disconsolate and very long. They are fatalists. *Che sara sara,* "What will be, will be!" If the God kills, he kills. There is always the hope of one more meal, and the sweeter hope that after death their bodies may be burned and the ashes cast into the motherly Ganges.

It is no wonder that Buddha—whose life began in Oudh—

urged his disciples to go forth "in pity for the world." To him existence was little more than a tale of sorrow and suffering, and he thought that it was well when the tale was told. "Let no man," he said, "love anything; loss of the beloved is evil. Those who love nothing and hate nothing have no fetters." And at this very moment of writing, when no less than 17,000 men and women are dying of plague in India every week, it is possible to understand how the teacher came to teach as he did.

Both Buddhists and Brahmans insist that meditation should form part of all practical religion, and those who hold to these beliefs certainly lack in India no opportunity for this pious exercise. India is a country which appears to foster meditation, and to the sombre-minded from any land it may be commended as a place to think in.

Another encouragement to melancholy in the native of India is the terrible incubus of caste which keeps the man of low degree from ever rising from the mire, and stamps out from the stoutest heart any pulse of ambition. Born a sweeper you shall die a sweeper, your children shall be sweepers, and there shall be ever upon your brow a mark as clear as the mark of Cain, but it shall be made in dirt instead of blood. Such is the form of curse under which millions start forth on the journey of the world in the heyday of life.

Finally no little of the gloom which hangs over the people is due to the degrading position which women are made to hold, as well as to the customs and traditions which deprive their lives of opportunities for pleasure and of facilities for advancement. The standard of enjoyment among any people, and indeed the touchstone of a nation's cheerfulness, depends mainly upon the women. Yet a reasonable merriment would be as little expected from the women of India as from the man with the Iron Mask. There may be female Mark Tapleys in this Peninsula of the Pessimist, but their efforts must be severely tried.

It is not to be assumed that a uniform melancholy is common to all the inhabitants of the country. Among the hills a more cheery people are to be met with, while with the inhabitants of Rajputana and the Punjab there is not that continued solemnity which would befit those who are conscious that their continent has merited the title of "the land of sudden deaths."

In the bazaars and in the markets there is more animation, more sense of ease, and some display of comfort. But the standard of comfort is not high. The delights of the native of India may be substantial, but they are not too apparent to the Western eye, and it is clear that those who enjoy them do not need "the stranger to intermeddle with their joys."

III.

THE WHITES AND THE BROWNS.

The English in India form an exceedingly small company among the two hundred and ninety millions of people with whose destinies they are concerned. It may not be unseemly to call to mind that England is not the only Western power which has endeavoured to establish its standard in India. The Portuguese first set foot in the country and founded the earliest outpost of European influence—for did not Vasco da Gama land at Calicut one day in May, 1498? But the possessions of Portugal in India are represented now only by the little settlements at Goa, Daman, and Diu. The Dutch made valiant progress in their efforts to absorb the mighty Peninsula, but there is no Dutch soil in India now. The Danes, the Swedes, and the Prussians came and established trading companies, but the memory of these alone remains. The French played a strong and determined part in an attempt to colonise the country, but the French flag now flies only over the towns of Pondicherri, Chandernagore, Mahe, Yanaon, and Karikal.

The governing of India is a wondrous thing to contemplate; wonderful to reckon by how few it is done, with what apparent ease and small parade of power; wonderful to see how difficulties have been moulded into gains, how prejudices have been turned to good account, and how strong bricks have been made from uninviting straw. Above all are to be admired those broad principles of justice, honesty, and kindness which are at the foundation of British rule.

What it has cost in human lives to carry the British flag from the Himalayas to the southernmost cape is terrible to contemplate. True, indeed, it is that the very earth of India "wears the red record" of the English name—the record of men who have died of heat in the burning plains, who have perished of cold among the snows, who have been cut down in lonely passes or have wasted away from disease in fetid swamps.

In the annals of the history of India there are no more graphic documents than those to be found in the English cemeteries throughout the country.

Gracious memorials, such as those at Lucknow and Cawnpore, do not cover all the heroic dead who have laid down their lives in this "Land of Regrets."

In the smallest cemetery in the least-remembered town there are the graves of men who died in the van of the column, but who now lie within the low walls of the compound, unknown and forgotten. And they died so young! Lads of nineteen and men of thirty; and not men only, for there are the graves of the gallant women who followed the men they loved—the wives, the sisters, and the mothers.

I am reminded of one very little burying-ground where a plain stone records the death of the wife of a subaltern. It states that she died aged "18 years and 11 months." One can picture her, a fair-haired girl, fresh from a west of England village, who went as a bride with her lad to this dismal land—a boy and a girl. She died in the fiendish heat (for she died in June) with her thoughts, I fancy, turned towards the ivy-covered house at home, with its kindly gardens and murmuring meadows. There is a pathetic apology in the added words "and 11 months" as if to show that she was not really so very young, but was indeed quite old in the dignity of wifehood. There is little on her grave but cracked earth, which turns to dust in the summer and to mud in the rains, and this has to serve for a covering of green turf within sound of an English trout stream.

In the study of the British residents in India one of the first problems which is presented to the newcomer is bound up in the word "cantonement." The visitor is told that the friend to whom he has a letter of introduction rents the best bungalow in the cantonement, or that another friend is all-powerful in certain phases because he is the cantonement magistrate. To this is added the advice that milk should be obtained from the cantonement dairy.

There may be some to whom it is necessary to explain that the cantonement is the British quarter—the camp or settlement of the army and people of occupation. The cantonement will, as a rule, therefore, be outside the town and in strong contrast with the town. One cantonement will differ but little from another, since the British have wasted no exuberant invention over the planning of their places of sojourn.

On alighting at a cantonement station one expects at once to see what a cantonement looks like, but a cantonement is not a thing that exposes itself immodestly to the eye. From the railway station there extends an ample road which is at once lost among trees. Of the camp there is probably nothing to be seen save the top of a barrack building or the spire of a church. The cantonement, in fact, is everywhere planted with trees by the tree-loving English, and is therefore hidden in green.

It consists of a series of roads which are wide and straight, with trees on either side of them, and beyond the trees white walls. One of these roads is always named "The Mall" in virtue of some undying memory which hangs about the precincts of Charing Cross. Beyond the roads are stiff rows of barracks as simple in design as the wooden blocks of buildings from a child's toy box. They are dotted about in just such a way as a boy would place them on a table when playing at town building. Near about the barracks are hospitals, stores, a racket court, "horse lines," a dairy, a bank, a post-office, and a church. The church professes a style of architecture which may be called amateur Gothic, but it is brave with whitewash and green paint.

A little removed are the bungalows where the English live. Some have thatched roofs, all have verandahs, and all have gardens within a low wall, for it is evident that the design of the bungalow has come from an English brain, filled with reverence for the thatched cottages and rose gardens in the old country.

Whatever may be the purpose of the building in the cantonement, whether it be a telegraph office, a bank, or a court house, it stands in a garden and looks like a bungalow, so that a cheque will be cashed at a table by a French window which opens upon a creeper-laden verandah, the while the bank clerk sits at the receipt of custom in white clothes under the ægis of a punkah.

Somewhere in the cantonement will be a line of shops reputed to be European. In one vile shed—as unassuming as a mule stable—will dwell a man who professes to be a "naval and military dress-maker." In another emporium "English tobacco" is sold, and a hovel that looks like a gutted cobbler's shop is defined by a board as the warehouse of a "coach and saddle builder." There are a chemist's shop and a grocery store for the residents, and a "photo studio," where post-cards and ancient Indian weapons are retailed for the benefit of the tourist.

Far afield are the parade ground, the polo ground, the race course, and the jail, with (in cantonements of high standing) a park, and the withered travesty of golf links.

Those who dwell in the bungalows are very pleasant folk, who are engaged in responsible work full of uncommon detail. They devote their leisure with some success to seeking for comfort in an uncomfortable country, and they are drawn together by the bonds of a common exile. To those of their countrymen who stray into their cantonements they offer a kindly welcome and a too lavish hospitality, and many of the most pleasant memories of a sojourn in India linger about the bungalows of friends whose acquaintance is to be counted in days. While the instincts of a generous host form the first motives in their kindness, there is possibly also in their hearts some desire to meet those who have so recently shaken the dust of Piccadilly from their feet, and who can bring with them the latest of the little news of home, and can talk of theatres and hansoms as of things of yesterday.

There are features in cantonement table talk which are indigenous. One hears always of the horrors of the last hot weather, of the sins of dhobies, of evils wrought by the rains, of cobras in bath rooms, and of intended migrations to the hills. It comes to be known that the most august ladies are the wives of the L.G. and the G.O.C., that the D.A.A.G. and the P.M.O. have played parts in certain "plain tales from the hills," and that the C.O. of R.E. is anxious to show you kindness.

In the British colony there are more who protest that "they like India" than who really like it. To the young subaltern India has actual joys. He has plenty of sport, he can afford to play polo, and he has more servants than he could dream of possessing in England. The young girl also finds that in India she can revel in the very best of "good times." She is a *rara avis*, and is made much of. In the cold weather there are dances and picnics, diversions at the club, and possible dallying on a river in an English boat propelled by an English youth. In the hot weather there are the hills, where heart-stirring things happen under the deodars.

With the middle-aged in India there is apt to be an abiding weariness and a never-dying longing for home. Some of the melancholy of the native has entered into their souls, the land has become a desert, and life a dreary tramp. Although the sky may be radiant with sun, they would change it for a November fog, if only the fog hung over London streets. Although they have a lordly house and many servants they would give it all for a flat in Bayswater. The jungle may be beautiful, but their longings are rather for certain muddy streets and bleak heaths, and, if mere wishing could do it, the palm, the bamboo, and the golden mohr would change to the lavender bush and the hollyhock in the gamekeeper's garden.

Upon those who have grown old in India there has usually fallen the peace of a tardy resignation. Friends at home are dead or gone, they themselves have become moulded to the routine of Indian ways, so that they fear that life in England might be strange and difficult now that the threads that bound them to the old country have been dropped so long. They have outlived the yearning for home, and would end their days wherever such end is easiest and, possibly, cheapest.

The natives of the country—as has been already said—are a woful folk, brown-skinned, with bright raiment, but dolorous countenance. That the great mass of the people are of Aryan descent is apparent enough, and the distinctions which separate them from the aboriginal tribes—such as the Goorkhas and the Bhils—are still unmistakable. The type of face which characterises the true East Indian is for the most part a high type—a lofty forehead, a well-shaped nose, with delicate nostrils, a finely chiselled mouth with parted lips, showing the whitest of white teeth, expressive eyes, shaded by heavy lids, while under the turban or hood is sleek, black hair.

But for the brown skin many would be handsome, and the peasant of few countries can surpass the Indian in the undoubted dignity of his mien. Many of the men might be swarthy Italians or sun-tanned Spaniards. At Simla I happened upon a few people of the hills, who wore caps and whose hair, long, black, and straight, was cut abruptly short at the level of the neck. These might have come from Florence in the days of Savonarola. They recalled the men who figured in old pictures of that time. One of them might have been a model for the brothers in Millais' picture of "Lorenzo and Isabella."

The Indian serves at least to show that the turban is one of the most picturesque forms of head-dress, as it is one of the most rational.

The women are for the most part abject, and are occupied in all manner of sordid work—grubbing about in the dirt or crouching before a mill stone or bearing most oppressive burdens on their heads. All but the youngest of them have managed to eliminate most of the distinctive attractions of their sex. There is nothing of suggestion in their dress, there is little left for the wholesome imagination as to the form their scant robes cover. There is an utter absence of coquetry, of any attempt to please, of any evidence of dressing for effect. A few extra bells on the toes, a brightening of the bangles on the wrist, or an exceptional nose ring would appear to be the limit to which the middle-aged beauty could extend her attractions.

They are bare-footed and bare-legged. The naked human foot is not pleasant to contemplate after the age of babyhood, but when it is brown and covered with mud it is not a thing to even look upon. Many a time in the streets of an Indian town prejudiced travellers must recall with regret the trim, tightly drawn stocking and the bright buckled shoe of the Paris boulevard.

There are two special attractions which the women of India can claim. They have, in the first place, a splendid carriage. They walk with a lissom grace and with dignified movement. In comparison with them in this respect the European woman is a stumbling automaton. A second merit is theirs. The heads of the Indian women are not disfigured by any hideous practice in the matter of the dressing of hair. The head of the Western lady is made uncouth by meaningless lumps and bunches decreed by fashion, so that while her brow assumes the shape of a pumpkin, her neck is bared like the neck of a plucked fowl. Beneath the thin hood the Indian girl wears is to be seen the simple, exquisite outline of the female head, unspoiled by any barbaric fancies of the hairdresser.

The young women and girls are pretty enough. The little girls have their "hair up" from the time they can run, and wear the hood and long skirts of their elders. While they are dressed to look like miniature matrons, their brown faces, their solemn eyes, their parted lips and brilliant teeth remind one of timid black-and-tan terriers. They are shy and modest. Their hands and feet, if unspoiled by unworthy toil, are singularly beautiful. The Indian girl dressed for a festa, with her many-plaited red frock, her blue hood and tasselled scarf, her sparkling rings and bangles, is a picturesque and gaudy personage, even if she appear a little weighed down by her splendour. It may be added, however, that the too often repeated blue and red of the Indian peasant woman's dress becomes in time monotonous.

Of the Indian lady, nothing that comes within the knowledge of men is known—she is "purdah." She is secluded within her house like a nun, and when she goes forth she is carefully protected from the light as if she were a photographic film. Strangely unlike the Western lady, she shrinks from the possibility of being seen of men.

If the grown-up Indian woman cannot look beautiful she can, at least, look old. She seems to possess, above all living things, the power of assuming in the most grisly form the phenomena which attend extreme length of years. He who would see what a human being might look like at the age of 200 years should seek out one of the toothless old women who crouch in the dark doorways in the bazaar. He would find a crooked, grey ghost in rags,

> "Whose shrivelled skin, sun-tanned,
> Clings like a beast's hide to its fleshless bones,"

whose face shows wrinkles which obliterate the features and seem to be graven down to the very skull. Such a poor soul may be no more than sixty, but Methuselah on his death-bed could not have looked older.

One such venerable crone I met with in a native hospital in a native state. She was attending upon her granddaughter who was ill, and her surroundings incidentally revealed some features of the Indian sick room. The room, very small and dark, was lit by one dim window near the roof. From the sill of the window a chance pigeon contemplated the sick bed. The floor of the room was of stone, while the sole suggestion of furniture was an iron bedstead without either head or foot and an earthenware water jar. A chair or a table would have been superfluous, as all visitors would naturally sit on the floor, and on the floor the belongings of the invalid would find a place.

The patient was a married woman of eighteen, plump and pretty. She was the wife of a Mohammedan pedlar, who had left her here while he had continued on his journey. As she squatted upright on the bed her eyes gleamed in the dark. She was radiant with earrings and necklaces and lit up by many bangles. She had a trouble in her thigh, from which she had suffered much at the hands of many Indian physicians. At last she had come upon an English surgeon, and was on the way to be well. She displayed her operation wound with whispered pride, putting her hands together to show how pleased she was that it had been done. For a native of India she was very cheery, and all things seemed to amuse her.

In one corner of the small room, and in its deepest shadow, a little old woman sat on a quilt on the floor. Her property, consisting of a blanket, an untidy bundle, and a small basin, was distributed on the stones around her. Her head was covered by a drab hood, and she was the brownest and most shrivelled human being that the mind could picture. She looked like a dried-up walnut kernel that had long rattled in its shell. Propped up on the brown cross bones which formed her knees was a heavy green book. This was the Koran, from which sacred volume she read aloud to her bright-eyed granddaughter the whole day through. She read "from morn till noon, from noon till dewy eve" without a moment for rest. The smiling girl from her bed and the stray pigeon from the window ledge looked down upon her with a pretty interest. The surgeon asked the ancient dame how old she was, to which she replied that "she had long forgotten."

The buxom girl and the wrinkled thing who read from the book formed a curious couple. They might have been the Princess and the Fairy Godmother of the story book, and the pigeon the Prince in disguise. The witch-like grandmother was proud at heart. It was the long reading of the Koran that had brought back health to the little maid. When she looked up at the laughing face she must have felt that the endless drawl of texts for many weeks had met with its reward, for although her conception of comfort in the sick room may have been ritualistic it was well meant. The patient was soothed by the crooning voice, while the pigeon, who had been attracted at first by curiosity, seemed to draw pleasure from the company of these two.

IV.

THE BAZAAR.

The term "bazaar" implies that quarter of an Indian town which is occupied by the shopkeepers and is devoted to business. The native bazaar at one place is very much like that at another. It is at Delhi, perhaps, that the shopkeepers' quarter can be seen at its best, and what is here written is based upon what was seen in that city.

The bazaar is made up of a tangle of streets, lanes, and alleys, which are crowded by a rabble of human beings and beasts of the field. The road is mere trodden earth, stained brown of black by the emptyings from casual pots. It is littered with garbage, which may still be green or in any stage of withering and decay. The houses, of no form or pattern, are often ruinous and never clean. The shops, which occupy the ground floor, are mere square recesses, as free from decoration or design as the interior of a cart shed. They huddle one after another, but at a wavering level.

Above the shops are the houses proper. Of one storey only as a rule, and built mainly of wood, they form an unsteady palisade of balconies with tattered awnings and dangling mats, overhanging windows, and plain white walls. There are no visible roofs, but on the housetops are often heaps of fodder or piles of wood. As no two adjacent buildings will be of even height, the skyline, along the streets, is notched like the edge of a rag. The street looks unsteady as if it had been shaken out of line by an earthquake. One house will be leaning across the road, and another will be staggering back from it. They reel like a row of drunken men linked together arm in arm.

The woodwork of some of the balconies may be fantastically

carved, or there will be here and there a stone building of some dignity. The timber is bare and burnt by the sun, while the plaster and whitewash which cover the bricks is thinned by the ravages of the rain. There will be in all streets the picturesqueness of broken lines, of careless informality, and of luxuriant neglect.

There is little about any native bazaar to suggest commercial prosperity, as it is understood by the European. The suggestion is rather that the quarter is the bankrupts' quarter, the city a city of ruined men, and the shops mere make-shifts in deserted streets.

Every lane in the bazaar is thronged with life and colour, as well as with an atmosphere of dirt and noise. It is hard to see the road for the tramping of feet, it is hard to see the road's end by reason of the burdens carried aloft upon men's heads. There is ever a solid stream of living forms and vivid tints. On the surface of the tide are heads turbaned with white or yellow, or green or pink, gleaming eyes, white teeth, with now and then a nun-like head shaded by a blue hood. At a lower level are tunics of every colour in a flower garden, brown backs, bare arms, white robes blending with red skirts. Among the stalky undergrowth of naked legs will be seen creeping a dog or a fowl fluttering with panic.

In the crowd are old men with staffs, and girls with water jars, bearers of palanquins, wild long-haired fakirs, water carriers, and coolies with bundles of every shape upon their skulls. Everything is carried upon the head, whether it be a bale of silk, borne by a servant before his master, or a basket of manure carried by a squalid woman.

Here through the mob a string of donkeys will plod along, and there will be a buffalo ridden by a boy, or a camel with a man rocking on his back, or a couple of cows pushed forward by a yelling harridan with a stick.

The vehicles in the bazaar will be represented by the bullock tonga, by the gharry (which looks like a bathing machine), and by the ekka, or two-wheeled pony cart. This latter—the hansom of the city—has the aspect of a Punch and Judy show, aloft on an ice-cream vendor's barrow, and those who ride therein squat cross-legged under the canopy.

THE BAZAAR, DELHI.

Women are chattering in the balconies, or, folding their brown arms upon the rail, are gazing down into the street. Above them on the roof may be a man in a gaudy turban driving importunate pigeons from his grain, while below them are the tattered awnings of brown canvas or coloured rags which keep the sun from the shops.

The shops are raised on a platform a little above the level of the street. As has been already said, they are merely square, cavern-like gaps. Their walls show traces of whitewash and of brown patches left by a generation of oily heads. There is neither window nor door, and at night the shop is closed by just such a gate of rough wood as will be used to shut in an English cow-house. The feature of the shop is the floor. The vendor squats on a mat on the floor, while his assistants or family crouch around him. The customer also squats on the floor or on the platform before the shop. The merchant's wares are deposited on the ground in shallow baskets, brass dishes, or pots, according to their kind. On the floor also are his books, his cash-box, his clothes, his *articles de toilette*, his great pipe, and the utensils from which he eats.

The dweller in the bazaar lives in the street, *coram populo*, and his inner life is generously laid open to the public gaze. In the morning he may think well to wash himself in front of his shop, and to clean his teeth with a stick, while he crouches among his goods and spits into the lane. He sits on the ground in the open to have his head shaved, and watches the flight of the barber's razor by means of a hand glass. The barber squats in front of him, and from time to time whets his blade upon his naked leg. The shopkeeper will change his clothes before the eyes of the world when he is so moved. He also eats in the open, and after the meal he washes his mouth with ostentatious publicity and empties his bowl into the road.

Every phase of the fine art of cooking—with a suppression of no detail—can be witnessed by the lounger in the bazaar. At the same time he can note how the Indian woman washes her head, by wetting it and rubbing thereon the dust from under her feet.

Indeed, in the bazaar, life is seen in its nakedness. There is little that is hidden from the gaze of the curious. There is no suggestion of "keeping up appearances," nor is any effort made to practise crude social deceptions. The mysteries of the household are as bluntly laid open as are the apartments of a doll's house when the front of the establishment is thrown wide by a delighted child. There are deeper shadows in courtyards and mean entries and behind hanging mats which the eye cannot penetrate, but if among the gloom there is the holy of holies of the Indian home, it may well be left in mystery.

The contents of the shops themselves are above all things interesting and endless in variety. Here a merchant sits, cross-legged, among trays and bowls of fragrant spices, the odours from which curl around him like incense. There is a vendor of grain squatting behind pyramids of rice and pulse laid out on mats, while birds watch his store from precarious perches in every corner of his shop. Here is a maker of sweetmeats busy with sticky cooking pots, and the piles of dainties which fence him in are black with flies.

There are shops ablaze with gaudy silks or green with vegetables and fruits. The twang of the cotton bow makes music among a hillock of white fluff on one side of the street, and the hammer of the gold-beater beats time on the other. The potter is busy with his wheel, moulding jars with his fingers, and the brassmaker or the blacksmith send the glint of metal and the glow of fire out into the murk of the road. Here is a meat shop, where the butcher, sitting amid acute smells, grips his knife between his feet and shapes rags of beef by drawing them across the blade with his hands. His neighbour on one side is making slippers, while he on the other bends with a graver over a silver cup.

In one shop two women will be grinding at a wheel, and the passer-by must wonder, when the plague comes, which one will be taken and which one left. Here is a dyer drawing dripping clothes from a vat of saffron dye, and near by is a weaver, or a maker of mats, or a rocking line of restless schoolboys with slates and pencils, learning to write and to add up sums.

Over all spread the sapphire sky and the burning glare of the sun, while from every shadow there steals the sickly odour of cooking oil.

It is at night and under the moon that the streets of an Indian town become filled with the most unearthly spirit of romance. I recall one such night in Bombay when the moon was high in the heavens.

The street was narrow, for the houses on either side of it leaned towards one another. They were lofty and fantastic in shape, so that the gap of light that marked the road made it look like a narrow way through a gorge of rocks. The white glory of the moon, falling from broken housetops, turned into marble the wood-carved mullions of an overhanging window, poured, slanting-wise, into a verandah and made beautiful its poor roof, its arches, and its bulging rail, and then dripping through rents and holes in ragged awnings, filled little pools of cool light in the hot, untidy road.

The shops were closed and were lost in the blackest shadows, although, here and there, a splash of moonlight would strike the stone platform which stood in front of them and reveal a bench, a barred door, or a heavy chest. A few steps of a rambling stair would climb up through the glamour and then vanish in the dusk. The pillars of a stone balcony would stand out like alabaster in the moon, appearing poised in the air, as if the corner of a palace projected into the street. A denser mass of shadow would mask an arched entry whose flagstones led through utter darkness to a courtyard flooded with light.

On the pale stones of one such courtyard was the recumbent figure of a man wrapped from head to foot in a purple cloak, like a corpse laid out for burial. Under the verandahs and in caverns of darkness many other figures were stretched out on mats, on low tables, or on bare stones, all wrapped up so that no face could be seen, all motionless, all lean like the dead. These mummy-like bundles (that were sleeping men) might all have been lifeless bodies put out of doors to wait for some tumbril to come by.

On certain lintels was the mark in red paint which showed

that the plague had visited the house, and so quiet was the place and so still the wrapped-up men that one could fancy that the lane was in a city of death. The figures looked so thin and lay so flat as to show, under the meagre covering, the feet, the points of the knees, and the outline of the head. One figure drew up a bony leg as I passed, and it seemed as if a man left for dead was still alive.

Some were wrapped in red garments, some in yellow, and a few in white. In every one the wrapping entirely enveloped the head, for the native of India when he sleeps—whether in a room or in the open—will always cover up his face.

Possibly a few of those who slept were servants lying outside their masters' houses, but the greater number of them were the homeless men of the city. Some were asleep in the very roadway, so that the passer-by would need to step over them.

The quiet in the place was terrible. The only sound came from the shuffling feet of two prowling dogs who rooted among the garbage in the gutter. It was just such a street as Doré was wont to paint, and such an one as has figured in many a rapier-and-cloaked-figure romance. It was a street that breathed murder, and to which would be fitting the stab in the back, the sudden shriek, the struggling body dragged into a dark doorway by knuckles clutching at the livid neck. It was the street of the Arabian Nights, and there was in it the hush that comes before a tragedy.

In one place in the street a bar of red light from an open door fell across the road and across a muffled figure asleep upon the stones. In another place a motionless woman bent over the rail of a verandah, her head outlined against the glare of a lamp in the room behind her. For what she watched, Heaven knows!

Beyond these two streaks of light, which burnt into the arctic pallor of the moon, there was nothing to suggest that the dwellers in the street did more than mimic death.

V.

AGRA AND ITS BOOK OF KINGS.

The great red fort at Agra was built by Akbar, ever to be known as "Akbar the Great." Its morose bastions and its dainty palaces are filled with memories of the valiant King, of his son Jahangir, and of his grandson Shah Jahan. Never was there such a cycle of romance as clings to the names of these three men. Their halls still stand, their pleasure gardens still blossom, and the sun still shines into the chambers where their ladies loved, languished, and died.

It was Shah Jahan who built the Pearl Mosque—the most divine of all courts of prayer. It was he who raised on the river's bank the Taj Mahal—the loveliest edifice that has ever been framed by the hands of men.

The name of Akbar came into the annals of the history of India in this wise. Somewhere about the time 1001 A.D., when the Normans were invading England, Mohammedan armies were streaming over the plains of India from the north-west passes in the Himalayas. The invaders were victorious, and they established in due time kingdoms and dynasties which were maintained—if maintained at all—by incessant conflict.

At last came Babar the Moghul, who invaded India in 1526, and found the country divided among many Mohammedan kings and as many Hindu princes. He concerned himself with no petty rivals, and sought no conciliatory alliances. His task was to conquer India, and he so far succeeded that when he died at Agra in 1530 he left behind him "an empire which stretched from the river Amu in Central Asia to the borders of the Gangetic Delta in Lower Bengal."

Thus was founded the great Moghul Empire which, before the

English came, was the most powerful dynasty which has ever gripped the sceptre of government in India. It was a dynasty which rose to majestic heights, which reached the supreme pinnacle of relentless power, of arrogance and of splendour, and which, at its zenith, could claim to be the most magnificent court in the whole world.

Of Babar the Lion no trace remains at Agra, unless it be a little summer garden by the river side, where his body is said to have rested before it was removed for burial in Kabul. His son, Humayun, succeeded him, and held somewhat feebly to the crown his father had established. He was King for twenty-six years, and his tomb, which stands on the great high road leading south from Delhi, is one of the finest in India. His wife was a Persian lady, and she bore him a son who became the Emperor Akbar.

Akbar succeeded to the throne when he was a lad of fourteen, and he reigned for nearly fifty years, from 1556 to 1605, and it is noteworthy that his reign was nearly contemporary with that of Queen Elizabeth of England. She came to the throne two years after his accession, and died two years before him. Akbar was a born King, a man of stirring talents, who showed himself to be both a daring soldier and a tactful diplomatist. His reign was a reign of conciliation; he fused the petty kingdoms into which India was split up into one united empire, while he reconciled to his rule as well the conquered Hindus as the independent Mohammedan princes. What he could not effect by statesmanship he attained by force. He it was who stormed and took the famous fortress of Chitor, and the gates of that citadel he carried with him to Agra, where they remain to this day. He was singularly tolerant in his religious views. His favourite wife was a Hindu princess. Another of his wives was a Christian lady named Miriam. At least, so the story goes, and those who tell it show still in his palace at Fatehpur-Sikri a house, in perfect state, called Miriam's House. He was an enlightened and just ruler, through whom the Moghul dynasty attained the highest peak it was ever destined to reach.

He built the great palace of Fatehpur-Sikri on a hill near by to Agra. The palace with its many halls still towers over the plain. It is empty and wofully deserted, but the hand of ruin has passed it by, so that if the dead King could once more ride up the cobbled way that leads to the palace gates he would find that four hundred years have wrought but little havoc upon his sturdy walls.

Akbar—as has been already said—built the red fort at Agra. At Agra he died, and he was buried in a stately garden at Sikandra, which garden lies some six miles from the fort towards the north. So the great Emperor slept with his fathers, and Jahangir his son reigned in his stead.

Jahangir reigned twenty and two years over India, and, in the words of the Book of Kings, "he did evil in the sight of the Lord." He was an indifferent ruler and an unsuccessful general. He spent his nights in drunken revelry, and it is said of him that "he talked religion over his cups until he reached a certain stage of intoxication, when he fell to weeping." *

An Englishman of distinction, Sir Thomas Roe, gives an account of a private audience he had with this monarch—who incidentally assumed the title of the "Conqueror of the World." The Emperor utilised the audience to enquire anxiously of Sir Thomas how much *he* drank in the day, how he esteemed beer as an intoxicant, and whether he could make it in Agra. It would appear that as soon as the Conqueror of the World was informed upon these vital points the interview closed.

Jahangir's palace still stands—in a state of perfect preservation—within the walls of the fort of Agra. It is a gloomy building, severe and grim. Owing, however, to the thickness of its walls and the seclusion of the royal apartments, the structure is well suited to the needs of a monarch who was in the habit of becoming tipsy after sundown, and of weeping and howling when sufficiently advanced in drink.

To Jahangir's merit must be placed the building of Akbar's resplendent tomb at Sikandra, and of the still more glorious structure which covers the remains of Itmad-ud-Daulah, the father of his favourite wife. Another matter in his life which should count

* Sir William Hunter's "History of the Indian Peoples," p. 141.

for righteousness was his undying devotion to this wife, Nur Jahan, and her unsparing love of him.

Jahangir died in 1627, and was succeeded by his son Shah Jahan, who was at the time of his father's death engaged in raising a rebellion against him. Shah Jahan was thirty-six years old when he came to the throne. His mother was Jahangir's second wife, a Hindu princess known as Jodh-Bai. Shah Jahan unfortunately commenced his career as Emperor by murdering his brother and such other members of the house of Akbar as might become rivals to the throne.

In 1615, when Shah Jahan was twenty-three years of age, he married Arjumand Banu—a lady whose name has been made immortal, for she was the lady of the Taj, the wife of his youth, over whose small body was erected the most glorious building in the world.

Arjumand Banu was of Persian descent. Her grandfather, Itmad-ud-Daulah, was an adventurer from Teheran, and the tomb that Jahangir erected over his remains has already been alluded to as one of the monuments of his reign. Her father was a minister of great influence in the court. His name was Asaf Khan, and his sister (the aunt of Arjumand Banu) was the Empress Nur Jahan, the favourite wife of the dead King.

The lady of the Taj died in 1629, so the two were married for fourteen years. She had seven children, and died during the birth of the eighth. If it be supposed that she was about seventeen years old when she married, she would have been about thirty-one when she died. It will be noticed that she died the year after her husband came to the throne; so the lady of the Taj was an empress for but one short year.

One might imagine that the happiest days of her life had been spent in Agra. It was there, by the Jumna, that the young Prince became her lover and her husband, and it was by the Jumna, no doubt, that she wished that her body might rest. She died far away from Agra; for she seems to have followed her husband on an expedition to the Deccan, and to have died in Burhanpur, a place many days' journey from the river fort.

Shah Jahan is said to have been a man of grave and solemn

countenance who seldom smiled. He was a good king who lived royally. In splendour and lavish magnificence his court was without an equal in the world, and there is little doubt that in his palaces the pomp and circumstance which surround an emperor were only to be surpassed by the glory of dreams.

He was the Great Moghul. Those who would see how an emperor should live must needs travel to Agra or to Delhi. There was nothing in Europe to compare with this radiant court. The halls in the palace of the King of England were humble and insignificant by the side of the gorgeous domes which covered the head of the Emperor of India. The throne upon which he sat—the famous Peacock Throne—was estimated to have cost six millions sterling, and the palace was worthy of the throne. The conception of "oriental magnificence" and of the "splendours of the East" has its prime origin in the courts of this most kingly of all kings. What the poet might imagine of the glamour which should encircle a throne he realised, while it would seem that he reached the end of those inventions which could minister to the possibilities of personal ambition.

Shah Jahan not only built the Pearl Mosque and the Taj Mahal, but he reared on the walls of the great red fort at Agra the palace of white marble, which crowns the fortress still. He founded the new city of Delhi, and built there another white palace, which in some elements of splendour was more magnificent than that of Agra.

All this and more he did during a reign of thirty years, but his end was not peace. One of his sons—a child of the lady of the Taj—rose up against him, deposed him, and made him a prisoner in that very palace of Agra which he himself had raised. There he lingered for seven years, and there he died one day in December, 1666. At the time of his death he was seventy-four years of age.

The son who deposed him—the Emperor Aurangzeb—although he bestowed upon himself the title of the "Conqueror of the Universe"—lived to see the great Moghul Empire fade. He ruled in sumptuous magnificence at Delhi, but before his end came the flaming cresset which had cast its glare over nearly the whole of India began to flicker and become dim.

The last of the Moghul Emperors was the paltry old puppet who ran out of Delhi when the British entered it in 1857 after the ever-memorable siege. This poor pantaloon monarch, who had no more regal reality than the king in a pantomime, hid in a tomb by the roadside, whence he was taken like a pickpocket back to Delhi, and finally sent as a prisoner to Rangoon. There he died in 1862, the sorry relic of a line of magnificent emperors.

VI.

THE FORT AT AGRA.

Agra figures very largely in the guide books, wherein both eloquence and adjectives are lavished upon it. For the various "objects of interest" encountered, the guide book has a severe classification and a graduated order of merit. Those objects which are peculiarly precious are defined as "imposing," as "most elegant," or as "miracles of beauty." They are admitted into a sacred coterie under the insignium of "the most interesting features of India." Such structures as just escape being miracles of beauty are received into the second class of the order under the category of things "which will well repay a visit." The third class embraces tombs and temples which are "pleasing," and which the tourist "should not fail to see if time permits."

Agra is happy in possessing examples of all these degrees of excellence, so that it can satisfy the pampered intellect which is only to be appeased by palaces, as well as the simpler mind which finds joy in "carvings in soapstone and imitations of old inlay work."

The fort at Agra stands upon an eminence near the banks of the river Jumna, a little outside the busy town it guards so valiantly. It is built wholly of dark red stone, and it is doubtful if there is in the world a fort which looks more fort-like. It has great walls rising like cliffs above flanking defences, a line of battlements for a legion of armed men, and loopholes for a thousand musketeers.

There is around it a huge moat, across which stretch ponderous drawbridges, and beyond the bridges are the most mighty and terrible gates that the timid could conceive. There are, moreover, huge bastions and frowning towers that care for nothing and defy the world.

Those who wish to see such a place of refuge as they have fashioned in their dreams should see the great fort at Agra. There is nothing they will have imagined so massive, so valiant, and so red. What a fortress of rock it must have seemed to the fluttering town folk as they hurried breathless under its portals, dragging with them their children and their clinging wives, just as the dust cloud of the galloping horde appeared along the outskirts of the city!

What a giant it is, and what terrible armaments its circuit must enclose! The very walls call up the clash of arms, the blasts of trumpets, the clatter of hoofs on stones, the thunder and glare of the bursting mine, the forest of scaling ladders, and the heap of dead in the moat. It is just such a fort as should figure in an allegory, or be engraven on a shield as an heraldic symbol. It is just such a fort as would delight a boy if he could have it in miniature and in copious red paint. It is to be feared that the modern soldier would regard Akbar's stronghold at Agra as a paltry place of arms. Still it looks so strong, it stands so gallantly in front of the town, and, when seen from the plain with the sun upon its eastern face, it looks so beautiful.

This eastern face is that which turns towards the river, and here on the summit of the great red height stands Shah Jahan's palace of marble. The fortress wall rises sheer from the ditch, as ponderous a mass of stone as is a precipice of granite. On the top of this rampart, where the battlements should be, is the frail palace. From afar it appears as a delicate line of polished walls pierced by tiny windows surmounted by gilded cupolas and broken by arcades with alabaster pillars. There one can see the chamber in the Jasmine tower where the ladies sat after sundown, the queen's white terrace, and beyond all these the peerless domes of the Pearl Mosque glistening in the sun like ice.

There could be no contrast more extreme than that between the savage war-tanned fortress wall and the gentle buildings which crown its summit. It looks as if a cloud had become entangled among the armaments of a stronghold, or as if a shower of white rose leaves had fallen upon a headsman's block.

VII.

THE PALACE IN THE FORT.

Within the fort and along its eastern face are two palaces side by side; one, built of red stone, is strong, dismal, and unlovely; the other, of white marble, is fragile, exquisite, and radiant. The red palace has dingy courts, its corridors are dim, its walls are austere, and it crouches sulkily in the shadow behind the ramparts of the fort. The white palace crowns the bastion like a creeping flower, lifts its domes towards the sun, lays bare its tender columns to the breeze, and its courtyards to the falling dews. One is a refuge for armed men, a place for stacked spears, for boisterous banqueting and ribald speech. The other is for women's feet, for the sound of lutes, the frou-frou of silk, and the stately pacing of a smiling prince. The red building is Jahangir's palace, the other the palace of Shah Jahan.

Jahangir's palace is built wholly of red sandstone, of the same stone indeed as the walls of the fort. It is an extensive building which has been well preserved. It is approached by a heavy gateway, with the look rather of the entrance to a stronghold than to a residence for kings. There is within the gate a noble courtyard, from which lead wide halls with many corridors. There are, besides, suspicious passages, and a maze of chambers fashioned all of the same ruddy stone. Beneath the great rooms is a wilderness of dark ways, and lines of chambers which never see the sun. There is everywhere a sense of heaviness and gloom. Most of the pillars and the brackets under the eaves are copiously carved, but the decoration is barbaric and truculent. Here and there is a moulding of lotus flowers cut out of stone, but they are not the flowers which dot the fountain pools in the garden. They are such buds as a soldier might carve with his dagger out of wood by the camp fire. In one hall the ceiling is supported by sloping beams of carved stone, but the things graven upon the beams are crawling snakes and loathly dragons. There are no arches in the building, and the substitutes for the arch, although always ingenious, are clumsy and harsh.

The decoration of the royal residence is—the guide books say—for the most part "pure Hindu." It is claimed that it is bold and virile, but it is not pleasing. Much of the dinginess of the palace is due to the fact that time has laid bare its walls and ceilings, for the harsh stone was once covered by plaster and gaudy paint. There are traces of this decoration still, and although the colours are now faint, it is evident that they were in old days bright enough, and were bestowed upon bold designs.

As one walks through the silent dust which covers the floors of the bald courts, it is impossible not to realise that the red palace of Jahangir was built for sturdy men. It was for men who had been hardened by life in camps, by angry marches, and the roar of battle. It was within its portal that the captain, hot from war, could throw down his arms in a careless heap, and stretch his tired limbs in the cool of its dim passages. The Hall of Audience was more suited for savage debate and the hammer fall of the determined fist than for leisurely discourse. Along the dark corridors and up the steep stairs one would expect rather the clang of mailed feet than the rustle of the courtly gown.

In that part of the palace where the ladies lived there is little to recall the gentle life. Rather do its walls suggest a prison, a place of safe keeping for timid captives who had been dragged to the palace with other spoils of war. It is easy to imagine on the verandah a fluttering woman, with terror in her writhing fingers, and the awful look of the hunted in her eyes.

It is pleasant to turn from the sinister courts of Jahangir to the White Palace reared by his son Shah Jahan.

This palace covers a great extent of ground, and is a wonder of courtyards and pavilions, of passages and corridors, and of domes and pillared halls. Within its precincts are pleasure gardens, fountain squares, mosques, a lady's market place, baths shimmering with glass, throne rooms for the court, and turrets to

THE GOLDEN PAVILION AT AGRA.

The Taj Mahal in the distance.

sleep in when the nights are hot. There are, moreover, secret passages which lead to hidden doors, and secret stairs which mount to unexpected roofs or plunge by whispering ways into the shadows of the moat. All the buildings are in a singularly good state—are, indeed, so little spoiled by time that no great labour could make the palace as it was when Shah Jahan was king.

The palace is entered through the Hall of Public Audience. This building, which looks out upon the tilt yard, is a vast piazza, the floor of which is raised a little from the ground. It is open on all sides but one, and is like a pine forest, where strong, white pillars stand in line instead of the trunks of trees. The columns are in aisles under a gorgeous roof, whose wide-spread eaves form a shelter from the sun. On the one side which is not open to the square is a raised alcove of white marble, made beautiful by inlaid stones. Aloft, in this recess, was placed the Emperor's throne. On either side of the alcove there were grilles in the wall which let light into closed passages, and through these fretted openings bright-eyed ladies of the Court peeped out upon the crowd.

Go back a few centuries and here is the great Armoury Square filled with a thousand men-at-arms, their horses in gay trappings, their elephants covered with cloths of crimson and tassels of gold. The courtyard is alive with colour, is dazzling with the gleam of spears, and hot with the noise and dust of impatient feet and clattering hoofs. In the Hall of Audience are the hushed people—a rustling, eager crowd of all degrees—the courtier, radiant as a peacock, the inquisitive boy, the sullen chief whose estate has gone, the pallid youth whose gaze is ever on the grilles in the wall, the sober merchant, and the man of law.

In the alcove sits the great king in a jewelled robe, effulgent beyond common speech, most valiant to gaze upon but yet filled with awe, worshipped as all-powerful, but sickly with a hundred fears. In the wall behind the Emperor's throne is a small door, which must have been watched with awful expectancy on the audience day.

Beyond this royal doorway is the gallery of the Machchi

Bhawan or Fishing Tank. This is a large square, with an arcade on all sides of it, both in the gallery and beneath the same. Grass now grows in the square under the shade of a pipal tree, but it is said that in days gone by the place was filled with water, and that the Emperor fished there surrounded by his Court. On one of the galleries, where the floor stands out beyond the rest, is a canopy of white pillars supporting a marble dome. Under the shade of this baldachino, if the story be true, the great Moghul sat and fished. The spot, quiet as it is, would not charm the meditative heart of Isaak Walton. To him the roof of stone and these stately cloisters would ill compare with an April sky in England and with a river bank green with willows and nodding rushes. Those, however, who would wish to see how an emperor should fish, or would care to learn what the gentle art might demand when it becomes the sport of kings, should visit the Machchi Bhawan.

From one corner of this strange enclosure a paved way leads to the Gem Mosque or Naginah Musjid. It was here that the Empress and the ladies of the Court came to pray, and if the peaceful beauty of the spot could avail them anything their prayers must have reached Heaven.

The mosque is very small, very unpretending, very white. It is built wholly of spotless marble, free of any but the plainest decoration. It is merely a little white square, with high walls open to the sky. The enclosure would be bare but for a miniature fountain and its baby stream. Over the mihrab—which is on the side nearest to Mecca—are three white domes. Under the domes is a tiny cloister, beyond whose pillars are such shades as lie beneath the wings of a dove. The little white square itself is dazzling: it sparkles in the sun. The spot is so chaste, so virginal, that it must needs be the court of a nunnery, and no sound could break its quiet harsher than a whispered prayer from timid lips.

Here on the cool stone knelt the ladies of the Court—exquisite little figures wrapped in glistening silk, one in rose, one in yellow, and one in blue. Black locks stray from under bright hoods as the shapely heads are bowed towards Mecca. Beneath the robe's edge are glimpses of bare feet and of gold rings, which tinkle on the marble as first one restless ankle is moved and then another. A pair of green parrakeets might watch the worshippers from the walls, but otherwise no eye can look upon them as they pray.

From the Gem Mosque there is a short passage which opens at once into the gallery of the Ladies' Bazaar. It is here that silks and jewels, feathers and pearls, singing birds and pretty toys were laid out for sale. The bazaar and the mosque stand side by side. The one leads directly to the other, and it is interesting to note—as a comment upon the ways of women—that the House of Prayer and the Market for Finery should be joined by a convenient corridor. It may be that visions of new possibilities in dress did enter the heads of the little ladies who knelt in the mosque, and disturbed their prayers. If such disorder was wrought in their minds it did not pass away with the century in which they lived, for it is probable that in modern times some of the most vivid inventions in dress have been revealed to women as they sat in church.

The bazaar by the mosque is as perfect now as it was in the days when it was thronged by sellers, holding aloft bright scarves and golden brooches, all eager to catch the royal eye. The place is in the form of a square with niches on all its sides, in which was displayed whatever could minister to feminine vanity.

The market place and its tiny shops are built of rude and common stone, but the royal gallery, which hangs over one side of it, is of white marble from no mean quarry. In this balcony is a canopy to shield the imperial ladies from the sun, and between the canopy and the doorway of the mosque is a screen of latticed marble—pale as snow—to hide them from plebeian eyes. The gleaming silken robes that flickered through the lattice, as the royal folk passed by, must have been good to see, and when the Empress took her seat by the balcony's edge the vendors of pretty things must have felt that their trinkets and embroideries had suddenly become dull.

Here in this miniature bazaar, within the palace wall, any who wish may still gaze upon the daintiest realisation of Vanity Fair that the world can show.

From that corner of the Machchi Bhawan which is farthest from the Ladies' Bazaar a devious and obscure passage leads to a mosque which is even smaller than is the Naginah Musjid just described. This is the Emperor's Private Mosque, in which he worshipped alone. It is hidden away from the brilliant terraces and the crowded halls of the palace, so that he who prayed here would find the silence broken by no sound of lute or singing, and by no clatter of arms. Only the murmuring of birds would fall upon his ear, and he would be as solitary as if he knelt in the heart of a forest.

It is a very small mosque of white marble, pathetic in its plainness and childlike in its simplicity. There is merely a narrow court—the smallest in the palace, and at one end—the end towards Mecca—are three little arches, so simple that they have no feature but their shape. The court is open to heaven, and the roof over the humble arcade of naked arches is flat. There are no domes, no carvings, no decorations. The place, indeed, is as bare as a hermit's cell. It lies buried among the walls of a palace whose magnificence is unparalleled. So well is the tiny mosque hidden that many a strutting courtier must have been at a loss to find it, and the waiting noble must have wondered where the great king hid. The people beyond the palace walls would picture the Emperor at prayer within a building of glittering domes, ablaze with precious stones, heavy with beaten gold, and luxuriant with the tenderest work of the artist.

There is nothing in the palace more touching than this poor little corner where the king prayed, where he knelt to thank God for victories, where he bowed in humility under defeats, where he poured out the tale of his weakness, and where he wrung Heaven to save him from the plotting rival, or the knife of the assassin.

Let those who would know something of the heart of the man who built the Taj recall this glorious palace of his at Agra; walk through the still more gracious halls he fashioned at Delhi; read of the splendours and unequalled grandeur of his court, and then seek out the plain little yard where the great king crept to pray.

The most sumptuous part of the palace of Shah Jahan—the heart of the mansion—lies towards the river on the edge of the fortress wall. It is built wholly of white marble, and wherever carving is seemly there are chiselled flowers or twining leaves, while on every arch and panel are fine patterns in inlaid stone in jade and jasper, in lapis lazuli or malachite, in bloodstone and cornelian. Whatever stone from the quarry can imitate the tint of blossom or fruit lies there embedded in marble like flowers in ice. In every wall that looks out upon the river are windows filled with marble fretwork, through which come glimpses of the wide stream by day and of the cold light of the moon at night. There may be princely palaces more gaudy and more lavish in gilt, and mansions more spacious in extent with loftier walls, but no abode of kings can excel the white palace of Agra in its delicacy and its lovable tenderness. Little has changed within its precincts since the time when:

> "By winding ways of garden and of court
> The inner gate was reached, of marble wrought,
> White, with pink veins; the lintel lazuli,
> The threshold alabaster, and the doors
> Sandal-wood, cut in pictured panelling;
> Whereby to lofty halls and shadowy bowers
> Passed the delighted foot, on stately stairs,
> Through latticed galleries, 'neath painted roofs
> And clustering columns, where cool fountains—fringed
> With lotus and nelumbo—danced; and fish
> Gleamed through their crystal, scarlet, gold, and blue."

Near by the fishing tank and overlooking a long stretch of the river is the Hall of Private Audience. It is the most beautiful pavilion in the palace, and is snow-white from its ample platform to the great drip stones beneath the roof—a wonder of glistening pillars, of exquisite carving, and of marvels in tinted stone.

The river front of this pavilion is open save for the aisles of pillars, but away from the river the great hall sinks into the shadow of many arches, and here in the faint and mysterious light the Emperor sat. It needs only a few obsequious nobles in cloth of gold and robes of ruby to be clustered around the solemn columns to bring back the scene as it was when the king held court in the pavilion. It needs little imagination to realise the trembling knees and fumbling hands of the pallid man, who, with his eyes fixed upon the jewelled presence far in the shadows of the hall, staggered up the white steps to seek an audience of the king.

Near about the centre of the palace is a closed square occupied by the Grape Garden. It is formal in all its planning, and on it from three sides open the windows of the ladies' apartments. It is a quiet spot, removed from the vulgar eye, and much frequented by birds, while through the middle of it, they say, a stream once ran.

On that side of the garden which looks towards the Jumna is the King's Private Pavilion. It is a brilliant building like in design to the Hall of Private Audience, but smaller and less extravagant in ornament. In front of it are a fountain tank in marble, a white terrace with a balustrade of trellis-work, and a flight of small steps which lead down to the garden. Rows of pillars fill the open side of the pavilion, and here the sun falls slanting-wise towards the evening; but that part of the hall which comes near to the river is in shadow, and in its panelled walls are windows filled with pale marble tracery. Through this lattice work can be seen the sweep of the great stream, with the Taj standing above it, and here on many a night

> "The moon has glittered through the lace-worked stone."

On either side of the King's Hall are courtyards of marble, as simple and as white as courts within convent walls. On the river side of each are the two Golden Pavilions. They are exquisite arcades of many arches, over which are gilded domes and pointed spires. They stand on the very edge of the fortress wall, and a flower dropped over the balustrade which holds them in would fall into the moat.

It is said that in these most dainty pavilions the ladies kept their jewels in recesses in the walls. Certainly the recesses are there, as well as the narrow holes that lead to them, and every tourist searches each hiding-place as he would search the bottom of an empty golf bag. From the Golden Pavilions, however, the perfume and the glamour of fair women and the enchanting incense that hung about them have gone as completely as have the trinkets that once were hidden there.

There can be little doubt that the most beautiful corner of this palace is where the pavilion stands in which the royal ladies spent their day, and in which they slept in the summer time. This is the Jasmine Tower. It rests upon the summit of the fort wall—a fabric of Sèvres china planted on a rampart of coarse stone. It crowns, indeed, a bastion in that rampart, so that it may as well be called the Jasmine Bastion as the Jasmine Tower. This boudoir among the battlements is as strangely placed as is the daisy which may crown in time the earthworks of a battery, or the nest which birds may build within the muzzle of a war-worn gun.

In the tower is an octagon chamber, crowned by a golden dome. This room—its walls, its columns, its floor, its ceiling—is brilliant with most lavish decoration.

> "O'er the alabaster roof there run
> Rich inlayings of lotus and of bird,
> Wrought in skilled work of lazulite and jade,
> Jacynth and jasper; woven round the dome,
> And down the sides, and all about the frames
> Wherein are set the fretted lattices,
> Through which there breathe, with moonlight and cool airs,
> Scents from the shell-flowers and the jasmine sprays."

This octagon room opens by five sides upon a white marble balcony, which hangs over the great wall, and but for the balustrade of lattice work, a careless foot might slip into the empty air.

On three sides the chamber leads into a hall, with an aisle of shadows. In the hall are a marble pool and a fountain, while beyond the sheltering pillars is a courtyard ablaze in the sun.

In the tower—open on all sides to the lazy breeze—the ladies idled; watching the ferry-boats cross the river, the men come home from work in the fields, the horsemen that galloped down to the ford, and the camels that trailed away from the city until they were mere dots against the sky. In this tower they toyed with their embroideries and their trinkets, listened to the singer and the teller of stories, and dozed over the half-touched lute. On the floor were carpets from Persia and rugs from the north, beyond the hills. On the walls were silks from the distant east, mirrors of silver and lamps of gold. Everywhere there were flowers and sparkling stones, and over all the odour of roses and the warm mist of laziness.

Now the tower is empty, and the whistling tourist tramps perspiringly over its dainty stones, with a red guide book in one hand and a camera in the other. He pronounces it "all ripping," and hurries off to "do" the Taj before the next train leaves.

Those who have seen all these things in the palace at Agra have still much to see. For the curious there is the Shish Mahal—a suite of royal baths, lit only by artificial light. The walls and roofs of this strange "palace" are lined with countless small mirrors and discs of glass. In one wall are recesses for coloured lamps, so that when water fell in front of them the stream should be tinted like the rainbow. A secret passage leads from these gaudy chambers to the Jasmine Tower, and another makes a way of escape by the water gate.

For the adventurous there will be discovered under the fountain by the King's Pavilion, and hidden in a quiet corner, a low entry. It leads by a black and narrow stair—which might be called "the conspirator's staircase"—to a labyrinth of passages which are in darkness, or are lit by occasional gashes in the fort wall. Among these passages will be found many rooms, both large and small, a great well, a place of prayer, and a variety of chambers which were intended to form a refuge from the summer heat. These subterranean halls and corridors are now much frequented by snakes, and have in consequence lost some of their attractiveness.

Last of all there is, in the older part of the palace and overhanging the fortress wall, a simple eight-sided room. It has within it two rows of columns, one inside the other, for the outer row serves to make a verandah for the chamber. It is a plain little place, in marked contrast with the superb palace within the confines of which it is found. There is a particular interest about this small octagon room, for it was here, so they say, that Shah Jahan died. He died a prisoner on a day in December, in the year 1666, at the age of 74. He had been a prisoner seven years.

As he lay on his couch in this tower, a wonderful view stretched out before him. The tower stands high. Below it and beyond the outer fortifications is a belt of green trees, and beyond the trees is the river Jumna, which here makes a great sweep, as if it bowed before the palace as it passed. In December the stream is so low that islands of fawn-coloured sand rise out of the water. Not a breath of wind ruffles the surface of the river, which glistens in the sun like polished metal. The banks are green and flat, and green is the country beyond the river—so verdant that it has the look of England. The eight-walled tower faces towards the east, and every day of the seven years that the old King lay a prisoner here he would see the sun rise across the river.

Two other things he could see from his windows. Towards the north is the Jasmine Tower, standing out over the moat. This is the tower which he had willed should be the sweetest pavilion in the palace, for it was to be the home of his Empress. On any day during his captivity he could hear the sound of laughing women there, and the northern wind would bear to his prison snatches of their songs and faint eddies of their perfumes, but the voices would be strange and the songs unfamiliar. There was, however, a thing more beautiful than the Jasmine Bastion that the King could see from his tower. In front of the palace, and standing high upon the river's bank, is the Taj Mahal—the very glory of his life—where the wife of his youth lay sleeping, and where his own body was to rest when his long captivity was over. In the morning the first light that dawned would fall upon the great white dome, and in the evening the last rays of the setting sun would flood the arches that covered the head of his Queen.

There was some bitterness in this, but, perhaps, some comfort in it. It is fitting that the last gaze of the dying King should be fixed upon the river and the Taj.

Within the fort wall, but some way removed from the palace, is the Pearl Mosque. This also was built by Shah Jahan, and it has been written of it that it is the most exquisite house of prayer in the world. It is raised high upon a gross platform of sandstone.

Its outer walls are red, dull, and plain. No building could appear more unattractive from the outside, and but for glimpses of white domes the four commonplace walls might enclose a store for goods or a tramway terminus. The mosque, moreover, is approached by a steep and uninviting staircase of rough stone, at the summit of which is a solid gateway, that, in guide-book language, is "very fine." The gateway breaks suddenly into a large square, open to the sky, and on the opposite side of the square is the Pearl Mosque.

The blaze of white is so unexpected and so intense that one needs must gasp. The contrast is so astonishing—on one side the enclosure of dull walls, the coarse, toiling stairs, the hot gateway; and on the other this ice-field of pure white. The square with its walls and its cloisters, and the mosque with its domes and pillars, are all of white marble, and when the sun fills the enclosure the effect is almost blinding. The onlooker, standing for the first time under the gloomy archway, draws a quick breath, as he would if he came suddenly upon a great stretch of sunlit snow, or a glacier revealed by an abrupt turning on a road.

There is some other charm in the Pearl Mosque beside that which is due to its absolute whiteness. There is a comfortable sense of proportion and of dignified design. On three sides of the square are colonnades, interrupted by great gates with cupolas. On the fourth side is the mosque, with those three white domes which can be seen so far off, and on each dome is a glittering spire. In the mosque are many columns arranged in three aisles. They support delicate Saracenic arches and a curiously vaulted roof.

As a place of prayer it is simple and chaste. Shadows of amber and brown fill its recesses as with incense. It is open to the sky, and the sky is blue. It is open to the sun, and the sun floods its courts and cloisters. The least devout must feel that it is a holy place, pure and spotless, and filled with the silent benediction of peace.

Anyone who would wish to fashion in their minds the most sufficing picture of a man in prayer could possibly find no spot in the world more fitting for such realisation than the Pearl

THE TAJ MAHAL, FROM A WINDOW
IN THE PALACE AT AGRA.

Mosque. The square would be empty save for the sun, shadows alone would occupy the white aisles, and, kneeling on the marble of the court, with only the heavens above him, would be the figure of a solitary man prostrate in prayer, with his turbaned head touching the stone.

The Pearl Mosque would better become this kneeling figure than would the steps before the high altar in St. Mark's at Venice, or in the Sistine Chapel at Rome. These places are grand, resplendent, and elaborate. The Pearl Mosque can claim only a divine simplicity and that access to Heaven which belongs to an unruffled mere of white water.

VIII.

THE TAJ MAHAL.

The Taj Mahal is a white marble mausoleum of immense size, erected on the high bank of the Jumna where the river bends to the east just below Agra. It was built—as has been already stated—by the Emperor Shah Jahan over the remains of his wife Arjumand Banu, the wife of his youth. She died in 1629, a little more than a year after her husband came to the throne, and in 1630 the building of the Taj was commenced. Thirty-seven years after the death of his queen the body of the Emperor was laid by her side, and under the great dome the two now sleep together. The mausoleum stands aloft on a huge platform of marble. In front of it is a glorious garden such as the East alone can produce, while behind it is the river. The height of the building from the garden walk to the pinnacle which crowns the dome is some two hundred and forty feet.

The Taj is constructed entirely of white marble, and is in general terms a square building surmounted by a single large dome and some minor cupolas and minarets. Its sides look to the four cardinal points of the compass. The south side is turned towards the garden, and here is the entrance to the mausoleum. The north wall looks over the river, while the west wall faces the palace of Agra. Each quarter of the building is the same. On every one of the four sides there is an enormous arch, which reaches to the base of the dome, and which encloses an equally great recess. This deep recess has a beautifully faceted and vaulted roof. On either side of each main arch are two small alcoves placed one above the other. These recesses also extend deep into the building. Each of the four angles of the mausoleum is cut away, and on the flat surface thus produced are two more deep alcoves in every way identical with those which flank the great arch.

On the far wall of each one of these arched spaces are windows of fine marble work with many square panes. Over the four principal arches is a floral design in coloured stone, together with a text from the Koran in letters of black. Inlaid work of simple character crowns the lesser arches, marks out the parapet of the building, and encircles the base of the main dome. With these exceptions the mausoleum is wholly white. Not only is the roof of every recess wonderfully faceted, but every wall is cunningly carved, and the same pattern is repeated over and over again.

On the four corners of the platform upon which the Taj stands are lofty and massive minarets, looking to European eyes a little like lighthouses. The individual stones, of white marble, are marked out by black lines, so that the towers are made to assume the aspect of great solidity and strength.

Within the mausoleum are passages and rooms and an inner wall which encloses the area beneath the dome, where are the tombs of the queen and her husband. As is usual in Mohammedan sepulchres, these tombs do not contain the bodies of the dead. These lie in a vault below, level with the surface of the ground. They are covered by plain tomb-stones, which are, however, exactly beneath the elaborately carved monuments in the hall above them.

The Taj is in a garden full of trees and palms, lavishly green. It has many shady paths, and these are so formally disposed that they may be alleys for the meditative. This garden sanctuary is shut in by a great red wall. On that part of the wall which faces the entrance to the tomb is a massive gateway of ruddy stone. No garden in the world has such a gate. Such is its extent that the way through it is dark, and so high is it that the twenty-six marble cupolas which crown its summit seem toys to those who look up at the point of its colossal arch.

All the way from the great gate to the Taj Mahal there extends through the garden a narrow strip of water between two stone causeways. On either side of the water is a line of cypresses in formal order, and beyond the paved paths are luxuriant trees.

Everyone who visits Arjumand Banu's tomb for the first time approaches it with curiosity, tinged probably by a faint disposition to be hostile. So much has been written about this wonderful building, so much rhapsody has been lavished upon it, that there is some suspicion of over-praise. The claim that it is the most beautiful building in the world is a claim that many at once resent. Its outlines are familiar enough from pictures and models, and it may be that they hardly warrant unrestrained ecstasy. The visitor proposes to himself to put sentiment aside and review the building critically. He is aware that it is very large, very white, and picturesquely situated. No doubt he will find it pretty, but he intends to submit it to a common-sense inspection, for he is inclined to believe that the masculine and practical brain will declare the Taj Mahal to be a much overrated monument. He has, indeed, already imagined himself, on his return home, giving to his friends evidence of originality of mind by asserting that "as for the Taj, he sees nothing in it."

The Taj Mahal should be visited late in the afternoon, when the sunlight falls upon it from the west. The first glimpse of it comes through the gloomy archway of the great gate. It stands aloft on its marble platform at the end of the garden causeway, a thing of white against the blue sky. It is poised between the masses of green trees which brush the terrace and the unruffled blue. It is like a white cloud, luminous, intangible, translucent.

With the first sight of the Taj Mahal there comes only a sense of indefinable pleasure. It is no mere feeling of admiration, still less of amazement, no mere delight in a splendid building, because it does not impress one as a building. There is a sudden vision, and with it a sudden sense of ineffable satisfaction, as if in the place of a marble dome the garden had been filled with divine music. All intended criticism is forgotten. There is nothing that appeals to the judgment, or that suggests the weighing of opinion. There is merely a something that touches the finest sense of what is tender, beautiful, and lovable, and brings with it a feeling of inexpressible delight.

The building is pale and unsubstantial, and its walls appear so thin that the fabric is like a shell. One would imagine that a blast of coarse wind would carry it away, or that it would melt before a vicious rain. There is no background for it but the sky, and in the sky are only wheeling kites.

THE TAJ MAHAL.

The four sturdy towers which stand guard over the Taj, like men-at-arms, look defiant and rough, while the pale palaçe they watch is so fragile, so feminine, and so queenly.

The great dome is white, and the great arch below it is filled with a bay of shade and of soft yellow light. The windows are like lace-work, and there is everywhere a suggestion of elaborate decoration, which can be no more detailed than can be the separate tints in a meadow of flowers when seen from afar. There is no impression that the building is large, for its size is lost in its daintiness, and no one could speak of it rightly as imposing or commanding. It rises modestly from among the belt of trees, and shrinks against the sapphire sky.

The secret of the beauty of the Taj Mahal lies in the great arched recesses or vaulted alcoves which burrow deep into the body of the building. These are throbbing with sensitive shadows, and they give the impression that the onlooker can see into the very heart of this gentle palace as one would gaze into the heart of a yellow rose, where, leaf by leaf, the tints become deeper, warmer, and more living. There is ever a sense of something half hidden and half revealed, of a tenderness which has deeper depths, of a beauty which is but partly shown, of a bosom shadowed by white lace. It is this abiding suggestion which makes the peculiar glory of the Taj, a glory which is beyond the reach of any model or any picture. To many the Taj Mahal will ever be the most beautiful building in the world, while there must be few who will not acknowledge that it is the most lovable monument that has ever been erected over the dead.

Beneath the great dome lies the little lady of the Taj, and if the man who loved her could come to the riverside once more he would feel that her memory had not faded. In the passion of his youth he longed that she should never die, and she lives for ever; he wished to make her the greatest lady of his empire, and she has become famous for all time.

It is advised that the Taj Mahal should be seen by moonlight, but under the light of the moon the most subtle elements of its charm entirely vanish. It appears of colossal size, but it looks dead and cold. It is a flower with its petals closed. It needs the warm light of the sun to make it live, to illumine those deep recesses which lead into its very heart, and to make the onlooker feel that there are tender secrets in its depths which are only just hidden by its translucent walls.

Those who are interested to know to what level the brutality of vandalism may sink, or in what fashion the solemn and saintly beauty of this great monument is regarded by some, should read accounts of certain festas, when the arches of the tomb have been lit by rows of lamps like a gin-palace, and when coloured lights have been thrown upon the white walls as upon a mountebank's folly in a circus.

Within the mausoleum itself a high screen of marble trellis work encloses the monumental cenotaphs of Arjumand Banu and her King. The lady's tomb is very small, and it lies under the very centre of the dome. It is so little that it is almost lost beneath the colossal vault. On her right side her husband lies, and his tomb is as great as hers is small. Everywhere—on the screen, on the walls, and on the cenotaphs—there is exquisite carving, together with fastidious work in inlaid stone of many colours. Both the carvings and the tinted designs show flowers, and flowers only.

A cream-coloured light steals through the windows, while through the open door can be seen palms waving in the sun.

The actual bodies of the dead lie in a low vault in the foundations of the building. The chamber is of white marble, its walls are absolutely plain, and it is approached by a long, narrow staircase. The tombs themselves, which stand within this humble vault, are of the utmost simplicity.

As is the custom with Mohammedan graves, there is carved upon the man's tomb a pen box, and upon the woman's a slate. The pen is active; the slate is passive. It is the pen that fashions the writing; it is the slate that bares its surface to be written on.

A ray of light comes down the narrow stone way, but it falls only upon the small marble slab beneath which sleeps the lady of the Taj.

IX.

THE TOMB OF A SCHEMER.

Over against Agra, on the other side of the river, by the Bridge of Boats, is a peculiarly squalid suburb. A little beyond the smells and dirt of this quarter is a mean enclosure, within which is a princely garden. In the centre of the garden is a little square building, wonderful to see. It is built wholly of white marble, crowned at each corner by a dazzling tower. In the centre of the flat roof is a raised pavilion, with broad sloping eaves and sides filled with marble tracery. Round the roof is a low balustrade of the same frail work. The walls of the main building are wondrously carved, being everywhere decorated with inlaid stone in many patterns, but mostly in the semblance of flowers. All the windows are filled with stone lattice work; all the doors are rich with sculpture. Within the house are beautifully painted walls and roofs, while on every panel that lines its chambers has been lavished most costly decoration.

The little pavilion is as exquisite as anything within the palace precincts at Agra. At a distance it looks like a casket, and seems as fragile as if its walls were fashioned from fine porcelain. Indeed, it would be easy to believe that it was built wholly of china which had been painted delicately.

As to the purpose of the little house, it may be in reality a kiosque built of costly ware and placed in this gracious garden as a prince's freak. It may be a lady's summer house, where her singing birds were kept, or where she played at gardening when tired with the bustle of the Court. It may be a tomb, but if it be, then this toy palace in porcelain must cover the limbs of some dancing girl who died in the zenith of her beauty, or hide the grave of a toddling princess who was the joy of her father's life and who made this garden her playground.

Curious it is to be told that this exquisite pavilion, which is so feminine as to be almost feeble in its prettiness, is the tomb of a crafty old man.

Here, indeed, in this quiet pleasaunce lies buried Itmad-ud-Daulah, a Persian adventurer who found his way to the Court at Agra, where he prospered exceedingly. His daughter became the Empress Nur Jahan, and his grand-daughter, Arjumand Banu, was the lady of the Taj.

It is a strange mausoleum for an old schemer, for a man of plots and plans, who was familiar with treachery and assassination, who knew the art of bribes and the possibilities of women's cunning. He lived in stirring and bloody times, and the dangerous part he elected to play he played well. His body might have rotted in a dungeon or in a castle moat, but here at peace lie the crafty head and the shuffling hands, under a chaste canopy of white marble, made beautiful by lace-work and flowers.

THE GATEWAY OF THE PALACE
AT FATEHPUR-SIKRI.

X.

THE CITY OF UNTRODDEN STREETS.

Twenty-two miles from Agra, a road, shaded by an avenue of trees, leads through cotton fields and by dusty villages to the wondrous city of Fatehpur-Sikri. Wondrous it is, for there is no city like it in the world. It was built by the great Emperor Akbar in 1570, and after a few years of occupation the palace and the township that had grown around it were deserted. No calamity fell upon the place, no earthquake rent its walls, no volcano buried its streets in ashes. All that is known is that it was mysteriously abandoned, and the Court quietly moved to Agra.

For three hundred years its streets, its market place, and its palaces have been empty. It remains, as it was left, in a state of astounding preservation. Those who walk along its empty terraces or through its deserted halls see it as it was when it bustled with men and women three centuries ago. It is uninhabited now, save by the leopard, the jackal, and the porcupine. They haunt its kingly passages, and crawl in the shadows of its haughty walls. Some who have visited the Queen's terrace at night have been terrified by two yellow eyes gleaming over the doorstep that led to her room.

The town stands upon an isolated hill, which rises from the centre of a wandering plain. Around it is a wall. seven miles in circumference, with many a gap and many a crumbling breach. The city is approached by a steep road, which leads from the wall to the palace court. On the way it passes under a brave gateway, crowned by a musicians' gallery, where music was made when the King passed up the road to the city.

The city is built of red sandstone, which [illegible] everywhere carved with the most profuse decoration, with strange geometric fancies or figures of birds and flowers. Its chambers were at one time gay with coloured designs, traces of which still exist. The cobbled streets are unchanged since the time when the last cavalcade climbed up into the town.

The hand of ruin has spared the colonnades where the nobles loitered, the galleries whence the ladies looked down upon the crowd, and the chambers in which the Emperor slept, or dined, or idled in conversation with his friends. Near one gate is a great caravanserai, near another a market place. There are barracks for soldiers, quarters for serving-men, and stables for an army of horses and elephants. There are Turkish baths which are still in a perfect state, a swimming bath, kiosques in which to sit when the sun went down, and underground chambers with vaulted halls to loiter in during the summer heat.

There is the Great Audience Hall of the King, with its paved quadrangle, its throne-room, its little anteroom where courtiers trembled, and its rows of seats for the great.

There is, too, the Queen's palace, with its stone stairs creeping up to balconies, quiet alcoves, and shy passages.

There are buildings innumerable, of which no history exists, but which ring with the enchantment of irresponsible legend. Among these are the treasury house, with its strong rooms and stone coffers, the mysterious Diwan-i-Khas, and a still more curious building of many storeys and more columns called the Panch Mahal.

This very lofty structure may have been the Eiffel Tower of the period. It would seem to have been as little sane in purpose as is the futile monstrosity at Paris, but it is infinitely less unsightly to look upon.

One dainty house, without a stone in it disturbed, is called Miriam's House. Another is the Turkish Sultana's palace, and a third called Birbal's House might have been lived in no longer ago than yesterday. This latter is a little mansion of two storeys, with walls most quaintly carved. It has, leading to the roof, a narrow stair, the steps of which have been made smooth by the patter of many naked feet.

THE GREAT GATE OF VICTORY
FATEHPUR-SIKRI.

In a quiet quarter stand, side by side, the houses of two brothers who were said to have been life-long friends, both of one another and of the King.

There are arid terraces and damp wells, squat gates and haughty towers, guard-rooms and gardens, and even a hospital, a doctor's house, and an office for the astrologer.

More than that, there is in the city a mosque standing in a many-acred square. In the square is the astounding tomb of the saint who, according to the legend, founded this city.

Above all, it is to be noted that the quadrangle of the mosque is overshadowed by the mighty Gate of Victory, and in all India there is no gate that can compare with this. There is none so lofty —for it rises to the height of one hundred and thirty feet—none so commanding, for when the sky is clear it can be seen for twenty miles across the plain.

It is at moonlight that this dead city on the hill is most wonderful to see. Its utter loneliness and the sense that it is forgotten are to be most fully understood when night has fallen upon the silent streets.

In the moonlight the harsh red stone looks beautiful, slinking shadows fill the gateways, and a wan light inundates the great courts; the moonbeams cover the roofs with silver, slant in through windows and illumine empty rooms, and make such silhouettes at the corners of the streets and in the sepulchral corridors that one expects to see a townsman of three hundred years ago step out into the startled light.

XI.

THE MAUSOLEUM AT SIKANDRA.

The body of the great Emperor Akbar, the grandson of Babar the Lion and the direct descendant of Tamerlane, lies at Sikandra.

Sikandra is some five miles from Agra to the north-west. The Emperor's tomb is in a luxuriant garden. The gate that leads to the enclosure is imposing both from its great size and its gaudiness. It is built of red sandstone, ornamented with inlaid designs in white and coloured marbles. There is a memorable view to be obtained from the summit of this gateway. It extends over a green, well-tended plain, on the confines of which may be seen the Taj Mahal and the fort of Agra, the Jumna, and, when the sky is clear, the great Gate of Victory at Fatehpur-Sikri.

The mausoleum is a pyramidal building of four storeys, each storey being less in size than the one below it. The three lower sections are of red sandstone, the crowning storey is low and fashioned wholly of white marble. Within, the vestibule of the mausoleum is radiant with blue and gold. The immense building, however, is not impressive. Its bald terraces, its wearisome pillars and arches, and its profuse array of kiosques suggest rather some eccentric place of amusement than the tomb of one of the greatest of kings.

It is impossible to resist the profane expectation of finding a row of round tables and a French waiter upon one of the spacious platforms, or a seller of trinkets and postcards in one of the kiosques.

The storey on the summit of the building is, however, very beautiful. It is open to the air, while around its sides is an exquisite pale cloister, with outside walls of marble trellis work. In the centre of the open space is the magnificent cenotaph of the king. It is white, and is carved all over with delicate designs of flowers. Upon it fall both the sun and the rain.

Akbar, it is well known, was a man with liberal conceptions of religion. He would fain have brought together the many conflicting faiths of his day, and to effect this end he founded a creed of his own. His followers were few, but they persisted in exalting him to the dignity of a being to be worshipped. Now, upon one side of his monument will be found, carved among the flowers, the words, "Allahu Akbar," "God is Greatest."

All his doubts, his aspirations, and his rebuke to his disciples would seem to be buried in these words.

Close to the cenotaph is a little purposeless pillar, with handsome chisel work upon it. It is said that it was at one time covered with gold, and that among the precious stones which decorated it was the Koh-i-noor diamond.

The most impressive feature of this royal monument belongs to an unpretending doorway in the lowest story of the mausoleum. The entrance leads to a pinched passage which, sloping underground, ends in a simple undecorated vault. Here, beneath a plain slab of white marble, upon which there is neither carving nor inscription, lies the body of the greatest of the Moghul emperors.

XII.

DELHI.

Probably there is no town in India that the traveller approaches with more expectancy than Delhi—the one-time capital of the country, the sacred city of India, the Rome of Asia, and the scene of the most critical episode of the Indian mutiny.

I reached Delhi by train, late at night, and the first glimpses of the romantic city were not particularly stirring. The train entered a new and bumptious railway station, which might have been at Bournemouth for any characteristics it displayed. The platforms were numbered 1, 2, and 3, and were lit by arc electric lights. My luggage was taken away in a bullock cart, while I entered the hallowed town in a wheezing carriage, which had probably commenced life at respectable livery stables in Camberwell.

The vehicle limped and reeled along a deserted road, by closed, hutch-like shops, and finally passed through a narrow way into open country which, in the moonlight, looked like an English park.

This was commonplace enough, and it was not until the next morning that I found that I had driven through the walls of Delhi, that the narrow way was the famous Mori gate, that what I had taken to be a ruined factory was the Mori Bastion, and that I had crossed the very flat between the walls and the ridge where the fighting had been the most desperate during the siege.

The city of Delhi lies on a plain by the banks of the Jumna. It is a city of great size, for the walls that surround it make a circuit of seven miles, and the people who live within these walls number nearly 200,000.

It is a city of small streets, so huddled together that they form a tangle of thoroughfares. There is one broad street, lined by an avenue of fine trees, which runs across the city from east to west. It is called the Chandni Chauk, and it has figured tragically in the history of the town.

About the centre of the city is the gigantic mosque, the Jumma Musjid, the white domes of which can be seen far away for miles upon miles. By the banks of the river, and within the city confines, is a ruddy fort, very like to the fort at Agra, and on the river wall of this fort is the famous marble palace built by Shah Jahan. The fort has two lofty gates, the Lahore gate and the Delhi gate, and these, like the domes of the mosque, can be seen from afar.

There are certain temples in the city belonging to ancient days, and some formal gardens, suited for nursemaids and children, appertaining to recent times.

The Delhi that now stands is not a place of remarkable antiquity, for it was founded by the Emperor Shah Jahan in 1638. It was he who built the Fort and the Palace, and also the great mosque.

The site upon which the city is built, however, is ancient beyond words. History has no record of the time when there was not a commanding town upon this bank of the Jumna. It tells, indeed, of no less than seven fortified places which were raised upon this spot by divers kings, and which were in turn pillaged, sacked, and brought to ruin.

Traces of the remains of these cities still exist. They do not cover a few bare acres; they cover the astounding area of no less than forty-five square miles. This great desert of ruin is without a parallel in the world. It is the most startling of the many remarkable features which are associated with this tragic place. Delhi itself is wonderful, but its wonder fades by the side of the awful country which lies to the south of its walls. Here, over a space of more than forty miles, there lies a land of stones and mounds, of crumbling walls, of dropping forts, of hillocks of earth which were palaces, and gullies of mud which were streets. Here is the most appalling picture of desolation that the mind could conceive, and the readiest realisation of the plains of Sodom and Gomorrah.

Two high roads lead to the south through this pitiable waste. One starts from the Ajmere gate of the city, the other from the Delhi gate. Along these roads the relics of centuries of destruction are to be seen, and the forts, as being the strong places, have best survived the hand of ruin.

On one of the roads—not far from the Delhi gate—is the fort of Firozabad. So strong was this savage old fortress, that, although it was built just five hundred and fifty years ago, there are still enough of the ancient stones left to show how sturdy it was. Two miles along this highway there is another fort. It stands upon the site of the long demolished city of Indrapat. It is called the Purana Killa, or old fort, and it is still a haughty and defiant stronghold. Its walls, its gates, and its huge bastions still stand, so that men could even now fight from its ramparts. Although within its circuit there is now little but a cluster of squalid huts, which have grown there like a mean fungus, and although there are many breaches in its battlements, the old fort still holds itself royally, an obstinate monument of grey and grim old age.

Far on the road that leads from the Ajmere gate are the ruins of yet another fort, as wonderful as any—the fort of Lalkot, built, it is said, in 1060. Its walls make a circuit of two miles, and its ramparts are some thirty feet in thickness. Its bastions are enormous, and besides these bastions there are many small towers. Around it, as far as the eye can stretch, there is nothing but ruin.

To make the desolation of these devastated sites more complete, and to accentuate the dismal roads that stretch across them, are many hundreds of tombs, which have been built along these Appian ways in less ancient times, and which have already themselves fallen into various stages of decay.

XIII.

TWO MOSQUES IN DELHI.

The city of Delhi, viewed from afar off, looks like a dingy swamp in an open plain. This morass of human habitations is level, brown, and misty. It is precisely circumscribed, while the lands around its margins are green. From the centre of the great dead-looking enclosure rise delicately into the air three immense white domes. They stand high, and when the sun illumines them they are by contrast as brilliant as three lilies springing from a waste of mud. These are the domes of the great mosque of Delhi, the *Jumma Musjid*.

The mosque, which has no equal in size in India, is more pleasant to look upon, when seen from a distance, than from near at hand. Indeed, it appears most splendid when viewed from a point so far away that the details of the town are lost, and there are only the three white domes to be seen rising over the city like three clouds of sacred smoke.

The Jumma Musjid was built by Shah Jahan. It stands upon a huge platform of red sandstone. Its court is approached on three sides by flights of stairs so wide that a thousand worshippers could mount by each entry at once. On the summit of these stone stairs are fine gateways, surmounted by galleries for spectators.

That gate which stands to the east is particularly magnificent, for, when the mosque was built, it was intended that no one should enter by it but the Emperor himself. These gates lead into an immense square open to the sky, and here the crowd of worshippers stands.

On three sides of the square is a colonnade with a balcony above it. On the fourth side is the mosque, fashioned of red stone and white marble blended in varying degree, and decorated with some inlaid work in black. As the sky is approached the deeper colours are less employed, so that the crowning part of each cupola and minaret is white.

The whole structure, therefore, is pure white where it reaches the sky, dull red where it touches the ground; while between the foundation and the pinnacle, red, white, and black are blended. The façade is of pale marble, toned with red and black. On each side of the mosque are two lofty minarets of red sandstone, slashed vertically with white. The three domes over the mosque are of exceptional magnitude. They are of white marble, faintly striped with vertical lines of black, and on their summits are gilt spires.

When the mosque is seen from the open space that extends to the east of it, or from the quadrangle within its walls, it does not convey the impression of being either a beautiful or a dignified house of prayer. It is of great size, but its proportions are by no means commanding, since there is little beauty in mere largeness. Its lines of colour are laid on heavily, and in harsh, angular patterns. The fabric is gaudy, bald, and aggressive. Its contrasts in colour are extreme. It is large without being really great, and its huge dimensions serve only to magnify the sourness of its features. It cannot for one moment be compared with the Pearl Mosque at Agra, nor can it be believed that the two mosques belong to the same period or were built by the same King.

The Jumma Musjid is strong, but it is blatant. It may be magnificent, but it has not the magnificence of holiness. It is a place where one would expect to find, not a quiet congregation, but a brass band of strident proportions. Indeed, the square structure which surrounds the archway under the central dome suggests the stage front of a theatre. It is a place which the casual visitor would associate with orchestral demonstrations of a Gargantuan type, or with noisy gatherings of the people hot with revolt. Its platform would seem better suited for the hoarse, red-faced demagogue who yelled sedition than for the priest breathing prayers to Heaven.

There is another mosque in Delhi which is in strong contrast to the Jumma Musjid, and is possessed of fine and honest features of its own. This is the *Kalan Musjid or Black Mosque.* It is half hidden in a slum of the town near by to the Turkuman gate. It was built as long ago as 1386. It is a small stone building, severe and quite pathetically plain. It scorns all ornament, for it is built like a fortress. It stands high upon a mass of stout masonry, and consists of a single room roofed by many small domes held up by rows of pillars.

This mosque belongs to a stern period when bloodshed and rapine filled men's minds, and when any place of assembly must needs be strong and safe from sudden attack. Men in those days must have worshipped with their arms by their side, and with sentinels posted to shout alarm.

There is a plain court in front of the mosque from which the door of the temple is approached by a straight flight of steps. They are narrow, so that a trespasser could be hurled headlong down them with some ease. The door, which passes through walls of great thickness, has all the features of a door in a fort, and those who entered could feel that they stepped into a strong place.

The most striking feature of the building depends upon two pillars which are placed one on either side of the portal and the steep stairs. These pillars are crude, are wide at the bottom, but taper towards the top. They are placed slantingly, like buttresses against the building, and it would seem as if their peculiar form had been suggested by a stack of spears piled upright on either side of the doorway.

It is a sturdy little mosque, black and stolid, with no pretension to be more than a place where men might pray in safety. It is easy to picture them standing in the gloomy aisles, savage and restless, with their loins girded, and with alert ears turned towards the plain to catch the first sound of alarm. There is little doubt that the voice of the priest ceased now and then so that all might listen.

There is a bluff honesty about this grimy place of worship, and a pathos in the tale it tells. It cannot—like the Jumma Musjid—pretend to "great variety and elegance," but it is a monument to the tender qualities of violent men, and a suitable shrine for the not mean figure of the kneeling buccaneer.

XIV.

AN INDIAN EDEN.

Shah Jahan's white palace at Delhi is built within the fort, and that part of it which is the most perfect stands upon the river wall. The fort is a little like the fort at Agra, in so far that its walls are of red stone and are surmounted by the same truculent battlements, but the stronghold at Delhi lacks those swaggering features which make the Agra fortress so very mighty and domineering. In the sacred city the fort is little more than a monotonous wall, which can only boast that it is high, and that it has two most stately gates—the Lahore gate and the Delhi gate—to make up for the much that the would-be strong place lacks. The greater part of the palace has been destroyed, while what remains is made inglorious by association with barrack buildings and sheds for stores.

There is the Diwan-i-Am or Hall of Public Audience, a fine pavilion, open on three sides, and filled with rows of sandstone pillars supporting graceful arches. On the fourth side is a wall, in the centre of which (and raised some way from the ground) is an alcove in which the Emperor sat. A staircase leads up to the place of the throne, and many a trembling wretch and many an elated favourite must have stumbled up its steps.

In the wall behind the throne is a little doorway which led from the Emperor's apartments. The wall is covered with pictures of beasts and birds, of flowers and fruit, worked cunningly in coloured marbles and precious stones. The tints are vivid and generously bestowed, so that this kingly wall looks a little as if it had been pasted over with the coloured pictures from a child's nursery book. The artist who wrought these gorgeous birds was one Austin de Bordeaux. He seems to have been a rogue of great parts, for he fled hither from Europe to escape the penalty of his sins in connection with the making of false gems. He might have died in the obscurity of a Paris jail, but he lives for ever as the deft craftsman who fashioned "Austin's Wall." He must have been cheery in his exile, for the fruits that grow upon "Austin's Wall" are exceedingly ripe and ruddy, while the birds that gather there are all of radiant plumage and blushing with song.

The Diwan-i-Khas, or Hall of Private Audience, is on the river wall. It is a white marble pavilion open on all sides, and it is the most glorious and most royal hall in India.

The massive columns are lavishly ornamented with gilt, and with unrestrained designs of flowers in inlaid stone. The arches they support are elegant, and the colonnades they form make a wonderful vista in white and gold. Beneath the floor of the hall there runs a wide stream of water in an alabaster bed to cool the terrace when the King gave audience. That side of the pavilion which faces the river is filled with lattice work in marble. In front of the four windows is still to be seen the platform on which stood the famous Peacock Throne. According to Beresford* this throne was of solid gold, and was so called from "having the figures of two peacocks standing behind it, their tails being expanded, and the whole so inlaid with sapphires, rubies, emeralds, pearls, and other precious stones of appropriate colours as to represent life." This remarkable monument of vanity, perverted art, and selfish extravagance was plundered and broken up by Nadir Shah in 1739.

A view of the Diwan-i-Khas enables one to realise that the Court of the Moghul Emperor at Delhi was not only the most sumptuous Court of its time, but that it was probably without an equal at any period of the world's history.

The stream of water flowing from beneath the Diwan-i-Khas follows an open channel across a court which surrounds the pavilion, and then passing under a rounded arch, makes a river through the centre of the Ladies' Apartments. The archway is filled in by a screen of nervous trellis work in marble decorated

* Beresford's "Delhi."

with gilt. In the centre of the screen is a small window, where there should be a silk curtain and a peeping face, and above the window is a pair of scales carved in the stone. The interpretation of this emblem on the wall is open to any invention of the ingenious.

The ladies' apartments are exquisite, but they fail to touch the superb refinement which belongs to the zenana at Agra. The walls are bright with frescoes in mosaic, and, as at Agra, there is a pavilion built on a bastion of the fortress which is called the Jasmine Tower. It is crowned by a dome, and its windows are shaded by tracery in marble.

The view from the Jasmine Tower is across the river, and it forms a sordid contrast to the luxurious splendour within the tower walls. The lady who leaned her jewelled arms against the pillar to look over the stream would see in the winter time a coarse, dry river bed of dull stones, with here and there a starving bush, and here and there a shrivelled gulley, while in the summer her eyes would fall upon a turbid torrent which eddied savagely under the ramparts.

Indeed, life in the palace and life without it were little alike in the days when Shah Jahan was King. Smooth marble and gushing wealth within the walls, and without a harsh people, struggling to live, and a horde of ruthless men who bore down upon them like a flood. The princess, who to please a whim would drop a pearl into the stream, might see, when she looked from the balcony to watch it fall, the corpse of a murdered woman drifting by. The Peacock Throne faced a spectacle of unequalled splendour, effulgent with colour and the dazzle of rare gems, but those who looked through the wicket behind the throne saw only the pauper river bed, monotonous and desolate.

There are in this imperial pleasure house two writings on the wall which serve to tell some part of the story of the place. On the arches of the Diwan-i-Khas there is written in Persian letters the distich—

> "If on earth be an Eden of bliss,
> It is this, it is this, it is this."

Such was the expression of the belief of him who built the palace;

it was the outcome of his hope, the object of his dearest endeavour. But beyond the Eden of bliss there were the shouts of war, the smouldering revolt, the muffled room filled with conspirators, and the assassin ready with his knife. If the Emperor looked over the wall of the palace at night it was not to see how the moon fell upon his Eden; it was to search for the stealthy creeping figure he had seen in his dreams.

It happens, then, that there is in this fair pile a second writing on the wall. It takes the shape of a small door at the very foot of the Jasmine Tower, where the ladies idled the day. The door opens through the fortress wall upon the sharp stones of the river bed, and leading to it is a secret passage from the royal apartments.

Some dark night the King might need this door to creep out of, and might be glad to change his Eden for the homeless waste.

The Royal Baths, which are close to the Diwan-i-Khas, afford perhaps a better conception of the luxury of the time than do any other buildings in the palace. They consist of a series of low rooms floored with white marble, and furnished with a dado generously decorated. One room is lit by windows which look over the river, the rest are lit from the roof. A stream, in a channel of alabaster, runs round the queen's bath, and on the floor of this water-way are ribs of black stone which alternate with raised ribs of silver. The silver has gone, but it is easy to see that when the water flowed these ridges of black and white would have thrown it into ripples.

Adjacent to the baths is the Pearl Mosque. It stands within a plain enclosure of four very high red walls, which are so commonplace that they might surround a racket court. The mosque is approached through a small gateway made glorious by a bronze door. The portal leads into a simple white court, on one side of which is the mosque surmounted by three domes. Built wholly of white and grey marble, it is a chaste, dignified temple. Those who pass into the little courtyard must feel that they pass into a place of peace. In construction it differs in no essential from the Pearl Mosque at Agra, but it cannot pretend to attain to the quite perfect beauty of the southern shrine. Those who have never seen the mosque at Agra will find this hard to believe, but so it is.

XV.

THE RIDGE AT DELHI.

A very living interest, and all that pathos and romance which belong to a deed of great heroism, are associated with the Ridge at Delhi.

The outline of the story of the Ridge can be told in a very few lines.

The first scene of the great Indian Mutiny opened at Meerut, a large military station some forty miles from Delhi. On one Sunday evening, just as the English soldiers were on their way to church, the Sepoys mutinied, set fire to as many bungalows as they passed, killed such Europeans as they met, and started for Delhi.

The actual date of this rising was May 10th, 1857. It was natural that the mutineers should make for Delhi, for it was to them the capital city of India and the heart of their country. There were a few English officers at Delhi, but no European troops.

The mutineers reached the sacred city on May 11th, and set to work to murder all the Europeans they could find. They were at once joined by the native regiments stationed at Delhi, and the men of these regiments, upon the arrival of the insurgents, turned upon their English officers and shot them down. Certain of the women and children in the city managed to escape to the Ridge, where they took refuge in a tower called the Flag-staff Tower.

"There, huddled together in a room smaller than the Black Hole of Calcutta, was collected a great company of every age and class, frightened children crying and clinging to their not less frightened ayahs, women bewailing the deaths of their husbands or brothers, others bravely bearing up against heat, and discomfort, and anxiety, and busily unfastening cartridges for the men." In due course these poor folk had to flee from the tower. "Then began that piteous flight, the first of many such incidents which hardened the hearts of the British to inflict a terrible revenge. Driven to hide in jungles or morasses from despicable vagrants, robbed and scourged and mocked by villagers who had entrapped them with promises of help, scorched by the blazing sun, blistered by burning winds, half-drowned in rivers which they had to ford or swim across, naked, weary, and starving, they wandered on; while some fell dead by the wayside, and others, unable to move further, were abandoned by their sorrowing friends to die on the road."*

There was in Delhi an important magazine under the charge of a certain Lieutenant Willoughby. "Warned of the approach of the mutineers, he had lost no time in sending to the Brigadier for help. He could not trust his native guards, and he had only eight Europeans to support him; but he could depend upon these for any sacrifice, and he could depend upon himself. No help came in answer to his appeal; the suffering and the glory of that day were for him and his gallant eight alone. His dispositions were soon made. Barricading the outer gates of the magazine, he placed guns inside them, and assigned to each man his post. But what if defence should fail? He had another plan in reserve. A train was laid from the powder store to a tree standing in the yard of the magazine. Here stood Conductor Scully, who had volunteered to fire the train whenever his chief should give the signal. If the enemy broke into the stronghold, they would find death, not plunder, within. For a time, however, the enemy seemed to hesitate. It was because they and their king feared the vengeance of the white troops from Meerut. But at last the king's scouts told him that no white troops were coming. Then he gathered confidence to demand the surrender of the magazine. The garrison did not even answer the summons; and, when the multitude no longer hesitated to advance, opened fire upon them from every gun. The most daring of the assailants planted ladders against the walls and came swarming in; but the guns, served with incredible swiftness, though the gunners were exposed to a fearful

* "A History of the Indian Mutiny," by T. R Holmes. London, 1898. pp. 107, 110.

musketry fire, poured round after round of grape into their midst. Yet so great were their numbers that the survivors, strengthened by the native guards, who had treacherously joined them, must have overpowered the little band of Englishmen. Still Willoughby hoped on. He had defended the magazine for three hours, and he would still defend it against any odds if only reinforcements were coming. Running to the river Castion, he bent over for a last look towards Meerut. No English were to be seen. Then, resolving that, though his countrymen had failed him, he would be true to himself, he gave the fatal order to Conductor Buckley: Buckley raised his hat as a signal, and Scully fired the train. In a moment some hundreds of rebels were destroyed, while many more without were struck down by flying splinters of shot and shell. Lieutenants Forrest and Raynor, Conductors Buckley and Shaw, and Sergeant Steward lived to wear the Victoria Cross; but Scully died where he fell, too cruelly wounded to escape; and Willoughby only survived to be murdered on his way to Meerut." *

Of the arsenal, which was the scene of this heroic deed, little now remains. There is no trace of "the tree standing in the yard." Post and telegraph offices stretch across the site, but the gateways of the place still stand to keep green the memory of this act of valour, and of the men who died "facing fearful odds."

Thus it came about that the great city of Delhi, with its powerful ramparts and its great fort, passed into the possession of the rebels. It was a matter of necessity to the English that the city should be retaken at any cost. A column of British troops was at once collected at Kurnal, a place some way to the north, and with as much despatch as was possible the march to Delhi was commenced. On the 5th of June the column reached Alipur, where it was joined by the British regiments from Meerut, and on the next day the whole force advanced towards Delhi. Six miles to the north-west of the city is a village called Badli-ki-Serai, where the rebels had posted a very formidable force to oppose the advance of the English. The English, however, continued to advance. On June 8th the battle of Badli-ki-Serai was fought; the mutineers were utterly defeated; the British column,

* Ibid., p. 108.

continuing their march, attacked and seized the Ridge before Delhi, and here they camped on the evening of June 8th.

The English general took up his position at four outposts. The outpost nearest to the city and the one most exposed to attack was a large, rambling country house called Hindu Rao's house. The next station was an old stone observatory in a state of partial ruin, but still a very solid building. The third outpost was in an ancient mosque, which also formed no mean place of shelter. The fourth post was the Flag-staff Tower, of which mention has been already made. These four positions were in a line on the Ridge—Hindu Rao's house at one end, the Flag-staff Tower at the other. The troops encamped on the flat below the far side of the Ridge. All four of the outposts could readily be seen from the city, but the camp was out of sight.

The British came to lay siege to Delhi, but soon found that they were themselves besieged. They had taken the Ridge, but now they had to hold it in the face of terrific difficulties. They were opposed "by full 40,000 soldiers," wrote Archdale Wilson at the time of the siege, "armed and disciplined by ourselves with 114 heavy pieces of artillery mounted on the walls, and the largest magazine of shot, shell, and ammunition in the Upper Provinces, beside some sixty pieces of field artillery all of our own manufacture, and manned by artillery men drilled and taught by ourselves." The force, on the other hand, that had the audacity to plant themselves before Delhi with the intention of taking it consisted at first of some three thousand British troops, one Goorka battalion, remnants of certain loyal native regiments, and twenty-two guns.

This daring body of men were in time reinforced, but at no period did the effective strength of all ranks reach to 10,000 men. They were attacked day after day and week after week. Between the 30th May, when the fighting about Delhi began, and the 20th September, when it ended, this undaunted column fought some twenty-four battles. Three times alone in June did the mutineers make a desperate onslaught upon Hindu Rao's house, but on these occasions and on every other, they failed to dislodge these stubborn men from the Ridge. They made attacks upon the Ridge in front and in the rear, but they never gained an inch of ground. The odds were so extreme as to be ridiculous, the weather was that of the height of the Indian summer, the heat was intense, there was no shelter on the barren face of the hillock, the supplies were poor, and the column had no help to look to.

In spite of the heat, the incessant fighting, and the incessant watching, these men clung to their Ridge. More than that, they were never beaten, although there were 40,000 against them. On the other hand, they crept gradually up to the city.

There was a little suburb called Subzi-mundi, gay with walled gardens, on the flat below Hindu Rao's house. It was on a convenient way to the town, so the gaunt men from the Ridge swooped down upon it. Better still, they held it.

There was near the Jumna a country house on high ground called Metcalfe House. It was on another way to the town, and so sinister men with uniforms in rags crept up to it one day and seized it. They clung to that place also, and no force could drive them out of it.

Near by the city wall was the Commissioner's house, called Ludlow Castle. The Commissioner had been murdered, and the house was empty. The spot was desirable, and the tireless men from the mound came down upon it, and took it, and this also they clung to till the end.

Above all, they held to their Ridge until it appeared as if no force belonging to the earth could drive them from it. Certainly 40,000 men were no company for such an enterprise. Sortie after sortie was made, but the British clung to their position, and to every other point of ground they had grasped.

They lost nothing that they had gained. They lost nothing but the lives of men. By the middle of July two generals had died, a third was prostrated by illness, while the Adjutant-General and the Quartermaster-General lay wounded. Worse befel them than that, for in time they had lost in killed and wounded 3,854 men, including forty-six British officers dead and 140 wounded. In spite of all this, they held to their heap of stones.

On September 14th they stormed the great city, and captured

it, and by September 20th they had done with Delhi. From June 8th to September 20th is a period of 104 days—104 days of an Indian summer, 104 days of continued watching, scheming, and fighting, and 104 days on every one of which some man died.

Nothing has altered the face of the Ridge. As it was in the summer of 1857, so it is now, and the Englishman who mounts to its summit must needs go reverently, and bare his head in memory of the gallant men who died there and of the valiant deeds that added such glory to the British name.

This famous piece of ground is a quite low, narrow hill—a mere long mound—which lies to the north of the city, in front of the Kashmir Gate, and is nearly "end on" to the town walls. It is about a mile from the city, while between it and the fortifications is a pleasant wooded flat, occupied by bungalows and gardens. The Ridge is of such trifling dimensions that it is only about a mile from Hindu Rao's house at one end to the Flag-staff Tower at the other.

It is a lonely place, deserted and quiet, and the native of Delhi has even now no love for it. It is a mound of rough boulders and stones, covered sparsely with bushes, and on the top is a modern road. In places the rocks are large, so that the face of the position looks like a rampart. Elsewhere it is green and no longer rugged, and children run up and down it. Here and there are pits and hollows with small dells among the stones. The prickly pear grows upon the face of the mound, and the mimosa trees and struggling bushes which cling there seem to find it hard to live. Boulders of a greyish blue make a pleasant contrast with the olive green undergrowth. They are smooth like the boulders on a beach. There can be few of these quiet-looking rocks on the face of the Ridge towards Delhi beneath which a British soldier has not sought shelter from the sun and the sepoys' bullets, and against many of these smooth, comfortable stones he must have leaned his head when he died.

The four outpost buildings on the Ridge are little altered since our soldiers held them. Hindu Rao's house is a fine, white, rambling house, with a commanding presence. Its many wounds have been healed, and it is now a convalescent home for sick soldiers. The observatory and the mosque are sturdy old ruins with thick walls and shady passages. Although they are in no way imposing they sheltered for many weary weeks the indomitable men who held the hill. In front of the observatory, on that side of it which faces Delhi, are still to be seen the earth entrenchments that these men made. The Flag-staff Tower remains unchanged, save for a coat or two of red paint. No one can stand before it without thinking of the haggard women and children who huddled there and watched the burning of their homes, and when the daylight came looked ever along the Meerut road for the cloud of dust that would mark the British troops that never came.

As the Ridge is the only high ground in the environs of Delhi, the view from the top of it stretches far.

The whole of the vast city lies spread out on the plain, a mysterious expanse of housetops and patches of wall. Struggling through this dense human stubble field is a line of trees which marks the Chandni Chauk. To the left a gleam of silver curving along the city wall is the river Jumna, while to the right is the dull flat. So level is the land that the entire circuit of the town can be seen, and beyond its farthest wall the eye can travel over the country that sweeps away to the south. Standing up against the sky in this dim distance is the white dome of Humayun's tomb, where the wretched King of Delhi sought shelter when the British entered the town. Far away beyond this dome, some thirteen miles from the Ridge, is the lonely column of the Kutab Minar, the great tower of victory, which first rose up in sight of these heights nearly seven hundred years ago.

Away to the east, across the river, is the poor, mean plain that leads to Meerut, and the picture of that flat must have been burnt into the brains of the many who watched from the Ridge in the hope of some sign of a relief column making for the city.

Within the brown walls of Delhi itself certain domes and minarets stand out above the housetops. On the left, near to the Kashmir Gate, is the dome of the English church. On that dome was an orb of copper surmounted by a cross. Both the orb and the cross are riddled with bullet holes, and they stand to this day in the church garden to bear record of the summer of '57. It was on the Kashmir Gate that the main onslaught of the British fell when they stormed the city, and by that gate and the breach near by it they entered the town.

It is a little curious that the guide to the Kashmir Gate was the cross on the English church.

To the right of this church there can be seen from the Ridge the high gates of the Fort, and farther away still the three white, nun-like domes of the Great Mosque. Beyond these domes there is nothing but a rabble of shabby houses crouching behind the walls.

Between the tumbled stones of the Ridge and the city wall is a pleasant expanse green with trees and dotted with bungalows, not unlike such a stretch of rambling green as may lie outside an English town. There, by the river, is the Metcalfe House as it stood in '57, a square white building, which, in the language of house agents, is still a desirable residence. Nearer to the moat is Ludlow Castle, also little changed, only that it is now a comfortable club house, while in the place of the battery that fired from its garden there is merely a memorial to mark its site, and the dining-room is no longer loopholed for muskets. Trees have grown with careless impudence over this deadly flat since the year of the Mutiny, so that the walls of Delhi are now less easily to be seen from the Ridge. But there, untouched since the siege, is the hideous rampart showing up between gaps in the trees like the sides of a great brown, watching snake.

There are the Mori Gate and the Mori Bastion that the British battered to pieces straight ahead, and a little to the left, the Kashmir Gate, with the Kashmir breach by which they rushed into the city.

Forty-seven years have passed by since this place was blackened and laid waste by the hot blast of war. Now the Ridge is deserted and as quiet as a convent garden.

There is little to be heard but the caw of crows, the chatter of the minas, and the whistle of the circling kites, for the place is much haunted by birds. A hare may now and then dart out among the bushes, or a couple of partridges may start up and flutter away, but otherwise there is little stirring, and the old sepoy who is the custodian of the Memorial on the mound has gone to sleep in its shadow. Some English children are playing at soldiers among the big rocks at the foot of the Ridge, and they are calling to one another in shrill trebles, and sometimes there comes the order "Fire" and often the order "Charge," but the city remains silent and makes no response, and none issue from the Kashmir Gate but a mincing regiment of brown goats.

XVI.

THE KASHMIR GATE.

They say—those who describe the siege of Delhi—that the city walls were seven miles round, that they were twenty-four feet high, and that the ditch in front of them was twenty-five feet wide and nearly twenty feet deep. As the walls were then, so are they now, for they have been left untouched. The Mori Gate and other gates on the north of the town have been removed, while at the bottom of the ditch is an unsavoury drain.

The wall that the British gazed upon so long stretches in a stiff line on that side of the defences which faces the Ridge, a cruel brown wall with tooth-like battlements. It was to many the dull thing their last gaze rested on, as, stumbling towards the breach, they fell headlong, dead, within a few feet of the goal. For many weary days eyes had been fixed upon these walls of Delhi as if they were the walls of Paradise, but the look was the look of hate, and if hate could destroy, then the battlements would long have crumbled into dust. There was no Peri at the gate, there was no river of peace beyond, but there was not a man on the Ridge who was not ready to sacrifice his life if only he could find his way to the shot-swept alleys within this accursed circle of stone. Here and there in the long stretch of the wall great gaps have been bitten out of the battlements by eager shells, and holes and gashes have been cut in the curtain by hissing shot. The great bastion by the Mori Gate is little more than a heap of stones, and goats graze on the grass which has crept over the ruin.

There is no need to tell again the story of the assault upon the city. It took place at daybreak on the 14th of September, and, according to the record, the morning was "fine and still." It will suffice to say that the attacking party was divided into five columns, and that the chief points of attack were the Kashmir Gate and the breach which the British had made in the wall to the left of the Kashmir bastion. The column told off to storm the Kashmir breach was led by that heroic soldier General Nicholson, while the column whose lot it was to make for the Kashmir Gate was under the leadership of Colonel Campbell. On the night of the 13th, Lieutenants Medley and Lang had explored the breach, and had declared it "practicable."

The story of Nicholson's dash upon the Kashmir breach is told in Holmes' "History of the Mutiny" after this fashion:—

"The columns fell in on the road leading from cantonements to the city. There were some four thousand five hundred men, British soldiers with bronzed war-worn faces, wearing uniforms which had been dyed dust-colour, Sikhs with their long hair twisted up behind, and tall, muscular Pathans with faces as fair as those of Englishmen. Eager as they were to move on, they were depressed and wearied by delay; for the enemy had filled up the breaches in the night; and it was necessary for the batteries to re-open. But at length the signal was given; and, while the heavy guns still thundered at the breaches, answered by the heavy guns from the city, and shells burst, and rockets, flashing along the dark sky, hissed above their heads, the columns tramped silently and steadily down. Near Ludlow Castle they halted and took up their respective stations. The engineer officers with their ladder-men moved on in front. Then Nicholson went to Brigadier Jones, who commanded the second column, and asked whether he was ready. The brigadier replied that he was. Nicholson put his arm round his comrade's shoulder and then hurried off to join his own column. The guns ceased firing; the Rifles, in skirmishing order, dashed to the front with a loud cheer and opened fire; and the columns streamed after to the assault of Delhi. The ladder-men moved quickly on: but the enemy, crowding in the breach, received the men of the first column with a terrible musketry fire, and, catching up the loosened stones, hurled them down upon their heads, yelling, cursing, and daring them to enter. For a moment it seemed as if the avalanche would overwhelm them: man after man was struck down: but in another moment two ladders

THE KASHMIR GATE, DELHI.

were thrown into the ditch: the stormers closed up behind; Nicholson, as ever in the front, slid down and mounted the scarp: and the rest followed: the enemy, feeling that the breach was lost, fled; and the victorious column poured into the city and took up its position in the main-guard." *

The breach is as it was when the siege was over. Time has smoothed its ragged surface, and the native with a hut to build has gathered up the loose stones that littered its base. Grass has healed over the gaping wound, but it is still a hideous scar. Children like no playground better than the crumbling rampart or the deserted fort, so the little people who play upon this haunted slope have worn a waving path upon its side, by endless running up and down; and any, who wish, can enter the city by the children's path, and can follow the steps of Nicholson and his gallant men on their way into the town. The children's path is a sorry one, but it is very glorious to tread.

The breach leads to the open space near by the Kashmir Gate, and here, in the great wall and the still more solid bastion, are some cavern-like barracks which belonged to the main-guard. This main-guard was associated with an episode which may be mentioned here by the way.

When the mutineers from Meerut entered Delhi on May 11th, the main-guard of the city was composed of Sepoys, for, as already stated, there were no British soldiers stationed in the town at this critical moment.

As soon as the wholesale murder of the Europeans in the city commenced some few of those who fled from their houses sought refuge in the main-guard by the Kashmir Gate, and even sheltered themselves in the guard-room. They trusted that the Sepoys who composed the guard would be faithful and would protect them. Suddenly, however, the men of one of these regiments fired a volley at their officers. "Three fell dead. Two of the survivors rushed up to the bastion of the main-guard and jumped down thirty feet into the ditch below. The rest were following, when, hearing the shrieks of the women in the guard-room, they ran back, under a storm of bullets, to rescue them. The women were

* Ibid., p. 374.

shuddering as they looked down the steep bank, and asking each other whether it would be possible to descend, when a round shot, whizzing over their heads, warned them not to hesitate. Fastening their belts and handkerchiefs together, the officers let themselves down, and then, having helped the women to follow, carried them with desperate struggles up the opposite side." *

Every detail of this moving episode can be followed by any who take the trouble to mount the wall, for nothing has changed since the memorable year when the horrors of war fell upon the city.

Here is the open space where the fluttering women gathered and huddled together in panic while the line of black Sepoys, that formed the main-guard, stood sullenly by the wall leaning upon their arms and talking in tragic whispers: the women in their bright summer dresses, a little knot of white muslin and gay ribbons, of white staring faces and clasped hands; the Sepoys in their English uniforms, restless and muttering—the cluster of sheep and the line of wolves. In the brains of the one the creeping, the numbness of terror; in the eyes of the other the red fever of murder and lust. Here is the very slope the tottering feet followed when the first cowardly volley was fired, and it has changed but little since its stones were stained with blood, and since among the dead who lay there were such strange things as a child's sash, a little shoe, and fragments of finery from "home." Here are the wall they dropped over and the ditch they crossed, and it is fitting that near by to this very spot is the Kashmir breach, where the deed was wiped out, and where, many months later, the hapless women were revenged.

To return to the events of the siege, the men who followed Nicholson over the Kashmir breach followed him along the narrow ways, that rattled with death, within the shadow of the city wall; until they had cleared the Mori and the Kabul gates, and were brought to a stand by musket firing that few could face. Nicholson could face it, and he did; for, rushing ahead of his men with his sword above his head, he fell before he had advanced many yards, shot through the chest. It was in a sordid lane that he fell, a lane that skirts the wall of Delhi between the Kabul and the

* Ibid., p. 110.

Lahore gates, and a small tablet on the wall tells where he met his end. He was taken back on a litter, and Lord Roberts, then an ensign, tells how he fared:

"While riding through the Kashmir Gate I observed by the side of the road a doolie, without bearers, and with evidently a wounded man inside. I dismounted to see if I could be of any use to the occupant, when I found to my grief and consternation that it was John Nicholson, with death written on his face. He told me that the bearers had put the doolie down and gone off to plunder; that he was in great pain, and wished to be taken to the hospital. He was lying on his back, no wound was visible, and but for the pallor of his face, always colourless, there was no sign of the agony he must have been enduring. On my expressing a hope that he was not seriously wounded, he said, 'I am dying; there is no chance for me.' . . . I searched about for the doolie bearers who, with other camp followers, were busy ransacking the houses and shops in the neighbourhood and carrying off everything of the slightest value they could lay their hands on. Having with difficulty collected four men, I put them in charge of a sergeant of the 61st Foot. I told him who the wounded man was, and ordered him to go direct to the field hospital. This was the last I saw of Nicholson." *

The gallant soldier was in this fashion taken back to the Ridge, the Ridge that he made so famous, and there he died.

His grave is in the little English cemetery just outside the Kashmir Gate, near by to the Kudsiya gardens.

The column which, under Colonel Campbell, was to attempt an entry by the Kashmir Gate could effect little until the gate was blown open. This desperate enterprise was undertaken by a company of six men, and the deed they did has few parallels in the annals of the British Army.

"Lieutenants Home and Salkeld of the Engineers, Bugler Hawthorne of the 52nd, and Sergeants Carmichael, Smith, and Burgess of the Bengal Sappers, started in advance of the column to blow up the Kashmir Gate. Outside the gate the ditch was spanned by a wooden bridge, the planks of which had been removed, leaving

* "Forty-one Years in India." London, 1897. Vol. I., p. 235.

only the sleepers intact. Passing through the outer gateway, Home, who was in front, crossed one of the sleepers with the bugler under a sharp musketry fire, planted his bag of powder, and leaped into the ditch. Carmichael followed, but, before he could lay his bag, was shot dead. Then Smith, who was just behind, planted his own and his comrade's bag, and arranged the fuses; while Salkeld, holding a slow match in his hand, stood by, waiting to fire the charge. Just as he was going to do so he was struck down by two bullets. As he fell he held out the match, telling Smith to take it and fire. Burgess, who was nearer to the wounded man, took it instead, but presently cried that it had gone out, and just as Smith was handing him a box of matches, fell over into the ditch, mortally wounded. Smith, now, as he thought, left alone, ran close up to the powder bags to avoid the enemy's fire, struck a light, and was in the act of applying it when the port-fire in the fuse went off in his face. As he was plunging through a cloud of smoke into the ditch he heard the thunder of the explosion, and barely escaped being dashed to pieces (by the masses of masonry falling from above) by clinging fast to the wall."*

Photographs of the Kashmir Gate, taken in 1857, after the siege was over, † show that the gate as it stands now is altered in no particular from what it was when Home and Salkeld crept up to it with their bags of powder on the morning of September 14th. It is a lowering portal with two gateways, and it was upon the right door that the desperate attack was made.

The parapet of the gate has been much battered by shell, and its outer walls are pitted in a hundred places by shot from the English guns. The place is haggard with grim memories. The ditch is spanned by just such a bridge as spanned it in '57, but the depth of the fosse is diminished, while its sides are less rugged than they were.

There is one feature, due to the exigencies of modern traffic, which would be new to the column who descended from the Ridge; for over one gateway is the inscription "In," and over the other the inscription "Out."

* Holmes' "History of the Indian Mutiny," page 379.

† See Fanshawe's "Delhi, Past and Present." London, 1902.

XVII.

THE GARDEN OF THE UNFORGOTTEN.

There lies, to the south of Delhi—as has been already said—a desolate plain covered with the ruin and wreckage of many cities. For miles it wanders, telling ever the one woful story of the hand of the destroyer. This country of things-that-were has been swept by a hundred armies, has heard the roar of a thousand battles, and none can tell the number of the dead who have lain stark among its stones, since the first human settlement sprang up on what was once green and gracious land.

For centuries the annals of this Golgotha have varied not—the prospering town; the rumbling of a savage storm; a curling, howling wave of rapine, murder, and outrage; and after the wave, a piteous swamp of ruin and dead things.

From the Delhi Gate a road starts across this desert and reaches to a kindly and wholesome land beyond. The road is straight, and it leads through a country of stones and dust. Its margins are marked by trees and deserted houses, and but for the shabby bushes it would be hard to say where the roadside ended and the plain began. The whole district has the look of a common of worn earth from which a million feet have scuffed whatever living thing has grown upon it, and upon which has been piled the débris of a score of Babylons.

Those who follow this melancholy track will pass by miles of ruins, by walls with breaches, shreds of turrets and relics of gates, by crumbling domes rent with cracks from spire to arch, by tottering pillars and half-seen vaults, and by prostrate blocks of matted stone which were bastions or buttresses. Around these ruins are acres of loose stones and clearings of drifted dust, with here and there a quarry-like hole, as if some fearful beast had scraped for dead among the bricks and tumbled masonry.

In a cranny or two, in coves and bays among the stone heaps, there are unexpected oases of cultivation, but the crops that shrivel there are grey with dust. Dust covers the weeds, the brambles, and the half-starved cactus, which slink like outcasts about this amphitheatre of death.

To add to the weariness of it all, many hundreds of tombs have been built in times gone by along the road, and these also are leprous with the all-pervading decay. Blinking vultures perch among these ruins, as if the very stones were carrion, and as if some fascination still drew them to the shambles where thousands of their kind have been glutted.

There are a few wells by the roadside, and a few goats that patter about, searching the ground as if for relics of the past. But for the wells, the goats, and the people on the highway, the whole land might have been deserted by the living many ages ago.

As far as the eye can stretch, the scene is the same—dust and crumbling stone, forgotten cities and forgotten dead. If there be a spot on the earth upon which all the woes uttered by the prophet Jeremiah can have fallen, it is assuredly upon this tract of land which lies to the south of Delhi.

Some three miles along the road there is a faint dust track not readily to be found. A mere trail of dirt, it stumbles over mounds and pits of refuse, and ends abruptly before a wall a little less forlorn than the disconsolate masonry around.

There is nothing to show that there is beyond the wall other than the same wandering waste. But there is a narrow white gateway in the wall, under the stone arch of which is a little paved road.

Any who enter this door pass at once into a new and unexpected demesne. The causeway leads, by a sudden turn, to a deep pool enclosed within four walls. A flight of wide steps slopes down to the water, and round the parapet of the pool is a trench-like path ending in a gallery with a balustrade of pierced stone. The arches of the balcony look down upon the cold surface of the spring. This is a strange thing to come upon in a desert of desolation, but the white gateway is the portal to a strange country.

In many a story told to children, the adventurer has passed through a mysterious doorway in a wall and has found himself in an unfamiliar land; and here, it would seem, is a realisation of the tale.

The wayfarer, turning his back upon the pond, passes into a narrow lane between high walls. This hushed passage is quite in the spirit of the story book, for it leads him to a white gate, and through the gate he steps into a silent court of dazzling marble, with snow-white walls and a polished floor, and with only the sapphire sky to be seen above it. There is no glimpse of the desert; there is no trace of desolation; there is no drift of dust.

The square is cool, gentle, and quiet, and motherly green trees overshadow it, so that only here and there does a splash of sun fall upon the spotless walls. There is no sound in this convent-like courtyard but the crooning of contented pigeons.

In the centre of the square is a shrine of marble, within a verandah of white pillars, and through the lattice screens that make its walls can be seen the outline of a tomb, covered with a cloth of green. In the white courtyard, before the tomb, a man in a red turban is kneeling on the stones in prayer, while others are sitting near him.

The cloister is old, and the trees that throw their shadows over it have shaded it for a hundred years, but the trees are as green as when they first bent to the wind, and the gleam on the marble is as bright as it was when the chisel of the mason touched it last.

The shrine is the tomb of Nizam-ud-din. He was the greatest of all the Chisti saints, and he died more than two hundred and fifty years ago. Yet his memory has never faded, and this most exquisite haven in the waste is tended and preserved by his descendants, who live still among the ruins near the shrine.

Assuredly this love in the wilderness, which has kept green so long a pious memory, is beyond all wonder. The bier is like a bed covered with a faded coverlet. Fresh flowers are strewn around it every day, and it is hard not to think that the good man's body lies just beneath the gilded cloth, that his features are still as they were in life, and that he died, indeed, but a day or so ago.

Within the courtyard are many other memorials to the quiet dead, as well as a solemn mosque where men still worship.

The tombs are enclosed within walls of marble fret-work, and they are but little less brilliant than the shrine within whose shadow they cluster.

In one of these enclosures lies buried the Princess Jahanara. She was a daughter of the Emperor Shah Jahan, and her mother was the lady of the Taj. When her father was deposed and made a prisoner at Agra she followed him into his captivity, and remained with him till he died. She would seem to have survived him fifteen years, and to have passed those years in absolute seclusion. On her tomb is this inscription in Persian characters:

> "Save the green herb, place naught above my head,
> Such pall alone befits the lowly dead."

The cenotaph is of white marble, the upper part of which is filled for its whole extent with earth in which there grows some weedy, melancholy grass. So her wish has been fulfilled.

There is another tomb within this delectable haven, which is perhaps, the most pathetic of all. It stands in a quiet corner outside the courtyard, and almost hidden in the shade of trees. The mausoleum is a little, low square building, with a verandah of rough stone. Compared with the dazzling monuments in the cloister, it is very simple, and it appears to shrink from view into the corner of the narrow court it occupies. Here, in peace, rests the body of Amir Khusrau, the poet, the "peerless singer" whose songs are still sung by the people of his country. Yet he died as long ago as 1324.

Nearly six hundred years have gone by, and still his memory is unforgotten. His tomb is covered by a decorated cloth, which is always spotless, and on one occasion when I visited the place the bier was buried beneath red rose leaves. Can there be any honour in the gift of man that can reach beyond the graciousness of this—to be still unforgotten after a stretch of years so long? It may be that when other centuries have passed there will still be one day in the year when the smell of roses will fill the poet's quiet resting-place, and when red petals will hide the feet of the pillars around the little stone verandah.

Without the wall of this garden of memories is only a desert of violence and oblivion; yet within there would seem to have fallen upon the white cloister and its mosque that Peace of God which passeth all understanding.

Strangest of all is this, that when once the white gateway in the wall is passed, and when once the dusty road is reached, not a trace can be discovered, in the famished waste, of this fair Garden of the Unforgotten.

XVIII.

THE PILLARS OF GOLIATH AND DAVID.

To the south of Delhi, some eleven miles from the Ajmere Gate, there stands near the outskirts of the great desert of ruined cities the Kutab Minar—a Tower of Victory. It has been described as one of the wonders of India, and as " the glory of Delhi as the Taj is of Agra." It stands alone, and rises to the height of 240 feet, so that it can be seen from the walls of the city itself.

It is a monument to the memory of one Kutab-ud-din, who began life as a Turki slave and rose to be King of India. He became famous in that he founded a dynasty which lasted for nearly ninety years—a long period as dynasties fared in those days. He died in 1210, and the king who reigned in his stead built the tower. It thus happens that this monument to the slave who became king has reared its shaft above the level of the plain for more than six hundred and fifty years.

Strange and terrible things it must have seen within this stretch of time. It has watched the rise of city after city, it has seen them prosper, reach to dignity and haughtiness, and then be laid waste and left lying mere skeletons of stone among the ashes. It has watched this desert of ruin spread northward century by century, with always a new town rising upon its farthest border; until at last came the Delhi of to-day—the city of Shah Jahan.

Beyond this city is the Ridge that the British held, and here the creeping plague of destruction would appear to have been stayed.

At the foot of the tower are some fragments of the Hindu city of Delhi, the city which was first swept away by the Mohammedan invaders; and at the farthest point, to be seen readily from the tower, is the town from which fled in the year 1857 the last

Mohammedan King of India. So in this flat, which extends far and wide for forty square miles, the tower of the slave who became king marks where the devastating fire began, and the famous Ridge of Delhi denotes where it ended.

Those who travel from the city come upon the great pillar suddenly, for it is long hidden by the trees which grow by the roadside. It stands in no garden, and in no well-tended enclosure, but springs up to the sky out of a rubbish heap of drab ruins and brown earth.

The marvellous feature of the tower is not its height, but its astonishing appearance of newness. It rises from the faded dust, a strong, jovial, fresh-coloured column of stone. It looks what it is, a tower of victory, and in spite of its six centuries it is the only young and hearty thing that starts out of the plain. The plain is dead, dismal, and hopeless, but the column is alert, living, and jubilant. It is built mainly of red sandstone, which has become beautiful in tone by age, so that the tower now is a rose-coloured tower with a glow of amber about it where the sun falls, and with shadows of red and brown in the depths of its massive mouldings.

It is made up of five storeys, and each storey is marked by a corbelled balcony. All up its sides are rounded flutings, vigorously cut out of the stone. The pillar is very wide at its base, and gradually tapers off to its summit, so that it looks like a gigantic stack of bamboos piled closely together; while the balconies are like bands fastened round the clump to keep the great shafts together. It tapers to the sky, and its evident message is to point skyward. The brackets beneath the balconies are honeycombed with carving, like buttresses of rock which have been delicately fretted by the sea. The mighty column is girdled by exquisite scroll work, made up of verses from the Koran in Arabic characters. These fillets are light and feminine-looking, and make such a contrast as would a ribbon of lace on a cuirass of steel.

There is nothing about this column which could compare with the Taj Mahal; but it is a virile Tower of Victory, radiant with majesty and triumph. It bursts forth from the plain as the blast of a clarion would ring out in a mist of silence, and it proclaims itself to be the token of a king who conquered.

By the side of it other towers of victory, such as the Vendôme column at Paris, are lisping and insignificant.

From its summit is a view of the great drift of wreckage left by centuries of war. To the north is Delhi, with its white mosque, and to the east is the titanic rock fortress of Tughlakabad, upon whose colossal walls neither war nor time have wrought destruction.

At the foot of the tower is a mosque, a shrinking cloister, and a plain pillar of wrought iron. This pillar is very small, and is, indeed, only twenty feet in height. It is as free from decoration as an engine shaft in a factory. It is said to be the only unaltered relic of the Hindu city which stood in this place before the Mohammedan invaders swept down to the Jumna. It has no name, and is known only as "the iron pillar." It may have been a monument of victory itself, but so old is it that its history has long since faded into nothingness. For some hundreds of years the plain iron shaft and the resplendent tower have stood side by side, and the tower has looked down upon the pillar as Goliath looked down upon David. The rose-tinted column was the standard of the conquering people, and the dull little iron shaft was the flag of the conquered.

The giant tower, valiant in its great girth, no doubt frowned contemptuously upon the stripling pillar, and left it to cringe in the shadow of its ridicule. But the little iron shaft had, like David, a "smooth stone out of the brook" in a shepherd's pouch, and a sling; so that after many years of humiliation the pillar brought death to the column, as it were by a stone from a sling, and as David slew Goliath. For the oppressed people of the pillar became victors in the end, and the power that boasted of the column as its standard faded out of the land.

Thus it has come to pass that the real Tower of Victory on the plain is not the ruddy giant of stone, but the bare shaft of iron which stands so meekly by its side.

XIX.

THE SURPRISING CITY OF JEYPORE.

Jeypore is a very surprising city. It is written of it that it is "the pleasant, healthy capital of one of the most prosperous independent states of Rajputana, and is a very busy and important commercial town, with large banks and other trading establishments." But it is not on account of its commercial importance, nor even of its large banks, that Jeypore is surprising.

The capital of this independent state of Rajputana was once at Amber—a wizened old city hidden among the hills at the end of a lonely gorge. So very ancient is this town that Ptolemy knew of it and wrote of it; while a century or more before the Norman Conquest of England Amber was already great and prosperous. Here many Maharajas reigned in splendour, and here in 1600 was built the great palace which still stands defiantly at the blind gorge's end with its back to the hills.

At last there came to the throne one Jey Sing. He was a Prince of unexpected talents and of original mind. In his hours of leisure he was an astronomer; he built observatories at Benares, Delhi, and other places, where they stand to this day, while the curious and mystic instruments that he made are preserved in museums, and fill the ignorant with awe. What Jey Sing the Maharaja learnt from the stars is not known, what portents he saw in the night have been revealed to none, and how the spirit of unrest fell upon him the wandering moon alone can tell. Although his palace was one of the stateliest in India, although centuries of romance and the memory of great deeds hung about the old city and its huddled streets, he determined to abandon Amber, and to rebuild a capital in the plains that opened at his feet.

Thus it was that he founded the surprising city, and called it Jeypore after his own name. He built it so that it was complete in every particular as if he were constructing an educational model. There was a high, embattled wall around it, with mathematically placed gates, a palace for affairs of State, and a palace for pleasure, suitable gardens, appropriate temples, schools and markets, and indeed all the appurtenances and belongings of a capital city. This he did in and about the year 1728. What was strangest about his building was this—that he anticipated by a century and more the aggressively modern town: the gridiron-plan town that springs up on a prairie in America in the course of a few feverish months. The new city is on a level and open plain. "It is remarkable," so the guide-book says, "for the width and regularity of its streets. It is laid out in rectangular blocks, and is divided by cross streets into six equal portions. The main streets are a hundred and eleven feet wide, and are paved, and the city is lighted by gas."*

The old city, on the other hand, clings to the hillside at the blind end of the ravine, a medley of winding ways, of steep causeways, and of houses built up on steps of rock, crowned by a palace. In Amber there is no street that could be called "straight."

Here, then, in a remote part of the continent of India, is a large city, "laid out on the American plan," but built by an astronomer Prince in the early days of the eighteenth century. It would not be unfitting, therefore, to describe Chicago as an American city laid out on the lines of Jeypore in Rajputana.

I am not aware that any record exists of the precise circumstances in which the populace of Amber removed to Jeypore. Certain it is that they left the old city just as it was, and as they left it so it remains to this day, save for such ruin as must needs fall upon a deserted town after a lapse of a hundred and seventy years. So radical and unconventional were the methods of Jey Sing that it is probable enough that he moved his entire capital from the glen to the plain in a single day.

One can imagine the deliberate building of the mathematical city of Jeypore, and can picture the people of Amber walking

* Murray's "Handbook of India," 1901, p. 127.

down furtively in twos or threes to watch how their new town was progressing. They would no doubt go down in chattering companies on high days and holidays, would gape about the torrent-wide avenues, and wonder at the amusing spectacle of houses in "rectangular blocks." The narrowest of these geometric streets was wider than the Great Palace courtyard at Amber, and there must have been much speculation among the gapers as to which trim-cut section of buildings would prove to be their home.

One could imagine how they would trudge back to Amber, to the twisting alleys and shut-in lanes, and fill the minds of the old and infirm with fearful pictures of a city which had no hills, no dark and cramped causeways, no places to hide in, and no steep stairs to climb.

They can hardly have thought comfortably of Jeypore. As well might a rabbit from a hillside warren contemplate with composure the marble courtyard of a temple as a future home.

Modern advertisements dealing with the subject of "Families Removing" enlarge upon the ease with which even extensive establishments can be transported "by Road or Rail." There can, however, be nothing in the records of families removing which can be compared with the great "move" from Amber to Jeypore.

There can be little doubt, I imagine, that the Maharaja went first—he and his wives and his ministers, his men servants, and his maid servants, his elephants, his oxen, and his asses, and all that was his. The procession would wind slowly down the hill from the palace yard. Slowly, because so narrow is the way in Amber that only one elephant can pass at a time The people would be so engrossed in their own "packing" that they would barely look up to see the great retinue go by. The procession would squeeze through the gate, and creep along the gorge to the flat, and then follow the empty streets of Jeypore to the new palace. The streets of the town being a hundred and eleven feet wide, well swept, and paved, would look unkindly bare.

After the great personages would follow the lesser folk, with their goods heaped up on bullock waggons, or laid astride of the backs of donkeys—a struggling, unsteady company, shuffling along with much noise, under a canopy of dust, eager, pushing, and hurried. There would be with them a rabble of bare-legged children, of dogs and goats, of swinging baskets and bulging bundles, the baggage train of a camp which had been pitched on one hillside for some 2,000 years, and had now "struck camp" for good.

Last of all would be the people of mean degree, the parasites of the city, the homeless, the men and women whose sole earthly possessions would be tied up in a loin-cloth or a scarf, and carried on a bewildered head.

When night fell the good old town would be empty for ever. It may be that none even were left to lock the gates after the halting man, who, by reason of his age, or his lameness, was the very last to limp through the archway into the trampled road. The walled streets of Amber must have seemed strange that night, all silent and all dark. The hush that, after centuries, had fallen upon this abode of men would have been terrible in its utterness. No doubt the jackal crawled in, when all was still, and was dazed to find that he had the city to himself, and that neither dog nor watchman challenged him as he crept up, step by step, the listening, suspicious stairway that led to the citadel. There must have been a guard left in the palace, and the light that shone from the slits in the wall would have intensified the sense of desertion.

It may be that the jackal and the moonlight had not the city all to themselves, but that here and there in the shadows was a nimble figure who had hidden until the last went by, and who was curious about many things, and above all, about his neighbour's house. There may, too, have been the dying, and those who stayed behind to be with them till they started on a journey longer than that to the new city of the Prince.

When the guard in the palace had fallen asleep, when the gorged jackal had crept back to his lair, when the crouching thief had slunk along the road through the glen, it would have been fitting if the silence of Amber had been broken for the last time by the moaning of a lonely woman over her dead.

There are other things about Jeypore which are surprising, besides its strange origin and its Chicago-like outlines. The whole of the city—its walls, its palaces, and its houses—are all painted in the same colours, and these colours are pink and white. Passing through a pink and white gate, in a pink and white wall, the traveller comes into a straight pink and white street, as wide as a parade ground.

This street is admirably paved, and sleepy bullocks from the country, who have waddled all their lives among either thick dust or thick mud, wake up with a start when they tread for the first time the smooth pavements of Jeypore. More than that, they stagger as do animals who walk upon ice.

There is no dust, for the streets are well watered. There is no mud, for the roads are well swept. The offal, rags, and dirt, to which the poorer native of India clings with such affection, are in Jeypore snatched from him, and are borne away by small trucks on rails, to a place beyond the city walls. The streets, therefore, are clean. They are also well lit; not, however, by mean oil, but by gas, which burns on a European lamp-post. It thus comes to pass that this pink and white city is strangely trim. The houses are made smooth outside by plaster, while the colour everywhere is uniform, as has been said.

Pink and white is not a usual tint for a metropolis. It would appear to exceed the bounds of frivolity, for example, if the Bank of England, the Mansion House, the Tower of London, and the House of Commons, as well as every street in London, from the north to the south, were to be painted uniformly in pink and white.

Indeed, it is impossible to take Jeypore, as a city, seriously. There is ever the idea that the place is unreal, that it is a card-board town, or that it is made up of the shifting scenery from a lyrical opera. The pink and white plaster with which the houses are covered is precisely like the pink and white sugar which coats a child's birthday cake. Moreover, these baby-like colours are disposed of according to the art canons of the nursery. The houses of the Jeypore Regent Street, for instance, are gay with patterns which might have been designed and executed by a fanciful child. Above a row of sober shops will be painted garlands of flowers of gigantic growth, and of the school treat type, with always the same pink and white bloom on both the blossom and the leaf. There will be wall paintings of pink elephants fighting with pink tigers, and pink and white kings issuing from pink palaces. A favourite form of fresco deals with scenes from English life, illustrative of the domestic habits of the race. A pink Englishman in a helmet is sitting on a sofa with his arm round the waist of a gratified pink lady, while on the next house is another Englishman—or it may be the same—still in a helmet, receiving a pink baby from a grinning pink-faced ayah.

Throughout the length and breadth of this birthday-cake city, and through all its ways, the same tone of rural decoration is observed. The great palace is pink and white, and so are the Public Library, the School of Art, and the local Downing Street.

The windows of the houses form another curious feature in this surprising capital. They are the shape of the windows of a ticket office, and are very small; so small that when a shock-headed child looks out into the street, the whole of the window is filled. The window is void of glass, but it has a wooden door which opens outwards, and this feature of the house has just the appearance of the window in a cuckoo clock from which the punctual and hurried bird pops out to announce the hour.

Such is the effect of the American streets, of the birthday-cake houses, and of the cuckoo clock windows, that the traveller who has visited many cities in a hasty journey, may be excused if he doubts in time if he has ever seen Jeypore in the flesh, or if the city he dreams about is a city made by hands. Many as are the wonders of Jey Sing's capital, its greatest wonder is certainly this, that it has acquired with startling realism the properties and attributes of unreality.

Jeypore would have pleased the heart of Hans Andersen, for here must have been the house of his little tin soldier; and the dancing girl, who inflamed the heart of that faithful warrior, must have first caught his gaze from a cuckoo-clock window in one of the birthday-cake streets.

The present Maharaja—like the founder of the city—is a Prince of great ability, and the results of his enlightened government are felt in every corner of this prosperous State. Thanks to the Maharaja, Jeypore has an excellent water supply—a blessing of some rarity in India—a flourishing college, and a hospital, the equipment of which is not surpassed by any institution of its size in England.

The public gardens in Jeypore are, moreover, among the finest in the country. In these gardens is an educational museum, constructed on the lines of the museum at South Kensington. It is maintained in a state of alert efficiency. The building is called the Albert Hall, and the foundation stone of it was laid by King Edward VII. in 1876. Here are graphically illustrated all the arts and industries which are peculiar to the district. Here can be seen the best work in gold and enamel that Jeypore has produced, and wonderful it is.

In the educational section, the casual visitor will probably be most interested in the departments respectively of Botany and Crime.

In the Botany division are *papier mâché* models—obtained from Paris—to show the intimate construction of flowers and fruits. For ease of demonstration these models are very large. The flowers have petals the size of shields, and pistils that look like war clubs. The individual parts are as gaudily painted as the outside of a circus car, and it is probable that the less intelligent natives who saunter round the galleries may leave with inaccurate impressions as to the flora of Europe, and with the belief that the flowers and fruits of France are as monstrous in size as they are prodigal in colour.

In the department of Crime the lesson to be taught is conveyed by groups of figures, small, but life-like, and elaborately coloured. These little puppets are engaged in every crime capable of being demonstrated by means of models, and the series soars from mere drunkenness to murder.

In the department of murder the collection is very rich, there being no accepted method of committing homicide which is not represented. As in other parts of the museum, so in this, thoroughness of execution is prominent. One model, for example, shows a murdered lady from whose wrists the miscreant is removing gold bangles. The wound in the deceased is of such length that it extends from the chin to the extremity of the trunk. It could not be longer unless made in a spiral manner.

Another group of little figures shows a Thug at work. He is strangling a British soldier, and so swollen, shiny, and purple is the soldier's face that it has the aspect of a bursting plum. Other models demonstrate how best to dispose of the body of a murdered person. The methods in favour in the department are by burial on the one hand, and by division of the remains into small pieces on the other. One little plaster criminal is evidently about to make use of the parcels post as a means of ridding himself of a body with which he has become encumbered.

Another group in the glass case is of encouragement to ladies travelling alone. The drama depicted is this. A native lady, travelling in a palanquin, has been attacked by three men, apparently her two bearers and another. The ruffians have evidently not informed themselves beforehand of the lady's character, for she has leapt from the palanquin in light attire, and has slain the three would-be assassins with the edge of the sword. In justice to the lady's powers it is to be noted that the wounds on the three are exceedingly large and red.

There is a very stately courtyard to this museum, and on the walls of it are inscriptions which embody the sayings of great men of India. The words are graven in both the original tongue and in English, and there is not one of these "writings on the wall" which is not admirable and memorable.

Among them is a saying of Akbar's—he who lies buried at Sikandra—and the message of the great Emperor might well face a man every day of his life. It runs in this wise: "I never saw anyone lost on a straight road."

XX.

AMBER.

Amber lies some five miles from Jeypore. After leaving one of the pink and white gates of the city, the road extends across a plain, and on both sides of the way are ruins. These ruins are widespread, and are the wrecks of comparatively modern buildings. There are the remains of gardens, temples, and palaces, and of the many houses, great and small, which hang about palaces. It is a matter of some surprise to see structures of so great a degree and of such recent growth abandoned to decay. But this is India, and in India can be seen outside many a city wall what desolation may be wrought by the whim of kings.

Along this road of mistakes the traveller drives for three and a half miles until he comes to a range of low hills, in the heart of which lies Amber. At the foot of the hills he changes a carriage for an elephant, both being provided by the princely hospitality of the Maharaja.

The elephant I travelled by was covered, as to his trunk and head, with primitive paintings in red, blue, and yellow. He knelt and on his back was a square seat covered by a white counterpane. As there was a low rail at either end of the seat it had the appearance of a bed prepared for two children. This bed is reached by means of a ladder, and on this bed the rider sits, while his feet rest on a thing of rope and wood such as men dangle from who paint the outsides of ships.

The driver of the elephant was more wonderful than his antediluvian beast. He was a little brown man, with a turban of scarlet and gold. He wore a dark green velvet jacket, trimmed with emerald green, and his forearms were enveloped in white linen sleeves. By a mere touch he made the ton of flesh move with the precision and delicacy of a hydraulic crane.

In the course of time the traveller will come from Jeypore to the foot of the hills in a motor car, and then, in the matter of travel, the very ancient and the very new will meet; but the turbaned mahout will always be more marvellous and more to be admired than the chauffeur with his goggles.

As the elephant moves he appears to be extraordinarily full of joints, and his tread is spongy as is that of an old butler. He stalks up a sloping road on the hillside and through a gateway in a wall. This wall marks the outer confines of Amber. It is cracked and rent, and presents many and grievous breaches, but it is for all that a fierce wall. It has tooth-shaped battlements, and it follows its course with savage determination. Nothing daunts it. It has to make a circuit of the city, and the circuit is made. This persistent wall can be followed for miles. It dives down into a ravine; it crosses the trench at the bottom; it climbs up the cliff on the other side. It winds over a stony down. It follows the sharp crest of a long ridge, so that the ridge looks like the body of a colossal lizard, and the battlements like spines along the back-bone of the beast. No obstacle stands in the way of this conscientious wall, and it turns aside for neither crag nor gully.

Beyond the gate the road enters a gorge between bare hills, ragged with stiff bushes or prickly pear, and with many loose stones. At the end of the gorge is a valley shut in by hills and by the still determined wall. On the summit of the highest hill is a deserted fort, while on a low ridge in the valley is the deserted place.

The town of Amber covers each slope of this ridge together with all that part of the valley which gives access to it.

The palace stands well—a fine, solid, square mass of masonry with white walls, stout buttresses, many cupolas, and domes. Its monotony is broken by arcades and passages with columns, by an occasional verandah, or the trellised walls of hidden courts. There are very few windows in the palace that look across the valley, so that the great bastion-sided edifice has rather the bearing of a fortress than of an abode of kings.

At the foot of the palace hill is a lake, with an island of gardens. The island has around it an embankment, in which are steps leading down to the water. Its gardens are in terraces, traversed by paved paths and covered walks, with here and there a summer house or cool court. Upon the island and its gardens a woful ruin has fallen. A wild undergrowth has spread over it, so that there is now reflected on the surface of the lake little more than a lonely arch, a crumbling balustrade, or a heap of stones covered with a cobweb of briars and brambles. So utterly desolate is this once laughter-haunted spot that the poor pleasaunce may be a garden of Babylon, and the little stairs may be hiding their broken steps in the waters of Babylon.

The way to the palace is by a long pinched street, paved with cobble stones, which winds up hill through narrow gateways and by old walls until it reaches the royal courtyard.

Of the palace itself there is little to be said. It is maintained in perfect state, and its halls and corridors are endless. It inclines to gaudiness, and serves to show how little is the step between what would be grand and what may be tawdry.

Near the entrance to the palace is a small temple dedicated to Kali. That Kali should be the goddess of the dead city is possibly not unfitting. Kali is the most terrible of all Hindu deities. She is the personification of whatever is horrible. Her breast is decked with human heads, and her girdle is made of human hands. Her raiment is stained with blood. Her lips breathe only murder and destruction. Venom fills her veins, and her tenderest mercies are cruel. Her shrine is the only one left at Amber where men still worship.

The temple is vault-like and gloomy, and the flaring red image of the goddess grins from the depths of a threatening cavern. At the feet of this Diva of the shambles is a heap of thick, unwholesome sand, upon which a live goat is sacrificed every morning, and the hideous iron knives with which the deed is done stand by the sand heap. Much red paint, much gilt and faded tinsel make hideous this place of execution, while a clammy shadow laden with the smell of incense and the odour of blood clings to all who enter from the sunlight which streams without upon the temple steps.

Such is Our Lady of Amber.

The whole city can be viewed from a balcony which juts out from the palace wall. It is a city of ruins, utterly silent, empty, and forlorn. It is "the woman who has been forgotten." The streets are narrow and tortuous; some are mere tracks between piles of stones, some are blocked by the débris of fallen buildings. There are houses which have survived the hand of ruin, but they are, for the most part, roofless, and pigeons roost in the upper chambers. Gates stand open: gardens are a tangle of weeds and cactus: windows have become shapeless holes, and verandahs are festooned by aggressive creepers.

Here one side of a house has fallen away, revealing bare rooms with doors that lead into space, and ragged stairs that climb up blindly to the sky, and stand above the crumbling wall like fragments of a turret.

From the palace heights one can look down into courtyards with still, on one side, a great gateway, and, on the other, steps leading to a barren hall. Trees are growing in the court. Their roots have lifted up the flags and have made of the fountain a jumble of marble.

The once walled-in zenana—the holy of holies—is now open to every breeze that blows; the sun pours into the ladies' inner chamber, and the rain beats upon its marble floor. Here and there is a temple with nothing of its dignity left but half a dome, a few broken arches, or a row of pillars held together by the twining branches of a sacrilegious creeper.

Peacocks strut among the ruins and haunt the untidy jungle that once was a market place or a noble's garden.

A tribe of monkeys who have taken possession of this skeleton of a capital, play about the housetops and such parapets as still lean over the streets. They are grey-headed, wrinkled beasts, and they look so like little chattering old men that, to those who believe in the transmigration of souls, they may be the restless spirits of people who once busied themselves in the old town.

A few peasants live among the unkempt ruins, with as little comfort as a tribe of cave-dwellers on a hillside. Their pretence of finding a home in the melancholy stone heap makes but a last mockery of the once arrogant and kingly town.

Amber is dead! The silence of eternity has fallen upon its dumb streets, its sightless windows, its altars that hear not; and those who still strive to dwell within its walls are as scampering rats in a mortuary.

XXI.

UDAIPUR BY THE LAKE.

In my small experience of the great Peninsula, Udaipur appeared to be the most beautiful place in India. It is the capital city of the native State of Meywar, and its name can be spelt in English in seventy-two different ways. The compliment thus paid to the elasticity of the English tongue would be of more practical value if seventy-two adjectives would exhaust the charms of this romantic town.

Udaipur lies on a branch line, sixty-nine miles from the junction, which distance the Meywar train accomplishes in five and a half hours. For this reason, among others, Udaipur is not well suited for the traveller who is in a hurry.

The way to the city is across a monotonous plain, sparsely cultivated, and much afflicted by famine when that trouble falls upon Rajputana. At the end of this plain is a circle of hills, within which the land is again level but for a solitary low mound upon which Udaipur stands. The girdle of hills is so complete as to form an immense encircling rampart, through which a passage has been cut for the railway, and the gap thus made is defended by walls and forts. If this natural amphitheatre could be viewed from an airship it would resemble one of those crater-like rings which are conspicuous in photographs of the moon, and Udaipur would appear to occupy the spot in the centre. The city and the land that lies around it are thus shut off from the rest of the world. Its fields are green and prosperous-looking, for they are well irrigated.

As the town is approached from the railway there is no indication that it stands upon the shores of a lake. The sheet of water lies hidden, so that there is only to be seen a pale city upon a hill,

THE CITY OF UDAIPUR, FROM ONE OF THE ISLAND PALACES.

with a great white palace on the summit of it. The mass of white is broken here and there by a brown roof or a clump of trees, and were it not for the domes of Hindu temples or an occasional minaret, Udaipur might be in Italy.

The city is surrounded by an ancient wall with many gateways—Bible story gateways common to all old Indian towns—where now and then a grave man with a staff walks through, followed by a woman with a baby, riding on a donkey.

Inside the walls the place is picturesque. It is picturesque without being evil-smelling, which is uncommon in the East. The streets are irregular, and they all lead in time either up to the palace or down to the lake. Every building throughout the city is white. Many of the houses are faced with fine carved stone, and it is evident that they were built for no mean folk. In the main street is a colonnade of pillars with a row of shops along the far wall—a shady walk lit by the vivid splashes of colour which are never wanting in an Indian bazaar.

There are many wells in the streets with dripping steps coming up from the water, and about them is always a chattering company of women and children with bright water pots.

There are many Hindu temples also, chief among them being the magnificent shrine of Jagannath, which can be seen from afar. These temples have that squat, bulbous spire, like an inverted urn, which is characteristic of the Hindu holy place.

The great god Jagannath is the *bête noir* of the weaker-minded missionary, and both the god and his car have been the subjects of melodramatic and child-frightening libels. At Udaipur, however, Jagannath would seem to dwell in peace with all men.

The glory of the capital of Meywar is the lake and the palace-covered islands which rest upon its surface. From whatever point it may be seen, the first glimpse of the lake is glorious beyond words, and the comfort of the sight is not lessened when it comes after weeks of travelling through a dried-up country, husky with dust. The lake is two and a quarter miles long, and one and a quarter miles in width. It is deep and blue, and in the time of the cool weather there is seldom a ripple to ruffle its surface. On one side of the lake is the white city; on the other are green flats, with forests of dark trees, while beyond, in the haze, are the purple hills.

Dominant over the lake stands the palace—a dazzling colossus of white stone. Its smooth walls rise sheer from the water, like a chalk cliff; the pinnacles and domes upon its heights tower far into the sky above the city. The city crouches comfortably at the foot of this majestic crag, while reflected in the mirror of the lake are every buttress and parapet of the palace, every terraced garden, every battlement of the city wall, its gates, the white houses, and the clusters of palms.

The palace, with its piled-up buildings, is over against the widest part of the pool. To the north the lake becomes so narrow that its waters lie under the city wall. Here, where it is little wider than a moat, it is crossed by a white bridge, which mounts to a point in the centre, and in some faint way suggests the Rialto Bridge at Venice. The bridge leads to a small peninsula, a suburb of the city, covered with mansions whose bright walls hang over the pool, and where are to be seen kiosques of marble among banana groves and flower gardens.

Between the ghost of the Rialto Bridge and the palace lies the town. Close to the lake's edge are a row of humble temples half hidden by trees, and steps where women in red and blue come to fill water pots of dazzling brass. Here also an elephant will now and then lounge down to drink with great display of leisure.

On this bank is a lofty water gate with three arches. It is built, with much nicety, of marble, but the patiently carved stone has been sullied by modern whitewash. There are rooms with screened windows and fine grilles above the gateway, and it is a matter of wonder who dwells therein, for common mats hide the sun from verandahs fit for princesses.

A steep road drops down from the city to the water gate, and it is probable that the traveller will have his first glimpse of the lake through the three archways, and catch the glamour of the water over the brass urns on the women's heads, or over the brown backs of the cattle who have come down to the ghat to drink, and who, with the women, form a constant band of loiterers in the shadow of the gateway.

AN ISLAND PALACE, UDAIPUR.

There are two islands in the lake, each of which is covered from shore to shore with a summer palace. The islands are small, and the buildings are old, for one was erected in 1628, and the other in 1734. Both are of pure white, and the older is fashioned wholly of marble.

The water of the lake is the blue of the iris; the cloudless sky has the tint of the forget-me-not, and the ivory-like walls which crown each island are overshadowed by palms and heavy masses of green trees. There is no lack, then, in Udaipur of contrasts and colours.

The palaces, as viewed from the land, are made up of a broken line of buildings of little height. White walls capped by fragile parapets or open towers rise out of the lake. Balconies hang over the water. Across a colonnade can be seen the blaze of the sun in a paved courtyard, while through the arches of an arcade is the soft foliage of an orange garden. From every column a clean shadow falls on the snow-white causeway. There is, moreover, a landing place of marble flags, where, on many a day, will be a man in a red robe watching by the prow of a boat.

Every detail of each palace is mirrored in the lake—the latticed window, the loggia by the landing steps, the towering palms, the drowsy man in the red robe.

Here, in the centre of a country of monotony and dreariness, are two of the gardens of the Hesperides shut away from the world by a circle of jealous hills.

There are lakes in Italy with wooded islands, but there are none so exquisite as these. This is Italy on the borders of the tropics, where the palm takes the place of the oleander, where spotless marble replaces painted stucco, and where a palace reigns over a lake in the place of a gaudy villa or a self-asserting hotel. Only the sky is the sky of Italy, and the water has the blue of the Mediterranean.

These palaces are not inhabited, but they are tended with pious care, and, by the hospitality of the Maharana, they can be visited.

They may be visited, but they cannot be fitly described, least of all by an uninspired tourist. The surveyor and the house agent would, no doubt, give an account of the isles of Udaipur in just such manner and with just such fluency as they would describe an Elysian isle should one of those "desirable properties" come into the market. This Indian paradise, however, can never be reduced to mere "premises and messuages." It would need a Tennyson to tell the idylls of the islands, and an Alma-Tadema to show what imagination fashioned their marble courts. They remain only in the memory as a lustrous vision of such Palaces of Delight as the dreamer has fashioned.

Step from the boat into a marble square dazzled with the sun! Pass across a piazza that overshadowing mango trees and palms fill with eternal twilight, and then a doorway in a wall will lead into an unsuspected garden, brilliant with blossoms and musical with the dripping of a fountain. Here is a bathing pool hidden among flowers, and a cloister fit for nothing harsher than trailing silk. Look up, and there is a white balcony with slender columns —it may be Juliet's balcony—hanging over a clump of orange trees. In one corner of the garden a stairway of marble leads to a perfume-haunted room ablaze with patterns in inlaid stone. Beneath the chamber window is the lake; across the water is a thicket of bamboos, while beyond the nodding brake are the ever-encircling hills.

These islands are the realisation of the landscape of romance. Here may be the scene of the love story of all love stories, for this is the land of the lotus eater where there is no last day to the month. These, too, are assuredly the palaces of the fairy tale where the prince and princess came after they were married, and where they "lived happily ever after."

XXII.

A PALACE GATEWAY.

The palace at Udaipur may, I imagine, be considered to be typical of the Indian palace of to-day, of the imperious edifice which dominates the capital of a native state. The building is, as has been already observed—colossal in size. Compared with it the ordinary native house is as a cottage by the side of Ailsa Crag. Those who dwell within its confines are to be numbered by thousands rather than by hundreds, so that in the matter of population it is a little town within unusual walls.

In a guide-book to Meywar, written by a native gentleman,* it is stated that "the city has little or no trade of its own, and is maintained by the expenditure of the court." The palace is not merely the residence of the reigning prince. It is a fatherly and comprehensive establishment which includes government departments, the treasury, certain barracks, the board of works, a potential county council, the Indian equivalent of a soup kitchen in famine times, a royal co-operative store, and an arena for elephant fights and other sports.

The buildings being of all ages, furnish a demonstration of the domestic architecture of the country as practised during the last few centuries. About the centre of this immense pile is the zenana, a great inscrutable, impenetrable block-house, into which none enter from the common world. A part of the new palace is devoted to magnificent apartments prepared for royal and distinguished guests with that profuse hospitality which is characteristic of the native prince. In the older wings of the edifice are Halls of Audience, with many suites of rooms, which are astounding in the brilliancy of their decoration, and which can be seen nowhere but in the East.

* "Handbook of Meywar," by Fateh Lal Metha. Bombay, 1902, p. 8.

There is within the palace a warren of corridors and courts, and of almost interminable passages. The visitor mounts up stair after stair until he expects to come to the palace attics—if such exist—but he finds himself in a garden full of shrubs and orange trees. A further flight of stone steps takes him to the palace roof, whence he can look over the whole town, the lake, and the hill-begirt plain. This view of the white city is only equalled by the view of Cairo from the citadel, or by that of Florence from the Torre al Gallo.

In passing from one hall to another the confused visitor comes upon a number of squatting men engaged in the making of embroidery, or upon a company of quiet jewellers or a noisy group of workers in brass. Incidentally there is within the palace a Museum of Arms. There are also a courtyard full of fodder, and a stable for elephants, which come within the minor details of a tour of the building.

Possibly the most interesting spot in this remarkable structure is the Main Gateway. It is a dingy and awful entry, to which a paved road leads from the palace court. This court serves the part of a general lounge or club enclosure for the unemployed of Udaipur. It is never without its company of loafers. It forms also a recreation ground for the boys and girls of the city. More than that, it is much frequented by cattle of leisure, for there are always a few cows strolling about among the loungers with an affected air of *ennui* and boredom. Pigeons sweep round this square in wheeling flocks, and somewhat disturb the torpid calm of the place. But for the pigeons and the children this rubbish-littered terrace might be part of the palace of the Sleeping Beauty, just before deep sleep fell upon its inmates and upon the cattle within its gates.

The main portal that looks down on this square is like the entrance to a stronghold. At the gate the road passes under the cliff side of the palace as through a tunnel. In the dark way a sentinel stands. On one side of the path is a great barred door, knobbed with iron, while on the other side is a narrow stair built in the thickness of the wall. This winding stair is, in all essentials, the stair of the historical romance. It seems to have been built to be defended by the fierce man with a rapier, or to provide an escape for the fluttering woman with a cloak drawn across her face. It opens upon a dark entry. It is well placed for a sudden attack upon the sentinel, since beyond are freedom and a wall to drop over.

A many-coloured multitude passes in and out of this gate during the day. Servants and retainers of all degrees stroll through, and now and then a company of untidy soldiers lurch up the road, not a little like hastily trained "supers" coming on a stage. Women carrying bales upon their heads pass by, and often there come men or boys with letters. Now and then a pompous man in a velvet jacket and a much-gilded turban swings into the palace yard followed by a grinning servant, and then all the loungers about the gate become alive and bow to the ground. Clerks, workers in silk, and workers in metals, jewellers, merchants, officials, and parties of indefinite status make up the items of the broken procession that winds through the gate.

Here can be seen to pass, in the course of a day, robes and turbans of every colour of the rainbow, and every one of the seven stages of man, from the half-naked urchin who clings to his father's cloak to the aged councillor, bowed down with cares of state, who hobbles through on the arm of his grandson.

Under the wall of the terrace that stretches beyond the arch there are generally men asleep in the shade. They are those—numerous enough in India—who spend their days waiting for somebody. A few are lying at full length, and others are sitting up with their backs to the wall and their heads on their knees.

XXIII.

CHITOR AND THE POOL IN THE CLIFF.

Chitor—like Fatehpur-Sikri and Amber—is another of the many dead cities of India. It was at one time the capital of Meywar, and a well-nigh impregnable fortress to boot. It is now deserted utterly. A few half-starving folk are its only inhabitants, and the least valiant tourist can enter its gates and picnic under its frowning fortifications.

Chitor has an unquiet past, for its annals are annals of violence and of heroic deeds. The story of the fort and of the men who held it can only compare with the legends of King Arthur and his Round Table. From its first days to its last the doom of war hung over the city like a thunder-cloud. The tale of the years of Chitor tells only of sieges, of night attacks, of fire and murder, of mad rushes from the sally port, of treachery and the crawling spy. To one thing only was Chitor a stranger, and that was the sleep of peace.

This strong city crowns the crest of a long lean hill, a solitary ridge in a homely flat, with nothing to end it but the horizon. The precipices which make up the sides of the hill are 500 feet high. The summit is a narrow strip of fairly level land three miles long. About the foot of the hill winds a bewildered river.

A steep road zigzags up the rock from the plain to the hill top. It is hidden from view by a heavy wall, and defended by no less than seven strong gates. Looking up from this road, the brow of the ridge is seen to be guarded by another mighty wall, supported by flanking defences, bastions, and towers. The hillside shows nothing but bare rock and adventurous jungle. Trees cling to every ledge, and bushes hold on to every cranny, but green and gentle as they are they fail to make the steep road hospitable.

On the way up there are, between the "Broken Gate" and the "Hanuman Gate," two chattries which mark the spot where the valiant Jaimall of Bednor and his clansman Putta of Kailwa were killed during Akbar's siege, in 1568. The latter was only sixteen years of age. When all hope was lost of saving the city these two rushed forth at the head of their followers and died fighting in the stubborn roadway. It was their last sally, and from the gallant venture none returned.

As the road nears the upper gate, the wall on the brow is seen to be old and very strong, and to rise straight from the cliff's edge. There are little windows with homely balconies in its blank masonry. They are like nest-holes on the face of a precipice, and many must have leaned from these look-outs to watch, with hope or terror, the wandering road below. So gently has time dealt with this veteran wall that a pot of flowers placed on the balcony ledge would complete the impression that someone still lived in the room within the window.

Beyond the last gate is the flat summit of the hill, and here are the ruins of an entire city, with its palaces, its temples, and its long streets. Chitor might claim to be the Pompeii of India, and those who find interest in the Italian town will find no less curiosity in this ancient citadel which has been buried so long beneath the ashes of neglect. Here are the bazaars and the line of little shops, the ruins of the guard-room, of the treasury, of the minister's house, and of countless tombs and shrines.

There are in Chitor clear pools enclosed by embankments, as solid as a quay, where birds have made a settlement with as much assurance as if the pond were in the depths of a forest.

Here is a pompous gateway that once led to a noble's mansion, but within the enclosure is only a heap of stones. A narrow paved alley, that winds through a shady thicket, was once a lane between two garden walls. Among a clump of shrubs can be seen an arcade of stone columns, or the arch of a gateway, and buried in green is a fragment of a temple rustling with birds. There, among the waving leaves, are the niche, the altar, the grey step.

Mud huts, steamy with squalid people, are built in streets which once rang with the clatter of princely arms. Within a cowshed that leans against a wall are fastidious carvings on the stone, for the wall once enclosed a fountain court. Goats wander in palace yards, or patter along terraces where kings paced in frowning meditation. There is no lane nor green walk in Chitor that the inquisitive may follow which does not open upon some surprising ruin, or reveal some fossil-like relic of the life of the old town.

There still stands, in the city's midst, the great temple of Vriji, with its colossal tower. It has stood there for over 450 years, and those who built it built well, for the ruin that has fallen upon Chitor has left the shrine well-nigh untouched. Trees grow within the sacred enclosure, and gaps in the masonry allow unusual lights to trespass among the solemn shadows of the sanctuary.

There are many palaces also in this hoary fortress. Their arrogant walls are yet erect, although on ledge and cornice vulgar weeds flaunt themselves unchecked. Through coarse breaches in the stone can be seen bare rooms and passages that hang over a chasm of ruin, fragments of stairs that lead no whither, and doorways that none can ever enter again. There is a hideous gash in the crowning dome of one palace, like to the wound in a skull that laid the living creature low. Some of the windows are still perfect, or have lost little of the feminine tracery that filled them. Centuries ago besieged men looked out of these windows across the plain and saw in every dust-cloud a column marching to their aid. Later they looked down upon the bloodshed in the streets and upon the clashing eddies of fighting men. Now crows fly in and out of the casement with some hauteur, and the street is like a green way in a wood. The desolation that has swept over the royal place is as a howling wind on a night in winter.

Two towers stand on the summit of Chitor—the Tower of Fame and the Tower of Victory. The former was, at the time of my visit, in process of repair, and was hidden by bamboo scaffolding. The building of the Tower of Victory was commenced in 1548, just 356 years ago. It rises to a height of 122 feet, and its whole surface is covered with tediously elaborate carving. The colour of the stone is a rich yellow brown, and the column is made up of nine storeys with appropriate windows and balconies, Every foot of every wall is covered with sculptor's work fretted by a thousand shadows.

It is as rich and gorgeous as a laboured piece of carved ivory, but, as a tower, it is somewhat more curious than imposing. The extravagant and restless decoration of its surface seems as little fitting as would be filigree silver work on the shaft of a spear. Compared with that other column of Victory—the Kutab Minar at Delhi—it is merely a clever and lavishly wrought erection of stone, interesting by reason of its age.

There is one spot in Chitor which will probably be the best remembered of all. It is the spring of Gaumakh, or the Cow's Mouth. Cut out of one side of the cliff is a rude, deep chasm in the rock, and at the bottom of this quarry-like hollow is a pool. Steep zigzag steps lead down to the water from the rim of the hill. The walls that shut in this place are precipices of rock, and from the many clefts in the stone lusty bushes are growing wantonly. Motherly trees lean over the edge of the chasm and fill it with shade. Here, indeed, there is always shade, for so deep down is the breathless pond that the sun can but rarely emblazon its surface. On the summits of the high walls which shut in this well of Gaumakh are the chattries of dead queens among the ruins of forgotten shrines.

The water below is blue and deep. So quiet, so cool, so green is the place, that to come upon it on a hot, dry day, when the shrivelled land is tormented with dust, is to step down into the Pool of Siloam. The inviting stairs lead to a place where there are healing waters, and where the weary day, the glaring sun, the heat and the thirst, can all be forgotten.

The pool itself has around it an enclosure of masonry with many steps cut into its sides. On one quay, by the water's edge, is a little low stone cloister. Its pillars, grey and simply carved, support a plain roof. The cloister is built along a ledge at the foot of the cliff, and is very narrow. Above it towers the precipice. That side which looks towards the water is enclosed by panels of pierced stonework, so the little colonnade is dark within.

Two springs of water gush from the rock wall of this quiet

cell, and, streaming in channels across the floor, drop over the steps into the pool.

What is the history of this shrinking chancel in the cliff I know not. It may have been a humble chapel to the goddess of cool springs, an altar to Our Lady of the Well. It may have been merely a bathing place for royal folk, or a retreat from the heat of the summer's day and the turmoil of war.

Whatever its purpose, this spring of Gaumakh is the only living thing and the only gentle thing among the ruins of the dead and savage city. Its waters still splash into the pool, as in centuries gone by, and the shadow that shuts it in is "the shadow of a rock in a weary land."

XXIV.

SIMLA.

India is a country of oppressive extremes. Its description requires a geography of exaggeration, and its physical features are to be expressed in capital letters which need to be immense and sensational. It is becoming, therefore, that the plain which makes a dead flat of the Peninsula for many thousand leagues should be shut in on the north by mountains which are the mightiest and loftiest in the world. That point on the earth which is in nearest touch with space is a peak of the Himalayas.

Among these mountains Simla is a comfortable outpost. On the road to this hill station the plain ends at Kalka, and where the flat dies out the hills begin. There is no hesitating country. When the man who travels on foot reaches the border of the plain he finds the mountains like a wall before him, so he must needs at once ascend or come to a stand.

Kalka certainly is 2,000 feet above the sea level, but the rise is spread over a continent, and is too gradual to be noticed. Simla is 7,000 feet in height, while the loftiest peak, Mount Everest, attains to the dignity of 29,000 feet.

The cart or tonga road from Kalka to Simla is sixty miles long, but by reason of its steepness, its many windings, and its dustiness, it would seem to be six hundred. A railway now takes the place of the purgatorial road. It is a fine tribute to the engineering skill of Mr. Harrington, and it follows the old track for much of the way.

From Kalka the hills mount up step by step, ridge by ridge, peak by peak, an appalling staircase. In the time of the cool weather these hills are brown and bare, and the gigantic lines of cowled heads rising one above the other make the place solemn.

The cart road winds along mountain sides and in and out of a hundred valleys, ever plodding higher and higher. Shrivelled grass, scanty trees, slopes of stones and barren cactus all make for monotony, and the most appropriate figure to find upon the way would be the Wandering Jew. A solitary man on the road is, however, not common. Most of those who are bound for the heights travel in companies. Here will be a squadron of dejected donkeys followed by silent, funereal men, and in another place a line of camels bearing miscellaneous burdens. The donkeys, the camels, and the men are all of one tint from a covering of dust. Indeed, a column of dust hangs over them all day long, like the pillar of cloud which led the Israelites.

Now and then there is the sound upon the road as of a rushing mighty wind, and something tears down hill, riding on a dust-cloud, and through the spinning mist may be a glimpse of a revolving wheel, a medley of hoofs, and possibly the head of a mud-faced man. This is a tonga making for the plains, and there is, perhaps, a satisfied Englishman within who is making for home.

Half-way up the road from the plains one learns how it happened that Simla—one hill among a host—was sought out and peopled. There can be seen, standing up against the sky line, and from among the ever-brown hill tops, one solitary peak which alone is green. It is very green. There is none other like it, and it seems to lord it over the sad-coloured mountains about its feet. It must have been when the uplands were brown that Simla was sighted by the first English settlers. To them it would appear as a green oasis, and they would climb to it as voyagers at sea would make for the one fair island in sight. After the rains the lower Himalayas are green with grass, but even then the peak of Simla stands out alone, for it is green with trees.

This peak, called Jako, lifts its summit more than 8,000 feet above the sea level. A portion of the town lies about its base, but on one side only, for Jako is steep. Round that part of the hill where Simla is not, there is a road called "The Ladies' Mile," made famous by the tales of Rudyard Kipling, and precious in the memories of many by reason of events beyond the emptiness of mere tales.

A town cannot well be built about a steep hill top, but it chances that ridges trail from the side of these heights, like the limbs of a starfish, and upon the crest of one such ridge the town of Simla is balanced. The ridge runs unsteadily from east to west, in the form of a crescent, and from one end to the other is about five miles.

Simla, therefore, like Humpty Dumpty of the nursery rhyme, sits on the top of a wall. The wall is narrow, and its sides are steep.

There is a drop of 1,000 feet on either side, with, in places, a declivity that varies from a wooded slope to a bare precipice. This cliff of many aspects is called the Khud, and horses and carriages, horsemen and men, have from time to time disappeared for ever over its evil edge. A runaway horse, therefore, is unsuited for Simla, nor is the position of the place convenient for the inebriated man after sundown.

When once the wall-capping town of Simla is reached there is little inducement to leave it voluntarily, and the inhabitants only descend to visit Annandale—a plain in a valley 1,200 feet below the ridge where are a race course, a cricket ground, and a wooded place called "the glen." From the main ridge run a few secondary ribs, upon the knife edge of which suburban Simla extends, until a precipice brings the bungalow builders' intentions to an end.

One such groin stretches north to the hill of Elysium, which name will show that Simla is not lacking in either invention or hope.

This Humpty Dumpty town is a holiday place, a city of forgetfulness. Here it is that the memory of the sunburnt plain, of the stifling office, of the sickly barrack square, will be blotted out. There are Government buildings in Simla, but they are as little like as possible to the official head-quarters in Calcutta. There are no straight, formal roads to recall the routine-ridden cantonement. There is no "Mall." Tumbling down the hillside, like a rubbish heap, and fairly well hidden from sight, is the native bazaar. There is no need to go there, nor any occasion to be reminded of India and its reeking cities. Those who come here come to forget. Simla—the make-believe—would have itself to be a little piece of the islands of Britain hidden away among foreign hills. Here are the Highlands of Scotland and the pine woods along the Portsmouth road. Here is that keen, fresh breeze which recalls the rustling north-east wind as it romps across the Sussex downs. Here are shops which will pass for those of Tunbridge Wells, and bungalows beaming with suggestions of Ascot. Here is a Town Hall with a library, a concert hall and a ball-room which must have been transported from some ambitious county town in England, while in the hospitable United Service Club can be breathed the very atmosphere of Pall Mall.

The places in Simla have no unsavoury Indian names, suggesting exile and the hard-earned rupee, but, as befits a homely fragment of Great Britain, which has dropped here like a magic carpet, every house and villa boasts an English name. Here are "Snowdon" and "Windermere," "Kensington Hall" and "Landsdown House," "Stirling Castle" and "Erin Villa," "Wildflower Hall," "Rose Cottage," and even "Windsor Castle."

Simla, in addition to such charm as depends upon agreeable suggestion, is a singularly beautiful town. Its position, on a height among immense mountains, would alone make it superb. Beyond this it is covered with trees from the summit of Jako to the valleys below. Some of these are natural to the place, but others have been planted by a tree-loving people. There are forests of firs and slopes covered with ilex, glades full of rhododendrons and pine trees, and hill-tops green with the solemn deodar, the cedar of the Himalayas. There are roads cut ledgewise along the mountain's face with only a bald peak above and a slippery grass precipice below, and shy lanes that dive into woods never to come out into the light again until the hillside ends on a sudden breezy bluff that hangs over space as it were over the edge of the world. There are paths that wind among gardens or hang about white-walled villas or lead to green-shuttered bungalows buried in shrubs and flowers.

There is nothing formal about the land of Simla, no highway that holds to the level long, few roads that do not twist round a rock buttress at one moment, drop into a glen at another, and bolt incontinently up a hill at the end. The rickshaw, which is the vehicle of the place, is either labouring up or sliding down, is either lost in the dark of a copse or is skirting a rim on a cliff slope white with the sun.

It was nearing the middle of December when I chanced to be at Simla. There was an honest black frost after sundown. The sky was blue and absolutely cloudless. No breath of wind was stirring, and so clear was the air that the peak the town clung to might have reached into the ether beyond the earth's atmosphere. So far as the eye can stretch there is nothing but hills, hills to the north, to the south, to the east, to the west, height after height, until they can be counted in hundreds and imagined in thousands.

Here from the scant plateau of Simla is the spectacle of an appalling multitude, of a motionless army of Armageddon, where the heads of men are mountain tops and their shoulders hummocks of rounded rock. The hills are bare, dun-coloured, and steep—so steep that the valleys are mere purple troughs, with an inch wide pass at the bottom. The hills seem to bear down upon Simla like lines of terrific smooth waves, so that this one green spot might be an island in a dull frozen sea. There is a sense of helplessness in the seeming isolation of the place and in the utter solitude of the encompassing waste.

Far away where the earth ends and the sky begins is a crescent of snow-covered peaks,

> "Ranged in white ranks against the blue—untrod,
> Infinite, wonderful—whose uplands vast,
> And lifted universe of crest and crag,
> Shoulder and shelf, green slope, and icy horn,
> Riven ravine, and splintered precipice
> Lead climbing thought higher and higher, until
> It seems to stand in heaven and speak with gods."

The peaks to the north look over Kashmir, and those to the east throw their shadows on Thibet. Among them can be seen the great snow mountains, from one side of which the river Ganges starts on its journey of 1,557 miles to the ocean, while on the other slope is the source of the Sutlej. This great stream passes by Simla on its way to the Arabian Sea, and the channel it has cut through the mountain barrier can be followed for many a league.

From the hills near at hand sharp-edged ridges push their way into every valley. Very sheer are these steep walls, while so scored are their sides by torrent tracks that they may be Titanic entrenchments, the deserted earthworks of the battling gods. They stand, row behind row, like ditch and wall, like scarp and counter-scarp, great battlements thrown up by unearthly spades, and hacked out of the startled earth by ghostly picks—a rampart to shield the sacred snows which touch the blue heaven.

The view is solemn, grand, despairing, and but for a single vulture poised in the air the awful solitude may be lifeless.

XXV.

THE MEN WITH THE PLANKS.

In Simla—as in other hill stations—are to be met natives of a very different type from those who people the plains. Here are dignified men from the hills, wild and tattered, but with a carriage which denotes freedom, manliness, and independence, and which contrasts vividly with the abject bearing of the dismal creature of the lowlands. Many of these men would be regarded as handsome by any European standard. It is possible to imagine that they may belong to mediæval Italy, and may have fought with the Guelphs or the Ghibellines. In spite of their rags and their uncouth bundles, they walk with no little stateliness and assurance.

Here also are squat people, who are not of Aryan descent, who are in no way dignified, and who, no doubt, must seek an ancestry among the aboriginal tribes of the country. Here are Mongolians also, and cheery, dirty-looking folk from Thibet, who have come from some lost place across the hills, who speak of their homes as "thirty days' journey" distant, and who have tramped every foot of the way.

Whatever their origin, they look, as they stalk through the English streets of Simla, as people from another world. They might have walked from the mountains of the moon, and have never been free all the way from the dust-cloud that still entangles their feet. Well might they stare at the trim Town Hall and at the mystic things to be seen through the telegraph office window. Between these men and the clerk who toys with a telephone there is a great gulf fixed. A Life Guardsman strolling through the High Street of a town in Mars would probably afford no more acute object for contrast than do some of these men who find their way into Simla from beyond the snows.

Something more about them can be learnt from a bluff a few miles to the east of Simla. Indeed, a strange thing is to be seen from there. The point commands an unbroken view across wide miles of hills right up to the wall of snow-clad peaks which look over into Thibet.

Along the sides of these hills, and not far below their summits, is a horizontal mark—like a high-water mark—which can be followed for leagues. It turns into every cleft between the many peaks, and winds around every bluff. It is lost to view a score of times, but it emerges again, always keeping to about one level, and, in spite of all obstacles, ever moving patiently towards the east. It is but a faint grey scratch upon the mountain side. It begins at Simla, and a telescope will show that it ends, only where all things end, at the horizon.

This old grey line is one of the great primeval highways of the world. It is a way from Asia into India. It is a road which has taken part in the peopling of the earth, in the formation of nations, in the primitive migrations of man. It is a solemn, fate-determining path, which has controlled destiny. Compared with it a Roman way in Britain is a thing of a year ago, a path in a child's garden, for men were toiling along this road before Rome was built. This track can only compare with the road in an allegory, with such a path as Bunyan saw in his dreams.

The actual highway is poor enough. It is very narrow, and only men on foot can travel along it, together with their donkeys, mules, and goats. Whoever would follow it to the end on horseback must needs ride well and have a trusty beast.

It was on this road that I met the men with the planks.

They are hillmen of the poorer sort who carry planks of sawn wood into Simla. Each beam is from twelve to fourteen feet in length, and two to three make up a load. The men are ill clad, and the sun and rain have tanned them and their rags to the colour of brown earth. They bear the planks across their bent backs, and the burden is grievous. They come from a place some days' journey towards the snows. They plod along from the dawn to the twilight. They seem crushed down by the weight of the beams, and their gait is more the gait of a stumbling beast than the walk of a man. They move slowly. Their long black hair is white with dust as it hangs by each side of their bowed down faces. The sweat among the wrinkles on their brows is hardened into lamentable clay. They walk in single file, and when the path is narrow they needs must move sideways.

In one day I met no less than fifty creeping wretches in this inhuman procession. Each dull eye is fixed upon the scuffled road or upon the plank on the stooping back that crawls in front. To the beams are strapped their sorry possessions—a cooking pot, sticks for a fire, a water gourd, and a sheep's skin to cover them from the frost at night. If there were but a transverse beam to the plank, each one of these bent men might be carrying his own cross to a far-off place of crucifixion.

No funeral procession of silent, hooded figures could be more horrible than this. The path is in a solitude among bare and pitiless hills: the road is as old as the world, and in the weary dust of it many hundreds have dropped and died.

There along it steals this patient line of groaning men, bending under the burden of the planks upon their backs. Behind them a rose-tinted light is falling upon the spotless snows, and it needs only the pointing figure of Dante, on one of the barren peaks, to complete the picture of a circle in Purgatory.

XXVI.

THE CITY OF TRAMPLED FLOWERS.

Benares, on the banks of the Ganges, has a population of 223,000 people. It can claim a sere antiquity, for "it was a most flourishing and important place six centuries before the Christian era."* It is the sacred city of India, and it has been the religious capital of the country from beyond historical times.

The temples and shrines in Benares number many hundreds, for there is not a Hindu deity who lacks a place in the holy city. Within its walls are idols of stone, of wood, of brass; idols daubed with red ochre or black paint, or smeared with a dubious white; idols with four arms; idols with three eyes; idols with faces of silver and bodies of stone. It may be that even among them all is the god with "feet of clay." Besides the temples there are holy tanks and wells, and sacred ghats or steps by the river.

There is to be found in Benares a refuge from every sorrow, a shelter from every calamity, a promise for every hope. There is a well in the city which can ward off fever, a shrine which will protect from snake bites, a goddess who can cure swelled hands and feet, a ghat which is all potent against small-pox, and a temple where plain women can pray for handsome sons.

In Benares one can buy peace. For there are charms for sale which will shield the purchaser from harm, and will ever encompass him with kindly wings. *Caveat emptor!* In Benares one can purchase comfort. By payment to the priest of quite small coin the haunted woman can be relieved of her secret sorrow, and the starving man can be recompensed for the failure of his rice patch. *Caveat emptor!*

There is nothing worth praying for in this world or in the next

* Murray's "Handbook of India," p. 39.

that cannot be prayed for in Benares at an altar mindful of the particular supplication. People are praying in public in Benares in many thousands the whole day through, from the gold-bedecked man of wealth who is anxious about his money bags, to the poor little ugly woman who kneels in a corner praying for a handsome son.

Along one bank of the Ganges are the sacred ghats, the sweeping line of stone steps which lead down to the stream. They extend through the entire length of the city, and here, every day, a countless host of the faithful come to bathe. The ghats of Benares, as seen in the early morning, can claim to be one of the sights of the world.

Benares is the Mecca of the pious Hindu, and an eager multitude of pilgrims pours into the city year after year. They come from all quarters of the Peninsula; as well from the mountains in the north as from the tableland in the south. Many of them come with infinite labour and pitiful patience by long and tedious ways. Day after day they tramp along, hugging the gifts they are to place upon the shrine, and the money they are to pay to the priest. They come filled with the one great longing to tread the streets of Benares, to throw themselves before the god they worship, to see the sacred river and be blessed by its divine waters. Every year there are hundreds upon the road in whose heart there is but one cry, "To Benares! To Benares!"

Little does it matter that the cost will mean pinching poverty for months. Little does it matter if the strength fail, if the blistered feet totter, if the brain reel from want of food. A few leagues ahead is the city of Paradise, with its Golden Temple, its Well of Knowledge, and its Sacred Stairs.

The pilgrim, when he reaches Benares, finds himself in a somewhat sordid Paradise, in a city indeed of slums and unholy smells. The "Golden Temple" is on no commanding height, and the "Well of Knowledge" sparkles in no echoing square.

Both these holy spots are hidden away in a stifling tangle of narrow lanes, lanes so pinched that here and there it is hard for two to walk abreast, alleys so full of bends and turns that the stranger is happy who does not at once lose his way. So shut in is the

Golden Temple that to see the gilt dome which gives it its name the visitor must mount to the upper storey of a flower-seller's shop near by. There, from a window, the dome stands but a yard or two away. From the walled-in street itself the great cupola is invisible. Those who look up see nothing but a bar of blue sky. The Golden Temple is one among a score of shrines which struggle to reach the light from out of this slough of crowding houses and hustling streets.

The Well of Knowledge is in a wet and stinking quadrangle, and yet it is precious beyond common words, for in it the great god Siva lives. The devout crowd here to drop their offerings into the well, offerings for the most part of water and flowers. But the throng about the well is great and eager, and savage with religious hunger. The square is small. Many can never reach the well, and these have to be content to throw their flowers and their gifts of water over the heads of the more fortunate. Their own scanty clothes are already wet by reason of the jolting of their water pots as they pushed their way up from the river, and the water they fling towards the well as often as not falls upon the heads and the robes of those who are nearer to the sacred brink.

Flowers fare no less uncertainly. The garland woven with such pious care is already torn apart by the struggle through the press. Flowers everywhere cover the ground. White blossoms lie upon the dirty flags, as leaves lie in an autumn glen, and with them are fragments of garlands scuffed into ropes of dirt. Flower petals have dropped into the hollows of unconscious turbans, or have stuck to wet patches on naked backs and on damp robes.

The sacred well must contain the dead flowers of ten centuries in one putrid pulp, and, in spite of attempts in latter years to prevent these gentle sacrifices, the great god has never yet lacked for victims. The stench is terrible. It rises to Heaven like an acrid column of invisible smoke—the incense of dead things from the censer of putrefaction.

The lanes about the well are filled to suffocation with the same jostling, serious crowd. They press along by walls once white, now brown and shiny from the rubbing of many shoulders, by great gates bound with brass, by cavern-like temples full of sickly shade and the dull flicker of stifled lamps. They struggle by courtyards packed with kneeling men bowed down before a fatuous red idol, who leers from a shrine of tinsel and coloured glass, and by the tiny shops of the flower-sellers and of those who deal in sacred emblems.

The narrow lanes are wet. They are slippery with mud and with a paste of trampled flowers, and here too are fragments of white garlands rolled by slipping feet into spindles of mud.

The crowd is wet. They jostle and push. Some still carry flowers or jars of water half emptied by repeated splashings. There is a roar of voices. The pilgrim has reached his goal at last. A fever-like eagerness burns in his face, and he calls out as a sick man babbles in his dreams.

Here among the rocking crowd will pass a fakir with tangled hair and glaring eyes, from whose foaming mouth come sounds like those from the throat of an animal. Here are half-crazy ascetics —men with whitened faces, who have smeared themselves with ashes and filled their hair with dust, or who have daubed their bare bodies with slashes of red paint. Here are vacant-looking priests, deaf to all sounds, blind to all sights. They move passively with the mob, but the lamp of their religious ardour has long since burnt out.

Now and then the road is blocked by a sacred cow, sleek and fat, who fares well while men starve, and who takes up the narrow way with an insolent, indolent unconcern.

Wherever there is a gap in the wall there will be beggars to fill it, the blind, the lame, the leprous. They hold up their mutilated limbs to the light, and bare their ulcerated breasts to the fetid wind.

Above the babble of those who talk, above the cries of the entranced fanatic, above the gasped-out prayer of the sick at heart, above the mumbled formula of the Pharisee, above the whine of the leper for alms, are the occasional tolling of a bell and the beating of a dismal gong.

The day is hot and the air stagnates. The close lane is filled with the stench of man, with the musty smell from damp rags, with the odour of incense, and the fetor of rotting leaves.

Now and then there comes through this murk, like an iced breeze, a waft of exquisite perfume from still living flowers.

The road to Heaven in Benares is dank and dirty. It is neither a path of pleasantness nor a way of peace. It is a road strewn with dead flowers.

When night falls and the bye-ways are deserted there is nothing left to mark the path of the worshippers but the wreckage of white flowers trampled to death in the lane

XXVII.

THE GHATS AT BENARES.

The bank upon which Benares stands is high, and the whole of the declivity, from one end of the city to the other, is lined with the stone stairways of the celebrated ghats. On the crest of the bank are temples and palaces, lofty houses with white walls, immense caravanserais for travellers, and steeples visible to the pilgrim from afar. Each ghat has its particular claim to sanctity, and there are nearly fifty of these holy stairways leading down to the stream. In one place the foundations of a wall and of a ponderous temple have sunk into the mud, so that the line of the ghats is interrupted by cracked masonry and helpless ruin.

The steps are wet, for they are thronged by a crowd of bathers to the number of many thousands. Devout men, gazing with rapt affection upon the river, are walking down to the water's edge, while those who have bathed are lounging contentedly home.

The steps are covered with booths and shelters, with little stone huts where the sick can be lodged, and die with their gaze fixed upon the sacred stream. Above each booth will be a flag on a bamboo pole, while many hundreds of flat grass umbrellas of immense circumference make a shade in favoured spots.

Children are playing on the steps. The pariah dog is everywhere, nosing among the rabble. Cows are wandering about wearily, or are slumbering, tethered to their owners' booths. Women are constantly toiling up and down the long stair, with water pots of earthenware or of dazzling brass upon their heads.

Now and then a woman will emerge from a dark gateway on the crest of the ghat, will empty water from a dish upon the steps as an offering to the God of the Ganges, will murmur a prayer and return through the gateway into the town again.

In one shadow on the stone a man is squatting while his head is shaved; and on a flat step wider than the rest another man is being rubbed and massaged. Everywhere is the figure of the devout offering his stumbling prayer to the divinity of the stream.

When the morning sun pours upon the ghats the display of colour is wonderful beyond words. The wet stair; the glistening brown bodies of naked men; the moving figures in white, in blue, in yellow, in red; the many-coloured flags; the primrose-tinted umbrellas and their round shadows; the glittering brass water pots; the green pipal trees; and, high above the restless crowd, the broken line of ancient and solemn buildings.

It is at the water's edge that the multitude is greatest, for here all the bathers are congregated. They bathe either from the actual steps or from one of the many frail stages built out into the tide. There will be a Brahmin in charge of each little jetty, and it is evident that he has regular customers. The bather steps slowly and gravely into the river, dips his head in the water, drinks of it, and rubs his limbs noiselessly with the divine stream.

The strangest thing in this enormous crowd is the silence which hangs over it. Bathing in the Ganges is a religious observance, a sacrament, and not a matter of mere pleasure. In contrast to this, one can only imagine the din, the yelling, and the splashing, if there were a line of ghats on the Thames from which ten thousand men and boys could bathe at a time.

There are some anomalies in the sacrament of bathing in the Ganges. At one point along the row of the ghats the main sewer of Benares pours the filth of the city into the stream near by to steps of great sanctity. Moreover, the bodies of the dead are cremated by the river's edge, close to the spot where the bathers are most numerous. The ashes are thrown into the stream, and human remains, which have escaped destruction by fire, are often to be seen floating seawards.

Thus it is that the bather may find a human bone left on the steps as the water subsides. Ever by the river's edge, too, are chains of dead flowers, either moving sadly down with the tide or cast up on the mud, at the foot of the stair.

Precious as is a pilgrimage to Benares in the eyes of the devout

THE GHATS, BENARES.

Hindu, there is still a dearer object in his heart, and that is to die in Benares, to die by the brink of the sacred river, so that his eyes may close their last upon the shining stream, and his failing sense feel the divine water ripple over his withering limbs.

So it is that the sick are brought to the ghat to await the end. The waiting is often long. But whether they die upon the open bank or in the shelter of home, their bodies are brought to the Burning Ghat, where they are consumed, and where the ashes are cast into the holy Ganges.

The Burning Ghat at Benares is of special holiness. It is a mere gap in the long embankment of steep stairs. In this gap the river bank is bare and black with the trodden ashes of centuries of pyres. Here is the mother bank of the old river, the one strip of untouched earth in the long array of temples, palaces, and steps. On each side of it are huge square blocks of masonry belonging to the river wall. The line of bricks and stones breaks suddenly at the Burning Ghat as if in awe of the place.

Upon the summit of these wide blocks stand the friends of the dead to watch the burning of the pile.

This shabby patch of earth is shut off from the city by a wall crowned with domed cupolas. Beyond the wall is a thicket of kindly trees which hide a temple. There are gates in the wall, and here is apt to be a group of clinging women who shudder and moan as they see the smoke rise up and hear the crackle of the flame.

Where the river sweeps by the dreadful slope there is an inky streak carried off into the stream which can be followed seawards like a stain of blood. There are always white flowers by the margin of the ghat. They are rocked to and fro among the cinders and the mud by the tiny wavelets which break upon this woful shore. By the side of the ghat are immense stacks of timber for the burning of the dead, and boats are busy here unloading wood the whole day through.

The bodies are wrapped in meagre cloth, the men in white, the women in red. The covering is scant, so scant that it fails to hide the sharp outlines of those who are brought, in this poor guise, to the Ganges for the last time.

On the occasion of my visit there were three bodies waiting to be burnt—one of a woman, two of men.

The wrapped-up corpse—looking strangely flat and thin—was carried to the water's edge and was placed upon the black beach so that the lower limbs were in the stream. The sooty water lapped over the senseless feet, and the rotting flowers that tumbled in the tide became entangled in their coverings. Over the body itself fresh white blossoms had been already scattered.

The pile of wood was built up, and upon it the corpse was laid. The chief mourner—distinguished by his white dress—set fire to the four corners of the stack. Then came

> "the red flame which crept
> And licked, and flickered, finding out his flesh
> And feeding on it with swift hissing tongues,
> And crackle of parched skin, and snap of joint;
> Till the fat smoke thinned and the ashes sank
> Scarlet and grey, with here and there a bone
> White 'midst the grey—the total of the man."

When the body was consumed the ashes were thrown into the Ganges.

The amount of wood employed in this ghastly ceremony depends upon the wealth of the surviving relatives. It happens, therefore, that so little wood is often used for the very poor that the body is only partly consumed, and what is thrown into the river is more than ash.

Poverty is always piteous. In India it is most piteous when the heart-broken man is unable to buy wood enough for the burning of his dead.

XXVIII.

CAWNPORE.

Cawnpore is a dull town near the Ganges which can boast of no attraction beyond that of being "a great emporium for harness, shoes, and other leather work."

At the time of my stay the city was bowed down by a disastrous epidemic of plague, and had in consequence become a place of undesirable importance. Those who could flee from the stricken town had apparently fled. The bazaars were strangely deserted, the hushed streets were empty, and there was an unwholesome languor about the inhabitants.

They must have looked at one another, as they walked on opposite sides of the road, with some such interest as would stir a company of condemned men who wondered who was the next to be named for execution and who was to be reprieved. It may be supposed that each regarded each with a sour suspicion, and no man dare boast in his timid heart that he was alive.

The interest of this city, however, is bound up neither in harness-making nor in the plague, but in certain vile episodes connected with the Indian Mutiny which must ever make the name of Cawnpore abhorred and accursed.

Here, in the summer of 1857 was played a tragedy which made the world shudder, a drama in which the dramatis personæ were mostly women and children, and the villain a more diabolical wretch than any tragedy writer has ever had the boldness to conceive. What can be endured by patient heroism, and what can be wrought by treachery, cowardice, and hate, the story of Cawnpore can tell.

There are three acts in this sickening drama, the scenes of which were laid at Cawnpore, viz., the defence of Wheeler's entrenchment, the massacre at the ghat, and the massacre at the well.

The following brief account of these episodes is derived from Holmes' "History of the Indian Mutiny":—

"In the spring of 1857 the English residents at Cawnpore were leading the ordinary life of an Anglo-Indian community. Morning rides, work in cutcherry or on parade, novel reading, racquets, dinners, balls filled up the time. Pretty women laughed and flirted, as they listened to the music of the band in the cool of the evening, and talked, perhaps, of the delightful balls which the Nana had given in his palace up the river. Suddenly the news of the great disasters at Meerut and Delhi arrived; and the life of the little society was violently wrenched into a new channel."

This same Nana Sahib was the great man of the district. He was the adopted son of the ex-Peshwa of the Mahrattas. He had some little grievance against the Government with respect to a pension, but nevertheless professed great friendliness to the English.

The commander at Cawnpore was General Sir Hugh Wheeler. Although an old man, he had lost neither his bodily vigour nor his activity of mind. He was not beguiled by the pleasing fancy that his sepoys would remain faithful though all around them should prove traitors, so he lost no time in securing a place of refuge for those under his charge.

Believing that the native regiments, when they mutinied, would hurry off to Delhi, and that he would only have to defend himself against the attacks of an undisciplined mob, Wheeler contented himself with throwing up a weak entrenchment close to the native lines.

"He asked the Nana to lend a body of his retainers for the protection of the treasury. He had been led to believe that it would be possible to win the cordial support of the Nana by offering to procure for him that pension which had been so long withheld. Besides, had not the Nana always lived on the most friendly terms with the English residents at Cawnpore? Had he not invited British officers to his table, played billiards with them, chatted with them, smoked with them? Might it not even be judicious to entrust the women of the garrison to his care? This last idea was not carried out, but the treasury was placed under his protection."

On May 22nd there was a general migration of non-combatants from the English quarter to the entrenchment.

On the night of the 4th June the mutiny among the troops broke out, and the Nana placed himself at the head of the rebels.

The treasury was at once seized and rifled, and on June 6th the attack upon Wheeler's entrenchment commenced. The siege of these poor defences became a memorable one. It was, writes Kaye, "a siege, the miseries of which to the besieged have never been exceeded in the history of the world."*

"The besieging army numbered some 3,000 trained soldiers, well fed, well lodged, well armed, and supplied with all munitions of war, aided by the retainers of their newly elected chief, and supported by the sympathies of a large portion of the civil population. The besieged were few in number, and had to contend against almost every disadvantage that could conceivably have been arrayed against them. Besides a few civilians and a small band of faithful sepoys, they could only muster about four hundred English fighting men, more than seventy of whom were invalids." There were within the entrenchment no less than three hundred and seventy six women and children. These poor creatures were huddled together, without the most ordinary comforts, in two stifling barracks, which offered the only shelter to be found within the precincts of the entrenchment.

The entrenchment itself was merely a weak mud wall, about four feet in height, constructed of earth so dry and friable as to be unable to resist the shock even of a bullet. The sky was a canopy of fire: the summer breeze the blast of a furnace.

"Day and night the enemy hurled a continuous shower of shot, shell, and bullets into the entrenchment: day and night the defenders, with ever lessened numbers, sent back a feebler discharge. . . . Within the first week fifty-nine artillerymen, all that the garrison could muster, were killed or wounded at their posts. . . . On June 11th a red hot shot struck the thatched roof of one of the barracks, within which the women and children, the sick and wounded, were lying; and in a few minutes the entire building was enveloped in flames."

* Kaye's "History of the Sepoy War," Vol. II., p. 316.

It is characteristic of the British soldier that when the flames had subsided, the men of the 32nd, regardless of the fire which their enemies continued to direct against them, began diligently to rake the ashes in search of their lost medals.

"The most trying period of the siege had now begun. There was so little food left that the daily ration of each person had to be reduced to a handful of flour and a handful of split peas. If the enemy were afraid to assault, their firing was as incessant as ever. Round shot plumped and bounded over the open ground, hurled down masses of timber from the remaining barrack, and sent bricks flying in all directions; bullets pattered like hail against the walls, and broke the windows to atoms. On June 14th a chosen band sallied forth, spiked several guns, and inflicted heavy loss upon their astonished persecutors: but more guns were soon brought to bear upon the devoted garrison.

"They were far less able to reply than they had been at the beginning; for one of their guns had lost its muzzle, two had their sides battered in, and a fourth had been knocked off its carriage. While fresh hosts of rebels and mutineers were daily swarming up to swell the ranks of their enemies, their own numbers were greatly diminished. Some were struck down by the sun, or wasted by fever; others pined away from exposure, from hunger, or from thirst; others went mad under the burden of their sufferings. More wretched still was the fate of the wounded; for the fire had destroyed the surgical instruments and the medical stores; and death, which came too slowly, was their only healer.

"But most to be pitied of all were those women who still survived. The destruction of the barrack had robbed them even of the wretched shelter which they had had before; and now their only resting place was the hard earth, their only protection the crumbling mud wall beneath which they lay. They were begrimed with dirt; their dresses were in rags; their cheeks were pinched and haggard, and their brows ploughed with furrows. There were some even, who, while stunned by horrid sounds and sickened by foul and ghastly sights, had to suffer the pains of labour, and gave birth to infants for whose future they could not dare to hope. A skilful pen might describe the acuteness of their bodily sufferings:

but who can imagine the intensity of their mental tortures? Yet they never despaired. They gave the artillerymen their stockings for grape cases; they handed round ammunition to the infantry; and they cheered all alike by their uncomplaining spirit and their tender, gracious kindness."*

The Nana was in a hurry. His thousands of well-armed men could not beat down the spirit of the hundred or two starved Englishmen who stood gripping their hot muskets within the entrenchment. In spite of his many and fine guns he could not make a breach in this poor rampart of mud, from behind which the hollow-cheeked men ever watched him. He therefore resorted to treachery. On June 25th a woman came into the entrenchment with a letter from the Nana offering a safe passage to Allahabad to the dwindling company under General Wheeler's command.

After some discussion it was agreed that the garrison should be allowed to march out with their arms and a certain proportion of ammunition, and the Nana offered to provide boats and provisions for the voyage to Allahabad.

Early on the morning of June 27th, the little band of British soldiers marched out of the entrenchment they had held so gallantly for three long weeks. With them went the women and children who had survived the fearful ordeal of these interminable twenty-one days, and the large company of the sick and wounded. The rest of the story is told by Holmes in the following words:

"About three-quarters of a mile from the entrenchment, a ravine, spanned by a wooden bridge, ran towards the river. Arriving at the bridge the procession turned aside, and began to thread its way down the ravine. And now the banks of the Ganges were close at hand. The unwieldy boats, with their thatched roofs, were drawn up close to the water's edge; and a great crowd of natives of every class was waiting to look on at the embarkation. There were some, too, who had not come merely to look on. More than a thousand infantry sepoys and several squadrons of cavalry were posted behind cover on the banks; and Tantia Topi, a favoured counsellor of the Nana, was there to execute his master's orders for the management of the embarkation.

* Holmes' "History of the Indian Mutiny." London, 1898, pp. 224 to 234.

"What those orders were, presently appeared. Those troops had not come to serve as a guard of honour. They had come to be the instruments for executing that plan which the Nana and his counsellors had devised. No mud wall separated them now from the men and women who had defied them. Their numbers and their artillery must surely be irresistible now. Now, therefore, was the moment to take the time-honoured vengeance of a besieging army upon an obstinate garrison.

"Hardly had the embarkation begun, when a bugle sounded. Immediately a host of sepoys, leaping up from behind the bushes and the houses on either bank, lifted their muskets to their shoulders; and a hail of bullets fell upon the dense crowd of passengers as they were clambering on board. Cannon roared out, and grape-shot raked the boats from stem to stern. Almost at the same instant the thatched roofs, which had been purposely strewn beforehand with glowing cinders, burst into flame. Then the sick and the wounded who had survived the destruction of the barrack and the horrors of the siege, were suffocated or burned to death. The able-bodied men sprang overboard, and strove with might and main to push off the boats into deep water: but all, save three, stuck fast. Women and children bent down under the sides of the boats, trying to escape the bullets. Some ten or twelve men swam for dear life after the nearest boat, but one soon sank exhausted: others, struck by grape or bullets, gasped and beat the bloody surf, and turned over dead; and three only reached the boat. Now the troopers rode with drawn sabres into the river, and slashed the cowering women to death. Little infants were dragged from their mothers' arms and torn to pieces. Suddenly, however, a messenger came from the Nana, saying that no more women or children were to be put to death. The slaughter therefore ceased; and the trembling survivors, a hundred and twenty-five in number, their clothes drenched and torn, mud-stained, and dripping with blood, were dragged back to Cawnpore."*

Wheeler's famous entrenchment is in the cantonement about a mile from the city towards the east. Its limits are now marked out by stone posts, but of the actual line of trenches little trace

* Ibid., p. 237.

remains. The encircling rampart was wofully scanty. The earthworks were only about four feet high, for the ground was so hard that it was almost impossible to dig it. Moreover, the earth thrown up was so dry that it formed in many places a rampart little better than a bank of sand.

It is not to be wondered that the rains of over forty years have nearly blotted out this frail, despairing defence. The entrenchment stands in a bare plain as level as an open common in England, without one single natural advantage. The buildings enclosed by the defences have long since vanished. The position, however, of the burnt barrack which served as a hospital is still indicated by its foundations. It was near the centre of the enclosure, where it was exposed, from first to last, to a deadly fire.

There is a well outside the entrenchment into which the dead were let down at night. Every evening, when darkness and some lull of peace fell upon the tormented camp, the dead were brought out by men who talked in whispers, and were lowered into the well one after the other—the war-tanned sergeant and the fever-wasted child, whose tiny body made so little strain upon the rope. The darkness was kindly, for it hid the tears that stood in the eyes of fearless men, and it hid the wretched mother who clung to the rope as they lowered her one baby into the heartless abyss. The well is now closed, and over it is built a fair memorial. Here were buried, within the space of twenty-one days, no less than two hundred and fifty of the little garrison, ladies and children, officers and private soldiers. They who shared a common trouble now lie together in a common grave.

There is this inscription on the memorial:

> "In a well under this Cross were laid, by the hands of their fellows in suffering, the bodies of men, women, and children who died hard by during the heroic defence of Wheeler's Entrenchment when beleaguered by the rebel Nana. June 6th to 27th, 1857."

The most noteworthy feature in this entrenchment is the very little space it covers. It is terrible to think that within this feeble circle of earth about nine hundred people were huddled together, and that nearly one half of this number were women and children.

They entered this miserable shelter on May 22nd, as has been already said. Those who survived marched out of it on June 27th, but only to march to the Massacre Ghat.

The heat was intense, water was hard to get, sleep was well-nigh impossible, and the poor garrison was dying at the rate of twelve a day. The defences were scarcely more formidable than those a boy would dig on the sands with a toy spade, yet there was a force inside the feeble ring of earth which enabled a few hundred British soldiers, hampered by every disadvantage, to keep three thousand well-armed and well-fed men at bay.

Those outside the circle dared nothing; there was nothing that those within it would not dare.

There was only one well within the line of the entrenchment. It still exists, little if at all changed. It is no more than the common well which is to be found everywhere in this part of the country. In just such a well the dead of Wheeler's garrison were buried, and into such a well the living and the dead were cast after the massacre of July 15th.

This one within the circle of trenches was in so very exposed a position that to approach it in the daylight was to court death. Yet the heat was great and thirst terrible. Many a man trying to draw water for a dying woman or a wounded comrade was shot down by the side of this tragic well; while even at night time the merciless enemy kept up a fire upon the spot.

It was, indeed, as Kaye puts it, "a service of death" to go to and fro to this well with the buckets and bags which brought water to the shrivelled lips of the famished garrison.* Yet one brave-hearted civilian, John MacKillop by name, appointed himself "Captain of the Well." He only held this desperate commission for seven days, when he was shot down at his post.

As he lay dying his sole thought was for those in whose service he had yielded up his life. With his last breath the faithful captain of the well begged a by-stander to take water to a lady to whom he had promised some, because he was troubled to think she might be disappointed.

There are many memorials of the Mutiny in Cawnpore, but this

* Kaye's "History of the Sepoy War," Vol. II., p. 332.

poor well—although no tablet adorns it—stands in its homely simplicity as a monument to a man who "laid down his life for his friend."

The Massacre Ghat—known in old days as the Sati Chaura Ghat—is about a mile and a half from Wheeler's Entrenchment. The road is across an undulating country, pretty and daintily wooded, which calls to mind many a spot in England. The actual ghat is approached by a winding ravine or glen, at the bottom of which is a nullah or dry water-course. There are many trees on the banks of this quiet grass-covered way, and it makes a shady path to the river.

As the approach was in '57 so it is now, and every step that the desperate defenders of the entrenchment took on their way to the river can be followed.

After twenty-one days of ceaseless fighting and of torturing suspense they were free at last. The hideous throb of guns was changed for silence. They were on their way to the boats. The deadly entrenchment, with all its horrors, was behind them. The Nana had promised them a safe conduct to Allahabad, and a leader's promise is good. After the long imprisonment there was liberty; after the stinking, fly-ridden enclosure there was the open country and green banks. After the thirst and the sickening heat there was ahead the swinging tide of a cool stream. The journey was to be by no dusty road, but they were to drift down the river by boat, and there is born in the English a love of boats.

The Nana Sahib was keener and more subtle in his cruelty than he himself knew.

The company that wound down the glen was a sorry one to look at—worn-out soldiers, ragged and lean; pallid women; terror-stricken, wondering children, clinging to their mothers' gowns and ever looking backwards; rocking litters with the wounded and the sick; together with much untidy luggage and hastily packed bundles. The march must have been slow and painful, and eager eyes must have kept a watch for the first sight of the river that was to bear them to safety. It is easy to picture it all.

A dazed woman walks by the litter that carries her wounded husband. He turns his throbbing head to look at the green slope of the gully, and she talks of a combe in Devonshire they both know well. She tells how the journey on the river will make him strong, and how there is no need any more to measure his water in a wine glass.

A soldier, with a bullet in his foot, limps along with his hand on a comrade's shoulder. They are wild, unshaven men, burnt by the sun to the colour of a lava stream. They go over the tale of the trenches and of the sepoys they have shot, and when something about the path to the river reminds them of home they lapse into rhapsodies upon beer.

A small, toddling child pulls at his mother's hand to show her two squirrels who are playing in a tree, but she hears nothing, and her gaze is far away. Her husband and two children are lying in the well outside the entrenchment, and she and the small boy are now on their way to the river alone. Poor soul, she might have turned to look at the squirrels, for in an hour she was lying dead in the river, with a bullet in her worried brain, and eighteen days later the toddling boy was thrown alive into the well at Bibi-garh.

The ghat to which the refugees came is on the river's bank some way below the town. It stands alone. It is merely a wide, stone stairway, with walls on all sides, except on that which opens to the stream. In the enclosing walls is a shady colonnade with a flight of steps in each corner leading from the road to the ghat. At the head of the stairway is an ancient temple to Siva—empty, ruinous, and hollow. Over this shrine to the "blessed" God are two friendly, garrulous old pipal trees. They must have been already advanced in years in 1857, and under their shadow many would have rested on this particular morning in June.

The ghat is now severely deserted. There are no houses within sight of the accursed spot. No natives come near it: no children play upon its steps: no women come here for water. It is shunned as a haunted place. It lies stretched out on the river's bank like a dead leper. This outcast stair is shabby and miserable to look at. The plaster is falling away from its walls, laying bare the poor bricks. The steps are covered with dry mud left by the last high Ganges, and in this drift there is not a single footprint to be seen.

The grass-covered banks on either side of the ghat are wooded and pleasant. It was among the genial bushes near by that the murderers hid.

The Ganges at this place is broad, and, in the time of the cold weather, its surface is a dazzling grey, as if the stream were made of mercury. In places sand-banks rise out of the wide flood, while across the water there is to be seen a flat land swept by a mist of dust.

This is probably the very bitterest spot on the earth, this murderer's stair, this devil's trap, this traitor's gate! The very stones are tainted and festered with mean hate, and, until it rots, the mud-covered colonnade will be foul with the sneaking shadows of cowardice.

The hundred and twenty-five women and children whose lives had been spared at the Massacre Ghat were imprisoned in a small house in Cawnpore called the Bibi-garh. It had been the home of a poor Eurasian clerk. The number of the prisoners was augmented by the few women and children who had drifted away from the scene of the massacre in one of the boats, and who had been captured and brought back. There were also some unfortunate fugitives from the fort of Fatehgarh, who had come to seek an asylum at Cawnpore of all places in the world. They were promptly seized and lodged with the rest in the Bibi-garh. The prison at last contained two hundred and six women and children and five men.

"Save that they were no longer exposed to the fire of the enemy, these poor captives," writes Holmes, "were worse off now than they had been in the entrenchment of Cawnpore, or the fort of Fatehgarh. English ladies, the wives of the defenders and the rulers of British India, were forced, like slaves, to grind corn for the murderer of their husbands. They themselves were fed on a scanty allowance of the coarsest food. Those were happiest among them who perished from the diseases which this food engendered. All this time the Nana himself, in a sumptuous building, which overlooked their prison, was living in a round of feasts, revels, and debaucheries. But on the 15th July, in the midst of his unholy mirth, an alarming announcement came upon him. That avenging army, of whose coming he had heard, was within a day's march of the city; and the force which he had sent out to check its advance had suffered a crushing defeat.

"Then ensued the last act of the tragedy of Cawnpore. . . . First of all the five men who had been suffered to live thus far were brought out and killed in the Nana's presence. Then a number of sepoys were selected, and told to go and shoot the women and children through the windows of the house. They went; but they could not harden their hearts to obey the rest of their instructions. They contented themselves, therefore, with firing at the ceiling instead. But such effeminate sensibility was disgusting to the Nana. At his bidding, then, two Mahomedan butchers, an Afghan, and two Hindus, armed with long knives, went into the house and hacked their victims to pieces.

"All through the night the bodies lay neglected in the room; and moans were distinctly heard proceeding from it by those without. Next morning a heap of corpses, a heap of wounded, and a number of children who had escaped the knives of the assassins, were dragged out, and thrown, the living and the dead together, into a well hard by."*

Of this awful massacre of July 15th all evidences have been wisely obliterated. Photographs taken in the year of the Mutiny show that the well was situated in bare and open country, and that the house—the Bibi-garh—in which the massacre took place, was a common building of one storey, with the aspect of a stable.

The place is now changed into a beautiful garden, very quiet and full of peace. The horrors of the spot have thus been blotted out, the ghastly house of one storey has been swept away, and the heartless earth has been covered with flowers and homely shrubs.

The site of the massacre house is marked by a small plain cross. In the lawns about the well are many mounds in which severed limbs and fragments of the dead, found about the well's brink, were buried by the avenging troops.

In the centre of the garden is the well. It is built over, so that no sign of it remains. Above the site is a memorial, made more familiar to the people of England by means of photographs and

* Holmes "History of the Indian Mutiny," p 241.

pictures than is any other spot in the whole of India. There must be few who do not know the octagonal Gothic screen of grey stone and the angel standing within with folded wings.

As a work of art the monument may be of no great merit, but the finest statuary in the world could not make this spot more lamentable than it is, nor invoke a sympathy more unutterable.

Poor dead women! Their bones are enfolded in those of their children, the garden in which they sleep is like a garden in England, and hardly a day passes but someone from the old country stands over their grave with bowed head and throbbing heart.

There are many wells which are famous in history, many which fill the scene of old legends, many which the poet has made memorable by song, but these three pitiable wells in Cawnpore will be, with many, the best-remembered of all.

XXIX.

THE RESIDENCY AT LUCKNOW.

The story of the siege of Lucknow will be humming in the traveller's mind as he nears the capital of Oudh—the state which has for its strange symbol two fish. Although Lucknow is the fourth largest city in India and covers an area of thirty-six square miles, there is but one spot within its wide limits which is of supremest interest, and this is the old Residency. Although the cantonement occupies what the estate agent would call "an extensive park-like expanse," and although it can claim to be one of the most charming places of residence in India, the visitor will discard fine bungalows and parks for certain poor ruins, for an old house with ragged walls, and for tumbled stones which still speak of the famous and tragic siege.

There are delightful public gardens in Lucknow, there are the Goomti River to row upon, and the regal club of Chatar Manzil to idle in, but overshadowing them all are memories of the deeds of Henry Lawrence, Havelock, Outram, and Colin Campbell. These memories are inseparable from Lucknow. Even the lounger at the club will now and then recall that the rebels fired upon Havelock from the club-house walls, and that they were in those days the walls of a hostile palace.

The siege lasted from June 30th to September 25th, during which time a mere handful of men held a weak position against a host. The fire of mutiny among the native troops showed itself in the city early in May, 1857, and by the end of the month it had burst into flame.

Sir Henry Lawrence, the chief commissioner, had already caused large quantities of provisions to be brought into the Residency, and had prepared that place for a siege which he estimated would last fourteen or fifteen days. Here in due course

gathered the English inhabitants of the town, the British troops, and the small number of Indian soldiers who had remained faithful. When the circle of muskets closed in around them and shut them off from the world, the number within the lines of defence was about 1,826—excluding servants and camp followers—and was made up of 927 Europeans, 765 natives, 68 women, and 66 children.

At the first sign of bloodshed the coolies, who had been engaged in the making of the fortifications, fled to a man, and with them went most of the domestic servants. The Residency and the buildings which were included within the beleaguered area occupied a low mound close to the Goomti. It was nearly in the centre of the river face of the city. The space enclosed by such hasty fortifications as could be thrown up was remarkably small and measured, indeed, only 2,150 feet in one direction by 1,200 feet in the other.

The Londoner can form some idea of the dimensions of this haphazard stronghold by the fact that the whole of the place to be defended could be put within the wall of Buckingham Palace and its garden, and that the greatest width of the compound was about equal to the distance from the Horse Guards to Westminster Abbey.

Within this very limited field were included the Residency and its garden, a banqueting hall which was turned into a hospital, a prominent house occupied by Dr. Fayrer, the surgeon to the Residency, an old mosque, a palace called the Begam Kothi, the English church and its cemetery, and a large number of small houses and out-buildings.

It contained also two or three little squares, with what may be termed one main street and numerous short lanes. There was a gateway leading into the enclosure. It was situated in the so-called Baillie Guard, which stood between Fayrer's house and the hospital.

The only steep part of the mound was on that side which faced the river, and here was placed the "Redan" battery, which proved to be the strongest post the besieged could boast of. Elsewhere, the mound fell away to a mere insignificant slope; while on that side farthest from the river the ground occupied by the garrison was level with that held by the enemy.

The fortifications consisted of walls, stockades, palisades, fascines, and earthworks, with loopholes made by sandbags. Crowding all around the English position were the houses of the native city, densely placed, and held in great force by the enemy. The spot to be defended was nothing more than a small corner in a populous city. Indeed, in one position there was only the width of a street—a few paltry feet—between the fortifications of the two forces. Native soldiers within the English lines would exchange banter—coarse enough probably—with the rebel sepoys in the houses just across the road.

The Residency was, at the time of the siege, the finest building in Lucknow. It consisted of a ground floor and two storeys, surmounted by a tower fifty feet high. It was a substantial structure, with wide verandahs and lofty rooms. It accommodated nearly a thousand people—men, women, and children. In its cellars women made for themselves a home, for in those days a cellar was the only "desirable residence" in the settlement.

The old palace, the Begam Kothi, another large and solid structure, occupied the centre of the enclosure, and here most of the ladies of the garrison were located. It was of all the houses in the place the one most removed from the enemy's fire.

The Banqueting Hall was an imposing hall of two storeys. It came to be used not only as a hospital but as a barracks, a store, and a place for charging fuses and cartridges. It was, unfortunately, in an exposed position, and sick men were shot as they were lying in bed. Fayrer's house was a picturesque house, built on English lines, typical of the residence of a prominent official.

The story of this siege differs little from that of other beleaguered places. There were the intolerable watching and waiting, the torment of unrest, the horror of alarm; by day the longing for the night, at night the longing for the day, the numbing monotony, the daily deaths.

A never-ceasing drip of shell and bullet fell upon the little settlement from dawn to sundown. No one moved from his shelter but felt a bullet whistle by. What the enemy lacked in valour they made up in persistency. Many times they hammered the earthworks with cannon until a breach was made, then came the boom

of a bursting mine, and after that a mad rush of yelling men towards the smoking gap. But they never carried an assault, and never, from the first day of the siege to the last, did a hostile foot find a place within the English lines.

"Hold it for fifteen days? We have held it for eighty-seven!"

There were night attacks which kept every heart in a turmoil and every limb alert. There were sorties, when men crept out silently with stern faces, and came back shouting with the tale of a gun spiked or of a house blown up. All the buildings within the Residency lines were battered and chipped. Some were hacked to pieces. Many were made roofless and ruinous. After the siege, from one house alone—the Brigade Mess—no less than four hundred and thirty-five cannon balls were removed.

On the 2nd July Sir Henry Lawrence was struck by a shell while lying on his couch in the Residency. He was removed to Dr. Fayrer's house, and there on July 4th he died.

On July 25th a spy brought in a letter from General Havelock to say that he was coming to the relief. A month passed, but he never came. On August 29th another letter was smuggled in with the glorious news that the garrison—now forlorn enough—might expect to be succoured in three weeks.

On September 22nd came the assurance that relief was near. All the next day the people in the Residency could hear the firing of guns outside the city. Those who had looked so long, so often, and so hopelessly towards the Cawnpore road, could now see puffs of smoke and signs of an advancing column.

On September 25th there was fighting in the streets; the noise came nearer and nearer, and in the evening of that day Outram and Havelock marched in through the Baillie Gate.

The relief of the worn-out garrison had, however, not yet come. Outram, Havelock, and their men were in turn beleaguered. They were able to improve and extend the fortifications of the Residency, and to make the position of the garrison less deplorable. The fighting, indeed, never ceased until November 17th, and on the afternoon of that day Sir Colin Campbell entered the Residency, and Lucknow was finally relieved.

On November 22nd the women and children, together with the sick, were removed to Dilkusha—a stately house in a rich garden. Here, on November 24th, the brave, patient, much-enduring Havelock died. He was fated to see the end.

The Residency and its puny ring of crowded outposts have altered much since November, 1857. The buildings are more or less ruinous, and of some of the batteries there is now no trace to be found. The spot has been transformed into a garden, with fair lawns and flower beds; and trees, new to the place, have made of it almost a thicket. On every wall that stands are marks of shot and shell, and everywhere are there ragged holes in the masonry.

But for this the ruins might be those of a pleasant country settlement. All the native houses for a considerable distance around the entrenchments have been swept away, so that now the mound with its curious medley of ruins stands isolated and alone. The little hillock is very green, and its gardens are tended with reverent care. An inscribed stone marks the situation of every post and battery, so that the line of the defences can be exactly followed.

The massive gate at the Baillie Guard stands up as defiantly as ever. It is pitted in fifty places with the basin-like marks that a cannon ball makes, and much of its stubborn brick has been blown away.

On the right of the road that leads up from the gate is the Hospital. It is now roofless and floorless, and there is little left of it but its long walls. Its square windows, which were once barricaded so that scant light came in except through shot holes, are now open enough to the heavens. Creepers have hidden many of the wounds on its surface, and the dignified pillars with which it was ornamented still proclaim it to have been a Banqueting Hall. There are long corridors and passages on the ground floor, and here many a time the dying—dragged hastily into shelter—heard the faint firing of the last shot.

On the left of the road is Fayrer's house, one of the best preserved in the compound. It is built like the rest—of brick and stucco—and it must have been a smart little place in its time. It is just such a house as is found in the most select outskirts of an English country town. The outer plaster is everywhere dotted

THE RESIDENCY, LUCKNOW.

with shot marks, as if there had fallen upon it some unearthly rain. There are orthodox steps to the entrance, and a cluster of columns to make a colonnade. Over each doorway is a quite English "fan" decoration. In the front an iron support of the verandah still projects from the wall. In one of the rooms Sir Henry Lawrence died, as a tablet on the wall records. Dr. Fayrer—now Sir Joseph Fayrer—is happily still alive, and no episode in his adventurous and most distinguished career can stand out more vividly in his memory than does that which has this little house for its background.

Between the doctor's house and the Hospital is one of the many wells to be found on the mound. One can imagine the longing look that was kept upon this well by any patient who could catch a glimpse of it through a crack in the shutter, and who—peevish with fever—moaned for the night to come when it would be safe to fetch water again.

Beyond the Hospital, and a short way along the road, is the Residency, towering high above every other building in the place. It is a fine old country house, spacious and lordly. The top storey has crumbled away, but the ground floor of the mansion is in good condition. The walls, it is needless to say, have been hammered with shot from every side. The tower still stands, in spite of its gaping wounds, and worn stone stairs still mount to the top of it. From that summit flies the British flag. It hung there through all the terrible months of 1857, and it hangs there still. The Residency at Lucknow was reduced to ruins, but the flag which waved over it was never hauled down.

"And ever upon the topmost roof our banner of England blew."

The stairs have winding steps, and those who walk up them now can picture with what stumbling haste they were traversed by the eager man who, for the hundredth time, climbed to the top to look over the country towards Cawnpore, towards the road along which the relief column would surely some day come. There is a narrow hall at the foot of the stair, where, no doubt, would always gather a few—also for the hundredth time—in weary hope of possible news. If the watcher stayed long at the top they would feel sure that some sign of the column was to be seen, and they would call up to him as soon as they heard his returning footsteps on the stairs. Only once in the long stretch of days did he bring good news.

Whoever looks from the Residency Tower towards Cawnpore has before him one of the most pathetic and most stirring views that the eye can rest upon. The view is across the narrowest part of the city—over an isthmus of houses, trees, and mosques—while beyond is the open country and the Cawnpore road. Was ever a stretch of country more eagerly, more desperately scanned? It was stared at until its details were branded into the brain. What looks of hope were shot over the unheeding way! What clamorous prayers were poured across the never-answering flat!

Think of the tower on the evening of September 22nd! The watcher would climb up to the look-out, slowly, languidly, mechanically, with little faith, with less hope. Those who waited dully at the bottom—more out of habit than with an expectancy—would hear suddenly the sound of a man dashing headlong down the stair, and the gasping cry, "My God, they are coming!"

The Mosque and the Begam Kothi have passed through the siege with slighter damage than has fallen upon less important structures. There is little sanctity, however, left to the mosque, and nothing palatial remains to the palace. Its walls are covered with gaudy paint, with scarcely more art than is bestowed upon the daubs of colour on the face of a North American Indian. In the Begam Kothi and the buildings around it most of the ladies of the garrison were lodged. They must have wearied of the sorry rooms and of the painted doggerel on the walls; but they had some measure of peace as they were well removed from the rabble about the firing line.

Many of the other buildings, such as Ommaney's House, the Brigade Mess, the Martinière Post, have fallen into such utter ruin that they are indicated only by the foundations of their walls.

To the south a pillar within the enemy's lines marks the site of Johannes' house. This building was very near to the English position, and it was occupied by an African whose aim was so deadly that he was complimented by the name of "Bob the

Nailer." On one happy sortie Johannes' house was blown up. In another rush of the English from beyond their ramparts the unerring Bob came to his death through a bayonet wound.

The famous Redan is now merely a grassy mound. The church is a ruin; and the cemetery—crowded with its tale of two thousand dead—is so like a burial ground in England that it needs only a hawthorn hedge and a lych gate to make it a piece of the old country.

The most impressive hour to visit the Residency is just after sundown, when the light is failing, and when the place is deserted. Let any who will walk once or twice round the line of the ever-silent outposts, and there comes back the scene as it was at a like hour of the day forty-seven years ago.

The tortured little place of refuge becomes peopled again. The beleaguering ring of walls, houses and pointing guns closes about it once more. The sun has gone down, and much of the sickening heat is over. There are still the stench of the camp and the ever-persisting host of ravenous flies.

The place has become quiet, for the firing has ceased with the light. Two or three pallid women have crawled out of cellars into the still air, holding their ragged clothing about their necks. They ask of the first passer-by the old monotonous question: "Any news? Any signs of their coming?"

There is a wine-coloured stain on the road, with rounded edges. It is plain enough to the women in spite of the dust which has been scraped over it. It was where a man, shot through the chest, died in the morning.

A slow-moving child has dragged her doll out with her, and a boy, made stupid by mere dreariness, is aimlessly scraping the earth out of a shell hole. There is a path to the well which has become piteously distinct during these sore months, and many are going to and fro along it.

A shuttered window in the Hospital has been thrown open, and white-faced men, who have gasped in the hot, foul gloom all day, are looking out. They look down upon piles of stores, casual rubbish, stacks of arms, heap of accoutrements, upon some comrades cooking under the shelter of a wall, and upon others who are playing cards by the light of the small fire. In what may be called the street men are already forming up for a night attack.

Within the darkened rooms of the Residency there is a kind of gipsy camp, with all its miscellaneous untidiness of dishes and clothes, beds, and cooking pots, mixed up with the sofas and chairs and delicate decorations of a drawing room.

Between the Residency and the Hospital is a bare waste of trodden earth, with here and there the stump of a leafless shrub. This brown waste was once the green, well-mowed lawn of the Residency garden. Across it now they are carrying a dead soldier in a blanket, on the way to the cemetery.

In front of the house a grey-headed man is pacing to and fro. No one disturbs his reverie. General Havelock is alone with his own thoughts.

XXX.

ON THE WAY TO BURMAH.

Calcutta—the last place I visited in India—is a city with no prominent individuality. Those parts which the traveller is apt to see are parts of a European town struggling with certain natural disadvantages—particularly with heat. It is evidently hard to assume the dignity and promiscuous bustle of a great capital under a sun which settles upon the brain like a weight. Calcutta is content to be busy languidly. There are wide, well-kept streets, admirable European shops, tram lines, and "fine public buildings" of all degrees.

The Hooghly is very like to the lower Thames. Its waters are quite as opaque and as brown, while up or down with the tide drift barges, floating crab-fashion, after the manner of Wapping. Hectic steam launches hurry about with great fuss and much whistling. By the quay side bloated liners slumber in the sun, with just a wreath of lazy smoke dawdling from the funnel to show that they still live. Compared with the small and active craft on the river they might be red-bellied hippopotami dozing on a mudbank.

Hanging over Calcutta, at this particular season, was a cloud of smoke, worthy of London. It was pleasant to see, not only as recalling a memory of the Great City, but as a relief from the ever-empty Indian sky.

The thing which of all others first strikes and impresses the visitor to Calcutta is the deadly smell which fills the place. A blind man could tell a street in Calcutta from any he had ever visited. Of this furious smell, Rudyard Kipling speaks in the following fashion:

"For diffused, soul-sickening expansiveness, the reek of Calcutta beats both Benares and Peshawar. Bombay cloaks her stenches with a veneer of assafœtida and tobacco; Calcutta is above pretence. There is no tracing back the Calcutta plague to any one source. It is faint, it is sickly, and it is indescribable. It is certainly not an Indian smell. It resembles the essence of corruption that has rotted for the second time—the clammy odour of blue slime. And there is no escape from it."*

If there be appalling slums in the capital there are also, about its borders, a circle of comely bungalows and delightful gardens, which are hardly to be equalled anywhere in India.

Government House, Calcutta, fulfils precisely the conception of what such a building should be—a large, white, dignified mansion, standing in a formal garden. It is the old English country house, haunted by the ghosts of tragic association, and, were it not for the statuesque native soldiers who stand as sentries on the wide steps, it might be a nobleman's demesne in a leisurely county.

The most admirable possession of the city is the Maidan, a wild, open common which extends from the garden end of Government House far away into the plains. On one side of it can be seen the masts and funnels of the ships in the Hooghly. They give to the place the semblance of a rollicking green about a seaport town. Even when the heavens are as brass, and the dull air is stagnant and sticky, the sight of the topmast yards of a barque is almost as good as a breeze from the sea. To perfect the illusion, there is, in the middle of the Maidan, a tall, white column, which every new arrival to the city believes to be a lighthouse. It is, as a matter of accuracy, a monument to a political resident, but it ever encourages the belief that from its summit might be viewed the dancing sea, and, possibly, white rollers on a pebbly beach.

If there were only a flag-staff or two in sight, a white-walled boat house, a capstan and a few rusty anchors, no one could come to believe that Calcutta lies (by river) ninety miles from the ocean.

Now and then, on an afternoon, a gentleman may be seen driving in a dog cart across this heath, attended by two native lancers. This is Lord Curzon, one of the most able viceroys India has ever possessed.

The voyage from Calcutta to Rangoon occupies about three and a half days, and not less than twelve hours of this time will probably be spent in the Hooghly. Although the river is suggestive

* "From Sea to Sea," Vol. II., p. 203.

of the Thames by reason of muddy waters, huddled shipping, and coal-stained banks, it differs from the English waterway in this—that as the lower reaches are passed, the river becomes greener and younger, instead of drearier and more senile.

Some way below Calcutta the steamer is stemming a delightful river, with banks lined by rushes and palms, among which are thatched cottages, or villages with the tints of autumn leaves, or sloping beaches with hauled-up boats. This is little to be expected. As well might a liner from Tilbury pass through the luxuriant reaches of Henley on its way to the sea.

There are curious boats on the Hooghly, craft with haughty poops, like a Spanish galleon, yet with thatched deck-houses as shabby as a cowshed. They are manned by men who are little like mariners, who are wrapped up in poor clothes which blow about in the wind. When the mornings are cold they tie up their heads with miscellaneous rags, as if troubled with toothache.

In due course the banks of the Hooghly become flatter, fainter, and more bare; until they fade, as if from mere weariness, into the void.

On the morning after leaving Calcutta there is a pleasant sight to greet the eye—the round disc of sparkling sea, cold, clean, and sapphire blue, which is framed by the porthole of the cabin. The sun makes it radiant with life, the wind makes it bubble with freshness. After the dust of India, after the dead roads, after the dismal view from rattling trains, this crisp circle of bonnie water is a vision of delight.

Long before the land of Burmah is sighted the sea becomes as thick with mud as the Tyne at its worst. This is due to deposits brought down by the Irrawaddy and other great streams which slide into the sea near about Rangoon.

So very flat are the banks of the lower Irrawaddy that they are at first mere sketchy lines on the drab horizon, and it is hard to say when the river is entered. In a little while, however, the steamer finds itself in a low country, green and pleasant, while, by some magic, river banks draw near until they are seen to be fringed by shock-headed palms and luxuriant trees, which are broken in upon, now and then, by brown hamlets or a row of black boats.

Now, too, are seen, for the first time, pagodas. They that are met with here are of little pretence, for they wait upon the pious of mere villages. For all that there is no structure with more grade than the slender, tapering spire which rises out of the bamboo thicket, or above the russet line of straw roofs, to point to Heaven.

As the river narrows, with many and pleasant windings, there is a Something to be seen afar off which inevitably attracts all eyes. The eager traveller is awed by the first sight of it, and the laziest sailor looks up from his work to gaze on it for the hundredth time. From the mutterings of those who gather on the deck it would appear that this object, which so strangely fascinates, stands above the invisible city of Rangoon. It is a wondrous spectacle. Not even Venice, when approached by sea from the west at the time of sunrise, is heralded by such a vision as this.

Beyond the glittering river, beyond the little beach of French grey, beyond the green, unbroken flat which sweeps inland for miles, there stands up against the sky a brilliant pinnacle of astounding height. It looks like a pink, snow-covered mountain peak as seen in the dawn. It rises up ghostlike against the blue, infinitely delicate, unsubstantial, marvellous. It is the Great Golden Pagoda of Rangoon—a wonder of the world.

As the steamer draws nearer there is some sign of the town. At first, all that is seen of it is a green hillock, about which cluster a medley of brown roofs and chubby trees. On the summit of the mound is the Great Pagoda. It has now become a dazzling spire of polished metal, a column of pure yellow gold, from its base among the trees to the spear-like pinnacle which trembles in the heavens. Just below its highest point hangs a canopy of tangled gilt and precious stones, and here are swinging mirrors which catch the light and sparkle in the sun like a circle of immense diamonds.

The Pagoda dominates the whole country. Nothing dares to rise above the awed horizon in the presence of this superb erection, this giant sword Excalibur which is lifted out of the lake-like level of the plain. Rangoon is nothing; the Pagoda is all.

Thus it comes about that Burmah—from this side of the sea—is to be known by the blaze of gold which shoots up into the sky over its city as if it were the beam of a divine pharos.

Part III

BURMAH AND CEYLON

RANGOON AND THE BURMAN.

As the steamer nears the quay at Rangoon, the city, which was so ethereal and so delicately hinted at, when viewed from a far-away reach of the river, becomes every moment grosser and more commonplace. The marvellous Pagoda is dwarfed and almost hidden from sight. Its glory is sullied by unworthy surroundings, by sheds and warehouses which flaunt themselves in the vain company of tall chimneys. Corrugated iron supplants the nut-brown thatch, and in place of solemn woods, ugly, dejected houses straggle stupidly about a crazy waste. There are oil-tanks where there should be clusters of palms, and the hiss of saw-mills is changed for the contented mumble of the river.

But for the low hill upon which the Pagoda stands, Rangoon lies on a flat. It is a prosperous and pushing town, modern to a fault, alive with new industries, alert with new ambitions. Every year its boundaries are extending; for out of the meek fishing village has come the arrogant metropolis. The structures in its amazed streets are passing rapidly from the state of shantyism to the dignity of "fine public buildings," from the stage of flannel-shirt-sleeves to the black coat and white collar. The town is still just a little weedy and wild, as are many young things during the stages of rapid growth.

The intelligent stranger dropped suddenly into Rangoon would know that he was in some active British settlement in the East, but there would be little to tell him that the place was in Burmah. The European shops might belong to Singapore, the last new streets to Penang, the tram-lines to Calcutta, and the drinking saloons to Port Said. He would be disappointed if he expected to find a distinctive populace. The Burmese, as a people, are slowly disappearing. They are becoming absorbed by alien races on the one hand, and are being pushed into the quiet country on the other. The reason for this will be explained later. Suffice it for the present to say that the Burman is little in evidence at Rangoon, especially in parts where work is being done. The apparent population of the place is made up of Chinamen, Malays, natives of India, and other less distinct Eastern folk. The native of the country is to be found in the delightful hinterland, away from wharves and unquiet quay sides.

The suburbs of Rangoon are supremely pleasant, especially to those who have made sojourn in India. The roads are red, the bungalows are of homely wood, the gardens are green and luxuriant. There is everywhere an atmosphere of content and comfortable prosperity. The dust, the glare, the barrenness of India are missing, and even the Hindu woman who comes here loses her love for grubbing in the dirt.

In these genial suburbs is Government House—a building little short of a palace—where lives the Lieutenant-Governor, Sir Hugh Barnes, whose admirable administration is doing so much for the progress of the country, and whose charming wife maintains a popularity as hearty as his own.

The Burmese are a people of Mongolian descent, who are in every particular distinct from the native of India. In stature they are short, their complexion is a faint brown, their faces are a little flat, with a tendency to high cheek bones. The men, on the whole, may be described as handsome—often as distinguished-looking—certainly as bright, intelligent, and good humoured. They are always clean, always tidy. They are, for the most part, slight, so that there will seldom, if ever, be found among these pleasant people any who would recall the inflated, greasy, half-strangled looking "baboo" of Calcutta. The men have long, sleek, black hair, which is twisted into a knob on the top or side of the head.

Around the forehead is a prettily arranged handkerchief of silk, usually of pale pink.

Their dress consists of a simple short jacket, most commonly made of linen, with a long skirt of silk in some bright tint. This is almost identical with the costume affected by the women, and—save for the handkerchief round the head and a possible moustache—it is at first not easy to tell the two sexes apart.

Although the Burmese man may look effeminate, he has not that character with those who know him. He is described as manly, as possessed of a great love for sport, and as generous and hearty. His habitual cheeriness is in strong contrast with the melancholy of the native of India. The Burman is, by nature, idle and a lover of pleasure. He is improvident and easy-going. He takes life lightly, while his view of the future is that of the Lotus Eater. As he does not like work, and as Burmah under English rule is a strenuous country, it is no matter of surprise that he is becoming replaced in all centres of activity by men who will work.

As for Rangoon, it is far too serious, too full of purpose, too absurdly in earnest, for the lover of ease. Progress bores him, and the strenuous man he views with dislike. He inclines to the park and the race course, but he finds no joy in quay sides or in wharves. He will watch men carrying weights or digging in the streets with picks and shovels, but his interest in these occupations ends with the watching. The Burman is adapted for an idyllic life. He would find congenial company among the polite and frivolous folk who people the glades of Watteau's pictures, but not among those who frequent tram-cars and factories. The river bank at Rangoon is no place for Strephon and Amaryllis, and Watteau himself would be ill at ease among scenery in the foreground of which a row of oil-tanks was prominent.

The Burman, therefore, must go inland. The gloriously wooded hinterland is beautiful, living is easy, and there is never the lack of a rollicking companion, who is as ready to gamble as to drowse in the sun.

II.

THE LADIES OF CREATION.

It is to be regretted that the traveller's first acquaintance with the fascinating Burmese woman will probably be made in Rangoon, as she is looking at French hats in a European shop, or as she is waiting for a train at a distasteful railway station.

The first glimpse of her should be on an old road, in a Burmese town—such a town as has remained unsullied by the West—where she would be found among surroundings which have known no change for centuries, and which are, above all, her own. The Burmese woman belongs to Burmah of the old world, over which the wind of change has not yet blown.

I can recall one such vision of the lady of the land in the country as it was. There was inland a grey, still road, shaded by trees and hushed by many palms, which made of the way a sleepy aisle. Small pools and splashes of sunshine lay in the road as if it had rained gold. Among the columns of the palms, low houses with walls of mat and roofs of velvet were dozing in the shadows. An inquisitive creeper had climbed to a verandah, and had tumbled over the slender handrail into the passage. Around each house was a yellow palisade of bamboo lattice-work, and against such a fence two naked children were leaning. The road itself was deserted. At one end of it a far-off pagoda of gilt shone in a jagged gap of blue sky.

From out of the cloister of the wood a girl came, who halted for a moment in the road, hesitating which way she should turn. She stood erect, like a queen. Her eyes were dark and expressive, and there was a smiling mouth with white teeth. Glossy black hair, with a red rose in it, made the covering of her head. A simple jacket of white linen hung from her shapely shoulders, and from her waist to her naked feet was a skirt of glistening pink silk that sketched in simplest lines her perfect form. Two plain gold bangles on her wrist complete the account of her—a delicate, cool little figure, with a splash of sunshine at her feet, and the vision of the pagoda at the road's end. Such is the lady of the land.

That her face is Mongolian in type is evident enough. She may hardly be pretty if judged by a European standard, but by no standard can it be declared that she is other than most fascinating. Her eyes, at least, are absolutely beautiful. Her expression is alert, vivacious, cheerful, so that she looks the embodiment of good temper. She is as neat as a nun, and as quaint as a Puritan maiden, but there is too much coquettishness about her to allow of these comparisons being made complete. She is a brilliant little personage, graceful in her slightest movement, infinitely feminine, full to her lips with the sparkle of life, yet dignified and even stately. She walks with a swing of her arms and a roll of her shoulders which mark her as one who thinks well of herself, and intends that all others should hold to the same belief.

She has excuse for some dignity of bearing, for it is the Burmese woman, and not the Burmese man, who is at the head of affairs. What business is to be done she does. She is ever astir in the market, buying and selling, since it is the woman who sits at the receipt of custom. Her husband or her brother may carry bales of silk for her, may unpack her cases of silver, may bring vegetables in from the country to her stall, but it is she who guides the enterprise and who manages the trading. She does it because she does it well, and because "he" is so indolent and uncertain.

She sits on a low, yellow mat in her stall, and holds up to you a piece of silk. Her hands are pretty, and there are many gold bangles on her wrists. A sleek head and smiling eyes are visible above the rim of the silk. She holds it up as a child would hold up its last new toy for admiration. You ask the price of this trifle of amber and rose, and she shyly suggests a quite fantastic sum, as if she were playing at "keeping shop."

You propose to give her half the amount she has ventured upon. This amuses her beyond words. She is filled with laughter, for the jest is evidently much to her liking. Smiling, moreover, becomes her, as her teeth are exquisite. There is more movement of shapely fingers and of supple wrists; the silk is dropped, and another piece is held up with mute questioning. You renew the offer of half the price named for the piece first shown. She again becomes radiant with laughter, and hides her mouth behind the edge of the outstretched stuff. With infinite shyness she suggests a less extreme mutilation of her original price. She half whispers the sum, as if it were a possible answer to some absurd conundrum. You finally take the silk for exactly one half of the sum originally discussed. She is perfectly delighted, and appears to regard the long bargaining as the best of fun.

It is all excellent fooling, this playing at "keeping shop" by a picturesque woman instead of by a child, but the woman—like the child—is never a loser at the simple game.

The ever-courteous little silk mercer is, without doubt, an alert woman of business, and yet matter-of-fact people who know her say she is careless, pleasure-loving, and hopelessly improvident. It would seem, then, that she is still a child, even when she is not playing at "keeping shop."

The blue-stocking lecturer on woman's rights should have one of these light-hearted, stockingless little people on the platform with her as an example. Harsh critics are apt to describe such a lecturer as sour of aspect, and also as lean, spectacled, and moustached. If there be any truth in this, the contrast between the advocate of women's rights and the possessor of them might be vivid. The association of the two may, however, arouse the suggestion that violent and perspiring speech, a creaking voice, and a bony and mittened fist are less strong aids to argument than an amiable capacity and a readiness to undertake loyally whatever the particular hand may find to do.

There is in the world one matter of taste upon which unanimity of opinion can never be obtained, and that is on the subject of woman's dress. It may as well, therefore, be stated—without the least hope of carrying conviction—that the dress of the Burmese woman is as nearly perfect as any female costume can be.

Its chief claim to perfection is that it is exquisitely, divinely simple. This will not appeal to the Western lady, who may hold that strict simplicity is only becoming to the workhouse inmate.

The dress of the Burmese woman consists of a white linen jacket of the plainest possible type, without collars, ties, or cuffs, and a skirt of unstudied silk wrapped closely round the body down to the feet. This robe is marred by neither flounce nor frill, and, so far as the uninitiated can tell, it has escaped even the touch of needle or thread. Sandals to the feet and gold bangles to the wrist complete the costume. Whatever may be the artistic value of this attire, it can at least claim to be perfect from the standpoint of health.

The Burmese woman " does " her hair also with equal simplicity, in a neat coil severely fastened by the turning of the same upon itself. It displays the outline of her head with perfection, and no hair arrangement of the ancient Greeks could be more " classical." A fresh flower, or, possibly, a comb is the sole ornament. There is no attempt to contort the human hair into puffs or rolls, or to make of it a grotesque, meaningless structure, held up by pins and cords and undermined by frowsy pads.

The dress of this picturesque people never varies. The Burmese woman knows nothing about " trimmings," nothing about " style," and her mind is not kept in a state of unrest by the contemplation of the anxious problems which centre about hats.

Here is a country of intelligent women where there is no such thing as fashion, and, therefore, none of the hopes, the petty strivings, and the sorrows which depend upon the blind pursuit of what is fashionable. Women reputed to be more civilised have to dress as the gospel of the fashion-plate dictates. A mysterious being, with the wand of the " latest style," drives them across the common of their little world, as a bumpkin drives a company of stiff-necked, cackling geese. No matter what the style may be so long as it is late. There is no option, no need of judgment; the fashion seekers will all go as they are driven so long as the goose-herd's stick embodies the last new thing.

The Burmese woman allows herself some latitude only in the matter of colour. Her silks incline to tints of pink and rose, of saffron and pale green. In the choice of these each follows her own taste. These dainty, delicate colours come as an agreeable relief to the unvarying blues and reds which seem to encompass the invention of the woman of India.

There are two other matters to be noted in connection with the woman of the country. She seems to be endowed with the privilege of preserving the youthfulness of her figure into advanced age. Indeed, it is hard to say with what lapse of years she will lose the quite girlish outline, the well-modelled shoulders and the slender hips.

Finally, she has at least one weakness, to wit, the smoking of Brobdingnagian cigars as large as wax candles from an altar. Some are white, some are green. They are compounded of tobacco and vague herbs, but however pleasant they may be to smoke, they spoil the pretty curves of a much pleasanter mouth.

III.

THE GOLDEN PAGODA.

The Golden Pagoda at Rangoon—rightly known as the Shwe Dagon Pagoda—is one of the most impressive of the works of man. It stands, as has already been said, on a low hill about the outskirts of the town. The whole summit of the sacred mound is occupied by a vast paved platform from the centre of which the pagoda rises.

This monument to the memory of Buddha has its foot upon an octagonal plinth of colossal size. From this base it springs upwards, a terrific spire, a solid pyramidal cone, plain and smooth, becoming as it rises less and less, until the far point that touches the clouds is a mere dizzy trembling rod. The girth of this wondrous column, as it rests upon its plinth, is no less than 1,355 feet; its summit a child could grasp in its hand.

The whole of the Pagoda is gilded from its foundations to its pinnacle, and it is to the eye a thing of absolute and refulgent gold. Its surface is polished as a surface of ice. At no level is it broken in upon by flaunting ornament or unquiet decoration. It is entirely plain, and it is this profound elemental simplicity which makes it so majestic. A Gothic spire as high as this would have its sides overladen with adornment, and would seem to be built up of arches and columns, of cornices and angles, of projecting ledges and masses of contorted stone. Here is a bare tapering column, loftier than the Cathedral of St. Paul's, in London, which from base to point is a smooth height of unsullied gold.*

This utter simplicity makes it sublime, endows it with primeval magnificence, bestows on it the grandeur of a fundamental truth.

The Golden Pagoda appeared to me, as it may possibly appear

* The height of the pagoda is given as 370 feet.

to many, as more imposing and more marvellous than the great pyramids of Egypt.

On the summit of the Pagoda is the Ti, or "umbrella spire," which is common to all erections of this kind. The *ti* is made up of concentric belts of beaten iron, hung with silver and gold bells which ring in the wind, and with mirrors, which flash all day in the light of the sun.

The Shwe Dagon Pagoda, while it is the finest in the world, is also the most venerable. All Buddhists hold it in supreme regard, and the ground upon which it stands is holy above all. Pilgrimages are made to its foot from afar, so that people from almost every country of the East may be found kneeling in its shadow.

The Pagoda is said to have been built in 588 B.C., and to have been originally only twenty-seven feet high. It was gradually added to from time to time, but has remained substantially unchanged since 1564.

This enormous spire of glowing gold must needs be a remarkable element in the landscape. The first sight of it, as viewed from the estuary of the Irrawaddy, has been already commented upon. The term "golden" is commonly enough employed in the description of scenery. Here, however, is a Titanic mass of plain gold introduced as an actual feature of the landscape. Such a feature would be impressive anywhere, but it could scarcely be more gloriously placed than here, in the tropics, on a soft stretch of land, luxuriant with trees, greener than any trees that grow, and with a ringing background of the bluest sky.

The platform of the Shwe Dagon Pagoda is approached on four sides by flights of stairs. The principal approach is on the southern aspect, and a most unusual ascent it is. The stairway is primitive and very old—as old, it may be, as the Pagoda itself. Its steps are of rude stone or of still ruder sun-dried bricks. They are very steep and much worn by centuries of eager feet. Where there is stone it has become burnished like glass; where there are bricks they have been scuffed into bays and gullies.

This tottering stair is covered by a roof of heavy teak, held up on either side of the way by immense bare wooden pillars.

The ponderous beams of the roof, as well as the architraves of the columns, are lavishly carved. The way to the sacred platform is dark except where some gap in the wall makes a panel of sunshine on the flags.

Between the pillars on each side of this long approach are stalls full of bright things, tended by brighter women. Here the loitering worshipper may buy flowers, rice, or cake for offerings, candles for the altar, sweetmeats for the children, as well as combs, gongs, jewellery, and tooth-brushes. He can also purchase playthings, mostly in the form of gruesome beasts. For here are articulated elephants which twine like snakes, and yellow tigers, jointed in sections like a toy train, with red open mouths, hot as ovens, and with horrible bristles bursting forth from their nostrils. The approach is not quite appropriate to a holy place. It would need but the overturned tables of money changers to recall the environs of another temple in the East. The busy, covered-in passage, the display of garish trifles on either side of the walk, and the sauntering crowd, suggest an oriental Burlington Arcade standing on end on a hillside, rather than the path to the great cathedral of Buddhism.

On a feast day the staircase is alive with moving figures, clad in gleaming silks of many hues, ever ascending and descending, a glorious throng, only a little less radiant than the company that Jacob saw upon the ladder of his dreams.

It is appropriate that the way to the great platform should be in shadow, for it makes the first glimpse of the paved terrace absolutely dazzling. As the visitor plods up the endless stair, he becomes a little weary of the dim light, of the monotonous pillars, of the ever-repeated stalls. At the end he steps suddenly out of this dark colonnade on to a stone plaza, white with the sun, shut in all round by a thousand little spires and roofs, a-glitter with gilt and silver and coloured stones, while moving every way about the flagged square is a crowd of people so brilliant and so strange that the whole picture is utterly unreal. Towering in front of him, far above the fluttering, chattering multitude, is the great majestic column of dumb gold.

The platform is occupied by a disordered litter of sacred structures. They close it in, as with a palisade, so that nothing can be seen, except through a casual gap, of the comfortable country which lies around the foot of the hill. Between these many buildings and the plinth of the pagoda is space enough, on the paved terrace, for the worshippers, the curious, and the idle.

The erections on the platform are of every shape and size. There are rows of little pagodas in white, in gilt, in silver, in red lacquer, each with its *ti* of dangling bells. There are temples and shrines with many roofs which mount up one above the other in diminishing tiers. Some of these holy places are of stone, some of wood, some have pillars blazing with coloured glass, while others are made marvellous by carving or deft chisel work. There are altars of brick, black with the smoke of legions of nodding candles, and heaped over with grease which has guttered into sooty stalactites. There are altars dripping with sacrificial water or loaded with rice, among the soft piles of which glutted crows are clawing mawkishly.

There are figures of monsters, half lion and half man, with curling lips and crab-like eyes. There are image houses without end, in which are sheltered a host of Buddhas. They are graven in alabaster, in silver, in brass, in teak. There are Buddhas who sit, Buddhas who stand, Buddhas who have shrunk to mere mannikins or who have swelled to elephant-chested giants. There are tall posts from which hang cylindrical streamers of bamboo pasted over with sacred paper. There are bells by thousands, shining on every spire, swinging from every roof, guarding every altar. They are infinite in shape and size, from the tiny gong that tinkles on the humblest *ti*, to the great forty-ton monster of green bronze that mumbles from under a mighty beam like a sullen thundercloud.

These many buildings are huddled together after the manner of monuments in an over-crowded cemetery, but there is none sombre in colour, none squat in design. They all mount up to the sky with lance-like pinnacles and are as lustrous as gold leaf or bright lacquer can make them. There is ever, over this army of spires, the sense that the colours move, and that there is a restless life in the myriad-flashing glint of metal.

As for the platform walk, it is astir with a pretty throng in robes of such colours as are seen upon butterflies or flower petals. The people are, for the most part, the pleasant folk of Burmah in holiday attire. Among them slouch smug priests in dull yellow cassocks, who hold up a fan to keep the sun from their shaven heads. Kneeling here and there are dismal beggars, often blind from leprosy, who strike monotonously upon gongs to attract mercy from the passer by. Here are also peasants from the country, gaping as if they saw visions, and wild men and women from the hills, whose costumes are coarse and unkempt, but who carry the sturdy breath of crag and pine through the perfumed atmosphere.

So far as mere colour is concerned the crowd which jostle one another at the pagoda's foot on high days and holidays must be one of the brightest in the world. The colours are all in rustling silks—shell-pink and apple-green, turquoise and garnet.

What of the worshippers? It is the many, not the few, who come to pray, and among the devout there are always more women than men. They come in twos and threes—two sisters, two friends, a mother and her girls. These cheery little women, who are merry enough in the market place, are solemn enough now. They bring flowers in their hands and offerings of cake or rice. Wherever there is a quiet place to kneel, they kneel, on the bare stones, with bowed heads, and with the flowers between their clasped palms. They may pray on the terrace edge, in full view of the great pagoda, or at the column's foot. They may kneel at some altar where their ancestors for generations have knelt, or before a shrine, beloved above all by reason of old memories. Every niche and spire on this familiar terrace must have precious associations for one or another, and the landmarks of many lives must have a place about the feet of this venerable monument.

The majority of those who come to pray seek out one of the numerous large temples to Buddha which are to be found upon the platform. These buildings are exceedingly resplendent, radiant with colour, bewildering with the flash of metal and mirrors, and weighed down with much ornamentation.

In the far shadow of such a temple will sit, on a large pedestal, a golden Buddha, obtuse, solemn, and well satisfied. The blinking lanterns, the swaying bells, the flowers, the dazzling ornaments of gilt and silver almost hide him from the view. The sparkle from every column and every panel makes him dim to the eye, while the smoke of incense shrouds him with a cloud.

Under the canopy, before the altar, the women kneel on the stones. Very dainty they look in their white jackets and soft silks. From out of the hushed shadow the great heavy-eyed Buddha watches them. So dead is he, so huge, so sullen, so tingling with life are they, that one may wonder which is the worshipper and which the worshipped. The sodden, toad-like god squatting in the gloom may well adore the "gay-sashed butterfly" kneeling in the sun.

The Golden Pagoda is an emblem of a great faith, of a religion which can claim to number more disciples than does any other belief in the world. Buddhism, as formulated by him who founded it, is a religion of singular simplicity. It teaches that life is sad, but that its sadness depends upon the man, and not upon his surroundings. He, and he alone, can work out his own happiness. By denial, and by persistent striving towards a blameless life, he can attain to Nirvana, where he will find peace—peace from the trouble of insistent desires, peace from those weaknesses which make the feet stumble and the road long.

It is a religion of kindliness, of compassion, and of self-sacrifice —a tender, womanly faith. It is a religion which encourages meditation and a searching of self—a quiet, cloister-haunting faith. It is a religion which recognises neither rites nor ordinances, but which holds that a man's future hangs upon his own deeds—a faith for the faint of heart.

As with many beliefs, the grand simplicity of Buddhism has been contorted by priestcraft and an extravagant idolatry.

To conceive of Buddhism as Gautama conceived of it, there must vanish from the great platform at Rangoon the whole crazy horde of spires and shrines, of graven images and tinsel-bedecked temples. The paved terrace then lies swept and silent. The green country opens up around it once more, for at the edge of the stone platform is only the drop of the hill.

In the centre of the white space, unapproached by any meaner symbol, is the august pagoda, as immense, as inspiring, and as simple as the truth it would teach—the silent emblem of the Great Peace.

Solitary at the foot of the column, the worshipping woman kneels, with an offering of flowers in her hands. The platform is deserted. These two are alone—the solemn pyramid so tremendous, the worshipper so little, the truth so imperial, the aspirant so lowly.

The hum of the distant town has died away. The silence on the terrace is broken only by the murmur of her lips, and by the tinkle of the bells among the clouds high up on the pagoda's summit. And here, in the golden shadow there falls upon her troubled heart

"The secret of the wordless calm."

IV.

THE FOREST OF YOUTH.

The journeying from Rangoon to Mandalay is over a green and bountiful country, infinitely pleasant to see. On all sides is the gorgeous vegetation of the tropics, while much of the passage is through a virgin forest innocent of roads and of the ways of men. Growth everywhere is luxuriant. So thick are the leaves upon the trees that the humble trunks and branches that bear them are hidden from view; so prodigal is the undergrowth that the mother earth is covered over and forgotten. There is everywhere a hurry to live, a passion to expand, a struggle to burst from the cramped crowd and reach to the limitless heaven beyond.

The land is the land of youth, where the pathless woods are astir with the rustle of growing things. In the exulting outbreak of verdure, all the forest over, is the parable of the extravagance and recklessness of youth. In the crush to gain the sky is the boisterous energy of the lad; his dreaminess is in the drift of lotus leaves upon the moody pool; his heedless ambition is in the towering palm, while in the close-set bamboo thicket is the tale of his effusive comradeship. On all sides are open-handedness and generous waste, thoughtlessness, and a forgetfulness of death.

This tropical jungle mimics every characteristic of the stripling. There are aspiring bushes, ablaze with blossoms, which are building his castles in the air; there are fanning leaves spread over the moss, which are types of his tenderness. Round a shrinking tree a creeper has twined until it has covered it to the topmost bough, has hung over it, and buried it in fervent embraces. Here is the fable of precipitate love. The creeper is quick of growth, but in time it dies and the tree lives on, covered with a cobweb of shrivelled stems and a cramping network of gripless tendrils. It stands in the forest an emblem of the dead heart and the still outstretched arms.

Moreover, in the dark places of the forest, in aisles and vaults full of shadow, there are crawling stalks that wind about the undergrowth like snakes, and long slender trailers that hang in festoons from the arms of trees, like loops of rope pendent from a gallows. These are reminiscent of the morbid fancies of youth and of the sickly projects which grope about in the dark of an unwholesome mind.

Such crops as are seen on the journey up country appear to grow in as easy a fashion as the weeds of the jungle. There is little evidence of a labòrious husbandry. A very happy-go-lucky air hangs about the Burmese farm, while the tiller of the ground seems to have realised a quite fine conception of the "gentleman farmer." Many paddy fields are passed, all dabbling in sludge. Some are stippled over with the stumps of the last cut harvest. These stalks are in regular bristle-like bundles, so that they give to the field the aspect of a worn-out brush. In other places the faint green of the new crops is spreading mysteriously over the mud. There would seem to be no uprising of individual plants, only the colour of the surface is changing from brown to green. The earth, indeed, is in the very act of giving forth life, and this budding tint rises from it like an exhalation.

Many banana groves are in sight, and many spinneys full of cocoa-nut palms. Here and there is a rabble of rugged cactus bushes—the wild men of the wood. Now and then an eddying river is crossed, so edged with rushes and overhanging trees that no brink is in view; or a polished pool is passed in which is mirrored a flock of white birds flying overhead.

So far as can be seen from the track the land is level, but wherever there is a clearing in the wood misty hills stand up in the distance.

At intervals a village is come upon, a small, comfortable settlement of russet houses. They are, for the most part, raised from the ground on piles. The high-pitched roofs are of bronze-coloured thatch or fine tiles, and have wide picturesque eaves. The walls, on one side or more, are replaced by swinging mats. There is always some pretence to a balcony or a verandah, and the place looks cool. Thus there is ever a shelter from the sun, and as for the wind, it can blow through the fragile tenement as through a patch of pines. The houses are simple. Their architecture is that of the buildings in a toy box, and are as artless as the productions of a kindergarten class. About these nut-brown huts and *châlets* is some sort of a garden, very green and wild, surrounded by a bamboo palisade of so sketchy a kind that, if it be intended as a line of defence, it would not thwart even an inquisitive kitten.

There is no formality about the village. The houses, scattered among palm trees and banana fields, are shaded by the margin of the great forest, out of which, indeed, they seem to be creeping. Rising above the green will be a pagoda or two, the humbler of dull wood, the more pretentious of gleaming gilt. If there be a hill at the back of the village it is likely to boast a pagoda on its summit. The elements of the Burmese village are, indeed, very primitive, for they consist of little more than a thatched roof in sepia, standing up above a plantain patch, with behind it a clump of forest trees, a few tall palms, and the spire of a pagoda.

There are signs everywhere of cleanliness and comfort, and over all a wide sense of most liberal leisure. To the occasional passer-by the native of Burmah appears to be occupied in a perpetual picnic, and his houses suggest that he and his friends are camping out in the woods while the weather is pleasant. Virgil might have placed the scenes of his Bucolics in Burmah, for the local swain lacks no opportunity for tuning his pipe, or for engaging in those dialogues which occupied the days of the Virgilian peasant.

Although there appear to be no poor in Burmah, the wealth of the country is not bound up in the efforts of the village agriculturist. The riches of Burmah depend neither upon flocks nor herds, but rather upon rice and rubies, teak and paraffin.

V.

THE PALACE OF THE KING OF KINGS.

Mandalay is 386 miles from Rangoon, to the north. It was, until 1885, the capital of Burmah and the residence of the king. Even now it contains some 180,000 inhabitants, mostly Burmese; and, as the guide-book says, "the traveller will find that he can spend several days very pleasantly" in the place. The city lies on a plain, not far from the Irrawaddy, and within sight of a range of low hills. A great part of the town is new, straggling and uninteresting, with shops boasting of glass windows, and streets with tram lines and telegraph poles.

There is a large native quarter, however, which is still green, quiet, and beautiful, and which is to the modern town as a sheep-fold to an engine shed.

But the iron has entered into the soul of Burmah. It has come in the form of corrugated iron. A roof of metallic corduroy is slowly supplanting the silken thatch of leaves. The blatant drab on the new house top is in bitter contrast with the soft covering on the old, with its tint of the thrush's wing. It is very hard, however, to mar the beauty of the tropics. Even the new Birmingham roof may be chastened when a cluster of areca nut palms hangs over it; and window frames, destined to grace an artisan's dwelling in West Ham, are robbed of much of their unseemliness when the house they mutilate is festooned with such a creeper as the tropical Bougainvillea. Even tram lines are more tolerable when the road they traverse is of red earth and is laid through a coppice of bamboo. A kerosene oil-tin with a loop of string is a wicked substitute for the native water jar; but when both lie side by side, all but buried by the reeds and flowers on the margin of the pool, there is a less cruel contrast in the companionship.

So far as the actual town of streets is concerned, the pleasure of a visit to Mandalay is largely bound up with the Great Bazaar, which is full of never-wearying interest. "Grain and vegetable vendors, silversmiths, toy, umbrella, and lacquer makers, silk merchants, and numerous other traders occupy streets of stalls. Burmese ladies, in the usual tight-fitting petticoat of gay silk and white jacket, attended by a maid, may be seen making their daily household purchases; groups of girls with flowers in their hair and huge cigars in their mouths, price the silks of which all Burmans are so fond. Many strangers to the city come on business or pleasure, wander about, deeply interested in the display on the stalls. Nowhere else can be seen gathered together representatives of so many widely-separated and little-known tribes, differing in dress, and forming a Babel of languages. Chins from the western mountains, Shans from the east, Kachins from the north, and Chinese from the little-known inland borders of the empire, all meet here; and Sikhs, Goorkhas, Madrassis, with many other tribes from India, are amongst the motley throng."*

The feature in Mandalay which is likely to prove of greatest interest to the visitor is the royal palace. The building is in the centre of an immense square fort, each side of which is a mile and a quarter long. The enclosing wall of the stronghold is of brick, machicolated at the top to serve the purpose of loopholes. The outer face of the wall drops sheer for twenty-six feet. The inner face has against it a slope of earth, so that the defenders could gain access to the battlements. Sentries and armed men, however, no longer look over the top of the wall, but on the mound of earth hospitable trees and palms have grown, and these alone keep watch upon the world. The wall, although it is a fortress wall, is not too severe, for there is little that is truculent about it. Compared with the stern rampart of the great red fort at Agra, this line of modest brick may enclose a mere garden.

There are many watch towers on the summit of the wall, but about them also there is nothing sinister. They are, indeed, dainty

* Murray's "Handbook of India, Burmah and Ceylon," London, 1901, p. 429.

and elegant, and each is rather more like a summer-house than the place for the spying eye of a man with murder in his mind. They are built of teak, and are surmounted by a tapering roof with as many spires on it as on the back of a spider crab. The roof is really compounded of six roofs placed in diminishing tiers one above the other. It would appear that dignity of position is indicated in Burmah, not by the number of quarterings on a shield, but by the number of roofs on a building. The chief spire over the palace, for example, has seven roofs—a climax of hauteur. The six roofs on the fort show magnificence enough, and are quite worthy insignia of the Burmese War Office. Some of these tiny turrets are much ornamented with gold, which makes them look still more frivolous.

There are many gates in the fort wall, all of which are massive, simple, and white. In front of every gate stands erect an enormous post of plain teak painted a maroon colour. There is an inscription on each giving the sign of the portal and the date of its making. "It is under or near these posts that the bodies of the unfortunate victims rest who are said to have been buried alive in order that their spirits might watch over the gates."*

Outside the wall, and surrounding the fort, is a broad moat, which gives to the stronghold a remarkable fascination. Now the conception of a castle moat is that of a stiff-walled ditch, filled with dull and venomous water, in which men are intended to drown. Ponderous bastions would rise out of the pool, and in the stone wall would be horrible slits, from which, in time of need, could pour arrows or bullets to make drowning easier. There should be, on the side away from the fort—a bank of surly masonry with an edge like a quay. On the water would be reflected a drawbridge and a portcullis.

The moat at Mandalay is as little like this as a moat could be. The water is as wide and clear and as gentle-looking as the Thames at Iffley. Its banks are of grass and rushes, while their verdant slopes are shaded by trees. The surface of the pool is covered with lotus leaves, and in due season with lotus flowers. Where there is a space of clear water between the lily fans are

* Murray's Handbook, p. 427.

mirrored the make-believe wall, the idle-apprentice watch-towers, and many palms.

The palace, as has been already said, occupies the centre of the fortified enclosure. There were at one time formidable stockades of timber around it, but these have been removed except in one place.

The last sovereign who dwelt in the palace was King Thebaw, who also was the last King of Burmah. He came to the throne in 1878, and commenced his regal life by murdering his brothers, his sisters, and other of his relatives. He proved himself to be a paltry and ignominious monarch. He treated the English with contumely, and on November 7th, 1885, he called upon his people to join him in driving them into the sea. His subjects responded to his call, and so did the English, with the result that on November 28th the Burmese troops laid down their arms; Mandalay, the capital city, with its palace, its arsenal, and its fort, was surrendered to the British; while King Thebaw was taken prisoner and transported to India, where he still lives.

This miserable monarch, in spite of his murders and other iniquities, was the possessor of many titles, and in his heaven-born body were collected distinctions that lacked not the quality of exclusiveness. He was "the Descendant of the Sun," "the King of Righteousness," "the King of Kings," and "the Arbiter of Life."

The palace of this demigod is a rambling, incoherent structure of one storey and many appendages, built wholly of wood. The buildings are of no great antiquity, as they are little more, it is said, than fifty years old. They form a disorderly collection of apartments and outhouses, which include throne rooms for the King and Queen, audience chambers, quarters for the Ministers and the regal retinue, a treasury, a watch tower, stables, and miscellaneous "offices."

The palace within is ablaze with gilt and red paint, and with decorations made from fragments of mirrors and tesseræ of coloured glass. The King's throne is called the "Lion Throne," and the daïs of the Queen "the Throne of the Lily." They are designed to be imperial and impressive, but they would not impress any but a child of six. These seats of the mighty are covered

THE MOAT, MANDALAY.

with gold leaf from balustrade to base, and are protuberant with carvings made with infinite labour, but little art. Inviting steps on either side lead up to the golden platform, so that the whole structure resembles nothing so much as the main entrance to a travelling circus. If there were in the King's place a man beating a big drum, with a tall hat tilted on one side of a rubicund face, the illusion would be complete.

The whole spirit of the palace is expressive of a feverish effort to be imposing, to attain to dignity by means of red paint, and to reach the solemnity of majesty through acres of gilt. The grandeur is puerile, the blazonry of kingship is that of the pantomime stage, and the poor attempt to be important is pitiable beyond words. It is pitiable because of its misdirected earnestness and its perversion of the possibilities of honest woodwork. It is pitiable because the frenzied struggle to grasp the divine afflatus which surrounds a king by sacrifices of paint and gold has failed so utterly.

But for the tawdry decorations, the palace and its scattered wings are very bare. The floors are of wood, and platforms of loose planks lead from one division of the building to another. Thus it comes to pass that the imperial residence has the aspect of last year's exhibition emptied of its show cases. A derelict ticket box with the inscription "Pay here" above it would not appear out of place, nor would a dusty glass cabinet of imitation jewellery be in any way unfitting. All about the palace roofs are pinnacles and spires innumerable, but even here the tone of the pretentious building is not lost, for these roofs are of corrugated iron.

The royal apartments, very lofty and very dark, are possessed of at least one character of dignity. They are upheld by stalwart columns of solid teak, immense bare pillars of heavy wood such as Samson might have grasped in his arms. They stand erect in the gloom as they stood in their solemn forests—honest tree trunks. Among the trumpery panels of coloured glass and spurious gold they alone are stately, true, and strong. The room called the Queen's bed-chamber shows a contemptuous lack of feminine refinement. The apartment is dark like the rest, and absolutely bare. Its walls are whitewashed, and it is windowless. Being narrow and exceptionally lofty, the high walls and wood pillars give it the appearance of a giraffe stable rather than that of the sanctum of a queen.

A cosmopolitan interest must needs attach to a prominent steeple, rich with spires and gables, which rises over the place of the Lion Throne. This pinnacle indicates "the centre of the universe." It has seven roofs, superimposed the one above the other, a little like the pile of hats which was worn by the Jew pedlar who tramped the streets in search of old clothes in days gone by. The seven royal roofs are of corrugated iron, and this all-important landmark, in spite of much gilt and gawdy colour, is supported by wires on either side. The chain of reasoning which determined its position as the centre of the planet was as follows. The modest Burman maintained that the steeple was in the centre of Mandalay. This premise being allowed, the rest was simple. For Mandalay, he further stated, was in the centre of Burmah, and consequently the seven-roofed spire was in the centre of the world.

What architects call the "elevation of the building" is not easy to appreciate, owing to the chaotic massing together of the parts of the palace. A picturesque little wing, however, projects towards the open land around the royal demesne, and is shown in the accompanying picture. It is a cheerful pavilion of wood with a laudable verandah, a steeple of seven roofs, and the usual covering of spires, gables, and stalagmite-like points which mark a self-respecting Burmese dwelling of high degree.

There is a small garden at the back of the palace with a memorable summer-house in it. The place is hardly a kingly pleasaunce, yet it was a favourite haunt of the monarch. Any who base their conceptions of what a regal garden should be upon the terrace at Versailles will be disappointed with this imperial retreat. It might be a tea-garden in the environs of Margate; for there are little oval flower beds in it, a little artificial pond, a little rockery, a little wooden bridge over an arm of the pond, and, indeed, all the scenic effects and appurtenances of a place where holiday folk expect to find round, white tables with shrimps and tea. The summer-house is, by comparison, quite august, for it has

A CORNER OF THE PALACE
AT MANDALAY.

a beautiful tiled roof and a handsome verandah with a royal spaciousness about it. This house in the garden is noteworthy, because it was on its balcony that King Thebaw was discovered when the English entered the place in November, 1885, and it was here that he surrendered himself as a prisoner to General Prendergast and Colonel Sladen. A brass tablet by the balustrade callously records this fact.

V

A BURMESE PUBLIC LIBRARY.

Among the sights in Mandalay which "will well repay a visit" are "the 450 Pagodas" and the Queen's Monastery. "The 450 Pagodas" are outside the town. They have always been associated with the figure 450, although the actual number of buildings assembled together is said to be 730. They are arranged in a precise square, shut in by a high wall and by crumbling guest houses which were intended to provide comfort for those who came to see this surprising spectacle. The attractiveness of the spot is evidently on the wane, for the place is wofully deserted, and grass has spread over the floors of the roofless caravanserai.

The 730 pagodas stand in a bare, paved yard, in long lines disposed with mathematical accuracy. The structures themselves are small, are built of brick covered over by plaster which once was white; they are now uniformly shabby.

The one terrible feature about this army of pagodas is that they are all exactly alike—height for height, dome for dome, niche for niche. They produce an impression which could only be equalled by finding in a silent square a great company of men standing in formal rows, and each man the very counterpart of the other. The alley ways of the square are in multiples, the path up and down them is without end, while the haunting sameness of the place is well-nigh appalling. The long passing by of one unchanging object may drowse some people into a mesmeric state, and those who roam along these never-varying streets lined with never-varying monuments may feel creeping over them a listless hypnotic influence.

This drear picture of monotony, this dismal realisation of unvariableness is as numbing as an ever-repeated "no." or as a chant droned over a thousand times. If the shut-in court were to reach for miles, and if a man were to lose his way among these interminable dumb lanes, he would have forced upon him some conception of eternity before he gained the outer air.

The loneliness and stillness of the place give it the aspect of a cemetery where everyone of the dead bore the same name, had reached the same age, and possessed the same countenance. To the trivial minded the place might be the yard of a pagoda-making company who had overstocked themselves with pagodas of one pattern and had then failed.

The enclosure, however, is neither a burial ground nor an architectural folly, nor a Golgotha for pagodas. It is a public library. King Thebaw's uncle—a Carnegie of the time—thought that certain holy books should be made accessible to the public, and should be preserved where neither moth nor rust could corrupt. He therefore caused the Buddhist commandments to be engraven upon slabs of stone. Every stone tablet is made upon the same pattern, and over each a pagoda is built which shows also no shadow of variableness.

If he intended to express the unchangeability of a commandment he has effected his end. If he hoped to show that each precept was alike in value he has taught the lesson.

Here are the sacred books so that all who run may read. Here, too, are endless avenues of stone where no unusual object can distract the mind of the contemplative reader. Those who pass through the deserted gateway which leads out of this sanctuary may thank heaven that

> "The great world spins for ever down the ringing grooves of change."

The Queen's Golden Monastery is an edifice of such magnificence that it is said to be the handsomest structure of its kind in Burmah. It is built of teak. Old it is, and wonderful, but little like a monastery to the European eye. From the lowest step to the topmost spire it is covered with faded gilt, as if a yellow hoar frost had settled upon it. Where the gilt is happily lacking there is wholesome wood; where the gilt is worn there is the eternal red paint. In the Western world the monastery roof is sober and plain, a homely slope of grey tiles tempered by moss and lichen, where pigeons can settle and watch the world in the cloister. Here the covering of the monastery is a restless erection of eaves upon eaves, of gables laden with ornament, and of steeples sprouting with a myriad gold spires. Such has been the builder's passion for points and pinnacles that the bramble-like roof is positively prickly with brazen thorns, while from every edge gilt seems to drip. The wandering dove would never find here a rest for the sole of her foot. Indeed, the only winged thing who could fitly perch upon this roof would be a heraldic griffin.

The building itself looks uneasy, for every wall, panel, and post is tortured by fretful and exuberant carving. The figures depicted by the carver illustrate tales of fairies and genii. Doors are casual and windows are lacking, but nowhere is there any respite from the all-pervading yellow glare. Around the monastery is a spacious wooden verandah raised upon pillars and approached by steep stairs. Encircling this balcony is a very magnificently carved balustrade of teak. There is a neglected garden, beyond the green of which is a rest from the blaze of perpetual gold leaf.

The Queen's Golden Monastery is very marvellous, and it may be fitting for the glaring sun of the tropics, but, as a contrast and an agreeable relief, there comes to the mind the picture of a like retreat where

> "Deep on the convent roof the snows
> Are sparkling to the moon."

Prowling about this uncomfortable monastery are the monks, clad in robes of dirty yellow. Their heads are shaven and uncovered, and they are for the most part of unpleasant countenance. A few of them look so dull and brutish that they seem to affect that aspect of sodden smugness which characterises the old images of Buddha. It is possible that they are not so slovenly as they look, and it is affirmed that their lives are by no means squandered in loutish idleness. To the casual onlooker they appear to be the licensed loafers of the country, so that if their days have a moral effect upon the youth around them, it escapes the superficial eye.

They toil not, neither do they spin. They do not pretend to work for their food, nor do they even buy it. They beg it, and that, too, with an air of haughty patronage. In the morning they slouch from house to house with bowls to be filled by the pious. They are a distinguished order of beggars in that they have succeeded in substituting condescension for cringing, and arrogance for hypocrisy. Their numbers are legion. They pervade the whole country, and in Mandalay alone there are said to be 7,000 of them. They are engaged in the teaching of youth, and nearly every Burman has been at one time or another a monk. Although they are likely to impress the hurried visitor unfavourably, they are much honoured and beloved by the people. Those who know most of the monastic system in Burmah speak of it in terms of the highest praise. No tribute, for example, is more critical or more generous than that furnished by Mr. Fielding in his most fascinating book, "The Soul of a People."*

* London, 1898.

VII.

THE IRRAWADDY.

The most pleasant route from Mandalay to Rangoon is by river. It is usual to take the steamer from Mandalay to Prome, a distance of 397 miles, and thence proceed to Rangoon by train.

The Irrawaddy is a mighty and glorious tide. It comes from the unknown, for it arises among the hills of an untravelled country somewhere in the highlands of Tibet. From the point where the geographer has a knowledge of it to the sea is some 1,500 miles, and of this distance no less than 900 are navigable.

It is a deep, majestic stream. In places it widens out into a lazy lake, two or three miles across, while elsewhere it narrows to a crazy rapid, hurrying through a fierce defile like a frightened thing. After this breathless passage it idles again—a leisurely current, dawdling through a languid jungle or by curving, coaxing bays, or drifting under the eaves of sleep-suggesting rocks. There is always a fine dignity about the river. It moves as moves a great determined multitude filled with such a blind solemn instinct as leads a migratory herd. It is as portentous as the river of an allegory.

The colour of the water is brown, and this, when the sun shines upon it, becomes steel-grey, so that the surface looks metallic. Here and there are bubbling sand shoals, and here and there, rising out of the stream, are sand islands dotted with birds. Around these straw-coloured eyots the tide eddies as if it mimicked the circles of a dance.

The banks change with every bend in the river. Sometimes they are covered with chubby, rounded trees that look, at the distance, as if made of pieces of green cauliflower; sometimes the bank is of brown rocks, which call to mind a moss-grown rampart

THE IRRAWADDY.

rising from a moat. Sometimes there are fawn-coloured stretches of sandy beach, edged with cactus, or there will be an ash-grey cliff of sand topped by a line of palms. The banks are most beautiful when there are smooth dove-coloured boulders by the edge of the stream with a yellow sand bank behind, on the summit of which are dark green bushes or creepers, which drop over the little yellow cliff in still cascades.

Many an untidy village of thatched huts will be passed, and many a well trodden gully where oxen come down to the river to drink. About the villages are women carrying up water in brass water pots which gleam on their heads like beads of gold, women washing on the beach, and children bathing. Here will be a rolling line of maize-tinted dunes with tufts of green rushes among the sand, and there, cut through a bank of bushes, is a white road leading from the water's edge to a village in a wood. Every few miles pagodas are to be seen, sometimes alone, sometimes struggling out of a cluster of banana leaves, or standing guardian over a little hamlet of seal-brown roofs.

Upon the drift of the stream there are strange birds and stranger boats. There are canoes and "dug-outs" which barely rise above the water, and great boats like gondolas, but with uncommon sails. There are house boats, timber rafts with mat huts on them and numerous wet men; also piratical-looking vessels with high poops—ghosts of the old Spanish caravel. On the poop is a throne where the helmsman stands shaded by a canopy. The vessel is marvellously carved, but the canopy is of corrugated iron. Dotted about everywhere are silent men and motionless birds, equally absorbed in fishing.

The steamers that trade upon the river are stalwart vessels, burning petroleum in place of coal. They are larger and more comfortable than any steamer on the Nile, so that the voyager will be hard to please who fails to find this river journey a delight.

By the wheel there stands a native pilot. He is usually a wrinkled old man with shrewd puckered eyes and bent shoulders. He stands with his hands behind his back and gazes ever on the stream. The monotonous drone of the man with the lead falls upon his ear, but he seems best to understand the chant of the river.

He lifts a hand, and the wheel is moved to the right. He nods, the wheel is still. He turns his eyes towards the helmsman, and the wheel circles to the left.

He is as placid as the river. The movements of his hand which guide the ship are as mystic as the river language, as the eddies, the line of ripples, the mirror-like ring, and all the other picture writings on her surface. He signs to the ship in this water language, in this wondrous dumb alphabet that so few can read, and the ship understands. He has spent his life on the whispering stream. In his little brown body is a great love for the river. He would tell you the stream is his mother. In his heart of hearts he would own she was his goddess, and he her prophet. He is the priest of the river. He passes his days in watching her face. He listens in his hut at night for any change in the chanting of her voice. He knows her as a mother knows a child—her waywardness, her petulance, her little outbreaks of rebellion, her dreaminess, her infinite lovableness.

The little brown pilot is part of the brown river, and one day his love, the river, will carry him away with her to the sea.

VIII.

THE CAPITAL CITY OF CEYLON.

Some six days are occupied in the journey by steamer from Calcutta to Colombo. There is the Hooghly to be traversed, a part of the voyage that is apt to be varied, for the Hooghly is a river of incidents. On one day there comes a wayward tide, and on another a sinister movement of a sand bank. Between the sand drifts and the pilot there is a perpetual feud. They play against one another as two play at the game of chess. The stakes are the lives of men. The river makes a move, and the pilot meets it. In the depths of the night the wily tide will glide a shoal across the fairway, as a player furtively pushes a piece across the board. Muddy as the waters are, the pilot's eye is not blind to the stealthy movement, and the ship goes safe. Sometimes the man at the wheel is checkmated, the good ship plunges on to the shallow and the greedy sand takes it.

How many wrecks this river has seen no record can tell. The most villainous shoal of all in the evil stream bears the unsuspicious name of "James and Mary." The very demon of the river must lie coiled here in the eddying mud. As long ago as 1694 he seized hold of a gallant craft, the *James and Mary*, and dragged her down to her death, whereby the bank came by its name.

By reason of some underhand operation of the river the steamer we sailed in was compelled to anchor all night in the centre of the stream. As soon as the sun had set, hordes of mosquitoes put off from the land and boarded the vessel like pirates. They came for blood, and they were probably satisfied, for the havoc they wrought was great.

It was a pleasant relief to most when the steamer was clear of the land, and was throwing from either side of her bows a curling wave of the bluest sea. It was pleasant to all who were homeward bound, for this was the same blue sea that bellowed into Plymouth Sound, and that swept the green slopes of Southampton Water. It was pleasant to those who were tired of India, of its heat, its smells, its flies, and its melancholy. As they looked back towards the "Land of Regrets" they could not fail to notice that the dust of India followed still, for miles out to sea, in the guise of the Hooghly mud.

The approach to Ceylon was heralded by a token in the sky, by a baldachino of white clouds. These were the first clouds which had been visible in the heavens for many months of this journey. In India the sky had been ever the same—a windless desert of turquoise blue, glaring, hot, and empty. This fathomless void faded upwards into space. There were no means of gauging its heights except by the poised hawk or the swinging speck of a vulture, watching for something to die. Such are the heavens, which, when filled with the yellow heat of the sun, are "as brass."

Now that we had come upon clouds the world had changed. The sky was kindly, and nearer at hand. It had stooped down to the hill-top, and had crept into the valley, while over the town it could be touched by the children's kites.

To the passengers on the steamer the clouds over the island recalled memories of England. One of the homeward bound, who through years of exile had ever cherished London as his earthly Paradise, declared that his present happiness would be complete if only the ship could glide into a cold November fog.

For many hours before Colombo is sighted the steamer skirts the coast of the island. The first impression of Ceylon is of a land of intense green. The shore is lined by cocoa-nut palms, not standing in twos or threes, as in India, but in dense forests, many miles long and some furlongs deep. Far inland the palms give way to other trees, for the cocoa-nut, they say, is only happy when within sound of the sea. All the far hills are covered so closely and so evenly with trees that, at a distance, the uplands look like grass downs; and it would seem as if one could walk smoothly over the dells and hillocks made by the topmost boughs.

As the vessel steams along close in shore, it is evident that we had come at last to the island of the story book. Here is the very beach which has figured so vividly in many a "tale for boys." Here is a coral reef where the indigo-coloured sea breaks up into roaring lines of foam, while within the reef the leisurely swell tumbles upon a yellow beach. This is the "adventurer's island," for here is a red headland, with a grassy knoll, and a clump of palms upon its summit which must have been a pirates' look-out. There is even a dark cave filled with the sea, and there can be little doubt that at its tunnel end is a small, dim beach where a boat could land with treasure to be buried. The cocoa-nut trees come down to the water's edge. They make a background of deep shadows, among which can be seen a forest of bare trunks, standing erect like a crowd of masts in a harbour. There is a rock between the forest and the beach, and from its shelter rises upwards a curling line of smoke—a wreath of Gobelin-blue against the purple aisles of the wood. By this fire a buccaneer must be sitting, counting his "pieces of eight," with his flint gun by his side, his faithful dog, his parrot, and his comic bo'sun. Though seen for the first time, the brilliant shore was familiar, and if Robinson Crusoe and Friday were searching in the sand for turtles' eggs it would seem more familiar still.

Colombo lies upon a level plain about the circle of its harbour. It looks bright and comfortable from the sea, and, like the rest of Ceylon, it is very green. Half the houses are lost among trees. A grey lighthouse dominates the town with no little dignity. On the sea face are the remains of an old fort which goes back to the days of the Dutch and the Portuguese. There is an ancient Dutch belfry also in the city, with other relics of the time when the sea-going peoples of Europe were struggling for possession of the favoured island. Many bungalows are to be seen, with chocolate-coloured roofs and creeper-covered walls, always in the shadow of palms. Very prominent from the sea is a long stiff building, with an interminable *façade* of drab arches. It is laboriously ugly and prim, and as little in keeping with the generous carelessness of the scenery of the tropics as would be a gasometer in the Elysian Fields. It is a barracks for English soldiers which would be a disfigurement even to Hounslow Heath.

The town is just an Eastern town which has been settled from the West. There are tram lines, of course, and along the metals of this modern road will be coming a creaking cart, with wheels of solid wood and a hood of mats, drawn by two dreamy, wavering bullocks. This is the cart of a thousand years ago. There are shops where anything can be purchased from patent medicines or flannel shirts to Paris hats or a gramophone. On the causeway outside the shop is a man, nude but for a loin cloth, crouching over a native basket filled with strange fruits. He is the merchant of a thousand years ago. There is a new colonnade, with the smart houses of shipping companies and banking firms, and in sight of it is a bee-hive hut made of bamboo fibre, palm-leaves, and mud—the house of a thousand years ago.

This mixture of the restless inventive European and the unchanging native is a striking feature of the settlement. If a motor launch broke down outside the harbour it would probably be towed ashore by a long narrow canoe propelled by paddles and steadied by an outrigger fashioned from a log of wood. Such a boat should be able to trace its pedigree to the days of Noah. At Colombo also can be seen by the side of great ocean liners, the catamaran—a scooped-out baulk of timber which was possibly familiar to prehistoric men.

Just outside Colombo is a delightful marine drive called the "Galle Face Esplanade." It is a fine red road, with a sandy beach on one side and a lawn on the other, bordered by bungalows and palms, and tempered by a blue-water lake. Along this road will be smart rickshaws, each drawn by a damp, never-tiring coolie, while now and then a trim governess car will go by, to which is harnessed a pair of trotting bullocks. Well-dressed ladies, half-naked Cingalese, wholly-naked children, Indians in gorgeous turbans and brilliant robes, and a couple of British soldiers, each with a cane under his arm, will be among the loiterers along the road. Everything is so strange, so unusual in colour, so anomalous, that it is a matter almost of surprise to note that the waves break upon the beach with just the same sounds as echo along the Marine Parade at Brighton.

All around Colombo is a country of glorious gardens. No other capital in the world has such suburbs. There are avenues of palms with just a glimpse of the white sea between their crowded trunks, hedges ablaze with the scarlet hybiscus, thickets of rustling bamboo, lanes that lead through banana groves, the apple-green fans of which shut out everything but the sky.

Such gardens, too, there are about the bungalows as can be seen nowhere but in the tropics! Such glens full of wildest undergrowth! For fields of wheat there are fields of cinnamon, for meadows there are rice swamps, for cherry orchards are copses of mango and bread fruit trees, for the hop garden is the brake of sugar cane. Here, too, as in Burmah, the cattle look well fed and comfortable, and in striking contrast to the half-starved ragged ghosts of animals who prowl sullenly about the wastes of India.

IX.

THE CINGALESE AND THEIR DEALINGS WITH DEVILS.

This beautiful country is peopled by pleasant-looking people. The Cingalese are evidently of Aryan descent, and there is little doubt but that they have come from the continent of India. They are a cheerful and amiable folk, who have shaken off the melancholy of India, and as the majority of them are Buddhists, they are not made gloomy by their religion. In the native bazaar the standard of comfort is evidently higher than on the mainland. The houses are trim and well-kept, and there is lacking that street of rags and ruins, filled with dust and the odour of goats and cooking oil, which recalls a memory of the native quarter in India.

The women are vivacious and comely. Such prettiness as they possess is that of the Hindu woman, but they want the weary, down-cast eye and the look of eternal nausea which is so common on the Peninsula. There is comparatively little squalor in Ceylon; life is easier, food is plentiful, while the women are not enslaved by the ignoble work which drags them to the dirt in India.

The Cingalese woman appears to be content. There is usually a smile on her cinnamon-brown face. Her head is bare, her black locks are arranged in a simple coil. Her costume consists of a skirt of coloured silk or cotton with a white linen bodice. This bodice is so scanty that, viewed by European eyes, it would seem to belong to the category of underclothing. Thus the native woman appears to have never completed her toilet. There is a suggestion that she has omitted to put on a jacket or some such upper garment. Between the white bodice and the gaudy skirt is a gap showing the brown skin of the waist, as if the wearer wished to place beyond doubt the fact that she is not tight-laced. The European affects a bare neck and shoulders, the Cingalese a bare waist. It is *de rigueur* to carry an umbrella. The jewellery worn is plain and unostentatious. The toe-rings, nose-rings, and other extravagances of the belle of India are lacking.

The clothing of the children is merely symbolic, while the men of the working classes have succeeded in reaching that limit in raiment beyond which any further reduction is impossible. Men of a less humble class wear a white linen jacket and a petticoat. They are peculiar about their hair in that they apparently decline to have it cut. It is drawn back from the forehead to be twisted into a prim knob at the back of the head. This knob is small, but is always decorously placed. It is very unlike the rakish knot of glossy hair which the Burman cultivates, and which is sometimes tossed on one side of the head, and sometimes allowed to droop on the nape of the neck. As age advances with the Cingalese man the effort to obtain enough hair to make a knob is evidently extreme. The enterprise, however, is never abandoned, for an old man will patiently scrape together the few remaining hairs of his head to form a button no larger than a Spanish nut. The average size of this boss of hair is that of an orange. Every man, whether well supplied with hair or bald, dons a semicircular tortoiseshell comb precisely like that worn by little English girls to keep their tresses from their foreheads. The man, however, wears his comb upside down, and at the back of his head. Its intention is not evident.

The feminine dressing jacket, the scanty, spinster-like skirt, the little girl's comb, and the hair "done" in a knob make the Cingalese man look very like a woman—and, it may be added, like a comic woman. This demure knot at the back of the head is a feature of the mother-in-law of the farce and of the aunt of the caricaturist. The typical "aunt" is thin and prim, has a sharp nose, and an almost bald head, the hair of which is collected into a frigid bulb behind. She has mittens, spectacles, and a faint moustache. The man of Ceylon does not wear mittens, but he often presents a feminine moustache; thus his near resemblance to the lean woman with a reticule over her arm is often remarkable. These men have agreeable, gentle faces, are often handsome, often pathetic-looking, while those who know them best are full of their praises.

Many of the educated natives of Ceylon have taken a high position in certain professions, notably in law and medicine. Apart from their specific learning they are as a rule gentlemen of culture and refinement, who have in addition to their attainments, the dignity of Eastern manners.

Through the kindness of a Cingalese gentleman and my friend Sir Allan Perry, I was able to see something of the native methods of treating disease—notably by "devil dancing."

The therapeutics of this measure is apparently based upon the theory that the sick person is possessed of a devil, that the disorder is due to that particular devil, and that the intruding spirit can be driven out of the body by appropriate means. The theory is old, and is as worthy of respect as are many less ancient theories as to the *fons et origo mali.* It may be considered to represent in an allegorical form the bacterial basis of disease, which is a leading feature of modern pathology.

In Ceylon the medical practitioner endeavours to drive the unsubstantial parasite out of the man's body by means of "devil dancing." This method of treatment is a little noisy and confusing, while it is as full of mystery as a physician's prescriptions.

I was taken into a room by the doctor and shown a man lying upon a bed. He was in perfect health, but he was playing the part of the invalid, and was for the moment the *corpus vile.* For the purpose of the demonstration he was assumed to be afflicted with typhoid fever, and the treatment was such as was applicable to that disorder. In front of the sick man was a board upon which was painted a gigantic demon or devil, in what may be presumed to be natural colours. He was very red, and his teeth and eyes were fearful beyond words.

He was so contorted by fury that the frown upon his brow was terrible to see. About him were many mystic signs, which would convey to the uninitiated some of the horrors of the unknown. The make-believe invalid held in his hand a string the other end of which entered the body of the demon about the region of the heart.

The quiet of the sick-room was now broken in upon by two grotesquely dressed men, one of whom beat hysterically upon a drum, while the other went through a series of contortions which included all the muscular possibilities of epileptic fits, mania, and demoniacal possession. I gathered from the native physician that his desire was to cast the devil of typhoid fever out of the man, and to make it enter the blood-curdling figure on the board. I was led to assume that this transmigration would be effected along the piece of string after the manner of a telephone message. As a method of procedure this driving out of devils appeared to differ little from that employed in driving an unquiet cow from a field, namely, by noise and the waving of arms.

Typhoid fever is an obstinate complaint, and the demon of it seemed to be but little influenced by noises which had already numbed us into deafness, or by movements which had rendered the sympathisers by the bedside giddy.

There came, however, a sudden crisis. The man who beat upon the drum now smote it like hail from a hurricane, so as to fill the bed-chamber with a crashing and chaotic din. His colleague at the same time fell into a series of the most fearful fits I have ever witnessed. Dreadful convulsions shook him as a terrier shakes a rat, he seemed to have as many revolving arms as a Hindu god, while the perspiration, streaming from his brow, washed the paint on his face into his foaming mouth. The contortions of hydrophobia, lock-jaw, and strychnia-poisoning combined would be languid and leisurely in comparison with the alarming movements of this healer of the sick.

The invalid trembled gently on his couch, like a kinematograph figure. The string twitched. Then in a moment the drum ceased, the convulsed man fell under the bed, the physician smiled proudly and bowed. He had triumphed. The demon of the fever had gone out of the man and had entered into the board. The struggle had been severe, but the art of healing had prevailed. Damp beads stood upon the foreheads of everyone—for Ceylon is hot—but all was well.

This treatment of typhoid fever differs in many essentials from that observed in this country. To those who hold that quiet in the sick-room is desirable, and who advocate "straw in the street," this method could not commend itself. The carrying out of the treatment, moreover, would harass the mind of the budding doctor who had heard much of what is called "a restful, bedside manner." In the case of an already delirious patient the cure might give point and individuality to his dreams, or it might serve to temper the tedium of a long illness in the case of a deaf child.

This one display had, however, by no means exhausted the resources of the native physician. It had served to do no more than demonstrate one procedure in treatment. There are, it appears, other means of healing which can be carried out beyond the confines of the sick-room, and are, indeed, quite effective if applied in the garden, or in the high road or jungle, in front of the patient's house.

The treatment consists in the dancing of one who is disguised to represent the particular demon causing the disease. The dancing is carried out amid a phenomenal beating of drums. Each disease has its own special devil, and these evil spirits vary considerably in feature, in complexion, and in the costume they affect. They are all very unattractive. Some have the heads of monkeys, some of tigers, some are as hairy as the wild goat, some glisten like fish. All are very rich in teeth, in tinsel, in vermilion and blue paint, and in jingling appendages.

I was fortunate enough to meet, among others, the demons of ague, of fever, of small-pox, and of cholera. The medical practitioner, to show that he was abreast of the times, introduced me, with special formality, to the demon of appendicitis. I was glad and interested to meet him, although he was unreasonably noisy, and had the look of a child's "jack-in-the-box."

The method in which the treatment is applied by this particular school of physic is as follows. A poor man lies ill, let us say, of the small-pox. The doctor is sent for. He identifies the disease. More than that, he knows the particular devil that caused it. A representative of this demon then comes upon the scene and, to the sound of drums, executes before the sufferer's hut a series of extraordinary convulsions, which for want of an appropriate term, are described as dances.

These contortions are of a high order, for they represent the struggle between man and the devil. Here the representative of human art—in the person of the physician's assistant—is, as it were, inside the devil, and the efforts he puts forth to rid him of the dire presence are exceptionally violent and heating. The dancing may last for hours or even for a night. The duration, so far as I know, may depend upon the severity of the disease, or even upon the physician's fee. At the end of the awful and Homeric contest, the champion of human genius, as a rule, conquers. Theoretically the patient should then recover, but in the East, as in the West, the destiny of a sick man does not always follow the dictates of theory.

I was assured that "devil dancing" was attended with considerable success in the relief of suffering in the island. It is as popular with certain classes as is physic drinking with some of the inhabitants of Europe. If a Cingalese child has measles its mother will long for a "devil dance" in order that the demon of measles might be cast out of the child. If an English child has measles many a mother will wish to give it medicine, not directly because the medicine may do it good, but because it has the measles.

Physic drinking has this advantage over "devil dancing"—it is quieter.

X.

THE WILD GARDEN.

The railway from Colombo to Kandy is probably the most beautiful that any train has ever traversed. The distance is seventy-five miles, during which the line rises to 1,680 feet above the sea level. The road winds up among hills covered to their summits with the glorious vegetation of the tropics, until it reaches the face of a commanding precipice at whose base lie stretched the domains of the evergreen island.

From this height one looks down upon the Wild Garden of the World, upon upland and dell, thorpe and towering crag, smooth slope and jagged ravine, all massed with romantic imagery, all budding with eager life.

Miles below is a river winding through a plain. By its banks are many palms, while beyond the palms lie yellow-green meadows of growing rice fringed by a village of brown huts. Out of the plain rise hills, one above the other, ever mounting skyward until they are lost in the range of damask peaks on the horizon. On to the plain valleys open, which wind away among the hills to end in a purple haze. Thesc are Valleys of Sleep, any one of which may lead to the Palace of the Sleeping Beauty. They are nearly choked by rustling leaves of every shape and size, and every tint of green. Out of the tangle a few areca-nut palms struggle into the air to breathe, or a lofty clump of feathery bamboos burst heavenwards like a flight of rockets.

Scattered over every dome of green are blossoms of white or blue, tassels of primrose, or sprays laden with crimson leaves. Where the open plain ends the jungle begins. The jungle in the wild garden is a real jungle; not a starving moorland as in India, but a forest through which a way can only be made with a hatchet,

A POND IN THE TROPICS.

and where in the first clearing reached one would fear to find, dangling against a gap of hazy sky, a writhing python.

There are terraces in this wild garden, but they are hewn from the face of precipices, while from their margins creepers hang into the void like drooping banners. There are alcoves and arbours whose roofs are groined with green, but they are as lofty as a cathedral nave. There are lawns that stretch away for miles, with hidden nooks banked round with moss that need only the moonlight and Titania with her court.

A scented and voluptuous wind blows through these silent glades, while in every still valley and breezeless bay among the woods a warm haze lingers like a cloud of incense.

As to the things that grow in this wild garden, it would need the acumen of the Swiss Family Robinson to discover and name but a few of them. Everywhere are there plants with strange pods, fabulous fruits, or unexpected blossoms. This tree crowned with a cluster of green melons is the papaw, and this bush hung with claret-coloured nuts is the cocoa plant. The nutmeg tree is tall and straight with a dark green trunk and dark green leaves. The tree that bears the clove mimics it in less sombre foliage. On the hillside is a tea plantation; in the plain is a field of ragged cinnamon bushes hemmed in by sago palms. There are many rubber trees, and it is some shock to the ill-informed observer to find that they bear no resemblance to the india-rubber plant of the Brixton parlour window. It would need one learned in plants to name the cactus and the ferns, to recognise the pimento and the pepper tree, or to tell which among the many unruly creepers bore the vanilla bean.

This great tree, with unwieldy fruit budding out of its trunk and branches, is the bread fruit, and this little weed by the roadside with its grey-blue blossom is the sensitive plant. In the English greenhouse it is a pampered fondling, in the wild garden it is as sturdy and plebeian as the school-children's buttercup.

XI.

KANDY, AND THE TEMPLE OF FRANGIPANNI BLOSSOMS.

Kandy is a little brown town in the hollow of a sumptuous tropical valley, where it lies on the margin of a quiet mere. Much of the romance in the history of Ceylon clings about this drowsy old city by the lake. It was at one time the capital of the island, and it has seen much of war and faction fights, as well as of the rise and fall of petty kingdoms. So many times has it been laid waste by fire that scarcely any of its ancient buildings, with the exception of the Temple of the Tooth, remain.

A wing of the palace still stands. It was built in 1600 by Portuguese prisoners, in the days of massive walls, small windows, and ponderous gates. There is a vivid suggestion of the fort and the prison about it still, of the strong place which was meant to defy both men and angels, both cyclones and earthquakes.

Now it is in the occupation of the chief civil officer of the province, who has made it worthy of its picturesque surroundings. The anomalous building is a curious meeting place of the old power and the new.

A frowning and savage portal, plain as a granite block, leads into a dainty drawing-room filled with nicknacks from Bond Street and the Rue de la Paix. It is a parlour in a donjon keep. The walls are prettily decorated, while in every nook and corner are traces of the hand of the English gentlewoman. The roof is a dome of solid masonry toned down with white distemper, but still grim enough to compel the impression of a boudoir in a vault. The window is a deep embrasure suited for cannon and heavy gun tackle, but it is occupied now only by a pot of violets and a lady's work-basket. The delicateness of the contents of the room is intensified by the surrounding of rough stone walls, thick as a castle rampart.

The lake of Kandy must needs be beautiful, as is every pool

THE LAKE OF KANDY

and pond in the tropics. About that part of the lake which is nearest to the town is a quaint wall, green with moss, and much shadowed by trees. Around the margin of the mere are avenues of palms. There are palms on every headland and every cape, and on the shore of every verdant bay. There is a little round island in the lake, and that also is shaded by a nodding palm. The lake is shut in all round by hills covered to their summits by a luxuriant growth of trees, the vanguard of a wild forest which sweeps down from the sky line to the grass-covered margin of the pool.

The hills guard the lake and hide it as if it were a sacred thing. A breeze can scarcely find its way through the jungle to trouble the surface of the pond, which lies bare like a mirror, so that on it are reflected the avenue of palms by the foot-path and the leafy hills beyond.

Roads wind up the sides of these slopes, but they are hidden by the crowding trees which sigh ever over the lake. On the wooded heights are houses with chocolate-coloured roofs and white walls, but they also are masked by the jealous thicket. Among them is a modest bungalow in which for many years lived Arabi Pasha, dreaming of the sand dunes of Egypt, of the great brown Nile, and of the sunset that changes the plains of Thebes into a mirage of coral pink. In the cottage garden is now a notice that "the house is to let."

There grow around Kandy certain trees which are, I think, the most beautiful in the world. They have tall, dignified heights, shapely and compact, which are crowned by masses of dark green leaves. Among this sombre foliage are scattered flowers so brilliant in hue as to dot it with a thousand splashes of vermilion. I am told that the tree is called the spathodia campanula. The name is pretty enough, but the growing thing itself might have been the glory of the Garden of Eden.

The most interesting building in Kandy is the Temple of the Tooth. The "sacred tooth" was no other than the tooth of Buddha. It was brought to the island of Ceylon, after many adventures, by a princess who hid it among the sleek folds of her hair. This was near upon 1,600 years ago. It was seized by the Malabars in 1315, and carried away to India. In due course, and after infinite persistence, it was recovered and secreted with pious caution. But the heedless Portuguese unearthed the tooth, and took it with them to India once more, to their settlement at Goa. Here the relic which the princess had wrapped in her hair was burned. It was burned by the blind unbelievers with boastful ceremony, for it was an archbishop who wrought the wicked deed, and the tooth was reduced to ashes "in the presence of the Viceroy and his court." There was no fond princess there to save it, and it was as long ago as 1560 that it came to this evil end.

"Wikrama Bahu manufactured another tooth, which is a piece of discoloured ivory two inches long and less than one inch in diameter, resembling the tooth of a crocodile rather than that of a man. It now reposes on a lotus flower of pure gold, hidden under seven concentric bell-shaped metal shrines, increasing in richness as they diminish in size, and containing jewels of much beauty."*

The tooth of Wikrama Bahu is, therefore, but an emblem and a shadow, only an Atavar of a tooth; but it lies under its seven bells at Kandy, one of the most cherished relics in the great realm of Buddhism.

Around the Temple of the Tooth is a curious and ancient wall, as old, it may be, as the little knoll it encompasses. It is fantastically machicolated, and is pierced by symmetrical holes, like the holes in a dovecote. Within the wall, for the greater safety of the tooth, there is a moat. Bloated fish and bored turtles move oilily in its waters, for they are fed by the devout as well as by the imitative tourist who casts food blindly to them as he casts coppers to a crowd of boys.

Over the moat is a bridge leading to old stairs which climb between older walls to a terrace. Here, for the further safety of the tooth, and the discouragement of the evildoer, are mural paintings showing the terrors of the Buddhist hell, with special reference to the punishment of the violators of shrines. Much scarlet paint has been lavished upon these terrifying pictures. They are rich in flames, in forks, in blood, and in the gnashing of teeth. The grinning face of the director of the tortures is so

* Murray's "Handbook of India, Burmah, and Ceylon." London, 1901, page 445.

occupied by teeth as to sacrifice his other features; but he has very dreadful hair on his head. His fell bidding is carried out by green devils, who differ in no important essentials from the demons of a Christmas pantomime.

The pilgrim who in his progress has passed the wall, the moat, the steep stair, and the writings on the wall, will find himself at last in the precincts of the temple. The building is in an enclosure. It is a simple house with a tiled roof, and barn-like walls covered by crude paintings. But the pilgrim is not yet within reach of its arcana.

From the terrace he is led along a whitewashed passage, where there are beggars on the floor, and heaps of rice deposited as offerings by the unostentatiously devout. He comes at last to the foot of a narrow wooden stair, like the stair to a cottage attic or a stable loft. When the summit of this ladder is reached he has lost all knowledge of the situation of the shrine, and is as a man in the turnings of a maze. He comes upon narrow rooms and passages, empty, swept, and garnished, with about them the look of by-ways in a prison. As he goes on he passes through many doors, which are covered with silver and brass and gilded metal. It seems that each must lead, door by door, into some nearer depth of the mystery, and that the last portal will open into the Presence itself. But they lead only through barren chambers.

In time he comes to a narrow vestibule. Is it the end? he thinks. Will he now know all? No. This is not the end. The anteroom is small and low, with bare walls poorly whitewashed. It is filled, however, with a heavy perfume which creeps upon the senses like the vapour of an anæsthetic. The space is so confined that the drugged air is stifling. This odour, so overwhelming in its fragrance, comes from masses of white frangipanni flowers, which have been brought here as offerings until they fill the little room knee-deep. Beyond this vestibule is another door, more gorgeous than any, with rich bestowal of silver and gilded plates, of studs and ornamented panels. It opens into a cramped cell within which no more than six persons could stand at once. The poor walls are windowless, the place is dark, the atmosphere oppressive, and the few who gather within talk in whispers.

Here is, then, the end of the quest. In this rude cell, as simple as a niche in a cellar, is the shrine of the Sacred Tooth. At one end of the recess is a cage of iron bars very crudely gilded. The door of the cage is fastened with enormous padlocks of archaic pattern. On the lower of the iron bars a few fragments of candle have been stuck, and the drowsy light from these tapers is the sole light of the cell.

Within the heavily-barred cage is the shrine, the outer of the seven bell-shaped coverings of the relic. It stands about four feet in height, is wrought apparently of gold, and is covered with crude jewels. In the gloom it looks old and unsubstantial, faded and a little tawdry. On either side of the cage, in the narrow space between the bars and the walls, is a half-naked priest. He stands in the steamy shadow, and the light falls fitfully upon his face, his brown skin, and his yellow robe. On a table in front of the bars is a silver dish, large and brilliant, on which is piled a soft pyramid of white frangipanni blossoms.

Beyond the imprisoned dome of gilt the vulgar eye does not penetrate. Far in the heart of it is the golden lotus flower, holding in its cup the carving of Wikrama Bahu, the *imago* of the precious thing the princess brought to the island hidden in her hair.

A suffocating heat fills the tiny chamber as if it were buried a mile deep in the earth. It is glutted with the smell of smoking candles and of dripping grease blended with the luxuriant sensuous perfume of the frangipanni. It is at best a meagre shrine, a village sanctuary, a peasant's treasure house, an Ark of the Covenant in a garret.

The one worshipful object in the cell is the dish with its burden of bright blossoms. They lie piled up before the barred shrine, an exquisite virginal offering, a divine sacrificial fleece. Neither the guttering candles, the gaudy jewels, nor the smoke-stained walls can sully the graciousness of these frangipanni flowers, nor can the vulgar air drown the queenly perfume that rises from their dying petals.

XII.

PENANG AND SINGAPORE.

It was while in Ceylon that the news arrived of the outbreak of war between Russia and Japan. The announcement had a disturbing effect upon the miscellaneous company of people who were travelling to seek pleasure or to escape boredom. Many of the latter, having decided that "war was a bore," returned home sulkily by way of the Red Sea, blessed with another grievance. Others fled westwards with some suggestion of alarm. A few elected to go to New Zealand instead of to Japan, feeling that in the former place they would be farther away from the sound of cannon and the tramp of troops.

A considerable number elected to continue on their way with much increased interest.

The next stage of the journey was through the Straits of Malacca to Hongkong, with Penang and Singapore as ports of call.

As our steamer sailed out of the harbour of Colombo it passed between a Russian vessel on the right and a Japanese on the left. They were both passenger ships. Each flew the flag of its nation, and it may be supposed that the two crews contemplated one another, across the strip of peaceful water, with a newly aroused curiosity. During the voyage the subject of war was a more unfailing topic of conversation than the weather. Certain of the passengers were English residents in Japan on the way to their homes. Others were naval officers hastening to join the British fleet at Hongkong, with minds full of conjectures. Among the company was a genial war correspondent who was going "direct to the front," or rather believed that he was so destined. Some months later I met him at Tokyo. He had approached no nearer than that to the fighting line, but he was full of that hope which "maketh the heart sick."

Colombo is situated in the parallel of 6° 56′ N. To pass through the Straits and reach the Yellow Sea beyond, it is needful to sail south to the edge of the equator. Singapore indeed is but a few hours from that magic belt.

The first part of the journey was very hot. The sea was as glass, the atmosphere sticky and enervating. In spite of wind-scoops, punkahs, and white clothes, the company on the ship was invertebrate and damp, while the discussion of impending events completed their feebleness. The men in the smoking-room played cards in their shirt sleeves, with handkerchiefs stuffed down their necks to prevent their collars from becoming as limp as their bodies. It was a voyage in a hot-house, and the crumpled man dozing flabbily in a chair would dream of a keen December wind sweeping over golf links and white cliffs by the English Channel.

On the morning of the fourth day some faint cliffs were sighted on the horizon, with above them a hazy shell-pink height. The coast was that of the island of Sumatra, and the peak was the Golden Mountain.

On the morning of the fifth day we came upon Penang, an island some fifteen miles in length, near to the mainland of the Malay Peninsula. The course of the steamer lies close along the shore, round a considerable part of the settlement. Viewed from the sea Penang is a very beautiful country, brilliant with every tint of green—an island of a thousand hills. The hills are small, but they make up in multitude what they may lack in height. They rise up, one behind the other, on the great slope which sweeps from the margin of the sea to the sky line, until the whole island is a mass of peaks and ridges, downs and knolls. So crowded together are they that the spot seems to have been the rallying place for a colony of exiled hills. Hard is it to imagine that there can be any level ground in the place, any wide plain, any staid stretch of fields.

Every height in this great array of hillocks is covered with foliage from foot to peak, with such vegetation as belongs to a land of eternal summer, to such a sun as rides over the equator, and to such warm winds as haunt the girdle of the world.

Between the sea base of these hills and the beach are a few

russet houses with mat roofs dotted among groves of cocoa-nut palms. The beach of pigeon-blue rocks serves to divide the green bank from the restless streak of breakers. Here and there is a dark inlet of rock, cut deep into the plinth of a hill, where there is no sound but the ripple of the rising tide, and the frou-frou of overhanging plumes of bamboo.

The town lies upon a great flat which runs out to sea for a distance of four miles. So low and level is this stretch of land that when seen from a distance it looks but a strip of verdant sedge afloat on the ocean. It is a mere line in the seascape, and everything upon it, the palms, the villas, the sheds about the quay, stand up clearly cut, like silhouettes against the white water beyond. Where the spit fades into the sea are some anchored liners which, from afar, are as tiny black toy ships on a silver mirror, with about them a cluster of masts, like a submerged tuft of dry grass.

As this streak of land is approached it is seen to be very green, and to hide among its woods an unaspiring town. There are splashes of bright colour about the spit. Here is a white block of Government buildings, and there a pile of offices faced by gaudy blinds. This canary-coloured house is a hotel, and this blue bungalow is a club, while between them an old drab fort sits brooding over the tide.

In the harbour are seen, for the first time, the sampan and the Chinese junk, with its high, box-like poop and battened sails. The sampan is a small boat, low and broad, with a double stern and pointed bow, which is propelled and steered by one long oar, rocked from behind. It is the boat of the Far East, to be met with everywhere in China and Japan, and not to be lost sight of until the homeward-bound passenger is well astride of the Pacific.

There was the usual bustle on the quay, the indiscriminate shouting, the aimless pushing to and fro, the evidences of that nervous fervour which fans the riot in a disturbed ant heap. The natives are more miscellaneous than are those even who crowd the landing stages of Rangoon—Malays, Klings, Cingalese, East Indians, and Chinamen. One of the most distinctive marks of a people is to be found in their hats, and here appeared a novel type of headgear in the form of the limpet-shell hat, which gives a character to the Malay Peninsula, as well as to the lands beyond. The Chinese form an apparent majority of the population, while the town itself is essentially a Chinese town, straightened by Western ideas of house building and of sanitation.

It is a busy, cheery place with formal streets in rectangular lines, whose original stiffness has been atoned for by many shanties, by an informal people, and the pleasant untidiness of the East. When the steamer touched at the colony it happened to be celebrating the Chinese New Year, and was, in consequence, exceptionally gay. Red lanterns waved everywhere, while lettered strips in black, red, or gold, hung from a hundred houses like tatters on a mountebank's back. The Chinaman had adopted, as the raiment of rejoicing, shiny black linen clothes, but his children were resplendent with tinsel head dresses and whitened faces.

At Penang, as at other ports, there was great pretence of providing news from the seat of war. The "news," however, in spite of large capitals and heavy print, never rose above the level of hysterical fiction.

After leaving Penang the steamer still moved south. It headed for the equator, for that fanciful band round the world where there is neither winter nor spring, but only autumn and summer, and where, between times of solemn and mysterious calm, the monsoons start on their wild flight towards the poles. So firmly is the conception of the equator branded upon the mind by early geography lessons, as well as by the familiar markings on maps and globes, that it is half imagined its site will be shown by some line on the sea, or that, as the ship nears the very outermost rim of the spinning world—there will be heard some hum in the air as the great circle turns in space.

In perfect silence, broken only by the mumbling of the screw, the ship glides, under a canopy of eternal sunshine, into a sea of islands. There is not a ripple on the blue-green water, and only a junk or two, or a party of idle sea birds, occupy the clear straits between the clusters of islands. The islands are small, but they are as beautiful as the imagination could devise. One is a mere crag, brick-red, where the sun falls on it, bronze-green where the rock is covered by trees. Another island is but a curved streak of yellow beach with three palms on it. A third is a dome-shaped clump of soft bushes resting on the sea. The lower boughs seem to touch the water, and so buried is this beehive-shaped hillock with foliage that neither shore nor bank is to be seen. A fourth is a wonder of white cliffs and woods with a bay in it, where a smooth lawn slopes down to the surf, and a crown of cropped green on its summit looks like a little breezy down.

The largest of the islands is Singapore. It is long and low, infinitely undulating, and intensely green. From one end to the other it measures twenty-seven miles. Its sea cliffs are marvellous in colour. Some are white, or of a dull yellow; others are salmon coloured, or even mauve-pink. They are crested everywhere with trees. Masses of green fill many chines or clefts in their heights, or cling to terraces halfway between the rippled beach and the summit. One entrance to the harbour is through a narrow strait, between steep headlands hung with green. It is the mouth of Dartmouth haven transported from Devonshire to the tropics.

The harbour itself is one of the largest and most picturesque in the world. It is a land-locked sea, a harbour in a garden of many leagues, a wide salt lake surrounded by the woods and groves of the far south. On a curving bay in this great harbour is the town. It appears as a low and broken line by the water's edge, made up of rows of masts, the hulls of ships, tall chimneys, banks of quays, long rows of sheds, and a spire or two. The far-stretching range is very hazy with smoke, while through the smoke can be seen the background of hills. Singapore, as first seen, might have been fashioned from a bank of the Mersey, about the busiest shipping quarter of Liverpool spread along the bay of a South Sea Island. Cranes, jetties, and coal heaps seem out of place on this gorgeous shore, where the hot wind breathes only of eternal idleness. Yet Singapore is one of the greatest ports in the world, and the population of its city is more than 160,000.

The quay the steamer makes fast to might be in the midst of a botanical garden, for just beyond the coaling shed is a bank of ferns on which is waving the beautiful traveller's palm, with its great leaves spread out like a fan.

Ashore there is a long, unsteady town, with that liberal air about it which belongs to places which have been able to spread themselves out over a virgin soil. A fine esplanade runs along the sweep of the bay, with ambitious public buildings and fine villas on one side, and on the other a polo ground by the edge of the sea. The Java sparrow, who in England is a pampered curiosity in a cage, takes here the place of the London sparrow, and haunts the roads and the house tops in quite a vulgar way. Singapore is prosperous. Its streets are alive with rickshaws, gharries, bullock carts, and a never-ending concourse of people. The chief business of the town would appear to be in the hands of Germans. Here, as in other generously-governed British settlements, is a certain sequence of events. The English do the colonising, the Germans follow after and do the trade.

The majority of the inhabitants are Chinese, and they give the colour to the colony. They form three-fourths of the population, do all the work, and fill the quay sides and busy ways with cheerful, half-naked men, grinning under limpet-shaped hats.

A MALAY VILLAGE, SINGAPORE.

XIII.

A PRIMITIVE VENICE.

The native Malay is of Aryan descent. He does not affect the strenuous life. Work bores him. The laziness of eternal summer has entered into his veins. He is content to enjoy the sunshine and the quiet of the creeks. When he finds such lotus-eating monotonous he goes a-fishing. He has already built himself a house of mats. He has his cocoanut tree, which supplies him with many things. What very few clothes he needs his wife can weave. All he has occasion to buy is rice. It is a simple, idyllic life with simple wants. He is happy and contented, and if work tries him, or makes him unhappy, why should he mar his life by carrying coal? Unlike the Western man, he has not the incentive to work which is provided by prospects of occasional intoxication. When the Malay needs excitement he indulges in cock-fighting.

The formal Malay village is a kind of rustic Venice. The grey and brown houses are built upon piles in the water, and are approached by slender causeways of wood. There was a time, perhaps, when the Queen of the Adriatic was as simple a settlement as this. Narrow bridges lead from hut to hut, and plank lanes separate one cluster from another. Bright rags hanging out to dry, fishing nets on a rail, a bunch of bananas, some naked children, and a few vacant-looking fowls occupy the queer streets of this Bœotian Venice. Each hut is covered by a sloping mat roof as if it followed the mode of the limpet-shaped hat. From one window is a view over the great sea creek, while another turns towards a thicket of palms.

Beneath the huts and lanes of the little township the tide ever rises and falls. The Malay baby is lulled to sleep by the lapping of the sea against the piles, and the naked boy finds the water and the canoe beneath the house a better play-ground than the dusty land.

XIV.

THE MANGROVE SWAMP.

The suburbs of Singapore are pleasant and beautiful, and, in the eyes of many, are more delectable than the outskirts of Colombo. Here, after following many yellow roads through many glades of green, by a score of gay bungalows and of exquisite gardens, the curious may, for the first time, come upon a mangrove swamp. The mangrove swamp is the slum of the tropical jungle, the squalid quarter of the imperial forest. It is dismal and dark, cramped, stifling, and ruinous. So thick are the boughs overhead that no light of the sun can ever pierce the dark, mildewed tangle of the place. So dense are the trunks below that none but a small, mean beast or a creeping thing could find a way through the network.

Dead creepers hang into the gloom of this forest morgue; dead boughs block every gap and path as with the *débris* of some grim disaster; about the ground are dead trunks, with shrunken and contorted arms, and bare roots, in worm-like bundles, that seem to be writhing out of the ooze.

In the undergrowth of this swamp of despair are horrible fungi, bloated and sodden. Some are scarlet, some are spotted like snakes, some have the pallor of a corpse. All seem swollen with venom. There are ghastly weeds, too, lank, colourless, and sapless—the seedlings of a devil's garden. Their sickly petals point skywards in a kind of hopeless mockery. Out of the slime come crawling things, and among them loathsome land crabs whose legs scratch among the black pulp of rotten leaves.

The air is heavy with the fumes of decay, and any ocean breeze which may wander into this thicket of desolation will become drugged by the vapour which bubbles up from the festering bog.

By silent and devious passages the soiled sea creeps into the swamp. It crawls in like a thief seeking to hide. When the tide is full the floor of the outcast wood is buried in fetid water; when the tide slinks out it leaves behind a reeking and evil mud, which is smeared over every bank and root like a poisonous ointment.

To make complete the picture of this Slough of Despond one might fancy a hunted man in its most putrid hollow brushing the vermin from his wet rags and listening with terror to the tramp of eager feet about the margin of the mere.

Part IV

CHINA

I.

THE ISLAND OF THE MIST.

AFTER leaving Singapore the steamer turned northwards into cooler weather, for we ran in the face of the north-east monsoon. On the third day out from Singapore the temperature had dropped to 70° F., whereupon the critics of the atmosphere decided that it was cold. Punkahs and wind scoops were removed, tropical clothing vanished, and cloaks, and even great coats, appeared. With them came the odour of camphor and naphthaline, for the last cold weather was long ago. Draughts, lately so much sought after, were now complained of, and the Germans on board put cotton-wool in their ears.

The colony of Hongkong lies just within the circle of the tropics, nearly 10,000 miles from London. The little island is separated from the mainland by a narrow sound, which constitutes the magnificent harbour of the place.

The mainland of China is represented by a much indented coast at the foot of a line of bare granite hills. The hills are a pink brown in colour, with lighter, almost yellow, patches about their sides where the barren rock shows through its thin covering. So smooth are these waving heights that they might be clothed with velvet which has become so thread-bare in patches as to show the faded woof. It is a featureless landscape of uninviting simplicity and an air of emptiness. It is as primitive as the coast-line of an archaic tapestry or of a water-colour drawing in its early stages. There is no hint that this deserted-looking place is China. There are none of those towers with curved roofs, none of those strange trees, bearing fruit after their kind, and none of those very round bridges which figure on packets of tea. Yet this is the country of the Willow Pattern plate.

Hongkong itself is a cluster of steep and lofty hills arranged with graceful irregularity. The one town, Victoria, is at the foot of "The Peak." The town has a population of 182,000 souls, and the peak a height of 1,800 feet. There is but little space between the steep hill and the sea, but along the low ledge the capital city of Victoria has perched itself with some sprightliness.

Viewed from the harbour, Hongkong appears as if compounded of different geographical strata. About the sky line is the bare summit of the peak, with fir trees and a few habitations clinging to its face. This is a part, surely, of the highlands of Derbyshire. Lower down the hill is well wooded. There are terraces, fine gardens, palm trees, and brightly-coloured houses. This reproduces the hillside at Monte Carlo. At the foot of the slope is the town, which is a strip taken from Hull or any other prosperous shipping centre. Even if it be made up of Hull, Monte Carlo, and a Derbyshire hill, Hongkong is still picturesque enough, and its crowning height makes it imposing. From the town to the top of the hill is a very steep funicular railway, which Rudyard Kipling found as a "tramway that stood on its head and waved its feet in the mist."

Hongkong can boast of at least one other astonishing thing besides the cable railway, and that is its weather. From about November to March the climate is charming—fine, bright, and brisk, like a June day in England. From April to October the whole island, peak and town, harbour and hillside, is liable to be buried in a mist. Any who want to know what a damp climate can do should visit Hongkong during the season of the mist. In the early morning they may amuse themselves by wringing the water out of the mosquito curtains, or by noting how much green mould has collected on boots during the night. In the daytime they must learn to breathe steam, to see the world through the atmosphere of a laundry, to write on damp paper, to keep their gloves in bottles, and to sit still and drip. In the evening they must send what clothes they wear in the day to the "drying room" with which every house is provided, and must feel, while they sit at dinner, the once stiff collar changing into a tie. Yet the residents in this Island of the Mist look well. The climate certainly fails to depress them, for they seem to have solved the problem "How to be happy though damp."

The view from the Peak before the coming of the mist is well to be remembered. On one side is the harbour—a blue sound full of ships of every kind, men-of-war, junks, passenger vessels, colliers, ocean tramps, and a myriad of sampans. On the other side is the Pacific and the silent side of the island—a place of valleys and slopes, of creeks and inlets, of mysterious channels and forgotten harbours.

Here, hidden away, is a small cove with a sandy beach. It is called Deep Water Bay. It is at a point, among the brown hills, where a valley descends, with a great rabble of trees and wild bushes, to the sea. Here, between the shore and the gorge, are golf links, constructed by the exiled British. Never has the ancient game of golf been played in a more romantic amphitheatre.

The caddie, who carries the player's clubs, is a Chinese boy with a face the colour of a new potato. He wears a trim blue jacket and black linen trousers, and there is a neat bow at the end of his pigtail. If the player makes a good stroke he expands into an approving smile. If the ball is missed he mutters "damn" with infinite sympathy. His store of English does not extend beyond the simple, primitive sentences, "All right," "God damn," "Gimme a penny." These phrases are evidently not learned at a mother's knee, but they are of practical service nevertheless.

He is a little versed in pidgin English, for when he is asked by appropriate signs if he plays golf, he answers, "No belong my pidgin," which is to say, "That is not my business."

He views the English player with an ever-delighted interest. He anticipates amusement from his every act, as if the white man were a clown with many humorous resources. If the man from the West takes anything from his pocket, the potato-faced boy runs forward to see it with rapturous curiosity. Possibly if a gorgeously dressed Chinaman were to essay to play golf on the links of St. Andrews, in Scotland, the attendant caddie would be as curious, even if a little less simple-mannered. At Deep Water Bay the Chinese boy finds as much enjoyment in an afternoon as does the Englishman he watches. What are the thoughts that flow so cheerfully through his subtle brain none can tell. If he could be asked himself he would probably reply in pidgin English, "Top-side savvy," which is by interpretation, "God knows."

There are many who think that Hong Kong, both its harbour and its town, are best to see at night time a little after sundown. There is a never-to-be-forgotten view from a certain garden on the hill.

In the foreground are an old stone balustrade on the edge of a terrace, and a single tree which stands out black in every leaf and twig against the pale sky. Beyond the balustrade is the moon-light, and an infinite depth of blue, as if, below the terrace, lay some misty pool. This great blue void is dotted with a thousand lights, some yellow, some white, some large and brilliant, and some the merest specks. They belong to ships in the harbour—the great sparks of light to men-of-war, and the tiniest dots to sampans huddled together by the shore in hundreds. The moon is too faint to show the ships, but sometimes a light will fall upon the blunt grey bow of a battleship, or illumine a wreath of steam from a red funnel, or touch the hanging topsail of a barque. The opposite coast of the sound is outlined by points of light, which follow each curve and quay of the little peninsula of Kowloon as it puts out into the harbour. Every light which is large enough is reflected on the water. There is in the Strait an island, called Stonecutter's Island, and the lamps on this little place also make a ring of bright dots. It is as if there were designs in stars on a shadowy surface of slate blue. In the haze, beyond the lights, are the silver-grey hills of the mainland.

Just below the balcony of the garden is the town, a mass of black roofs with glimpses of glowing channels here and there, which are streets. There is just one block of buildings in view, every window of which is a square of warm yellow light in the black wall.

There is no sound stirring in this pool of blue, except the tinkle of a ship bell or the rhythmical creak of rowlocks as a man-of-war's galley is rowed ashore. From the town float up the striking of the church clock and the occasional sound of singing in the street.

The town itself, as seen in the evening, is bustling with life. The streets are wide and admirably kept. The offices and public buildings can put to shame many a town of equal size in the old country. Hongkong is flourishing. The actual trade of the colony is represented by twenty million pounds sterling per annum.

The inhabitants are Chinese, and they seem to live in the streets. Rickshaws pass by in never-ending lines, and with them are many sedan chairs, each swung by a pole from the shoulders of two coolies. The rickshaw and the chair represent the public conveyances of the island. Of horses and carts the busy colony knows nothing. One motor-car I saw driven by a Chinese gentleman in the brilliant raiment of his country. He had neither goggles over his almond-shaped eyes, nor had he tucked his queue into a motor cap.

The streets in those parts of the town which are more exclusively Chinese are exceedingly lively and bright. The Chinaman is a cheerful individual with a love of shining things, and a gregarious instinct which makes him seek the company of his fellow men. The street is his club, his Stock Exchange, his lounge; it does duty for the park of the city and the esplanade of the seaside town. It is a play-ground for his children and a drawing-room for his women folk. After sundown, when the lights are lit and the air is heavy with the steam of tea and the reek of cooking oil, the road is the scene of one continuous informal conversazione.

The shops are brilliant with lamps and coloured lanterns, and are fantastic with unfamiliar wares. They are open to the street, for they boast of neither windows nor doors, and are hung with vertical wooden signs on which the name and trade of the merchant are inscribed in letters of gold or scarlet on a background of brilliant lacquer.

On a sudden there may be a hush in the lane, while all eyes are turned towards an advancing procession headed by immense Sikh policemen in red turbans—bearded and sombre men. The procession consists of a number of sedan chairs with white canopies.

They are swung from long poles, which rest on the shoulders of four bearers, two in front and two behind. The leading chair is borne aloft by no less than eight men walking in solemn pairs. These bearers are Chinamen in brilliant attire. They wear scarlet tunics, and as they walk they swing their arms with considerable pomp and circumstance. On the head of each is a black silk hat shaped like a pie and decorated by a swinging red tassel. The costume is completed by white breeches, white leggings, and white shoes. On the arm of each scarlet tunic is the Tudor crown. The cortège, which moves through the gaping streets with such a dignified tramp of feet, is that of the party from Government House on their way to the Chinese theatre. In the chair with eight bearers is Mr. Francis May, the Acting Governor, with whose admirable work in the colony the tale of its progress will always be associated. In the second chair is his wife, who can claim to be the most popular lady in the island.

II.

A THEATRE AND A HOSPITAL.

There is in Hongkong a substantial native theatre in the form of a permanent building. As a rule the Chinese theatre is a temporary structure of bamboo and matting—a mere shanty put together when occasion needs. The theatre in Hongkong is an immense square building, as bare as a goods shed and as ugly. The auditorium is one vast pit, stuffed to suffocation with a chattering blue and black crowd. The theatre opens at 11 a.m. and closes at 11 p.m.; but those who may find these hours too short are consoled by the knowledge that a play will usually extend over many days.

The stage is a rough platform occupying one end of the hall. It possesses neither footlights, scenery, nor curtain. The orchestra sits on the stage itself, on dilapidated chairs or boxes. They are in the shabby working dress of the ordinary coolie of the quay. They smoke and talk a good deal, while their friends drop in casually during the performance to discuss at leisure current events.

The musicians beat upon things of iron and things of wood, they clash enormous cymbals, they blow upon horns and flageolets until their yellow faces become blue. The noise they produce is astounding and extremely violent. It comes forth in deafening bursts. The gentler tones are those of an iron foundry where many anvils are at work. To the accompaniment of such dulcet notes the Chinese Romeo pours the tale of his love into Juliet's ear. It may be that the sound of the riveting of boiler plates would be to the humbler Chinaman the melody of love.

The less soothing notes of the orchestra convey a sense of some fearful structural disaster. Should the hero be especially magnanimous, or the villain particularly vile, there comes a deafening crash, as of the collapse of a resounding building, with infinite smashing of glass and shrill shrieks. The human brain is not constructed on invariable lines, so it may be that mere noise can arouse in the Mongolian cerebrum emotions and raptures which the Western sense fails to appreciate.

The actors enter by two doors in the rough brick wall on either side of the stage. Boys and hangers-on stroll on to the boards during the performance, and when their number or their noisiness exceeds a liberal limit the Sikh policeman, who stands on duty on the platform, drives them through the doors.

The play I saw was not intelligible. It dealt with mediæval times, with princes, and generals, and mildly distressed women. The costumes were gorgeous. Each of the more esteemed folk wore on his head an ornament like an electric fan, while meaner people paraded a thing of fur, like a lamp-cleaning brush. Beards —most obviously false—were common to the men, while the women's parts were taken by boys, who dissembled well. When a lady was spoken to she gave a little high-pitched squeak and twirled round on her tiny feet like a top. This rotatory movement seemed capable of expressing a variety of emotions. The villain is easily identified because he has a white nose, which, among the Chinese, is a recognised mark of vice.

The principal *dramatis personæ* were always surrounded by banners, painted staves, umbrellas, and strange emblems on poles which followed them about like an obsequious toy-shop.

The actors spoke in a shrill, staccato voice, which was apt to be raised until it faded into a thin shriek. There was much bowing and bending of the knee, much stroking of beards, much aimless posturing and waving of hands. These movements, I was informed, were accepted as evidences of acting, and conveyed a dramatic sense.

Those, however, who are in search of sentiment, are not likely to find it on a Chinese stage. As a contrast to the din and unreality of the native theatre I would commend the English hospital.

At the time of my visit to the island many Russian sailors, who had been wounded at the disastrous engagement of Chemulpo, were brought to Hongkong. They had been rescued from drowning by H.M.S. *Talbot*, by a French vessel, and the Italian cruiser *Elba*.

Their injuries were mostly due to shell wounds. As soon as possible after their arrival, they were taken ashore and housed in the excellent hospital of Victoria Town, under the charge of Dr. Atkinson, whose name is famous among colonial medical officers.

These Russians were all fine, stalwart men. Some of them were giants. They were evidently well content to find themselves between the spotless sheets of a hospital bed and under the British flag. They were cared for by English nurses, but neither nurses nor patients could understand a single word that the other spoke. Still they managed well. The men needed no language to show their gratitude, nor the nurses any to demonstrate their eagerness to make them well.

In one bed was a great burly sailor with a beard like a bush. He had been badly injured by a splinter, and was likely to lose a limb. But a few days since he was aflame with the passion of murder, on a sinking ship, amid bursting shells and dying comrades. There was a good deal of the savage in him no doubt, and when he was ashore and well aroused by gin he was probably little better than a wild beast. He was the sort of man who would wreck a grog-shop with his fist and empty the little street of a seaport town by the bellowing of strange oaths.

By his bedside sat a pale English nurse stitching with a needle at something white. The huge fighting man gazed at her as he would at a sacred ikon. Although they spoke no language her least touch controlled him, her least service comforted him, her presence gave him peace.

A strangely assorted couple these two, as strange as Una and her lion.

III.

THE PEARL RIVER.

A pleasant journey over smooth waters will take the traveller from Hongkong to Canton in about seven hours. Such a steamer as the *Kinshan* lacks nothing in the matter of comfort.

Moreover the passenger can use the ship as a hotel during his sojourn at the great Chinese capital. The part of the vessel devoted to Europeans is luxuriant, the part given over to the native is bare, but it will accommodate him to the number of a thousand or so. These two sections of the ship are separated from one another by very substantial iron bars suggestive of a prison grating. There is a reason for this penal settlement barrier. It is no mere rail to indicate the separation of one class from another, no commonplace wicket to restrain the curious third-class from wandering into the habitations of the first, but it is concerned with nothing less than the stirring possibility of piracy.

With a sight of these iron bars comes a moment of a lifetime! To be afloat on a ship with contingencies, no matter how remote, which are involved with living pirates!

The Chinese passengers lie about between decks in astounding numbers—a crowd, motley in colour, surrounded by their worldly possessions—boxes, packages, and baskets—unlike any other luggage in the universe, together with cages, kettles, umbrellas, and items of a fabulous wardrobe. Some sit in cane chairs, some lie on mats on the floor with their heads on peculiar bundles; others squat and smoke, play cards, or chat, or fan themselves in a bland reverie. The passengers of the better class are on one deck, and are disposed of as just described. The lower deck is given up to coolies. These form a dense thicket of human beings whose individuality is no better marked than that of a flock of live quails in a basket. The massed blue and black of their raiment is relieved by yellow faces, bald heads, pig-tails, and bright handkerchiefs.

The atmosphere of the hold is thick, partly with tobacco smoke, partly with a mixture of human fumes, which are as horrible to the sense of smell as an ulcerated limb is to the sense of sight.

The steamer makes its way between islands, through narrow channels filled with the eddies of a hustling tide, by bare capes and blue water fiords. The scenery is very like that of the west coast of Scotland, save that the land is a little barer and, in the season before the coming of the mist, a little less green.

One island, called Lintin, was a great place in its time. It is deserted now. Its period of glory belonged to the 'thirties, to the "good old days" before the opening of Canton to foreign trade. British merchantmen came here, sometimes empty, sometimes full to the hatch combings; and many an ocean tramp, with the swagger of rascality, brought up under the lea of the smooth downs. Fat junks would creep up to the island after sunset, while now and then a white-winged clipper, laden with tea, would flutter around the anchorage. There was much business in the place of a kind, but it was hardly a port where the industrious apprentice would come to learn commercial integrity. There was a little of the freebooters' haven about the island, and a good deal of the smugglers' rendezvous. While over all was ever spread a liberal air of lawlessness.

Some day the story of the romance of this island will be told, for the surroundings were picturesque. The sailors of that time wore pigtails. The poop of the ship was raised aloft, and was marked off from the main deck by a carved wooden rail and a flight of steps. It made a fitting stage for nautical drama. There would be a great deal of cursing hurled down from the balustrade at times, and the dropping of the Chinese trader over the schooner's side would be hastened now and then by a pistol shot from a deck house.

Some miles beyond Lintin the vessel enters the Pearl River, the river on which Canton stands.

The waters of this dull stream are thick and muddy, and that it should be compared to a jewel is only to be explained by the recklessness of Oriental flattery.

THE CANTON RIVER.

The way into the river is through a narrow strait called the Tiger's Mouth. Here, on the side of a bare but valiant hill, is a Chinese fort. It defends Canton. It is very rich in walls and aggressive battlements, but the whole place seems to have fallen upon sleep. There are many sentry boxes, but no sentries. There is a stone terrace, but not a sign of a man to parade thereon. There are numerous guns, but they are covered over with fragments of packing-cases to keep them from the rain. There is so little evidence of life in the place that it might be merely a corral for savage cattle. Yet over the topmost rampart is a flagstaff from which is flying proudly the Chinese flag.

There is a little quay by the water's edge with a crane for the unloading of the munitions of war. Here, on the stone, a solitary man is fishing. There can be little doubt but that he it is who hoists the flag in the morning and lowers it at night, and that he devotes the intervening hours to the art of Izaak Walton. He must be the soul of the fortress, and incorporate in his person the commandant, the constable of the tower, the armourer, and the faithful garrison.

On second thoughts, I am disposed to think that this solitary holder of the fort, this gentle fisher who alone keeps the flag flying over the stronghold, is a woman.

This same Tiger's Mouth has been the scene of stirring events concerned with battle, murder, and sudden death. In 1841 England and China were at war, and then the mouth of the Pearl River saw much of fighting, of conflicts between junks and gunboats, of cutting-out expeditions, of the deeds of boarding parties, and of such scenes as belong to the most romantic periods of the British Navy.

As the river narrowed, junks of all shapes and sizes were come upon. They are venerable-looking craft, with no little dignity about them. They move through the water with all the lofty pride of a company of village geese. Some were crowded with merchandise, and others with people. No matter what the cargo was, they had this common feature—they all carried cannon. The number of guns varied from two to eight, according to the size of the ship. They were very ancient weapons, such as are seen in the vestibule of a county town museum, or about the bandstand on a marine parade. Some were of brass, but most were of baser metal. It is hard to say who would suffer the more from the firing of these pieces of ordnance—the gunner or the object fired at.

It is with some degree of emotion that the traveller learns that these guns are carried as a protection against pirates. More than that, he is told that the steam launches which ply between Canton and up-country villages are not only armed, but have often around them a netting of wire to prevent pirates from boarding their decks. This is, in fact, a pirates' country, and the estuaries, creeks, and rivers of the coast have been pirates' haunts.

If there be an English schoolboy on board he will be thrilled with delight. Since the age of five it has been the ambition of his life to be either an engine-driver or a pirate. He has played at pirates in the chalk caves at Margate, he has terrified his sister with a toy pistol and the most lurid homicidal threats. It has been upon the pirate, his ideal, that he has lavished the fondest hero worship, and when he has been lying ill in bed with chicken pox, stories of piracy and rapine read from a book by gentle lips have brought to him the utmost consolation and peace.

Such a lad will fancy strange things in the Pearl River. He sees sailing down upon the steamer a vessel with a dark hull and an indistinct pennon at her masthead: that flag must be black, and upon it there must be wrought in ghastly white a skull and crossbones. He sees ashore a bamboo tied to an upright rock; that is a pirates' signal. It is either a guide to hidden treasure or a token to meet at night, in a certain cave, to plot the spoiling of a merchantman. He sees a riverside village with a great crowd of junks in the little harbour. These have fled here to escape the pirates. They are huddled together with fear, and none has the heart to put to sea.

One thing, however, he will observe that is apparent to all, and that is an island which forms a most perfect background to any scenes of violence that the most fertile writer of books for boys could conceive.

A league or so above the narrows of the Tiger's Mouth is Tiger

Island. It is beyond doubt the deadliest, cruellest, and most vile-looking island that rises out of any sea. If ever there was a pirate's lair framed for every kind of infamy and crime it is this. It is an island of black-domed rock, so rounded and smooth as to scarcely give footing to a goat. At the sides are fearsome cliffs, so sheer that those who slipped upon the summit must glide to their destruction, however frantically they clutched at the stone. The outline of the mass is such that it looks like some maleficent monster lying dead on the sea and half submerged. There is the ugly black bone of his occiput covered with a little withered grass, as if there were thin grey hairs on his skull. There is his rounded snout, a quarter of a mile long, smooth and black, stretching out to be lost in the tide. One can see the tips of huge black ears and the bony points of his elbows thrust upwards, as if his claws rested on the bed of the strait. Beyond are his heavy shoulders and the line of vertebræ on his back.

Just at one spot is a sullen beach under the dark cliff, where there is a strip of green and a few bare trees. Here shrink some drab wooden huts. They look sinister, and must have the tale of some tragedy to tell. This little beach is a perfect realisation of the villains' meeting place; and if there is a duel to the death to be fought by two inhuman men let it be fought on the strip of green between the sand and the black cliff.

The affable captain of the steamer had tales to tell of pirates, which he related with much vividness. The most recent encounter with these desperadoes within his personal knowledge was after this wise—if Mr. Barlow were telling the story in the pages of "Sandford and Merton" he would call it "The Story of the Pirate and the Ticket Collector":—Just before one Chinese New Year a steamer, proceeding from Hongkong to Canton, was laden with many passengers. They were mostly Chinamen returning home to celebrate the great festival, bringing with them copious presents and their earnings of the year. Certain pirates, suitably disguised, took passage in this ship, and located themselves as near as possible to the wheel. At a certain lonely spot in the estuary they were to rise, kill the helmsman, and run the steamer ashore. At this point less unconventional pirates were to be lying in wait, who were to board the helpless ship and despoil their fellow countrymen in approved fashion. It so happened that the ticket collector on the steamer noticed a pistol projecting from a passenger's pocket. He promptly had him seized. The other passengers were thereupon examined. The pirates stood revealed. They confessed all, and in due course an appropriate number of executions brought the episode to a happy close.

This incident serves to illustrate the decadence of real romance in modern times. In the good old days the proceedings of pirates were always conducted on dramatic and picturesque lines. The man who foiled the pirate had black ringlets, and a bright belt full of weapons. He stood with a pistol in each hand, his legs wide apart, a dagger between his teeth, so that none could withstand him. In the twentieth century this saviour of men has come to be represented by a ticket collector, earning a pound a week and his board, who is armed with no more deadly weapon than a ticket punch.

IV.

A FLOATING SUBURB.

From Tiger Island to Canton is a distance of thirty miles. The river gradually narrows, the country it passes through becomes flat, and with each mile of the way the stream is more and more crowded by boats. Canton stretches away across a bend of the river, a level sweep of dingy roofs, low-lying as if crouching in a swamp. Over the monotonous flat of housetops there rise up against the sky three curiously assorted structures, viz. the graceful white spire of the French cathedral in the European quarter, the fantastic column of the Flowery Pagoda, and certain square lofty stone buildings like blockhouses. The last-named have the look of a Norman keep, for they are almost windowless. So strong are they that they might be towers of refuge, or strongholds for the defence of the city. They are, however, neither of these: they are pawnshops. Their massive strength is intended to withstand not only flood, fire, and the sneaking burglar, but also the attacks of mobs, bent upon looting whenever there is a rising in the city.

Such is then the first glimpse of one of the most amazing human settlements in the world. A muddy river winding through a flat, some square miles of level housetops, out of which arise the spire of a French cathedral, a many-roofed pagoda, and a company of pawnshops.

By the time the strange place is reached the river is alive with boats, not in hundreds merely, but in many thousands. In Canton 400,000 people spend their lives in boats. They are born on the water, live their days on the water, and finally die in the cabin of a junk, or under the awning of a sampan.

Prominent in this river of boats are the great sea-going junks. Curious, unwieldy vessels they are, with high, square sterns, and nothing particular for a bow. Their decks are covered by unintelligible lumber, among which a more or less definite house is pitched. The battened sails of bamboo matting arise aloft like enormous wings. The "lines" of a junk are like the lines of a packing case. They are at least so unusual that it is a little difficult to tell whether the craft is sailing stern first, or bow first, or is gliding sideways.

The entire family lives on board, and the wife is the chief mariner. She stands at the tiller with a baby strapped to her back, and has a real nautical manner. Towards evening the fire is lit on the poop, and here the woman with the baby does the cooking while she guides the ship. She stops her dallying with a saucepan to put the helm "hard a lee." As the ship comes about she attends to the mainsheet, and then returns to her cooking. Children lean out of the portholes, and the family cat prowls about the cabin roof. Some clothes are hanging out to dry as if the deck were a back garden. Things dangle from the vessel's stern as did weapons from the knight in "Through the Looking-Glass." Among them are nets full of vegetables, a live chow chow in a cage, many noisy fowls in a wicker basket, certain boxes, spare oars, and a few china pots with flowers. The passenger junks carry hundreds of people, while the junks which take in lodgers and boarders will accommodate as many as a modern hotel.

Among the crowd of vessels are trim steamers from over the seas, as well as nondescript craft with a single paddle-wheel at the stern, worked by the feet of a score of coolies hopping on a treadmill, Thames barges, out-of-date steam launches, and a species of "dug out" belonging to the days of prehistoric man. Moored by the bank are the famous Flowery Boats, gaudy as a line of circus cars. Each is a kind of floating *café chantant*, where the lighter vices flourish exceedingly to the sounds of vile music, and under the glare of many scarlet lanterns.

The boat of the river is the sampan, which is here a wherry with a rounded bottom, a wide stern, and a narrow, low, flat prow. The middle part of it is usually shut in by a mat canopy or awning, which makes a little tunnel of its waist. In the sampan, small as it is, the whole family lives—the husband, his wife or wives, his children, and possibly his friend. With them are the domestic cat and dog, a few live fowls, a litter of mats, bowls, old relatives, and other impedimenta of a home. Some of these little vessels are poor enough, but others are exceedingly smart. The boat is propelled by a long single oar projecting from the stern and worked by a woman.

This woman of the sampan is a remarkable being. She directs the boat and all that is within it. If she is not rowing, she is cooking, or washing the deck, or re-dressing the baby. She is a mixture of the man at the wheel and the woman at the hearth. She is the gondolier of the Pearl River. She wears a jacket of blue, black, or brown, and loose trousers of the same colours. Her feet are bare, and her peculiarly sleek, black hair is ornamented with bright pins, red worsted, or artificial jade. As she rocks the oar to and fro she stands on a springy plank. Her movements are graceful, especially the coquettish swing of one bare foot. She is very lithe, very alert, so that her sampan darts about the river like a wild bird. Sometimes her mother, her daughter, or possibly an aunt will help her at the sweep, and then they all swing to and fro together. She often has a baby strapped to her back. Indeed, the woman of the sampan wears a baby much as a graduate of a university wears an academic hood.

When the rain comes on, she dons a large circular hat with a steeple top like the roof of a kiosk, and a yellow cloak made of bamboo leaves. This garment is a kind of Inverness cape of straw. The ends of the dry leaves that form the cape stream loose like untidy feathers. As she rocks her wherry through the rain in this wild costume the lissome woman of the sampan looks most bewitching.

The sampan family earn a living by ferrying passengers or goods, and, incidentally, by taking in lodgers at night. The cargo may be composed of live pigs in wicker baskets, of piled-up vegetables, or of boxes of tea. One boat I watched took across the river a horde of noisy ducks, and returned with a Mandarin in a blue sedan chair, poles, bearers and all. Within the chair, which had a roof and little side-blinds, sat the great man with fan in his hand.

The scene on the Pearl River is not only curious and most

wonderful, but it is unique. It provides a panorama of river life as it was in primitive times. Take away the steamers, the paddle boats, and the telegraph wires, and the scene goes back to ten centuries ago. As the river was then, so is it now, for the banks, the boats, and the people can have changed but little.

The houses by the riverside are of wood, and, creeping out into the mud on piles, they hang unsteadily over the brown tide. They form a medley of uneven roofs, verandahs, loft-like rooms, stages on poles, and steps to the stream. The lake dwellers' houses could scarcely have been more simple.

In the channel are junks at anchor as old-world-looking as the archaic craft painted on Grecian vases or Egyptian tombs. By the banks at sundown is a fleet of sampans, twenty deep, huddled together until they look like a pile of timber wreckage, of spars, of bamboo mats and shipyard rubbish cast up on the shore of the river. Under the covering of mats, however, is a swarming, restless hive of human folk.

It is at night time that the sampan looks its best, as it lies drawn up in the shadows by the bend of the river or the side of the canal. Five hundred boats will crowd together in a single bight of the stream. The arch of each mat cabin is then a cave of light. On the floor is a small round table laden with the bowls and saucers of the evening meal. About it the family of the sampan are clustered, kneeling or squatting. In the centre of the table is a lamp which fills the little place with a furnace-like glow. Its light falls upon a circle of yellow faces bent eagerly over the common mess of rice. Everyone is chattering. The lamp casts long distorted shadows of shaven heads and coiled-up pigtails upon the roof of the cabin, while an occasional ray touches a piece of china on a shelf or a shining thing of brass in the distant gloom.

Moving in this shadow, outside the circle, is the woman of the sampan. She has been busy all day as a ferryman, and now she is the housewife, the cook, the waiting-maid. As she leans over her husband's shoulder to reach the table, the light of the lamp illumines her face as with a glow from a sacred fire. For a moment the gleam transfigures her, and makes her beautiful, for by the light of day the face of the sampan woman is pathetically plain.

V.

THE NIGHTMARE CITY OF CANTON.

Canton is a city, with two million inhabitants, shut in on three sides by an old fortified wall, and on one side by the river. It is a strange and terribie town, for there can scarcely be a walled city on the earth where so huge a multitude of human beings is herded and hustled together in a space so cramped.

In this fearsome city there is no way which could be called a street, no open square, no gap free to the breath of heaven. There is, moreover, within its confines, no still spot where the weary could rest or the leisurely stroll. From wall to wall every alley in the place is swarming with life, bustling with restlessness. Such peace as is to be found in Canton lies only on the green hillside without the walls, where the dead are sleeping.

The city is intersected by a myriad of narrow passages from six to seven feet wide. They are the sole streets of the town. These alleys push in among the swarm for miles, tunneling in every direction. Shops and houses of blue-grey brick close them in on either side. The sky is almost shut out by high verandahs and projecting eaves. The narrow space between the roofs and the causeway is filled by signboards hanging vertically. These narrow strips of wood are covered with Chinese letters in gold or red, on a background of black or green lacquer. With them are many swinging paper lanterns. They would sway in a breeze if ever a breeze could find its way into these choking passages. The lanes, therefore, are sunless and dim, and are filled by an unearthly and rueful twilight.

The alley is paved with narrow blocks of granite placed transversely. The stones are wet with water jerked from a thousand buckets, are slimy with a fetid sludge, and are so loose and ill-fitting as to rock under the foot and throw up an occasional spurt of putrid mud. Dotting the stones everywhere are fragments of red paper. They look like soiled rose petals, but they are torn shreds of the crimson wrapping in which every bundle of joss sticks is tied. When a temple is neared the mud in the lane is entirely red because of them.

No cart, no vehicle with wheels, is to be found in the cuttings of Canton, nor will there be seen there a mule or a donkey. A few ducks and fowls, with an occasional rat, are the only animals to be met with in this city of footpaths. The rickshaw has no place here. The only conveyance is the sedan chair swinging from a pole and carried on the shoulders of two coolies. So narrow are the alleys that when a chair is swaying along there is only room for one foot-passenger on either side of it. Still less space is there for two chairs to pass. When such a meeting does occur, one chair has to be put down, or to be partially backed into a shop while the other goes by.

The shops give some kind of brilliancy to these twilight lanes. They are gaudy with much gilding, with much red paint and handsome lacquer, with cryptic hieroglyphics and fantastic carvings. They are open to the causeway, for they possess neither windows nor doors, while at night they are closed in by double-leaved gates of planks heavily bolted. On the ground by each shop is a gaily painted recess wherein is a porcelain cup full of sand for the joss stick. This is the little altar of the house from which incense arises to the comfort of departed spirits. The shops are for the most part tidy and bright, the proprietor alert and dignified. He sits within with his dish of Indian ink and paint brush before him in place of a pen, and uses an abacus or counting frame in place of arithmetic.

As the sedan chair swings along the coolies never cease to yell, in order that those who crowd the narrow passages may keep out of the way. As it is, many have barely time to dodge the chair, and so get bumped by its corners. Its sides rub against the meat hanging at the butchers' stalls, and it will now and then knock over a chest of tea or a faggot of charcoal. It once happened that the hood of my chair was torn off by coming into contact with some coffin planks in an undertaker's shop. And on another occasion the coolies and the chair were brought to the ground owing to the slipping of the leader's foot upon a dead rat. Some of the swinging signboards and the paper lanterns hang so low that they catch the roof of the conveyance, or its projecting canopy may sweep a dried fish from a hook or set a cluster of brass utensils jingling.

Everybody in every lane is busy. Some are gambling or drinking tea, or are having their heads shaved. Others are making bracelets or embroidery, are fashioning red lamps out of paper, or are mixing the incense for joss sticks. The chair passes actually over the heads of men on low stools who bend over jewellery work, or the cutting of printing blocks, or who are graving designs in brass or in sandal wood. They sit out in the path to catch what little light comes down from the slit of sky.

Here is a lane with a quarter of a mile of shoe shops. Here a warehouse for pictures on rice paper, and there a depôt for blackwood cabinets. Here are piles of fresh green vegetables by the side of an emporium of stinking fish and of shark fins, which in the matter of smell have a monopoly of nastiness. There are shops where they sell boxes and baskets, articles in lacquer, fans and screens, silks and unique embroidery. There are shops full of idols, full of rare teas, full of fancies in tinsel, full of wonders in carved jade.

Every alley is swarming with people. They are all Chinese, all of sallow countenance, all clad in dull colours, in blue or black, brown or grey. Most of the coolies are naked but for a loin-cloth. They crush and hurry through every by-way in the city, a crowd of many thousands of bare, sweating backs and yellow, panting chests.

There are two million people in Canton, and it will appear to a visitor who has spent a day in its crowded trenches that he has met every one of them.

In India all things, from street rubbish to a piano, are carried upon the head. In Canton everything is slung from the shoulder. A single coolie will rest a bamboo pole upon his shoulder, from the two ends of which his burdens are suspended like the scales of a balance. Heavier things are carried on a pole between two men.

No matter whether the weight be great or little, these half-naked men of burden trot along with a kind of rocking movement and a low, guttural chant.

Among the crowd are coolies carrying rice, sugar-cane, stones for building, water in buckets, charcoal, street garbage, live fish in tubs, furniture, and endless baskets. Now and then a mandarin will pass, in a sumptuous sedan chair, with considerable fuss. There are women marketing, and children gaping at the shops, while once in a way a cheery funeral jogs along at a great pace, with much noise of music, and a man in front scattering joss paper.

Possibly the most unpleasant objects exposed to view in the shops of Canton are articles of food. At the present day, when every second civilised person is "on a diet," and when the introduction of any new thing in a dietary is an act of merit, some interest may attach to the food shops of China. The Cantonese live mainly upon rice, fish (fresh or dried), pork, fowls, and ducks. Everything but the rice is very unpleasantly exhibited. Hanging from a hundred hooks in one shop will be hideous brown strips of cooked bacon. They might have been torn from the flitch by dogs' teeth.

There are cooked ducks, oily and sticky, which seem to have died in convulsions, or to have been rudely crushed to death. They have, in fact, been flattened out during the process of "preparation for the table" until they look like greasy lumps of compressed rag. There are disgusting fowls, so cooked as to be white and shiny, like blanc mange. There are cooked dogs hanging up in select restaurants. They are equally white and glazed, and seem to have been blown out to make them appear round and fat.

There are shops where they sell nasty fragments of meat such as might be hooked, half masticated, from under a tiger's paw, and white broths in basins which might have come from an operating theatre, with loathsome lumps of food of an unknown kind. I was shown a depôt where I could purchase rats, either dried or fresh, or prepared for cooking. I could also obtain them ready boiled.

A conspicuous restaurant in one squalid lane was little more than a witches' kitchen. It was full of a sickening steam hanging over cauldrons bubbling with loathsome stews, or filled with dead-looking soup in which floated awful fragments of bird or beast.

The eating of fish in Canton would appear to be made as revolting as an unwholesome ingenuity could devise. The fish are carried about alive in tubs, or lie gasping in buckets in the fish sellers' shops. Some are scaly and green and vilely spotted like lizards, others have gargoyle heads on bodies yellow with leprous marks. They look as poisonous as tropical fungi. They are sliced up alive in such a way as to make the cut surface as bloody as possible. In these reptile shambles, festoons of fish entrails are hanging up for sale to tempt the appetite of the less fastidious. As for the dried fish shops, they resemble depôts for discarded museum specimens, while the stench that arises from them is beyond all words.

As Mr. Dyer Ball observes: "It is not every foreign stomach that can stand the sight of hundreds of greenish-brown worms, fresh from the rice fields, hawked about the streets for sale; nor do salted and pickled eggs, getting discoloured by age, and eggs high from long keeping, prove agreeable to our palate, though why we should take our game high, and turn with disgust from an egg in a similar condition, is a mystery to a Chinese. Silkworm grubs do not sound very tempting to a foreign ear, yet the Chinese are very fond of them."*

So many "cash" go to a penny that very small purchases are possible in Canton. The economically minded can buy three monkey nuts, or six matches, a quarter of an orange, a slice of pomelo, or half a cooked fowl's leg. Whatever the purchase may be, the article is secured by a thin string of fibre, which the happy buyer dangles from his finger's end. Thus I have seen a man returning from marketing with a single raw kidney at the end of a thread. Another, who was evidently something of a gourmet, had, swinging from his string, half a green fish, some fowl entrails, and two onions. He was no doubt the envy of many.

One of the most dreadful things in Canton is the stench which fills the cramped streets. It is a charnel-house smell, a smell suggestive of mawkish disease, of rottenness of bones. It is no

* "Things Chinese," Hong Kong, 1903, p. 288.

mere compound of open drains and the reek of perspiring men, streaked by the odour of cooking oil, of incense, and of putrid fish. It is an aggressive smell. It strikes upon the sense as a crash of discordant sound beats upon the ear. It is cruel in its persistence, and as horrible, in its suggestion of suffocation, as if invisible fingers were clutching at the throat.

No little of the vileness of this acrid stench comes from certain creeks which crawl through the city. They are crossed now and then by narrow stone bridges. From the parapet of the bridge one looks down upon no prattling rivulet, no Venetian canal, but upon a gutter of black mud, and a slimy track bestrewed with pots and pans, dead animals, rotting rags, and the general offal of the town. The filth oozes seaward as if it were the dark blood of a diseased city draining away. Tumble-down houses hang over these creeks, like faint and sickly people. Not even a live rat is to be seen on the banks, nor is there a single blade of grass in the length of the gully, for the shores of the creek are of festering, bubbling sludge, which would poison anything that had life. Yet two million people call this city "home," and the country they name the "Flowery Land."

Canton is a nightmare city, and it is hard to conceive of a more ghastly dream than to be lost in its maze of cruel streets. Everything is strange, the dark ways are cramped and sinister, and shut in from the sky. They seem to lead on for miles and miles, so that one might wander for days before the outer wall and the green fields are reached. The streets are like corridors in a prison, like subterranean trenches, like cuttings in a mine. The high walls on either side seem to be creeping together. There is a fear that the causeway will become narrower and narrower, until at last the wayfarer must be crushed between the greasy stones. The stench in the air is unbreathable as a gas. The alleys are full of a sallow crowd, some in dingy clothes, some with bare yellow skins. They have shaven heads and grinning teeth. As the terror-stricken man in the dream hurries by like a hunted thing from lane to lane, they all stare with curious faces. There comes to him a memory of the devilry of the people, of their murderous risings, of their fiendish cruelty.

He is filled with piteous alarm. He is imprisoned. He is seized with a frenzy to escape before the painted walls close in, before the fumes of the place stifle him, or the growing crowd trample him into the mud. There is no sound about the place like the sound of cities, only a muttering in an unknown tongue, and the slimy tramp of thousands of bare feet. More terrible than all, the panting man in the dream is utterly alone.

VI.

WHITE CLOUD HILL.

The basis of the Chinese religion is Ancestor Worship, and the extreme and wide-extending form of filial piety which that worship involves is the basis of Chinese morality.

The spirits that pass after death into the other world need necessities and comforts, and so the faithful descendants of the dead have need to send them houses, boats, clothing, and money. It is a make-believe offering, for the luxuries bestowed upon the spirits are in the form of paper models or emblems. Money, for example, is in the guise of joss paper with a little dab of silver on it. These paper things are burnt, and their substance floats away in smoke to the arms of the expectant dead. That which a Chinaman desires above all is a son, who will keep green his memory after his death, who will minister to his needs in the other world, and who will, before all things, secure for him an appropriate burial.

The son has, moreover, an object in this worship which is bound up in his own happiness and security. Ancestor worship includes "not only the direct worship of the dead, but also whatever is done directly or indirectly for their comfort; also all that is done to avert the calamities which the spirits of the departed are supposed to be able to inflict upon the living, as a punishment for inattention to their necessities."*

Moreover, there are "beggar spirits, who may have been neglected by living relatives, or who may have no relatives living, and the spirits of those who have died at sea, in war, of starvation, or abroad."†

The Chinese "believe that nearly all the ills to which flesh is

* "Things Chinese," p. 30.

† Ibid., p. 31.

heir,. such as sickness, calamity, and death, are inflicted by these unfortunate and demoniacal spirits."*

The mourning for the dead in China involves a ritual which is extremely elaborate, together with a series of observances which extend over months and years. The future of those who survive hangs in large degree upon the precision with which the ceremonial acts are performed.

Among these acts that which is of the very first importance is the actual burial of the deceased. There is, indeed, a Chinese saying to the effect that "the most important thing in life is to get buried well."

In the case of the poor the ceremony must needs be scant, and the time involved in its performance brief. In Canton those who are ill-to-do are buried for the most part on the slopes of certain green hills just outside the town. The place is picturesque. Round the great city winds an old drab wall with many gates and towers in its length. It is ever deserted and lonely. Grass has grown over all its paths, moss covers its stairs, and many a tree has sprung up among its forgotten ramparts.

From this height one looks down upon the town, upon its thousands of pointed roofs which hide, happily, the squalid lanes and the seething crowd. So very slit-like are these alleys that no trace of any one of them is to be seen. There is nothing but a stretch of roofs. Of the mighty horde of two million folk there is no sign except that a few children are playing about a distant gate. To lift off the crust of roofs would be to turn over the flat stone which covers a huge nest of ants. No sound even of the hideous turmoil of the town reaches the old grey wall.

Here is monastic peace, broken only by the twittering of birds. The air is clear and fresh. Far away the great river winds seawards, with a gleam upon it which makes the name of the Pearl River a name that can be understood. Even over the nightmare city there is a ripple of sunshine. Just at this point of the wall is a fine pagoda, the Five Storeyed Pagoda. It brings prosperity to the town, they say, for, in some guise, the fortunes of Canton are mysteriously hidden away within its red and black walls.

* Ibid., p. 32.

On the other side of the ramparts is a range of grass-covered hillocks where the poor of Canton lie buried. On these hillsides are cut ten thousand notches. In every notch is a small, plain stone. Each little scooped-out place marks a grave. So closely placed are they that the hill looks honeycombed or waterworn, or as if it had been gnawed at by gigantic worms. Still these little downs are green and pleasant, and upon them has settled an eternal quiet.

To many a poor coolie carrying sacks in dockyards across the Pacific, or dragging a rickshaw in Penang, or working in a laundry in Calcutta, this hill is the one spot to which his thoughts are ever turning. In the confines of his little world it is the one sacred place that is treasured above all. However dismal his lot may be, however dire his exile, he is still cheered by the memory that

"There is a green hill far away."

Here rest his great hopes of a happiness which will come in time, his faith in a power which will be with him to the end.

In the case of the rich, the disposal of the dead is by no means a simple matter. His coffin cannot be hurried through the lanes of the city, to cheerful, but immature, music and a plentiful scattering of joss paper, to be buried on a worn hillside just beyond the walls. The location of his grave demands profound reflection, indefinite enquiry, and a knowledge of the mysteries of Fung-Shui.

Fung-Shui is an ancient form of geomancy which teaches that the whole of nature is alive with influences which affect, for good or evil, as well the living as the dead. The site of a tomb may be rendered favourable or unfavourable by the slope of a hill, by the bearing of a clump of trees to a roadway, by the curve of a stream, and by other natural combinations too complex to be detailed. The Chinese people "believe not only that the comfortable sepulture of their ancestors will redound to their own comfort, but that if the union of the elements, the nature of the soil, the configuration of the ground, and all the other things which enter into this farrago of nonsense are such as to produce a felicitous combination, that riches, honour, and posterity may be vouchsafed to them. It is these beliefs that cause the coffin to be so often kept for months or years unburied, while a site is being searched for which shall combine all that is productive of good to the children and grandchildren. Even when the eldest son has discovered such a site, and is confident that happiness and prosperity will be his lot, it may be that another son has found out that what will benefit his brother will not be productive of good to him, but of evil; consequently the whole search will have to be gone over again till one favourable to all parties can be discovered. So many different elements come in in determining the lucky sites that the professors of geomancy are easily able to make a living out of the gullibility of their employers."*

During the progress of these intricate and baffling researches, where is the body of the dead to rest? It has already been placed in a substantial coffin made of curved logs, so that the whole structure has the aspect of the trunk of a tree. The surface of this uncoffin-like coffin is coloured a deep rich brown, is brilliantly polished, and glistens with copious lacquer. Its temporary resting-place will be in a garden on "White Cloud Hill."

Here is a still, retired spot in a most comely enclosure. The entrance is through a gateway made of brick, so as to form a perfect circle. Within are paths lined by many porcelain pots full of flowers, while beyond the paths are the details of a formal garden. In this pleasaunce are a number of houses of two rooms each. These are the lodging-houses for the dead. Here they linger until the troublous question is settled as to the happiest place of burial, and here they may sojourn for weeks or months, or even for years. In this strange caravanserai one coffin had been lodged for seven years, and still none could say when at last it would come to the close of its journey.

In each small house the front room is furnished with an altar, blushing with colour, and decked with cheerful images, with tinsel and much bright paper. On the walls hang vertical scripts, covered with a strange lettering, which tell of the titles and virtues of the dead. There are chairs, too, where those can sit who come to visit the lost friend, and do homage to his memory. On the table is placed every day a cup of fresh tea for the departed man, so that

* "Things Chinese," p. 313.

he can drink and be refreshed. The altar, the gaudy emblems, and the writing on the wall convey but little meaning to the profane; but the chair and the cup of tea are pitifully vivid tokens of the reality of the mourner's faith.

The back room of the house is very plain. It is meant to be a bedroom—a place for sleep. Here stands the huge coffin, supported on trestles, and those who enter the chamber step gently, so as not to disturb the sleeper's peace.

If life be a pilgrimage, this garden of summer houses is an exquisite conception of the Last Inn, of the Last Resting Place between this world and the next. In the language of the West the little spot would be "a Necropolis: a City of the Dead"; but in the dainty imagery of the Oriental it is the "Garden on White Cloud Hill."

VII.

THE HEALING OF THE SICK.

There are, it is needless to say, in China many educated medical men who have studied in the West, and who have supplemented the knowledge so obtained by a critical appreciation of the practices of the East. They are not, however, the doctors of the people. The native doctor in China differs but little from the "medicine man" who ministers to the woes of the North American Indian, or from the quack who masquerades at a country fair. The Chinese practitioner is not troubled by any education. He has no hospitals to "walk," and no examinations to disturb his peace. An absence of ceremony marks his initiation into the mysteries of medicine, for to the dignity of a healer of men he elects himself. If his father has been a doctor before him it is well. If both his grandfather and his father have been members of the profession, he at once takes a place of some eminence, for he will possess the books of recipes of these ancestors, and to the sick Chinaman the most commendable feature in a prescription is its antiquity.

To the Oriental the science of medicine goes backwards into the past; it is spoiled by progress. It has no future. A prescription, like wine, improves with age, gathering power and mellowness with years.

The stock-in-trade of a native doctor consists of a bundle of recipes, a knowledge that the pulse is on the thumb side of the wrist, and a pair of goggles of circular glass set in heavy copper frames. These latter give him an appearance of learning, and are more valuable in his particular practice than an academic degree. If any man will only observe a reasonable silence it is easy to look profound; so it is probable that the Chinese doctor, by the bedside, commits himself to few utterances.

The physic he prescribes is for the most part nauseous, if not actually disgusting. This much can be learned from a study of the native drug shop, while writers on Chinese customs give details of prescriptions which are nearly as filthy as those in vogue in England in the seventeenth century. It may seem unkind to give a child ill with fever an infusion of cockroaches, but the English apothecary in ancient days never hesitated to do worse than that.

A belief that medicine to be effectual should be odious is a primitive faith common to all peoples. The Chinaman holds to it still, and even in the enlightened West it has not yet died away. A patient at a metropolitan hospital goes away best satisfied when he is given something to drink out of a bottle. The drinking, according to ancient ritual, must not be less often than three times a day, and the ceremony must have some reference to meals. The draught to be efficient should be coloured. It must have a marked odour, so that he may invite his friends to smell it. It should be loathsome to the taste, so that the taking of it may call for some heroism. Above all, it needs to possess an evil-looking sediment which will require a formal shaking of the phial. The Chinaman who is sick will appreciate all this and think well of it. He will intensify every detail of nastiness in the compound, so that the potion, when it reaches him, is too impossible to be thrown even to the dogs.

From the drug shops in Canton it would appear that plasters are in much esteem for the cure of disease. They have the advantage of being small, cheap, and of unpleasant aspect. Three little bile-green plasters stuck on a shaven head would seem to be the popular remedy for headache. I have no doubt also that many a child playing in the street has a constellation of plasters about its stomach.

It is well, however, that those who are sick in China can "take higher advice" than that tendered by the goggle-bedecked doctor. There is the temple, and notably the temple to the memory of a great exponent of the healing art. I was taken to one such in Canton by a guide who felt that he was bringing me in touch with the departed spirit of a professional brother.

Most of the temples in this part of China are very gaudy without, and very squalid within. Their most beautiful feature is the roof, whose graceful curves are swept by brilliant ridges of glazed tiles. There is often running around a court a frieze, constructed of porcelain figures moving among porcelain scenery, gods and dragons, emperors and imps, with fantastic beasts ranging among a gaudy flora. Pillars of stone or columns of timber, shrewdly carved, support the roof, while there will be besides much deft woodwork in the form of railings and little gates. Within is a cavern filled with dirt below and smoke above, relieved fitfully by structures in gilt, tinsel, and meretricious lacquer. In one corner, probably, a cheap European lamp will be hanging before an idol who looks red, stupid, and bored.

To the temple which was medically inclined—it was the temple of Cho-Sing—I saw many come in search of relief and comfort for themselves or for others. The ritual appeared to be as follows:—The devotee first of all lit a joss stick and stuck it erect in a pot of sand by the shrine. He then burnt some joss paper before the idol. This worthless paper with its dab of silver paint on it is supposed to represent money. The money, in the act of burning, passes away to those poor spirits who bring death and disease to men, but who may be propitiated by a timely bribe. The compliment thus paid to the powers of the Universe is not high, but there is a kindred mercenary taint in other faiths. The devotee then prostrated himself before the image.

In this temple, I believe, the prayer is ever the same—a prayer in the words of Christian litany—"that it may please thee to succour, help, and comfort all that are in danger, necessity, and tribulation."

One poor woman I watched, whose distress was piteous to see. She planted many joss sticks in the sand, but her hands trembled so that she could hardly light them. She burnt paper with distressful recklessness, and the red flare fell savagely upon her drawn features and her streaming eyes. She then fell before the uncouth idol in a paroxysm of misery, her knees on the stones among the dirt, the ruin of joss sticks, and the fragments of red paper in which they were wrapped.

I imagine she was a woman from a sampan—one of those cheery, lithe gondoliers who rock their boats to and fro across the

Pearl River. In the cabin of the sampan one could picture the dying child on a mat, with its baby pigtail, with its almond-shaped eyes almost closed, with a strange tint creeping over its yellow skin, and the flies of the river beginning to settle on its face. Whatever may have been the true cause of the poor woman's anguish, it needed little to tell that the scene in the dismal temple was a fearful presentation of the tragedy of the Forlorn Hope.

In this same temple is provided another means of obtaining relief from disease which is much more worldly. The sick man, or his friend, after suitable devotions, dips his hand into a bowl and draws out a number. Near by the bowl is a row of papers in bundles, the series being methodically numbered. The invalid extracts a paper from beneath the figure which corresponds to that he has drawn. This document is a medical prescription, which he presents at a drug counter in the temple, where it is duly "dispensed." Having obtained the physic the sick man swallows it with the conviction that he has found a sure remedy. By this simple process—which differs in no essential from that known as "the penny-in-the-slot method," the victim of disease obtains a potential diagnosis and a prompt treatment.

This is a practical development of the faith cure, with the additional feature that the physic is hurled against the malady by a bow drawn at a venture.

In one of the dull alleys of Canton can now and then be seen a woful illustration of the truth that "faith is the substance of things hoped for." A miserable mother, dazed by grief, may step out from her desolated house and wave a child's jacket in the air, looking all the time skywards with intense eagerness, as if she watched for something to come. Her child is dead. Before it died it became unconscious, and it is her belief that while the child was insensible its spirit wandered away and has been lost in the lanes of the city. She waves the jacket so that the soul of the child might see it and be coaxed back to it again, and the fond mother thinks that she may still take a warm, tired baby into her arms and carry it back to its home. As she stands in the street, with a wistful light in her eyes, she croons a kind of cradle song that the child would know.

The jacket is new and very bright in colour, for it was made months ago for the little thing to wear when the New Year came. It had been so pleased to look upon the coat, even when it was lying ill! Now the New Year has come, but the child has wandered away.

VIII.

THE UPHOLDING OF THE LAW.

A week or so before we reached Canton a man had been strangled to death on the quay by the upholders of the law for a robbery committed on a steamer. He was brought to die at the scene of his crime. Those who landed at Canton for the first time on the day of this event must be haunted by this "street scene" in the nightmare city. The man is suspended in a pyramidal framework of wood. On the summit of this is a horizontal board with a hole in it, just large enough to take his neck. His toes barely touch the ground, so he hangs by his head. Death comes slowly to those who find themselves in the grip of this fiendish trap. They may live a day or more, I was told.

The man who came to his end on the quay in this wise could see from the height to which his strained neck was lifted the Pearl River and the sampans skimming to and fro with light-hearted indifference. He would, no doubt, catch sight of one he knew now and then. He could see the crowd of stokers and seamen leaning over the rail of the steamer alongside, watching him die while they smoked; and the string of coolies, tramping to and fro, unloading the ship. He could see the gaping crowd about him, the man with the savage's insane glare of cruelty in his eye, the pitying woman, the half-weary friend, the curious boy, munching a handful of nuts. He would look until the blood burst into his cracking eyeballs and made all red, and in this whirling eddy of crimson his soul would pass from out of the company of men.

The identical instrument of death can be seen outside the common gaol, and shopkeepers who sell souvenirs to tourists sell photographs of men with black, bloated faces dying in the embrace of this machine.

There are other forms of torture sanctioned by the law, either for the purpose of extracting a confession or of inflicting punishment. They vary from mere flogging, or kneeling with bare knees on chains, to suspension by means of the thumbs or fingers, the crushing of the ankles between boards, and other less lenient processes.

Capital punishment is carried into effect by means of rapid throttling with a rope and pole, by slicing the victim to death slowly with a knife, or by the merciful process of hacking off his head with a sword. There is so little open space in Canton that the executions are performed in a potter's yard—a little muddy gap in the midst of the straightened lanes of the city. On one side is the potter's cottage; on two sides are low grey walls; while at the fourth end is an alley of shops filled with the usual pressing crowd. Men are busy in the yard moulding coarse bowls and clay stoves. They make a few less on the mornings when the upholders of the law march into the place with a criminal or two.

The victim has his hands tied behind his back. He kneels facing a blank wall, where are some rows of pots put out to dry, and his head is cut off by an expert coolie. If any blood spurts upon the potter's goods it is easily rubbed off. Children like to play in this place, because it is open, and the potters are interesting folk to watch. In a photograph of an actual execution, the faces of pigtailed children are to be seen in the gaps between the apathetic row of clay stoves. They appear to be watching the man of the sword with great admiration.

The crowd, the potter's handiwork, and the children are all human enough, but there is a presentiment of the terrible about that bare grey wall, grim and pitiless, upon which the eyes of so many have looked their last.

The common prison of Canton is a woful place. There is a cavernous guardroom, dark and smoke-stained, where, amid the fumes of cooking-pots and tobacco, gaolers are squatting playing at cards. A sombre passage, jangling with keys, leads to a grating of iron which looks into a court. Here are the prisoners, huddled like beasts. The court is a mere grimy yard, a bear pit, a sty. The prisoners crowd to the grating, hold on nervously to the ironwork with filthy hands, thrust grinning yellow faces through the bars—a company of human wolves—with among them the bland, smiling countenance of the idiot, and the frowning brow of the insane. Here and there are a few pleasant-looking people, and one wonders how they have found themselves in this hellish pen.

The fate of these trapped wretches is hideous to think upon. The torture instruments are just without, while the execution yard is but a little way off. Which of these jabbering men will have his voice silenced and his neck crushed by a cord twisted with a pole? How many of these thumbs, which grip the bars, will serve to swing their owners by, and how many of these almond-shaped eyes will close upon the dreary grey wall in the potter's field?

In the daytime the endless alleys of Canton fill the wayfarer with a disquieting sense of insecurity, which could only be abolished by meeting a London policeman, in full uniform, strolling along the lane. At night the feeling of helplessness may deepen into actual dread. The shops are barricaded, as if to anticipate the roaring past of a rioting mob. The fronts of many houses are closed in by mats. There are voices behind some of these, and faint lights. Possibly they hide a group around the family meal, or a solitary man counting the earnings of the day. The fearsome mind, however, would picture, behind the screen, men plotting murder, or the crouching figure of a robber in ambush.

The lanes at night are strangely deserted. The noisome air is drugged into a deathly quiet. Many who go by are shoeless, and the scuffle of naked feet upon the stones makes little more sound than the rustle of a snake. The passages are dark, for there are no street lamps. To look down one of these alleys is to look along a black, deep trench. Here and there a little streak of light from some sepulchral interior falls across the way. A few of the loiterers in the street carry lanterns, which serve only to throw fantastic shadows on the walls. Those without lanterns are mere black, slinking shades, formless and well-nigh invisible.

The signboards which hang overhead are dun and ominous, like banners in the vault of a catacomb. Wherever the stranger wanders there is always the long black lane, the red specks of moving lanterns, the groping shadows, the dangling boards.

It is pleasant to come upon a house of lamps, which flood the little lane with light, so that those who step from the gloom into the glare change from spectres into common men. Such a house will be a gambling place, where the game of Fantan can be watched. It is quiet but for the rattle of counters and the tinkle of scooped-in coin. The faces of those who crowd round the table are more agreeable to look upon than is the ring of eyes at the roulette tables at Monte Carlo. A Chinaman is a born gambler. He gambles steadily, without either excitement or feverish paroxysm.

In any one of the haunted lanes the wanderer may come across a band of men—four or five in number—tramping along with some show of hurry. They slouch on their way untidily. Their slovenly heads are bare, while their dirty red tunics are emblazoned with a circular white badge on chest and back. From each man's wrist a revolver is dangling, and with the company is a rogue with a drum, upon which he beats at times, as if to the unheard music of some evil march. This is the city guard patrolling the town.

At occasional points in the lane are iron gates to be slammed when there is a rising in the place. The closing of certain of these barriers will shut in a section of the city, and so limit the spread of riot. For some reason, neither the upholders of the law nor the iron bars inspire much confidence. A memory of the gaol engenders the suspicion that the tender mercies of the city guard may be cruel, while the gates, with their clanking locks, induce only terror of the prospect of being locked within a maze in purgatory.

Out of a vague doorway there will now and then stagger a gaunt man. When a light falls upon his face his eyes are seen to be glaring, his amber cheeks are flushed, and a fearful smile hangs about his mouth. He draws in a breath of the stinking air of the lane as if it were a March breeze on a moor. He has reeled forth from an opium den, starving and penniless. He is going home to sleep, but his bed will be the garbage of a ditch. For the moment he is in a celestial city, strange lights flash in the causeway, stirring sounds break upon his ear, he is happy, he has fared well, money is dross, and fit only to be flung to the sneaking shades which pass him by and elude his reeling steps. The filthy pavement is of gold, and the dead banners that swing above him in the dark are hung with stars.

The light of the dawn finds him on a mud bank, wet and cold, empty and racked with nameless pains. The brilliant city has vanished, the mist that clings about him is peopled with gibing things of horror. He is haunted by terrors worse than those of death. During his stertorous dream a rat has nibbled at his hand, but the man must crawl away to the quay to work. If he is strong enough to carry bags of rice he can earn a coin or two, and after sundown he can buy peace, and find himself once more in the valiant city of stars.

IX.

THE MAN OF THE WORLD.

The population of China is said to be four hundred millions. An ingenious person has estimated that if a man stood by a roadside and watched the whole of the people of China walk past him, at the rate of one individual per second, more than twelve years would elapse before the last member of the procession went by.

The visitor to China is likely to make early enquiry from prominent European residents in the matter of the "Yellow Peril." It will be with some little disappointment that he learns that the "Yellow Peril" does not exist. The Chinese have no desire to spread themselves over foreign lands in devastating hordes like the Goths and the Huns. They are fired by no desire for conquest, nor for new territory. The wish dearest to their hearts is to be left alone. The cry of the people is "China for the Chinese," and the extreme bitterness of this cry has led from time to time to trouble, in the form of risings, riots, and indiscriminate murder. On each of these occasions the Chinese worm has turned, and turned unpleasantly.

The mass of the people are ignorant, superstitious, and credulous as children. They find the foreigner mysterious and uncanny. He frightens them, and his ways fill them with alarm. They are distrustful of his ships, which move against wind and tide, of the dreadful things he does with steam, and the terrifying things he does with wires. They call him a devil, for his ways are not of this world. He will run a cutting through a graveyard, will store his goods in a pagoda, and will appear neither to fear idols nor regard his ancestors, and yet he does not fall dead. He is unnatural and unearthly, his face and his clothes are utterly strange, while his habits are unpleasant. Few know whence he comes. He is pushing, insistent, and, at times, violent. They are terrified to think what he may do next, and they want him to go away.

If a horrible stag beetle of the tropics were to crawl on to the white hand of an English child it could scarcely cause more alarm and uneasiness than does the foreigner who drops down into an unsophisticated part of China with an eye to business. The child's instinct would be to knock the awful thing off, and that is the impulse of the Chinaman.

The Boxer rising was an outcome of this impulse. It was due to the working of a secret guild, with a name which is, in literal English, "The Harmonious Fist Society," by which was implied an organisation of men banded together to obtain freedom from the foreigner by force. The motive was honourable and patriotic; the method of application was faulty, and worse.

The prayer of the Chinese is for peace, not for power to run riot over the earth; for remunerative work, and not for the privilege of filling the dramatic part of a Peril, yellow or otherwise.

The average Chinaman has no ambition as the Western mind understands the term. He wants to be comfortable in his own station, to have sons who will revere his memory, watch over his grave, and attend to his needs in the other world. The wish nearest his heart is to be buried well. He has little desire to open up the country, to develop waste lands, to worry over public works, or to be for ever grubbing the earth for minerals. As a trader he is a man of wondrous parts, but he has no leanings towards big ventures, "booms," or the making of "corners." He has no initiative, and small sense of the lack of that quality. By nature he is a conservative of so old a school that he would rather be fossilised than take upon himself anything that is new.

Unfortunately for the home-loving Chinese, the "Flowery Land" cannot comfortably support four hundred millions of people. Thus it is that, year by year, thousands are turned forth into the wide world to shift for themselves. Those who have seen even a little of the emigrants, on the one hand, and of the Chinese at home on the other, must feel that they have come upon a remarkable race, upon a mysterious people, full of unfathomed forces and of the strangest incongruities.

The Chinese are by nature kindly, affectionate, and docile, yet when the firebrand of riot glares over the city, they are yelling, maniacal demons, monsters of murder, arson, and rapine. I have watched, in a garden in Burmah, a Chinaman who was nurse to a little fractious English girl. That he was trusted absolutely was evident, while his gentleness, his patience, his much tried forbearance were wonderful to see. Yet take this very man back to the slums of Canton whence he came, strip him, and turn him into a coolie again, touch some spot on his brain with a spark that is just aglow in the town, and he changes into a devil, venomous with treachery, and fevered with the most fiendish cruelty.

Conservative as the Chinaman is, he is quick to learn, and can adapt himself to any position he comes upon. He soon develops into an experienced mechanic, and an adept at any European industry. He may burn joss sticks before a daubed and dirty idol in a secret corner of the stoke-hole, but he is nevertheless a first-class electrical fitter. His face and his clothing may be strange, and he may eat weird food with chop-sticks, but he can work a pianola in a Californian drinking saloon better than any in the district.

He can stand all climates. He can go anywhere, and he does. Whatever land he reaches he there makes himself serenely at home, dropping into the life of the place as if he had been born to it. He will be found mining along the Yukon, working on the wharf at Cape Town, cooking on a steamer down the Irrawaddy, taking in sewing in San Francisco, running a laundry in the Sandwich Islands, driving a smart victoria at Bombay, or keeping a tailor's shop in Borneo. Wherever he is, he settles down like a philosopher, and whatever his surroundings may be he will be genial and contented.

The Chinaman, indeed, is the Man of the World, or has at least a better claim to that title than any other of the many peoples of the earth. Nothing comes amiss to him, and so easily and amiably does he mingle with any tide that he drifts into on his voyaging that he seems never out of place.

He is an excellent servant, obedient, shrewd, polite; an excellent manager, quick and trustworthy. He is always busy, always ready, and strangely uncomplaining. Bret Harte did the native of China an injustice in his vivid rhyme of the "Heathen Chinee"; for there are many, possibly, who base their conception of the

Chinaman's integrity upon that famous ballad. The world has not yet produced a people who can resist the temptation of occasionally cheating at cards. The Chinaman has, however, no exclusive claim to this particular weakness. The average Chinese man of business is rigidly honourable, his word is as good as his bond, while he shirks no obligation he has incurred. Throughout the East the cashiers of the banks are nearly always natives of China. The shroff, or detector of base coin, is a Chinaman, and so, as a rule, is the comprador, or merchant's agent.

Before leaving the topic of the relation of the Chinaman to other men, it is impossible to avoid notice of one factor which is at work among the foundations of the land, and that is the almost imperceptible invasion of the country by Japan. To the Chinaman the native of Japan is hardly a foreigner. The two peoples both came originally from the same Mongolian stock. For centuries they have been intimately associated, both in the paths of peace and in the clamours of war. In all prominent arts and industries Japan has learned at the feet of China, so that the influence of the great continent has left a mark for ever upon the genius of the islanders. The two peoples are alike in aspect, in costume, in their methods of living and eating, and, above all, in the elements of their religions. Ancestor worship is the basis of all moral and devotional life in China, and, in spite of modern changes on the surface, it holds deep down a kindred position in Japan. The Japanese may not be much in evidence in the busy marts of China, but they are to be found in a more important quarter, in the schools and colleges, and notably in the naval and military academies. The Western foreigner has made his way into China by force of arms. The Eastern foreigner is growing gently into the country, is growing up with the country, and is busy with the springs of its national life. The Japanese invader has crept in almost unobserved, has mingled with the crowd, and in the crowd he is for the moment lost. The European visitor is still the armed man who has landed noisily out of a boat, has built his strange shanty on the beach, and declines to leave.

The Man of the World, when he is seen in large quantity, in his own country and in the busier streets of his towns, is a little monotonous. There is a remarkable sameness about him as well as about his womankind. The colours of his clothes are blue and black, while the colour of his face is that of a new potato. The crowd that encircles the race course at Hong Kong, for example, looks like a wreath of blue and black with dots of yellow, lying on the wide green.

To wear a blue jacket and stiff trousers of shiny black cotton is to be smart; and as the men are, so are the women, save that their jackets are larger and longer. The men, being often thin and lanky, have a little the look of mechanical dolls, so that one would not be surprised to find that their legs were made of wire. Their garments have the severe simplicity peculiar to the cheap toy which is made by the thousand from the same mould.

Those women who have the tiny foot, which is so great a feature in female loveliness, are still more like mechanical figures; for they have precisely the gait of a clockwork man, and the peculiar stilted lameness of the puppet of watch spring and wheels. When the tiny-footed lady reaches a dirty road, her maid or amah lifts her up, and carries her on her ample back across the mire. In this passage she has precisely the aspect of a helpless automaton whose works have failed, or whose key has been lost, or of a model which is being carried home in triumph from an exhibition. The amah may smile, but not her mistress, who preserves on her decorous face, during the process of transfer, the vacant calm of a wax figure.

To make the resemblance to a mechanical toy more complete, the Chinese woman pastes her black and glossy hair flat against her skull, so that it resembles the cap of rich paint on the head of a Dutch doll. More than that, she whitens her face with so little skill that her cheeks and forehead appear to be made of papier mâché.

There is a strong suggestion that the resemblance of a Chinese lady to an automaton is not quite accidental. I infer that to appear helpless is a sign of gentility, while possibly it is an expression of female charm. Not only do the crumpled feet prevent her from walking and the whitened face make it impolitic to smile, but the sleeves of her jacket are so long as to extend half a yard beyond her hands, of the use of which she is thus deprived. The Chinaman may yield to the fascination of utter uselessness in his adored, and, if he has many wives, he may fill his house with the sentiment of a cripples' home, but he will not convince the rest of the world that a woman who can use her hands and her feet has thereby lost all enchantment.

I imagine that no more dire or lamentable spectacle could be presented to a Chinese woman than that of an English girl playing lawn tennis, with a smile on her face and her hair " coming down."

The women with small feet who are met with in the ways of the city belong, for the most part, to the tradesman class. The lady of high birth is seldom to be seen. She lives in seclusion, and when she ventures forth she is hurried along in a sedan chair.

When the Oriental does devote himself to the question of colour in dress he exhibits little restraint. The man of high degree will adopt *en masse* all the tints of an Egyptian sunset, all the glitter of a bird of paradise. The young girl—arrayed for a festa—will be in the fashion if she wears a mauve tunic, under a large blue collar, and bright green trousers edged with a band of black like a mourning envelope. She will whiten her face to the utmost. Her hair she will twist into a sticky black knob over her right ear, and then cover the protuberance with artificial flowers, pins, and tinsel ornaments. Like the man, she dallies with no half measures.

The dull, yellow face of the native of China has remarkable capacities for expression, both positive and negative. No one can look so utterly expressionless as a Chinaman, nor can any assume an aspect of more bland vacuity. On the other hand, he can smile like a negro, and scowl like a stage villain. His children are more childlike than any, and none can rival the solemnity of his solemn men. No balloon-chested Guardsman can swagger like a Chinaman, while those who seek the supremest expression of smug dignity and patronising pompousness, must seek for it among such Chinese traders as have become both prosperous and fat.

The Chinese woman is never beautiful, but she can yield to no female in the world in her capacity for expressing the state of being coy.

A STREET IN SHANGHAI.

X.

SHANGHAI.

On the way from Hong Kong to Japan the ship sailed into a yellow sea among many bare and miserly islands which shuddered under a cold, sunless, and forbidding sky. For the first time there was a suggestion of winter in the world, and on the way up the chilled river to Shanghai it was noticed, with some relief, that the everlasting palm had vanished, and that trees were to be seen which were bare of leaves, and had thereby come more in touch with human sympathies.

Shanghai is a Chinese town which has been Europeanised, or which, rather, has grown up under a strict European eye. There is a fine promenade along the Bund with grass lawns and public gardens, a red clock tower, and a cab stand, quite on the lines of the self-respecting English town. We landed on a Sunday morning, when steeple bells were ringing, and the English colony was going stiffly to church. The fine streets of the city were filled by a great concourse of people who constitute, probably, the most cosmopolitan crowd in the world. The majority were Chinese, but they were leavened by the folk of every country in Europe—Russians, Germans, Italians, and French—by natives of India, Burmah, and Ceylon, as well as by men from Manchuria and Korea, by Japanese, and an occasional African negro. Like a pharos in the tide, in the English quarter, stood a London policeman dressed in the familiar uniform of Piccadilly.

In addition to the inevitable rickshaw were many smart carriages driven by Chinamen in old-world European liveries, who had absorbed with their uniform all the stiff-necked immobility of the family coachman. The cab of Shanghai is a wheelbarrow. It is a structure with one huge wheel in the centre, and a seat on either side of the same. The passenger from the quay will place himself upon one ledge of this modified jaunting car, and his luggage on the other. The wheelbarrow is more commodious than a London hansom. It will accommodate a man and his wife and a couple of children. On one barrow we met with were four elaborately dressed women and two children—a load for an omnibus—but the whole company were trundled along by a solitary man.

The roads are well kept. There are stone pavements on either side of the way, street lamps, electric lights, and a general air of order and decorum.

The chief streets of the town are exceedingly brilliant. The roofs of the houses are covered by gay tiles which are broken in upon by many gables—like cocked hats—resplendent in colour. The fronts of the shops are as bright as lacquer and gold can make them. They are tattooed with the strange hieroglyphics of the country, and are relieved from monotony by verandahs of carved wood, by hanging signs of every tint of the rainbow, by red lanterns, and much emblazoned symbols. A smell of incense fills the air, as well as of spices and of odorous woods, which is entirely consistent with a street made up of houses like lacquered cabinets.

There is little that is reminiscent of the slimy lanes of Canton or of the stench which creeps from out of its dull slums. There is the knowledge, too, that the hand of Europe has turned the executioner's sword into a ploughshare, has swept away the torture chamber, and has fixed its grip upon the demons of cruelty and lawlessness. The white man in Shanghai is not stared at as if he had dropped from black clouds, nor is it impressed upon him that he is both a foreigner and a devil.

Prominent pagodas are dispensed with in Shanghai, while temples do not flaunt themselves abroad. There are slums, of course, and mean streets, but they exhibit a becoming restraint in their nastiness; while whatever there may be that is vile lurks nervously in unsearchable shadows.

China, as seen at Shanghai, is an agreeable country. It is a China which has been amended after the manner of an Anglicised French farce. Those who would study China and its people at Shanghai must remember that they have before them a Bowdlerised version, an edition de luxe suited for the European reader, or even for the young.

A SHANGHAI WHEELBARROW.

Part V

JAPAN

I.

THE FIRST SIGHT OF JAPAN.

It was in the passage from Shanghai to the coast of Japan that we came nearest to the seat of war. There were great expectations among the more sanguine of the passengers, but we fell neither upon battle-ships nor upon sounds of battle. On approaching Japan the steamer slowed down, in order to enter Nagasaki harbour by daylight, for the entrance was mined. When we reached the port we crept in timorously at the heels of a little fussy steam tug sent off from the guard ship.

It was a brilliant morning, crisp and clear, and the first sight of Japan was afforded as the ship sailed into the mouth of a long sinuous inlet among low hills. This was the seaward end of that green fiord, whose far away point is buried among the brown houses of Nagasaki. Precipitous cliffs climbed out of the blue water, on the summits of which were rolling downs with many pine trees. If the country were more verdant and better wooded, this beautiful sea entrance might have been an estuary in England.

As the vessel glided up the long channel, we fell in with certain small islands made up of nothing more than a grey cliff, rising sheer from the sea, a crest of stiff grass, and one or two contorted pine trees on the tiny sky line. These were the islands of the Japanese screen and of the kakemono; while the trees were matsu, growing as the Japanese love them to grow, and as they train their dwarf trees in pots. A little further on was a lad sculling a sampan with all the squat spread-out vigour which is common to the man of action in Japanese drawings. His arms and legs together made a kind of X. His bare head was covered by short cropped hair, his brow was wrinkled, and he wore a monkish garment with wide sleeves. He also—like the small island—was very familiar, and by the sign of these two it was evident that we had come upon Japan.

Nagasaki—as seen from the inlet—is as dull a town as the mind could imagine. At a distance it is merely a disorderly crowd of sepia roofs on a slope, like the backs of a herd of brown swine running violently down a steep place into the sea.

The first impression of the place is one of utter dinginess. Ashore is a long quay with European houses, banks and offices, a forest of telegraph poles, electric light standards, and a few dull factory chimneys. The first individuals fallen in with on landing are French-looking policemen with white gloves, together with a crowd of rickshaw coolies bawling in rickshaw English. These latter wear white hats shaped like mushrooms or basins, with blue jackets and tights. On the back of the jacket, near the neck, is a square white tablet with strange letters upon it. On their feet are sandals. They seem to be more the men of the country than the little gendarmes.

On the road between the quay and the town it is possible to come upon the Japanese peasant. He also is clad in a jacket of deep blue and in tights of the same colour. On his head is a white handkerchief. He looks like a mediæval retainer, or he may be one of the crowd of varlets and villeins from the stage of an ancient play. He leads a bullock, on whose feet are straw slippers. In a little time there must come along a Japanese woman—one of the women of the fans—with elaborately fashioned black hair and a kimono of silver grey, with glimpses of a red lining in the sleeve. She and the peasant will fulfil the assurance that the country is really Japan.

Yet it is not the Japan that was imagined. The first impressions of the wonderful island and its people are very disappointing. So much was expected. It may be supposed, however, that expectations based upon fans and screens and the literature of romance are not likely to be satisfactorily realised. Those who are familiar with the artistic temperament of the people,

JAPANESE HOUSE AND MATSU TREE.

and with choice specimens of their art, are discouraged to find the streets flaring with vulgar advertisements, and the shops full of tawdry wares. With this spectacle vanishes the belief that the Japanese could never be inartistic.

Those who only know of Japan as the land of the tea house and the Geisha, as the country of brilliant silks and quaint costumes, will be vexed to find the towns so dull and the dresses of the people duller still. The kimonos of the men and women, who are encountered in the street, are in sombre blues, drabs, browns and greys. It is the dancing girl who dresses in crimson, in green and in sapphire blue, and who has gilt dragons on her gown and red peonies on her sash. There is little doubt that to many the representative of the race is this same dancing girl, and all such will be disappointed not to see a town of tea houses, whose streets are crowded with Geishas, and are brilliant with the florid colours of the comic opera. To those with such hopes it will be a shock to find that the Japanese woman, met with in the ways of the town, is very plain, and that the man (it may be added) is apparently very obtuse.

Japan, like other countries, does not wear the heart of its sentiment upon its sleeve, nor does it present to the casual eye a formal display of its characteristics. Any native of Japan, who has read much of England and English ways, may be dissatisfied, when he lands at Southampton, not to see at once the ruins of a Norman Keep, not to meet the counterpart of Mr. Pickwick or of Dolly Varden, and not to find upon the wharf, in front of an old hostelry, the "plump head waiter of the Cock."

Nagasaki is the Portsmouth of Japan, and those who are chagrined by their first sight of its streets and its people must remember how little just it would be if the looks of the English girl were to be judged by the first half dozen factory hands met with in a seaport town, or if the intelligence of the British race were to be gauged by the face of the first dock labourer on the quay. It would be as reasonable to estimate the influence of Shakespeare and Turner on national taste by the study of a row of riverside shops at Liverpool.

In a little while—in the matter indeed of a few weeks—the charm of Japan takes possession of whatever stranger finds his way within its gates. The first thing that delights him, in the first town he enters, is neither the houses nor the shops, but the children. They are the children he has learned to know by a hundred sketches and photographs, and in whom he sees the living ideal of the famous Japanese doll. They toddle along dressed in the brilliant colours of toys. On their shaved heads is the same circle of hair the dolls affect—a thing like a mat made all of fringe—while they have the same brown lacquer eyes.

Then there are the dainty houses with their paper walls, the primrose-coloured mats, the niche with the single flower in its pot of blue china. About the outskirts of the town is a monastery close, shut in by solemn pines, in whose shade stands the grey stone lantern, while in every little thorpe and through every garden door will be a glimpse of the cherry blossom. In the air is the monotonous boom of the temple gong, the sound of clogs that clatter on the temple steps, and the murmur of exquisite human voices. There is in all this the delight which attends the incarnation of old impressions, the coming to life of old pictures, the actual realisation of scenes which have been long imagined.

There is such charm, too, as follows upon contrast. India with its melancholy, its vastness, and its tragedies is changed for an island with little hills and downs, little cliffs and bays, peopled by little folk who are cheerful and dignified, and who spend their days in cultured simplicity. The wild, reckless vegetation of the tropics is changed for trim trees, for the miniature garden, for the well tended and elaborate orchard. The wanton, luxurious palm has given way to the ascetic pine, while the reeking alleys of China have faded into pretty wynds, where plum blossoms hang over white walls.

II.

THE INLAND SEA AND CERTAIN TOWNS.

It is probable that the visitor to Japan will not disembark at Nagasaki, but will travel by the Inland Sea to Kobe, and thence to Kyoto, Yokohama, or Tokyo. The voyage from Nagasaki to Kobe is 387 miles, the greater part of which distance is occupied by the passage of the Inland Sea.

The western entrance to this sea is through the Straits of Shimonoseki, which are some fifteen miles in length, and which wind through the hills like an eel. It was at 5.30 in the morning—while it was yet quite dark—that this waterway was approached. The dawn broke over the ship's bow, and in a while the silhouette of a ragged coast stood up against the rose-tinted sky like a black saw edge. For this dark bank we steered, and by the time the daylight came we were off the island of Rokuren, which guards the Straits.

From out of the channel there rushed a roaring tide, which made eddies of domed water and hissing whirlpools, as if the spirits of the sea were dancing in mad circles.

Then came a track of blue—like a flooded mountain pass—among low hills with yellow cliffs, by valleys and gorges, and by ruddy hillocks which came to be islands. Twenty times it seemed as if the passage were blocked by a precipice, but the ship swung round, and the blue Straits shone ahead again. Sloping down to the brink of this great sea river were mountain sides covered with pines, or bare of all but rocks, so that the colours upon them changed many times from deep green to rose brown. We glided by many capes and creeks, by coves with beaches of pearl-grey pebbles, by doddering villages hanging over the sea on tottering posts, by harbours full of junks and long sea walls.

There were islands in hundreds, some rocky and savage, some

moss covered and meadow like. Most beautiful of these was a boy and girl's island. It was no longer and no loftier than the steamer, yet on it were three small hills covered with fir trees. In one mimic valley was a tiny temple, devoutly red, and, where the valley opened to the sea, stretched a bay of white sand with a small path that wound across the grass from the beach to the shrine. At one end of this island were frowning, brick-coloured cliffs, as if the little place had the pretensions of Gibraltar, and a rock-girt harbour which suggested that it encouraged commerce and possessed a safe haven for ships from over the seas.

The Inland Sea itself is 250 miles in length, while its width varies from eight miles to forty. In it are a thousand islands of every possible size and shape, from an eyot of biscuit-coloured boulders to a land of woods and forests and cultivated fields. The sea is blue; a porpoise will now and then leap out into the sun; and following seagulls ever make circles about the ship. The coast is a coast of low hills, deep inlets and verdant capes which change their outlines so unceasingly that there is scarcely a phase of mountain, headland, or bay that does not come into view before the day is done.

The beauty of the Inland Sea has been much exaggerated. Its prettiness is monotonous, and has the effect of a popular tune which is played over and over again until it becomes wearisome. It cannot compare with the west coast of Scotland, nor with the passage northwards from Stavanger to Bergen, nor with such a majestic fiord as that which leads from the Adriatic, far inland, to Cattaro.

Kobe is a town which maintains an aspect of cheerfulness in spite of its being neither beautiful nor interesting. An unpicturesque middle age is the characteristic of Kobe. There is, on the side towards the sea, a large Western town which might have been transported bodily from America—streets, sidewalks, banks and hotels. The Japanese quarter has been marred by what is regarded by some as civilisation. In the main streets are still the Japanese houses, but they have been, for the most part, hopelessly defaced by the introduction of plate glass shop fronts, which are as fitting as a Paris *toque* on the head of a statue of Artemis. At the back of Kobe are delightful hills and downs, but like everything else in Japan, they are by comparison little.

Yokohama—the most important port in Japan—has a population of 193,000. In 1854 it was an insignificant fishing village.

Those who make their first acquaintance with Japan at Yokohama can scarcely fail to look around them, when they land, with eyes filled with disappointment. To go ashore in a steam launch, and step out upon a great black pier embodies no novelty. Along the sea wall stretches a European town, clean and open, with an orthodox church, appropriate hotels, club houses and banks. At one end of the Bund, or Marine Parade, is a well-wooded hill—" the Bluff "—dotted over with the villas of Torquay and Atlantic City. A sorry crowd of Japanese men in Western dress hang about the pier end; and until the enquiring gaze has alighted upon a rickshaw coolie, or upon one or two women in kimonos, there is no promise that this quite charming seaside town is in Japan.

The Japanese city lies inland, but the streets of it show a sad falling away from the homely brown lanes of Kyoto, the street on the hill at Nara, or the one long road of Nikko. The thoroughfares of Yokohama are a compromise between the Far East and the Recent West, and they are creditable to neither of them. At first sight it would appear that the only thing the natty, artistic native of Japan has absorbed from Western civilisation is its dirtiness, its untidiness, and its vulgarity. In the noisy, blatant Theatre Street, with its flags and placards, its tinsel decorations and its gramophones, there is little that is in tune with the gentleness and the quiet of the Japanese people.

Those who stay long in Yokohama would do well to live in the pleasant European quarter, and try to forget that they are in Japan.

Early in May in each year there is a great popular festival in honour of the boys. The exemplar that is held before the boy, as worthy of his ambitious imitation, is the carp. The carp is strong, he is undaunted, he makes his way up stream in spite of all obstacles and all difficulties. If the torrent be fierce he will fight with it; if there be rocks in the way he will leap over them. Thus it is that about the fifth of May the sky all over Yokohama and the villages around is alive with fish. Fish flying from poles like flags, and fish, too, of no mean kind, for many of them are ten or fifteen feet in length.

They are made of paper or cotton, and are all most brilliantly painted. As they are hollow, and as their mouths are wide open, the wind fills them and makes them flap their tails and their fins and struggle gallantly. Their movements are indeed strangely realistic. There is some ferocity about the gaping mouth and about the great eyes, made of discs of silver paper, while their scales, whether they be blue or yellow or red, have the look of armour plate. These great fish twist and roll and wriggle in the blue sky, ever battling against the strong stream of the May wind. Never do they turn round and float away lazily with the current. They can be seen at night, still struggling up stream, over the house tops; while the early sun falls upon an ever-moving shoal of stout backs, white bellies and gleaming eyes. Over some houses there are as many as four fish dangling from one pole, in graduated sizes, and it may be supposed that the large carp at the top is the big boy of the family, and that the small one at the bottom is the baby.

Only the well-to-do can afford to have calico fish fifteen feet in length floating over their houses. The poor must needs be content with paper fish of less stately proportions. The most meagre fish I saw was over a squalid hut in the outskirts of the town. It was of paper, of course, but its colouring was very faint. It lacked the bold silver eye and the heroic scales. Moreover, the seam along its back had become unstuck so that it looked very wasted and flat. A breeze had sprung up, and the mother—a mere ugly girl—had come out of the hut to see how bravely her boy's fish could swim. She held the baby up to see the fish, and chattered with delight as the poor thin rag fluttered at its pole.

The boy seemed hardly to notice it, and when I drew nearer I saw that the little thing was blind.

III.

THE CAPITAL OF OLD JAPAN.

As a type of a Japanese town it would be well to select Kyoto, because it is an ancient city full of old temples and monasteries and because it has played a romantic part in the history of the country. For many centuries the Palace of the Mikado has stood within its confines, and for as long a time the roads leading into the city were apt to see many regal and noble processions winding into the dim streets of the capital. Kyoto, moreover, is not a progressive town. Its population is declining, and it is pre-eminently the metropolis of old Japan. It has not become Westernised, for its people cling to the houses of their forefathers and to the costumes of bygone days. A native woman in the attire of Europe will not be seen in its pleasant lanes, and such men as have discarded sandals and kimonos belong to the official classes.

Kyoto lies in a dead plain surrounded by a ring of hills which opens only to the south, as if to make a way to the sea. There are many dips and valleys in these hills, while on those slopes which lie to the east there are luxuriant trees. It is at the foot to the eastern hills that the city is stretched.

From among the pines on the sunset-facing slope is the most pleasant view of the town. It is a wide city of pewter-grey roofs, jumbled together about the same dull level, as if it were a pond grown over with stiff grey leaves which had been tilted by the wind at many angles. Rising above the surface is the mighty roof of Higashi Hongwanji, the St. Peter's of Japan. Through the drab expanse there are, here and there, flashes of the white river which runs through the town, whilst a waving line of yellow green marks an avenue of budding willows by the side of the canal. Between the dun city and the distant hills are patches of brilliant green where young corn is growing. In the foreground a few ragged matsu trees stand out from the hillside. Below them is a brown house with a garden of pebbles and little firs in its courtyard, and a steep road dropping down into the town. Cherry trees in blossom hang over the road, and there are glimpses of red lanterns by the way.

The streets of the town are straight. The roadway is of honest earth, for pavements are unknown. The houses are of two storeys, with the charm that no two of them are precisely alike. The most striking part of the house is the roof, which is made of strongly marked drab tiles vigorously rounded. The rest of the structure is fragile and subservient to the roof. It would seem as if the roof had been sketched in bold strokes by a masculine quill pen, whilst the walls and framework had been delicately drawn by the finest nib of steel. The houses are of chocolate-coloured wood, disposed in kindergarten lines. There are no windows, for the outer walls are fashioned of paper screens which admit a wan light in the winter, whilst in the summer they are thrown open to the heavens. There will be a frail balcony of wood under the solid eaves, where are cupboards for the shutters which close in the verandah at night. On the ground floor is a species of "bow window," made of lattice work and paper, which has a little the aspect of an idealised larder.

About each private house or about some part of it will be a fence of bamboo or pine, a mere quaint arrangement of lines, but always admirable in effect. The Japanese have brought the art of fence-making to perfection. The little palisade is a beautiful setting to the house, the delicacy of which can be judged by comparing it with the gawky lines of iron railings around a suburban villa in England. Many of the houses are within little courtyards, over the tiled-capped wall of which will rise a plum tree, a pine, or a tuft of bamboos. Through the gate, leading into the court, is a sight of a mimic garden made of pebbles, a few boulders, and a grass lawn six feet square. Here will be a dwarf maple in a blue vase, a grey stone lantern, or a bronze stork.

By the banks of the river, which tumbles through the town, are many tea houses. They crowd along the brink—a medley of

A STREET IN KYOTO.

glazed roofs, of brown balconies and paper windows, of wooden terraces which hang over the stream, and of steps which drop into the water. Here and there, in this long line, is a paper lantern hanging above a hidden court, while a mass of plum blossom or a Japanese willow marks the place of a tiny garden that opens on the river.

In the business part of the town are miles of streets full of shops. These shops are without either windows or doors. They are open to the causeway, like the lower storey in a doll's house, and are closed at night by shutters. Within is a low platform covered with mats on which the shopkeeper sits. Here are the lacquer boxes in which he keeps his treasures, his smoking table, his bronze brazier full of glowing charcoal, and his favourite dwarf tree in a jade-green pot.

A lane of shops displays an incongruous variety of things for sale. Here is a little *magasin* for ladies' fans. It forms a splash of colour between a shop full of bronze lanterns on one side, and a mat maker's on the other. Here will be a stall brilliant with green vegetables, and there a pastry cook's, a shop hung with clogs, a place for the sale of granite lanterns and rocks for gardens. On the opposite side of the road may be a little kiosk filled with head ornaments and curious productions in artificial hair, a shop resplendent with gilt shrines, a depôt for dwarf shrubs, or a fragrant counter for the sale of teas. Shops of a kind are apt to cluster together, so there will be a lane of curio shops, a long row of houses where ladies' finery is dispensed, and a street of carpenters, or of lacquer makers, or of workers in silk.

There is no formality in the lines of a Japanese street. The town builder knows nothing of the monotonous "terrace," with houses in a row like drilled men; of the "colonnade"; or of the geometrical "quadrant." Hanging over the road are innumerable signboards, many of them glistening with gilt; with them are paper lanterns of every size and shape, and now and then a Japanese flag to mark a recent victory. Here a balcony will lean over a lane with gaudy paper umbrellas on it which have been put out to dry, and there a cherry tree in blossom, or a matsu will stand up above the wall of a tradesman's garden. There are little restaurants on wheels in the road, as well as the barrow of the tobacco seller and of the merchant of sweets.

Each lane is thronged by bare-headed men and women in the delightful and familiar costumes of the country, by innumerable solemn children, some walking about, full of mere delight of the street, some with drums and flags playing at soldiers. A rickshaw will swing by with two smart and stately Japanese girls in it, then a blind shampooer feeling his way with a long stick, then a company of curious pilgrims in white, dazed and tired. There will be occasional tourists also, with cameras and guide books, who seem as out of place as the French modelled policeman, or the everlasting avenues of telegraph and telephone poles.

There are no carriages in Kyoto. The only vehicles are the rickshaw and the two-wheeled trolley which is dragged along indifferently by red-faced men, puffy-faced women, or oxen with straw slippers on their feet.

Ever in the lanes of a Japanese city is a sound which is pleasant to hear and which is unlikely to be forgotten; it is the clatter of clogs, "the clang of the wooden shoon." It is no mere noise, for there are a hundred musical tones in it like the notes of a flute. When the road is hard the sound is that of a shrill brook tumbling over hollow stones, where each note is echoed back by resounding rocks. To a native of Japan it must be one of the sweetest sounds in the world. To many an exile in the blaring unmusical streets of Europe, to many a soldier, tramping in unfamiliar guise across a weary country, no music could fall more divinely upon the ear than this babble of the clogs.

IV.

THE BUYING OF AN INCENSE BURNER.

Among the simpler arts which are open to the resources of the humblest is the art of shopping. There are many in the Western world who devote much time and ingenuity to this butterfly-like pursuit; but it is only in the East that the art and science of shopping has reached to heights which may be considered great or satisfying.

It is in Japan, above all other Oriental countries, that this mere phase of commerce has attained to a development which is little short of idyllic. Shopping in Japan is no mere question of sitting on a chair and turning over goods on a counter, in the presence of an unsympathetic shopman who sees no delight in uncertainty of mind and nothing but ill in infinity of leisure. It is hard to dally pleasantly with a man who is so gross that he merely wants to sell goods for lucre, and who is so lacking in the artistic sense as to talk of "fixed prices" and of things "marked in plain figures."

Bargaining in Japan recalls the limitless inactivity of the pastoral play and the speech of shepherds in an ancient eclogue. It carries one back to the mediæval market place, even if at the end there seems to be, "but one half-pennyworth of bread to an intolerable deal of sack."

Many visitors to Kyoto will need to buy some specimen of the cloisonné enamel, for which that town is famous. To satisfy this need they will make their way to the house of Namikawa, the great cloisonné maker. In this particular shopping you come upon no shop, but upon a plain Japanese dwelling in a plain street. The rickshaw deposits you in a little yard, where you remove your shoes and step at once on to the primrose-coloured mats of an exquisite room. A man in a brown kimono leads you, with many bows, through other rooms, bright with the primary colours of plain wood, and bare but for a black and gold cupboard, a bronze stork, and a single flower in a porcelain jar. At the end of a verandah which crosses a courtyard is a room looking over a garden. Here are a European table and some lodging-house chairs. Without them the room would be faultless.

Sliding paper screens open upon a little balcony, built over a pond, where are innumerable gold carp lounging through the bistre water like fish made of coral-pink lacquer. The garden is as pretty a Japanese garden as the town can show. Besides the pond is a river, also many bridges, together with paved walks in a forest of dwarf pines. There are old water basins, too, with wooden dippers in them, the familiar granite lantern, and a circle of trees, which give the impression that the garden is in a wood.

It is a fanciful little landscape, and I have no doubt that the yard long beach, at the edge of the lake, is "the Coast of the Early Dawn." The whole of the make-believe country is but little larger than the room with the lodging-house chairs.

An amused Japanese girl comes out upon the balcony and gives you rice cakes with which to feed the fish. You are joined, in due course, by an old and most courtly man with a fine ascetic face. He is thin and pale, and his dark robe gives him the aspect of a monk. He is no other than the great cloisonné maker himself. He speaks no English, but he points out certain fish as curious and joins in the feeding of them.

There are things in the garden to be seen, and time passes quickly. After a while you sit down at the obtrusive table, where now some incense is burning, and the man who led you thither brings from a cupboard a white box, out of which he draws a tiny vase of cloisonné wrapped up in a rag of lavender silk. You tell him it is not the kind of thing you want, whereupon he brings other boxes out of the cupboard, which also contain the kind of things you do not want. In time the table is covered and the incense has burnt out. One of the carp can be heard splashing in the pond, and the day is waning.

At last, from out of the twentieth box, comes the ware you have talked of. You carry it on to the balcony, over the pool, for the better seeing of its workmanship, and notice an old gardener tending the moss on a bridge. Then follows much talk about yen, together with a disquisition on the costliness of art. Finally you leave, amid infinite expressions of amiability, and promise to come the next afternoon.

The next afternoon you walk in the garden a little, watch workmen who are busy in a room as neat as a boudoir, and who only take their eyes off their work to look at the "Tree of the Setting Sun" on the "Elysian Isle." Then comes the eating of rice cakes, more talk about yen, copious bowing and smiling, to the accompaniment of which the box of cloisonné is deposited under the seat of your rickshaw. Thus is shopping elevated to a fine art.

Wishing to buy an incense burner, I took counsel with a Japanese friend on the matter. He knew a potter who made such things, but he added that the potter in question was also a poet of some note, and that the business would occupy an afternoon. It did. We went in rickshaws to the outskirts of the town, where we stopped in front of a rustic gate. The gate opened into a garden, about eight feet wide, which ran between the house and an enclosing palisade of bamboo. The house was approached by stepping stones which crossed a strait of raked earth intended to represent a rushing trout stream.

The garden showed a sweep of green, undulating downs, with storm-blown pine trees here and there, a thicket of shrubs, and some lichen-covered boulders from a moor. Although this stretch of country was but fifteen feet in length it was easy to fancy that it would be a Sabbath day's journey to tramp from one end of the downs to the other against a March wind.

In England the backyard of a potter's house would present a water butt, a perambulator, and a ruinous dog kennel, together with a dust bin, some packing cases, and a pile of empty bottles. Any attempt at landscape gardening would end at a circular flower bed circumscribed by tiles.

A verandah looked into the potter's garden, and here we removed our shoes, and entered the house. The poet received us. He was a solemn man, who looked more like a poet in his long sleeved kimono than he would have done had he adopted the orthodox velvet jacket, the loose flying necktie, and the flopping hair of the West.

The room we came into was purely Japanese. It was disfigured by neither tables nor chairs, so we sat on the floor. On the mats was a bronze charcoal stove and a low, black lacquer table, upon which was served, in due course, tea and cakes. The prevailing colours of the room were French grey and maize-yellow. The simplicity of it was relieved by small cupboards with sliding panels on which flowers were painted upon a background of dull gold, by a kakemono in black and cardinal red upon the wall, and by exquisite rammas or friezes of carved woodwork between the ceiling and the wall. The semi-transparent screens which divided this room from the next were furnished with sunken "finger plates" in dark bronze. The ceiling was of seaweed-brown wood—cryptomeria in tiny beams—relieved by yellow rods of untouched bamboo. Paint or varnish in this dignified chamber would have been as out of place as a wall-paper or a firestove ornament.

The Japanese room is a room in outline, a sketch in water colours, a few masterly lines drawn to make a setting for the blue vase of azalea which forms the centre of the little salon.

After a most leisurely tea drinking the potter poet opened an old gilded box, and taking out a piece of incense put it in a bronze burner, which was older still. The smoke, as it rose, he gathered up in his hands and carried to his nose, and he invited us to do the same. Then out of various cupboards he began to take treasures —one by one—and absently he placed them on the floor beside us. During this stage in the ceremony of shopping it was his pleasure that we smoked. In due course he sat down again and smoked also, the while he handled the pieces of china with evident affection. Among them, however, was there no incense burner.

We then went through the kitchen of the house—where was a small shrine to the Fox Goddess Inari—to see the potter's shed at the back of the building. After watching two leisurely men at work for a while we returned to the grey and yellow room, and ate sweet cakes with ostentatious disregard of time.

Finally from a cupboard was produced—as an after thought—an incense burner. It was a little pot of mushroom coloured china, on which was wrought a pearl grey dragon moving through white clouds. The cap was of the plainest iron. The whole was the product of the potter's own imagining, and both the pot and the iron cover were the work of his hands.

There then came some dreamy talk about yen, which talk was dropped on occasion and then incontinently resumed. Finally, and by unconscious steps, the incense burner, with its pearl grey dragon, passed into my possession. When the rickshaws finally took us back to the town the day was far spent.

V.

THE JAPANESE GARDEN.

There is no garden like a Japanese garden. It is as little comparable with the garden of the West as any tended plot of ground could be. The Western garden is an aristocratically planted enclosure. It is indefinitely informal, for its formality is eclectic, being based upon uncertain codes of horticultural deportment. It presents gravel paths of a type, trees in rows, trees in pairs, shrubs which are foreign to the climate, plants which are cherished because they are costly or curious, vases bought at a famous sale, flowers which have obtained prizes at a show, and incongruous summer houses.

Very often its main claim to attention is as a vehicle for display. The features which then call for admiration are the extent of the grounds, the number of gardeners employed, the size and billiard-table surface of the lawn and the cost required to maintain the same, the fountain containing carp bred in a ducal pond, the myrtle bush grown from a cutting from a notable wedding bouquet, and the yew tree clipped to resemble a peacock. Above all are the hot houses, the glory of which is only to be expressed in the coinage of pride. He who has "an acre under glass" owns a garden indeed. There may be floral freaks and big gooseberries under the glass, but the enviable charm is the covering of an acre. The flowers in the garden are apt to be disposed in strong blotches of colour, so as to produce an effect like that of an "art" Persian carpet. The summer house may be a Grecian temple, or a hut made laboriously rustic.

The gardens of Japan can compete in no way with attractions such as these. They, on their part, aim at reproducing the spirit of a landscape, the memory of a well-beloved corner of the

A JAPANESE SUMMER-HOUSE.

country; while at the same time they attempt, in every detail of their planning, to express some sentiment or pleasurable fancy. The manner in which this purpose is attained may be conventional and pedantic, but it will always be full of subtleness and fine suggestion.

In his intensely interesting volumes on landscape gardening in Japan, Mr. Conder writes of this subject as follows: "In these compositions, as in the pictorial works of painters of the old school, there is an absence of that perfect realism which we are accustomed to look for in a naturalistic art. The same subjection to conventional canons noticeable in the works of the Japanese landscape painter, is paramount in the compositions of the landscape gardener. A representation of nature is, in neither case, intended to be a completely realistic reproduction. The limits imposed by art in Japan require that all imitation should be subject to careful selection and modification."*

To the Japanese gardener would never occur the attempt to make his garden the medium for mere display, either in the matter of flowers or plants, or of horticultural skill. His ambition would be satisfied if his garden could recall a cove by a familiar sea, the hillside bordering on a lake, a valley among the mountains, or a scene that was precious from old associations. Further, he would wish no more than that he who walked in his garden should

> "Find tongues in trees, books in the running brooks,
> Sermons in stones, and good in everything."

Thus it is that many a Japanese garden professes only to embody an abstract idea, such as that of quiet and solitude, of hope or of contentment; while others seek to picture the scene of a bygone legend or the landscape of some traditionary spot.

"Landscape gardening, as taught and practised by the Japanese, reveals an art of considerable refinement, built upon a charming system of ethics. . . . Whether or not the Japanese conception be the ideal art expression of nature, it is undoubtedly governed in its execution by a scrupulous attention to æsthetic rules. Considerations of scale, proportion, unity, balance, con-

* "Landscape Gardening in Japan," Tokyo, 1893, p. 1.

gruity, and all that tends to produce artistic repose and harmony, are carefully preserved throughout the designs."*

There are numerous schools of garden-makers, each with distinctive styles and jealously preserved systems of procedure. Each garden is planned as a writer plans a drama or a sonnet, or an artist a picture. There are precise rules for the securing of suitable perspective as well as for the fitting indication of height and distance. Every detail is as gravely formulated as are the items of a ceremonious ritual. The outline of a lake is determined by accepted types, not by mere whim. Each island in the pool follows a familiar model. There are the "Master's Isle" and the "Guests' Isle" for the inland lake, the "Wind Swept Isle" for the sea. The lake islands will have bridges, but the sea islands will have none.

Every stone employed in the decoration of the garden must conform to an established figure. There is a form for the "Kettle Stone," on which the tea is made, as well as for the "Shoe-removing Stone," and the "Children's Stones." Each boulder has its name, whether it be the "Water-dividing Stone," the "Torrent-breaking Stone," or the "Guardian Stone." So also, among the hill scenery of gardens, will be found the well-defined outlines of the "Mountain Summit Stone," the "Way Side Stone," the "Mist Envelopéd Stone." To build a rockery of burnt bricks and clinkers, after the manner of the British gardener, would be to the Japanese an offence beyond imagining. There are many ways of placing stepping stones, but in Japan each manner is determined by rigid canons of the art. A water-worn boulder could only be employed in connection with water, real or suggested. In the cascade in a Japanese garden—as a matter of fact—there need be no water. The fall is suggested by a torrent-worn rift in an upright rock, and then by a pebbly course across a stretch of green.

It has been said that the trees and bushes in a Japanese garden are so clipped and contorted as to be unnatural. In the treatment of every tree, however, there is an artistic object. Thus a little matsu is so trained as to look both old and tempest-worn,

* "Landscape Gardening in Japan," pp. 6 and 7.

and if it then be planted upon the summit of a far peak it looks fitting. The disposition of every tree in the pleasaunce is ruled by a definite scientific scheme, by which a place is allotted to the "Principal Tree," to the "Distancing Pine," and to the "View-perfecting Tree."

The Japanese garden is a garden of suggestion, a scene from the land of make-believe, the little world of a child.

There are many different kinds of garden which are classified under various heads. The actual arrangement is, however, of little interest except to the enthusiast. The hurried visitor to the country, who has seen many of these quaint spots, will group them according to a method of his own. For my own part, the gardens I have come upon in Japan range themselves in an easy fashion in some such way as this—the King's garden, the Monastery garden, and Endymion's garden.

Of the King's Garden there is a fair example within the prim palisade of the Katsura Palace near Kyoto. This little summer retreat is by the banks of a tumbling river, but both the house and the garden are hidden from common eyes by an encircling thicket of bamboos. The house is exquisite, with its delicate verandahs, its faded paintings, its doll's house cupboards, its tiny courtyards, its fragile screens. From a balcony built out over the grass, and called the "Moon Gazing Platform," is a fine view of the garden. It is large, as Japanese gardens go; while it is full of many and ancient trees, pines and firs, cryptomeria and maples.

There is a winding lake which seems to lead on for ever, for its end is hard to find. In it are steep islands, covered with storm-blown trees, as well as lazy-looking islands, fringed with iris. There are bridges between the islands built of both stone and wood. One—"The Full Moon Bridge"—is like a section of a water wheel.

Mossy slopes, so shaded by trees as to be almost dark, lead down from the woods. There are silent back waters where strange ducks find a home. Devious paths lead across hills and along valleys, over stone planks, by lonely obelisks, and by summer houses. One path ends on a green, far-reaching cape with a single pine on it. Another wanders to a spit of pebbles, which creeps out into the lake until the water covers it. Here stands a stone lantern, as if it were a lighthouse at the end of a shoal. Elsewhere are the open hillside, the savage gorge, the pine-clad crest, the moody forest, as well as the beach at low tide—a sonnet in stones.

It is a mimic world, a toy garden of Eden, a piece of such a country as Alice saw in Wonderland. All this it is, but it is not regal; neither is there any feature in it which lends itself to the pomp of courts. It is neither a place for a pageant; nor for an imperial reception. It is merely the garden of an idyll, bare of any hint of palace precincts.

Of the Monastery garden an example will not be far to seek, since there is scarcely a temple in the country which has not a garden of a kind, and many of these are ancient and noteworthy. Kurodani, near Kyoto, is a Buddhist temple and monastery, beautifully placed upon a hillside among the pines. The temple has a sweeping roof of drab tiles upheld by immense pillars of good brown wood. Without is a time-worn pine tree which figures in the romantic traditions of the place. Within is the shrine, a wonder of crimson and gold, of brilliant black lacquer, of gilt brocade, of tinkling ornaments and priceless bronze. The ample eaves and the paper screens make it dim. Moreover, it is filled ever with the mist of incense. Beyond the sounds of the woods, the silence is only troubled by the droning of priests, by the monotonous heart beat of a gong, and the clatter of clogs in the court.

Behind is a little garden 500 years old. It is a mere child's pond in the corner of a wood. The hills shut it in on all sides, except where the monastery stands; while the slopes which come down to the pool are thick with cedar and pine, cherry and azalea, bamboo and moss. There is a mimic island in the pond with a stone lantern on it. It is approached by a bridge made of one slab of granite. Another bridge, covered with green turf, crosses an arm of the tiny lake. There are stepping stones across the grass, while many paths lead among rocks, through green glades, and by azalea thickets. The sound of the temple gong reaches

A BUDDHIST TEMPLE, KURODANI

the drowsy nook, but that is all. The garden is the monastery cloister, the place for reflection. The priest paces its paths at sundown with his head bowed and his lips fashioning a prayer. It is full of fancies, full of memories, and the voice that speaks in the garden is the voice of God.

If there be in the world a place to think in, it is such a monastery close as this at Kurodani.

In another garden like to it, at Ginkakuji, there is also a pool hidden in a wood. The pool is so small that a stag could leap across it. Yet it is full of rocky, fir-covered islands reached by bridges. It has, too, a wild coast of cliff and bay, of sandy beach and wind-haunted inlet. The matsu trees crowd about the pond and make it silent. A tiny waterfall drops out of the steep hillside from among wet rocks and bejewelled moss. Here and there, around the margin of the haunted mere, is a glimpse of a path of white sand.

This little make-believe garden, which is lost to sight, is one of the sacred books in which the priest reads, for it portrays the scenery of the most cherished traditions of his brotherhood.

Last of all there is Endymion's garden, the garden of fancies, the garden of the dreamer. There are many of these in Japan. The one I remember best was shut away from the world, and we entered it through a wooden gate, with a creeper covered roof, called the Gate of Summer Sleep. Just inside was a beautiful lawn, leading down to the margin of a lake. There was a great stone at the edge of the water called the Angling Stone, while a pigeon-blue boulder on the tiny beach of the lake was the Moon Shadow Stone. On the other shore of the pool, hills covered with trees came down to the brink, while clumps of oleander and bamboo hung over the water and were reflected in it.

Winding through these far away trees, as through a ravine, was the River of Loneliness. The trees met over it so that it was almost dark, and faintly in its far shades a stone bridge crossed it, the Floating Bridge of Heaven.

In the mere was a large, undulating island approached by a trestle bridge, known as the Bridge of the White Crane. The way to the crossing was along a line of stepping stones which reached the bridge through a swamp of soft moss. There were many hills in the island, while through one valley of maples a small track wound and vanished. It was the Eternal Narrow Path. From a clearing on the island one could look into the Pool of the Autumn Wind, and to the country on the other side of the lake. Here a bare hill stood up against the sky called the Ocean Viewing Hill, below which could be seen the roof of the Mountain Village Tea House.

Hence, by another bridge, we passed on to the main land again, where was the Magician's Pool, almost buried in dim bushes. On its reed-covered margin was a ghostly obelisk to mark the Tomb of the White Dragon. Following a path by the lake we came upon the Shuddering Wood, a sombre copse of dull green pines, against whose melancholy shades a slender cherry tree, crowned with white blossoms, rose up, alone in the solitude. It was the Tree of Good Hope.

A path then led to a bare part of lake, where were the Sand Blown Beach, the Seagull Resting Stone, and the Tree of the Salt Breeze. Off from the shore were a few bleak islands—Wild Moor Island and Dry Beach Island, with, in the distance, the Misty Isle. On the grass that came down nearly to the pebbles was built the House of the Sound of the Sea Shore.

Another turn of the lake brought into view the Island of Leave Taking with two stone lanterns on it. It was approached by the Bridge of Remembrance, made of a single smooth rock. At one end of it was the Idling Stone, at the other the Waiting Stone. An arched wooden causeway—the Bridge of Regrets—led away from the island.

Thence by the Garden of Mountain Grass we came to the tea house. It was on a land-locked cove fringed with rushes, through a gap in which a river crept into the pool. The stream came from under an arch of camellias, and followed a rocky ravine between steep cliffs. It bubbled over bright stones, making much noise for its size, for it was only two feet in width, while the precipices of the gorge were little more than a yard in height. The whole garden—with its lake, its sea, its forest, and its hills—covered barely an acre of land.

The tea house hung over the water, for it stood on brown piles, around which ever idled a listless crowd of golden carp. The little house was built on fine lines, of bare, bright unsullied wood. The floor was of mats, the windows of paper screens. A red kakemono hung from the French grey walls. Near it on one side was a cupboard of black lacquer with doors of gilt. On the other side was a recess with some peach blossom in a drab vase. When the paper screens were drawn aside there opened from the front of the house a view across the lake; while at the back was a glimpse of a secluded garden with a path among rocks, a copse of dwarf pines, and a miniature pagoda.

On a summer's evening, when a cool breeze would eddy lazily out of the lake, the paper screens would be closed. The light in the little room would become so faint that the colour of the kakemono would fade, and the figures of the two who sat within would blend into one. If either spoke it would be to quote the little Japanese poem:

> "The window itself is dark,
> But see!
> A firefly is creeping up the paper pane."

VI.

A RELIGION OF CHERRY BLOSSOM AND OLD MEMORIES.

By the shore of Lake Biwa is an old temple gate. It is covered by a roof of thatch which time has turned from brown to bronze green. The wooden gates have become ash coloured from age. They are carved modestly, but the work is delicate, and has remained ever untouched by paint or varnish. By the side of the gate is a plum tree in blossom. The exquisite white flowers hang over the old thatch, and many petals have dropped on to the grey moss-covered wall near by and upon the steps that lead up from the road. Under the faint shadow of the plum tree stands an ancient stone lantern also grey, and covered with moss and lichen. The place is quiet; while the path from the gate winds solemnly uphill through a wood of pines and cedars to the temple.

It is an old Shinto worshipping place which may have relapsed of late years into Buddhism; but the gate, the path through the wood, and the shrine on the hill, looking over the lake, are all expressive of the ancient religion of Japan.

The Shinto faith belongs only to Japan. It is the indigenous religion of the country, and although it may have been much modified by the teaching of Buddha, it remains still the religion of the people.

It is the simplest of all the faiths of the world. Shinto merely means "God's way," and to the founders of the sect "God's way" must have been a way of pleasantness and a path of peace. Shintoism possesses neither sacred books nor an austere code of ethics. It has burdened itself with no dogmas, while the unseemly cackle of theological discussion has never come within its tree-encircled walls. Of the malignity of religious hate, of the bitterness of religious persecution, the Shinto faith knows nothing.

It has been to the people the familiar friend, not the pedagogue; the comforter, not the censor.

Shintoism is represented mainly by two elements—by ancestor

THE TEMPLE GATE.

worship and the adoration of nature. Ancestor worship has made it the religion of the state as well as the religion of the family. With that phase of devotion has come the inculcating of loyalty, patriotism, reverence, duty, unselfishness, comradeship. With it has also come the veneration of those who have passed from out of the sight of men. It has made itself a religion of Hero Worship, in whose Pantheon God's good man has come to occupy a place that is worshipful. It has made of great men demi-gods; and it has done more than this, for it has served to keep their memories green.

The Shinto faith is the religion of old friends, the religion of lovers, since high among the objects of its homage is fidelity in human affection, unforgetfulness of human ties.

Another aspect of this homely creed concerns itself with the adoration of nature and whatever in it is beautiful and lovable. It recognises that in the sunshine, in the mountain torrent, in the cherry trees about the meadow there is a glory which is divine. That glow of pleasure which stirs the senses when the eye opens upon the stretch of Biwa Lake, or upon a nook full of iris flowers in a monastery garden, is worshipful, for it is the reflection of the divine presence.

So simple is Shintoism that it may have been founded by a coterie of serious boys and girls whose lives were bound up in kindly homes, and in the woods and meadows of a fair country. A reverent remembering of those who have gone away, a love for the beauty of thicket and field, and an instinct to uphold the right need only be expressed by a power which could be deified and worshipped, and there arises the foundation of a boy and girl's creed.

To such creed makers it would seem that human tenderness was no mere phase of mind to spring up, pass by, and then be lost for ever; that the thrill of delight which comes with the contemplation of the world was no mere mood of the sense of sight, and that the incentive to do no wrong was founded upon some influence which was not wholly man's.

The temple gateway by the lake is an emblem of this religion of cherry blossom and old memories. The common thatched roof is the cottage roof, a token of homeliness and simplicity. By the gate is the worshipful plum tree, and under the tree is a granite lantern placed there to keep alight the memory of a friend.

The temple stands high up on the hill, on a terrace that juts out over the lake. It is reached by long stone stairs which climb up among the dark passages of the wood, or by contemplative paths which wind by old walls and through silent courtyards, where are yet again stone lanterns and a plum tree in bloom.

On the terrace is a little pavilion close to the drop of the hill, whence is a view over the great Lake Biwa. It is a view of a blue lake within a circle of pine-covered hills. On its shores are many a brown-roofed village, many a green flat busy with husbandmen, many a cape of rocks crowned by fir trees. In places a bamboo copse creeps down to the water, or a company of sighing rushes wade out into the shallows. Here and there is a fishing boat drawn up, or a tiny island of emerald dotted by white birds.

The Shinto faith would teach that the contemplation of this gentle stretch of water was a religious exercise from which the troubled man would gather peace, and which would lead the man with evil in his heart to turn homewards in a purer spirit. It is indeed something of a sacrament to sit by the terrace edge on a still day (when there is no disturbing sound but the temple bell), to look over the lake and be filled with the divineness of its presence. Thus it is that the nature-loving Japanese have evolved some kind of ritual for those who worship at this wondrous shrine. There are eight views of the Lake of Biwa, they say, which are commendable above all. They are these: "The autumn moon seen from Ishiyama, the evening snow on Hirayama, the sunset at Seta, the evening bell of Miidera, the boats sailing back from Yabase, the bright sky with a breeze at Awazu, rain by night at Karasaki, and the wild geese alighting at Katata."*

If there be many who can see no element of religion in this, there are, at least, not a few who can.

There are two temples at Kyoto near by to one another. The smaller of these—the temple of Hirano Jinja—is considered to be an example of "pure Shinto." Its garden is so full of cherry

* "Things Japanese," by Prof. Chamberlain. London, 1902, page 355.

OVERLOOKING LAKE BIWA.

trees that it might be regarded as a type of the temple of the cherry blossom. The other—Kitano Tenjin—serves to illustrate that phase of Shintoism which has ripened into hero worship, for it was erected to the ever-sacred memory of a scholar who died in exile precisely one thousand and one years ago.

Hirano Jinja is a very humble shrine, very modest, very bare. At its entrance is a homely unpainted wooden gate, such as may lead into a farmyard. Within is an open garden very beautiful to see. A little stream wanders about it affectionately, and over the stream are bridges. At one spot the mimic river encircles an island with a shrine on it. It is quite a child's garden, and the flowers in it are planted with a lovable absence of art. Over against the garden is a copse of cherry trees which—when I saw them—were covered with bloom. Every tree has a name, a pet name associated with some pretty fancy, such as a child would construct for the things that grew in her garden. It was evident that to the crowd of worshippers the trees were themselves familiar, and that some were the favourites of one and some of another.

Beyond the garden and the cherry copse is the oratory—a mere open shed—and before the oratory is the temple. The temple is made up of five small wooden shrines in a row, under a long plain roof of cedar bark. They stand within a kind of miniature gallery, while in front of them all is a low fence of meekly carved wood. Everything is grey and bare. Before each shrine is placed the wand with the dangling paper, or gohei, and the tassels of straw and hemp, which are common to all holy places of the Shinto faith. The plainness, the scantiness, the simplicity of the wizened building is befitting to an ancient village.

Behind the motherly thatched roof of the shrine a clump of bamboos makes a background of brilliant green, whilst beyond them stands a monkish company of solemn pines and sombre cryptomeria to shut the sacred close away from the world.

The prayer uttered before the shrine by those who came was very short, but I think that many, as they passed out through the gate, would have murmured that it was good to see the cherry blossom at Hirano.

Kitano Tenjin—the temple of the exile—is a more florid and pretentious building. It belongs to a decadent form of the faith, to the sect of Ryobu Shinto. Still it serves to keep in reverent memory a man who had a claim to be unforgotten. Tenjin is said to have been a great minister and a scholar. In A.D. 901 he was degraded and banished to the island of Kyushu. What was the offence that brought upon him this dire punishment I know not. He would seem to have carried away with him the sympathy of the people, and to have held it from that time until now.

In the Imperial Museum at Kyoto are a series of pictures illustrative of the life of Tenjin. They are the work of one Nobuzane, who is said to have wrought upon them in A.D. 1206. The most vivid painting deals with the passing of the scholar into exile. He is seated in the stern of a boat rowed by ten men. They pull in the face of a terrific and unearthly wind. The sail is furled and lies, with the mast, on the roof of the galley. The efforts of the rowers are so frantic as to be pitiable to see. They fight their way against this blast from the nether world until the oars are bent double under the awful strain. The sea is horrible beyond words, a sea more gruesome than any the ancient mariner ever reached in his dread sailing. Its colour is a livid blue green, the tint of a bruise, and it is contorted into gnawing waves, sharp like the curled teeth of a gigantic saw. The waters, moreover, are full of loathsome fish, red and slimy, while on rocks near by are snaky black cormorants—portentous birds of evil. In the bows of the ship kneels a distressful man in white. As he prays his raiment is being dragged tight across his bones by the direful wind. In the hold, among much luggage, are limp women wan with weeping. They are blown prone by the storm, like wheat in a hurricane. Tenjin, the scholar, alone sits in the stern, wrapped in a brown robe, unruffled and unmoved.

The temple stands among trees, and, through these and by many lanterns and many gates, a stone causeway leads up to the shrine. The encircling trees are mostly the matsu and the cryptomeria.

The temple is in a paved square. It is a little more than a great solemn shed with a comfortable roof of warm brown thatch, which mounts in the middle to a surprising gable. The shrine,

TEMPLE OF KITANO TENJIN
AND ITS PLUM-TREE.

with the tablet of the exile, is far away at the back of the temple, where it is lost in inscrutable shadows. Before these shadows are ranged mighty wooden pillars; while from unseen beams lanterns in gilt and in bronze hang down into the dusk. In the cabalistic gloom is the outline of a black table, with brass incense burners and candlesticks on it, as well as dishes for offerings. There are mysterious screens, too, that hide something; while, here and there, in the unfathomable depth are glimpses of silver emblems, of mighty timbers covered with red paint, and enigmatical panels glistening with black and crimson lacquer.

In front of all—so that the wholesome daylight falls upon it—is a delicate branch of plum blossom in a blue vase.

The favourite flower of the banished scholar, who was rowed away in the teeth of so ruthless a storm, was the plum blossom. Thus it is that in the courtyard of the temple, surrounded by a wooden fence, there stands a venerable plum tree laden with pink flowers. It is the exile's tree, and it blooms in the little paved square to do honour to the man who loved it in his life-time and who loves it still.

In the temple precincts are thatched buildings of plain bare wood, granite lanterns and small shrines. In every byway, by every moss-covered wall, and by the side of every flagged path are plum trees in blossom. The flowers of most of them are white; a few are pink.

In the early spring the temple close is buried in clouds of plum blossom. The masses of flowers stand out, in exquisite contrast, against the old drab walls, the seal brown thatch, and the dark green of the encircling pines. The ground is snowed over with frail petals which, along the temple step, have been swept into a white drift by the March breeze.

For those who come here to worship the ceremonial is very simple. They go first of all to a stone cistern, where they wash their hands and their mouths, dipping up the water in a small wooden cup at the end of a long stick. In front of the temple is a bell from which dangles a wide linen rope. There is also a receptacle for alms not unlike the hay-rack above a horse's manger. The worshipper approaches, makes an obeisance to the shrine, and throws an offering of money into the rack. Then, after ringing the bell, he kneels or bows before the altar with clasped hands while he prays. He prays to the scholar who died in exile, and to whom the plum blossom was dear. He then claps his hands, makes another obeisance, and retires.

Before he leaves he wanders about the temple gardens to see the plum trees. His eyes light up as they fall upon the wondrous bloom, his mind is aglow with unspeakable adoration. To him the temple plum blossom with the sun on it is an emblem of the Great Peace.

In a place called Shimo-Gamo, near Kyoto, on a much-wooded spit of land running out into the river, is an old and deserted Shinto temple at the end of an avenue of maples. It was founded, they say, in A.D. 667.

It seems now to have been forgotten by the world, to have faded into the sightless grey of centuries, and to have become deaf to the voices of living men. There is no rattle of clogs upon its stones, nor is there any sound of the temple bell in the gloom of its ancient eaves. Once a year, I understand, there is a ceremonial visit to the place, when it partially awakens. As soon as the day is over the shrivelled old sanctuary wraps itself once more in the silence of sleep.

In one corner of the temple square a spring of water creeps from under a rock and, after loitering in a pool banked by stone steps, it runs as a small river across the courtyard, to be lost among the trees. There is a tiny round bridge over the stream arched like a bow, and, near by the bridge, a well, with a wheel and bucket, under a wooden roof. Shading the well is a plum tree in blossom.

The only living creature met with in the temple grounds, on the occasion of my visit, was an old woman carrying a ruddy-faced baby—her grandson. My companion asked her why she had come to a place so solitary. She said, " she thought it would do the baby good to see the plum blossom." In such wise commences the education of the Japanese child.

VII.

THE GENTLE LIFE.

Not a few of the more highly educated Japanese—especially the younger of them—are apt to assert that, after some critical enquiry into the subject of creeds, they have abandoned all religions on the ground that they are neither useful nor convincing. It is stated also by competent writers on Japan that the people of the country generally are undevotional and irreligious. A residence in the island of a few months only leads one to doubt the correctness of both of these statements. The erudite Japanese may discard as unsound the professions of Buddhism or Christianity, or may even repudiate the gentle and unassuming pretensions of the Shinto faith, but all the same he will remain a devotee to Ancestor Worship, and in the religion of ancestor worship he will find the code of morality he observes. He has not, therefore, thrown aside all religion.

In spite of fluttering manifestations of particular beliefs, or of unbelief, there is a religion in Japan, the foundations of which are set in Ancestor Worship, and these foundations neither ancient Indian creeds nor modern agnosticism have in any degree disturbed. Both Buddhism and Western civilisation are opposed to ancestor worship, and although both have entered very intimately into the life of Japan they have left this old-world faith untouched.

To refute the general charge of irreligion it is only necessary to note the immense number of temples which exist throughout Japan, the constant crowd of worshippers, their obvious sincerity, and the enthusiasm which attends their great sacred festivals throughout the year. The religion of the humbler classes, whilst it does not express itself in mere parade and exacting ceremony, yet influences every circumstance of daily life. Their devotional acts are simple, but they are not confined to public places where they can be seen of men, nor are they regulated by social requirements, nor employed as a means of "appearing respectable."

But for the comments of those more competent to speak I should have regarded the Japanese as a devout people.

Ancestor worship lies at the bottom of it all. The worship of the Imperial Ancestors is, as Professor Nitobe says, "the national worship."* Upon it is based the government of the country. The present constitution of the Empire of Japan, promulgated in 1889, is definitely founded upon the worship of the Imperial Ancestors, and, in the preamble of the charter, this fact is very prominently set forth. The worship of clan ancestors—the dead of the district—serves to maintain that love of country and of home, that attachment to the land, which is so strong and wonderful a factor in the Japanese character.

The worship of family ancestors influences and directs every act in the worshipper's life. It is the sacred soul of the ancestor who watches over the family, who is ever mindful of the dignity of his kind, and who has in his keeping the memory of old ties and old associations. The living feel that they are never forgotten, and that they in turn should never forget. The same father—although he is long since dead—keeps ward over the son, in whose every action he still remains intently concerned. "When a young student goes to Europe to pursue his studies, when a soldier sets out on a campaign, when an official is sent abroad on some government service, he invariably visits the graves of his ancestors in order to take leave of them."†

With the devout Buddhist in Japan there are four days in the year—in the height of the glorious Japanese summer—when the spirits of the dead come back to the old house and live in it again. On the evening of the first day a fire is kindled before the door of the house, or in the little garden, to guide the spirit home. On the evening of the fourth day another fire is lighted; it is "the farewell fire," and it is intended to cheer them on their way. During these four days the house is filled with tender memories, with the dearest presence, with longings which, though

* "Japan by the Japanese." London, 1904, page 286.

† *Ibid.*, page 289.

unutterable, will one day be satisfied. It is during these scented summer evenings that those who still live on can feel once again "the touch of the vanished hand," and can hear once more "the sound of the voice that is still." The offerings of flowers and fruit, which are placed on "the spirits' shelf," are a repetition of the presents which are bestowed in life with such infinite pleasure and such graciousness.

It is little to be wondered that the Japanese are loyal to the death, are devoted to their country and their people with a fervour that few have knowledge of, are filled with the fierce partisanship of the clansman and the pride of birth, but are yet gentle and tender, considerate and full of sympathies. It is small wonder, too, that their everyday life is peopled with fancies, and that they traffic much with the world of dreams. The basis of their worship is affection and gratitude, the motive of their ceremonial is the ever-present voice, "Do this in remembrance of me."

The daily acts of the Japanese man are moulded upon the resolve never to degrade in any way the name of those who have gone before him. He is always under their watchful eyes, and it is the purpose of his life to do nothing which may occasion them offence, or may alienate their affection and good will. The Japanese woman, facing the great crisis of her life, would speak in the words of Pompilia's prayer:—

> "O lover of my life, O soldier saint,
> No work begun shall ever pause for death!
> Love will be helpful to me more and more
> I' the coming course, the new path I must tread,
> My weak hand in thy strong hand, strong for that!"

One passing comment upon ancestor worship, made to me by a Japanese gentleman with whom I was speaking upon the subject, brought this antique religion lightly in touch with modern criticism. "There is considerable doubt," he said, "as to the precise origin of the human species. That origin, at least, is the subject of difference of opinion, and has been the matter of much philosophical discourse. Amongst all the clouds of argument and of dogma one thing alone stands out as certain, and that is, that we all come from ancestors."

The standard of Japanese morality is high. It is influenced not merely by the logical outcome of ancestor worship and by the teachings of such religious creeds as Shintoism, Buddhism, and Confucianism, but also by an ancient and curious code of morality called Bushido. The literal significance of Bushido is "fighting Knight ways," or, in freer English, "the precepts of Knightly behaviour." This code of honour was that professed originally by the Samurai class, and in time by the greater body of the people. Bushido is of indefinite antiquity, and is reputed to be an outcome of the old Shinto religion. "It professes no revelation from above, and it boasts of no founder. Its ultimate sanction lies in the inborn sense of shame at all wrong-doing, and of honour in doing right. It offers no philosophical demonstration for this belief."* It is embodied in the form of no statutes, and its teachings, such as they are, have never been systematised.

It enforced care of the body in that it is, for a time, the habitat of a divine presence. It taught that a man should be master of himself, should be capable of effacing himself, should be so unselfish that he should regard it as the highest praise to be spoken of as "the man without a me."

Bushido insisted upon the power of the voice of conscience, taught the nobleness of self-sacrifice, of valour, of patriotism and of benevolence. It inculcated gentle manners, courtesy, and an ever-mindful regard for the feeling of others. If any man were insulting and violent it was wrong to be cross with him. He had offended against himself and not against you, so that he is only to be pitied and helped.

Bushido is an expression of "the inborn race instinct of honour" of the Japanese people, the sum of their natural estimate of right-doing. It is the outcome of an intuition, and not of a cult, just as what we call in England "the dictates of common sense" depend upon no carefully constructed formulæ, but upon the judgment and perception of the English people. Bushido presents this element of strength. Its code of precepts does not rest upon a revelation, the reality of which may become a matter of doubt, nor is it framed from the utterances of a teacher whose authority

* "Japan by the Japanese," page 265.

A SHINTO TEMPLE.

may be disputed. It is the feeling of the nation. It is the country's ideal of what is right, its ideal of what is wrong. He who breaks its unwritten laws sins against the unanimous conscience of his fellow-man.

If anyone upon this side of the world will tabulate "the instincts of a gentleman," or will place in order the accepted principles of the Gentle Life, he will be laying the foundations of a Western Bushido.

VIII.

THE JAPANESE THEATRE.

There is in Kyoto a jingling street, full of trivial shops, called Theatre Street. It is given over wholly to frivolity, so that the sign of the street might as well be "the Cap and Bells." No rickshaws are allowed in this lane, neither may a cart nor a pedlar trespass upon it. The crowd, therefore, can wander within its limits aimlessly, can gape at the booths and the finery without fear of being knocked down by anything in a hurry.

The street is aflame with colour from one end to the other. Besides lanterns and flags there are hanging silks and gaudy umbrellas, which wave in the wind, shop signs in black, red, and gold, together with brilliant pictures, framed in tinsel and paper flowers, over a score of theatres and booths. These places of entertainment show no restraint whatever in the matter of colour. Any tint that is bright is acceptable. If there be one façade in pink and yellow, the next will be in crimson and green. They seem indeed to shout at one another in colours. At some playhouses can be heard tragedies which deal with much shedding of blood, or comedies which, according to the placards, are embowered in cherry blossoms and moonlight on lakes. In other places it is possible to see dances, or men juggling with plates, or women strolling with bare feet on red-hot iron. There are waxworks also and peep-shows, as well as displays of animated pictures.

The shops, which fill up the gaps between the booths and theatres, deal with no serious articles of commerce. In some are revealed all the mysteries of the Japanese lady's dress, together with the splendours of her silks; while in others are fans, cosmetics, trifles such as hair-pins and pipes, children's toys, and posies of artificial flowers. The street traffics, indeed, only with vanities, for the place is none other than Vanity Fair.

It is at night that it is most crowded and most brilliant. The booths and theatres are ablaze with light, which illumines the amused faces of the restless crowd. The many-coloured lanterns are lit, while even through the paper screens of the houses there filters the glow of the yellow light within. So great is the clatter of clogs and the rustle of sandals that the gong of the conjurer is hard to hear, while the drum of the exponent of the panorama is but a mumbling echo.

The chief theatre in this gay thoroughfare is very large, and had devoted itself to a bustling play illustrative of the great war. The building itself inside is low roofed and bare, like an unfurnished mission hall. There are neither seats nor footlights, neither boxes nor orchestra. The stage occupies one side of the hall, and from the foot of the platform the floor slopes upwards as if it were an undecided roof. The whole of this tilted area is divided into little square compartments by boards which are only some four inches high. Thus it comes about that the auditorium has the look of a seedsman's counter marked off with shallow compartments for seeds. Each square has a mat and "kneels" two people, for the whole of the audience are dumped down upon the floor. At the back of the hall, facing the stage, is a gallery to "kneel" about one hundred.

A curious feature of the theatre is due to the circumstance that the actors enter by the front of the stage instead of by the back. A raised wooden causeway runs along one side of the hall from the stage to the street. If applied to a Western theatre it would traverse the pen for the orchestra, the stalls, and the pit, and end somewhere in the foyer, or outer hall. By this causeway —which suggests an embankment across a flood—the actors make their entries and their exits. By it also the audience reach their "kneels," the waitresses their customers, while upon it inattentive children play.

As the actors have to stalk through the company their exits are, in consequence, a little drawn out. The suicidal woman, rushing riverwards, has to maintain her agony until she has traversed the causeway; while the hero, who is making for the rescue of the afflicted, appears to be hurrying to the street. It is possible that a playgoer, on his way to his seedsman's compartment, may collide with a Japanese Ellen Terry, who is leaving the stage heavy with tears. This long extended fading from the public gaze, moreover, compels the funny man to continue to be funny for some time after he has made his last jest upon the boards.

The auditorium is dull in colour, for all the playgoers who huddle together on the floor affect dull dresses. Although the theatre, on the occasion of my visit, was full to its paper walls, there was not a European costume among the crowd. There are, therefore, no matinée hats. By stepping from one compartment to another it is easy to ramble over the whole theatre, while in case of fire it is only necessary to walk through the wall.

As the performance could only appeal to me as would a drama acted before a stone deaf man, I took the opportunity of noting the observances which attend the going-to-the-play in Japan. An illustration was afforded by a young couple, who, if there were a "smart set" in Japan, would certainly be of its fellowship. The man had a fine intellectual face, and his black robe was evidently of the most approved type. The wife was very young, as well as exceptionally pretty. Her hair was a triumph of art, and she was exquisitely dressed. Her kimono was of the dull grey of a moth's wing; her legs were bare; her socks were white. Beneath the skirt was a glimpse of some garment in bright coloured silk.

The little couple came in late, just as the "smart set" do in England. They were shown to their places, with some ceremony, and as they stepped from one little pen to another they bowed to their friends. It is evidently the "proper thing" for the up-to-date playgoer and his companion to take two seedsman's compartments and turn them into one by removing the intervening strip of wood. This they did. A low-bowing waitress brought them cushions to kneel on, programmes, a bronze stove full of glowing charcoal, and a smoking box with a bamboo receptacle for tobacco ashes. Later on she followed with a tray, on which were a teapot and two cups. The lady, as soon as she had settled down, drew a mirror from out of her sash, inspected her hair with some anxiety, altered the position of a coral pin, wiped her face in places with paper and applied powder where necessary. The powder puff also came from the depths of her sash. There were still other things buried in this broad band of silk, for when she had put away her mirror, powder box and puff she drew out a showy pipe case along with an exquisite tobacco pouch. She smoked three pipes with infinite grace, taking about three whiffs from each, and knocking out the ashes into the bamboo cylinder, with or without the aid of a hairpin. Having returned her pipe and accessories to her obi she proceeded to take tea.

As soon as the tea was disposed of the waitress brought in dinner. It was a jumbled little meal made up of elegant trays, dishes of lacquer, and tiny basins of porcelain, very suggestive of a doll's birthday repast. The grace with which the lady ate was more wonderful to see than anything on the stage. She used her chopsticks as if they were sensitive antennæ and fed like a butterfly. There was a bone in the fish, so she picked it from between her teeth with the chopsticks and let it drop into the bamboo tube. Her neatness and quickness of movement were amazing. She and her husband sipped saki out of doll's house cups. I noticed that he helped himself quite liberally before she ventured to take any, and that she usually poured it out for him. He had forgotten his handkerchiefs; whereupon she dived into her sleeve and brought out a dozen. With some of these he wiped his face and his hands, and dropped the used paper into his own sleeve so as not to litter the prim enclosure.

When the many dinner dishes had been removed the little people lapsed into tea drinking and smoking again, and the lady was now more in a mood to smile at the play. In due course the baby was brought in by a nurse. The baby—about three years old—was as radiant in colour as a tropical bird. With the arrival of the child the mother's interest in the drama vanished, for it was evident that the baby provided her with a delight which absorbed all others.

The acting on the stage appeared to me to be admirable, so far as it is possible to judge of acting in an unknown tongue. Certainly the scenery and the management of the play were near to perfection. As soon as the curtain came down upon an exciting episode those of the audience who were nearest to the stage jumped up, and lifting the foot of the curtain, put their heads under it to see the veritable end. It might be thought that persistent disillusions would have discouraged them, but the same heads dived under the curtain time after time.

When the play is over the calling for cabs and carriages is replaced by a calling for clogs. It is impossible to step into the muddy road in spotless white socks; and as everybody wants to leave at once there is much importunate holding out of wooden clog room tickets.

IX.

TOKYO THE REFORMED.

At the extremity of a long bay which ends in a tired water—like Southampton water—stands the city of Tokyo, the capital of Japan. It is a place of astonishing extent, as those who cross it in a rickshaw come to learn at the cost of some weariness. It needs to be large, as it shelters one and a half millions of people. Up to September 13th, 1868, the city went by the name of Yedo. Since that date there has dawned upon it the unhappy light of Western civilisation, under which it is reputed to have advanced amazingly. Yet there are many in Japan, as well as without it, who would long to see come back again the city of Yedo the Unreformed.

Civilisation fell upon the gracious city like a disfiguring disease, and if good has come of it, it has been at no less a sacrifice to the capital than the loss of its beauty and its individuality. Progress has changed the homely brown lane into a wide and glaring street, with two lines of tramways and broad pavements. It has made the winding path straight, while the alley, whose tiny gap of sky was almost shut out by paper lanterns, it has taken entirely away. Saddest of all, it has fallen upon the Japanese house—the exquisite little house of chocolate-coloured wood and paper screens—and has turned it into a horror of stone or brick. The white paper it has replaced by glass, the dignified plain wood by stucco. The ill that has thus been wrought is beyond all weeping for.

In the main street of Tokyo there are now scarcely any wooden houses to be seen. In their stead are two storied buildings of brick, no two of which are alike, although they all possess the common quality of ugliness. They are daubed with coarse colours like a tattooed Indian, while in the features of meanness and vulgarity they leave no opportunity for further development. Their style of architecture is that known as "foreign," which means that no country in the world would acknowledge it, or give it a home.

It is to be hoped that far at the back of the tawdry shop front, and out of sight of the flaring advertisements which cover it, there is still a quiet Japanese home where the relieved shopkeeper can throw off the mask, can don his kimono, and smoke his pipe, sitting on wholesome yellow mats, with the companionship of a sprig of cherry blossom in a cherished vase. He must often question what it is he has gained by the pursuit of progress. He has gained neither charm nor ease, nor has he secured any advantage in the matter of health. The Japanese house with its liberal ventilation and its paper walls—permeable to air—is well to live in. The same cannot be said of the brick and stucco casement which has taken its place.

It would seem as if some sinister Aladdin had walked through the dignified byways of the old city crying, "New lanterns for old," and that the people had come out to exchange paper windows for glass, coarse iron railings for the bamboo fence, corrugated iron for the old grey tile, the sound of rattling tram-cars for the rustle of sandals and the whisperings of the street.

The picturesqueness of the Japanese dress may well be the envy of any civilised people. In Tokyo—lamentable to say—the delightful costume of the country is vanishing. The women (to their great credit be it observed) still cling to their own beautiful dress, but the men are succumbing to the infection of reform. It is to be regretted, for the Japanese man in his kimono has a natural dignity which vanishes miserably when he takes upon him the costume of Europe. There is no spectacle in the streets of Tokyo more distressful than that of the dandy who has attempted a compromise, in the matter of his attire, between the Far East and the Far West. Such infirmity of purpose will lead him to wear a kimono, with above it a "bowler" hat, and below it knickerbockers and elastic-side boots.

Tokyo is noisy and smoky. A black forest of factory chimneys is springing up around it, while the incessant shrieking of steam whistles has already made the city famous. Against the sky in every street are lines of electric wires concerned with telegraphs, telephones and incandescent lamps. These wire entanglements cross the city in every direction and at every angle, so that there seems to be creeping over the troubled settlement a cobweb of iron.

About the centre of the town merciless clearings are being made. The picturesque old houses, with always the warm tints of autumn about them, have been swept away; just as a ferocious builder would mow down bracken and fern to make a brutal waste for his castellated villa. The defiant outer moat, which in heroic times served to guard the King, is being filled up, so that soon its place will know it no more. On the bald spaces thus made in the improving city appear, in fulness of time, wide roads, open squares, and line after line of immense public buildings in red brick and stone. At a period but little distant, Yedo the Imperial, the Sacred, the World-ignoring, will become a "modern capital," the simulacrum of Brussels, the echo of Pretoria.

Near about the centre of the reformed city an opportunity is afforded to the English of seeing themselves as others see them. The mirror that is thus held up to the Western country is in the guise of a small public park—a European park—with evidences that it is modelled upon like enclosures in England. It is girt about by assertive iron railings, exulting in their ugliness. It is entered by lofty iron gates of the well-known, much lamented suburban type. Within are wide gravel walks, precise flower beds, a waste of confused and vacant grass crowned by a purposeless mound, to show the end of the art of landscape gardening. Near the mound is an up-to-date open-air gymnasium.

And this is a country that has been civilised for a thousand years! The land with such a garden as that at Katsura, such walks and terraces as those at Nikko, such a park as that at Ueno on the outskirts of the very city itself!

Those who look into the mirror provided by Tokyo's new public park will recognise the face, but will be startled to find that it was so much more unsightly than they had ever dreamed. One thing about this park must count for righteousness. In May it is glorious with azalea trees in bloom, with such an outpouring of dainty colours as would make a halo about even a boot factory.

The two ancient parks of Tokyo, Shiba and Ueno, are suffering a little from the close association with a population of one and a half millions. They crown certain low hills, over which they stretch with many avenues of trees and wide slopes about old temples, with occasional ponds and carved pagodas.

The temples, once among the most beautiful in Japan, are becoming a little shabby. Their precincts are neglected and untidy, for casual paths have been trodden about the woods by some of the three million feet of the city. About these sacred parks there is a suggestion of Hampstead Heath as it appears on the morning after a Bank Holiday. The great pines and the stalwart cryptomeria keep up, in some manner, the dignity of the old feudal days, but the magic of their presence is waning.

In the Ueno Park is the once beautiful Lake of Shinobazu-no-ike, famous for its lotus flowers in August. Western civilisation, however, has no sympathy with people who waste the early morning, by the margin of a pool, watching for the lotus to open; and thus it is that the shores of the lake have been turned into a race-course.

A river traverses Tokyo, and besides the river there are many half-forgotten Dutch-looking canals. From them arises all that stench which is proper to any town canal which has come under the influence of useful progress. Many of these waterways still retain the beautiful old wooden bridges of the Japan that was, the tumble-down timber houses which hang half across the stream, and the quaint craft which, with sail and oar, have passed by the riverside tea houses in so many an ancient picture.

There are bridges across the river of recent erection which can, I believe, claim to be the ugliest constructions of the kind in the known world. One bridge of iron girders especially leaves on the mind the impression of a hideous nightmare in which a colossal humpbacked insect with stilt-like legs is crawling across a tainted river. Near by to this fearsome thing is one of the old bridges of the city. It is called Ohashi, which is by interpretation "The Honourable Bridge."

The Honourable Bridge is fashioned wholly of wood, and honest planks have not been spared in its building. An old coloured print by Hiroshige shows the bridge as it was in the leisurely days before the city became regenerate. As it was then so is it now, except for differences which matter little. In the print the bridge leads over into a place where there are a few contented houses among a stretch of comfortable trees. It is raining in the picture, so that two women have drawn up the skirts of their kimonos, while the man behind them in a limpet-shell hat is pulling down his sleeves. Further on the way are three coolies hurrying along under a paper umbrella, following a fourth who has wrapped himself in a mat. On the river a man clad in a "mino," or rain cape of straw, is poling a timber raft down the stream.

The Honourable Bridge leads no longer from the town into the green country, for across the river are factories and wharves, tall chimneys and telegraph poles. When the rain falls now the women on the bridge open French umbrellas. The coolie turns up the collar of a discarded Norfolk jacket, or dons a London cabman's waterproof cape. There is a timber raft on the river, but it is being towed by a tug, belching black smoke and whistling hysterically, while the "mino" is replaced by an oilskin coat from Chicago. The bridge has been left behind with its gorgeous past and its ancient memories; the relic of a dead romance. There is now little to keep it fitting company, but it is still The Honourable Bridge.

As a relief from the imposing courts of the Imperial Diet, from the new University Buildings, from the girder bridges and the Industrial Exhibitions of the reformed city, the visitor might go to Kameido—an old Shinto temple in the undecided suburbs of the town. The place is called Kameido because of a stone tortoise, which still rests there on the brink of the well.

The temple itself is of no particular interest, but the garden by which it is approached—if seen about the end of April—is not likely to be forgotten. A plain wooden gate opens into a court traversed by a stone causeway. This causeway leads across the middle of a pond to the temple, going by way of strangely shaped islands, on which—among green lawns—are rocks and azalea bushes with some venerable matsu trees, looking crazy with age. The islands are approached from one side, and are landed from on the other, by wooden bridges, which are very round and steep and which, by reason of their shape and the little steps upon them, have the look of paddle-boxes emptied of their wheels. To cross these bridges when the planks are wet is a feat creditable to an acrobat.

The pond is called the "Pond of the Word Heart," because it is supposed to be the shape of the Chinese character for "Heart." All around this Pool of the Heart, extending from one fantastic bridge to the other, are arbours laden with wistarias. Towards the end of April every climbing shrub is in full blossom. The flowers are either white or mauve, and they drop from the trellis in great cone-shaped clusters, hanging over the water and over the flagged walk which skirts the margin of the pool.

The water of the pond is clear and has the yellow-brown tint of the oak leaf in autumn. Upon it are reflected the grey trellis-work and its burden of green, partly hidden by clouds of white and clouds of mauve—the shadows of the flowers. Under these shadows swim golden carp. The air is full of the sensuous perfume from thousands of drooping flowers; and if only the little square could be emptied of its clattering holiday folk, it would be a garden court with scarcely an equal in the world.

Let the emblem of the reformed city of Tokyo be, by all means, a steam tug floating under a girder bridge. But the emblem of the old untroubled city of Yedo shall be a golden carp floating under the mauve shadow of an overhanging wistaria blossom.

X.

THE ST. PETER'S OF JAPAN.

The largest Buddhist temple in Japan, the most recently built and the most magnificent to see, is the temple of Higashi Hongwanji at Kyoto.

It will probably be a matter of little interest to know that the structure cost eight millions of dollars, or that it needed seventeen years to build. There are many holy places which have cost ten times that sum, and which have occupied a score more years in the building. But the money for the uplifting of this temple was for the most part provided by the peasants of the country, who saved up their pence, week by week, with unstinted labour, and then carried the little offering by long miles into Kyoto.

Still less interest may attach to the fact that there are ninety-six mighty pillars of solid wood in the shrine, together with beams which are forty-two feet long and four feet thick. But these huge timbers were dragged to Kyoto by singing folk, who raised them on high by the might of their arms and placed them where they stand, and who—be it noted—would take no wage for the work they did. They would tramp home through the length of the night, hungry and sore of limb, but with a great comfort in their hearts.

In an outbuilding by the temple is a curious thing which may arrest the attention of some. It is a gigantic rough cable or hawser, curled up like a Titanic caterpillar in a stone court. It measures three hundred feet in length and boasts a diameter of three inches. There are many cables longer than this and larger, yet there is no other rope like it in the world. It is curious in colour, being a faded and musty black. It is unusual in texture, appearing at a distance as if made of fur. Its peculiarities are readily to be explained. It is made of human hair contributed by thousands of poor people from the country around. In this dull warp are the glossy locks of many a smiling Japanese girl and many a sober matron. Wound up with such rich tresses also are grey hairs from the head of the old grandmother, who longed to help in the building of the sanctuary. This hawser of hair was used to drag the timbers along, as well as to hoist them into place.

Higashi Hongwanji, indeed, was built by the love of a people, whose unselfishness and devotion are without end. Much money was bestowed upon it, but it belonged to that coinless wealth which is "beyond the dream of avarice." Much gold was poured forth for seventeen years, but it came from a land of Havilah, of which it could well be said, "and the gold of that land is good."

The temple, of immense proportions, is beautifully placed in an open square, where are the cistern, the great bell, and the ponderous lanterns of bronze. The roof shows one majestic sweep of grey tiles, with a curve like the hollow of a foam-crested wave. The pillars are made of untouched baulks of keyaki wood, brown and bare.

Within is a wide hall, the pine ceiling of which is held up by huge columns of timber, free from any trace of decoration and standing in four rows. The walls are of paper screens, so that the light within is dim. Before the shrine is a coarse wooden barrier, and then a broad mat-covered passage for the priests. The shrine and the open chantries on either side of it occupy the whole of one length of the building.

The shrine itself is of red and black lacquer and brilliant gold. Its gilded screens are thrown aside, and within is the figure of Buddha, black and grave, sitting in an alcove of gold. The altar before the image is of gold lacquer brilliantly burnished. On its dazzling surface stand the golden lotus, the candlesticks, the dishes for offerings, and the incense burner. Amidst these effulgent emblems, and almost lost in the blaze of brass and bronze, silver and gilt, is a blue china vase with a sprig of cherry blossom in it. The ceiling is lost in darkness, but from it hang metal lanterns, glistening tassels, and curiously shaped ornaments.

The unenclosed rooms on either side of the shrine are extremely beautiful. Around each runs a dado of black lacquer with panels of gold. The wall above the dado is wholly of dull gold; and on this background are painted white and pink lotus flowers adrift among eddies of blue green. On this wall hangs a solitary kakemono in Pompeiian red. The ceiling is too dim to see. The floor is of black lacquer polished like a mirror, and in it are reflected the gold panels on the wall and the drifting lotus flowers. Stealing through the gorgeous chamber is the perfume of incense; from some corner comes the sound of the beating of a gong; without is the kneeling multitude.

Such is the temple the poor people built with their coppers, and for which, moreover, the men gave the wealth of their muscles, and the women the glory of their hair.

XI.

THREE TEMPLES IN KYOTO.

The three most frequented temples in Kyoto are Kiyomizu-dera, the Inari Temple, and Chion-in. Kiyomizu-dera stands on a precipitous hillside looking down over the town. It is hardly a temple, but rather a little hamlet of sacred buildings perched half way up a height which is covered with trees. A ledge has been hewn out of the slope to provide a foothold for this holy place; but so steep is the incline that the wooden platform which widens out before the main temple, and which makes a way round the terrace from one chapel to another, is built upon lofty timbers stepped on the sides of the declivity. The pines with which the great hill is shrouded gather around Kiyomizu-dera on every side, like a multitude of eager worshippers. Thus it is that the venerable roofs and the sun-tanned pillars stand out always against a background of eternal green.

The spot is reached by a long, steep street, given up to the sale of earthenware dolls and fancies of many kinds in homely porcelain. At the end of the street the worshipper is faced by towering stairs of stone which he needs must ascend. On the summit of these are two-storied gateways; while beyond, and still higher up the hill, is a stately pagoda, from the foot of which is a glorious view over the town and the misty plain in which it lies. The paved path thence climbs ever up and up, mounting towards the solemn tree-covered hill. It winds through avenues of stone lanterns, by the great fountain of bronze, by the stone cistern and the belfry, past the hall for offerings, and by many little chapels and shrines. It is, as it were, a street clambering through a village of monastic buildings.

At last the wide platform before the chief temple is reached. It is a stage of plain wood with a railing round it, over which those weary with the climb can lean and look down into the wooded gorge below. The temple is old and bare. Its roof of velvet brown cedar bark is streaked here and there with green moss, for the thatch lies under the damp shadows of the trees. On the platform is always a loitering crowd—just as on the platform of the Golden Pagoda at Rangoon—old men and maidens, young men and children, all attired in their best. There is much chattering among the friends who meet here, but their voices are drowned by the musical babble of clogs on the hollow boards. Always can be heard, too, the throb of the temple gongs, and the chink of copper money thrown by the worshippers on to the altar floor. In the still air the odour of incense mingles with the smell of pines.

The mysterious shadows in the depths of the shrine mimic the shades among the pine woods which gather around. In the one are the flickering flame of a swinging lantern, the gleam of gilt figures and the glint of brass. In the other are patches of burnished moss, bright tufts of ferns, and wet rocks that reflect the light of the setting sun.

The temple is sacred to Kwannon, the goddess who looks after the unhappy. So it comes to pass that those who every day climb up to this worshipping place among the trees come hither to find peace. It is a goal of pilgrimage for the sad at heart; and many, walking townwards, down the long paved way, stop at the edge of the hill to gaze across the dreamy valley with its white river, and in the looking lose some of the burden of their trouble.

Kiyomizu-dera is, however, no mere shrine to Kwannon. It is a sanctuary which supplies, to all sorts and conditions of men, a religion sufficing for every need.

There is, for example, on the platform the squatting figure of an aged man who ever looks amiably towards the distant hills. He is the god Binzuru. He is a deity "with a past," and certain slight failings in his early days have brought him in closer touch with the sympathies of the people. He now busies himself with the healing of the sick. The method of the healing is after this fashion: The believer rubs Binzuru on such part of his body as corresponds to the seat of his own trouble, and then rubs himself. This rubbing—although it may be a form of celestial massage—has done the god Binzuru no good. His image is of wood, which has been heavily coated at some time with red lacquer. Thousands of hopeful hands have rubbed all the lacquer from his brow, have lowered the height of his forehead, and have rubbed away his nose. From this it is to be inferred that headache and cold in the nose are common in Japan. Binzuru also has been worn to the wood in the region of the stomach as well as over the great toe, which losses of structure suggest that indigestion and possibly gout are not unknown about Kyoto.

It may be added that the constant abstraction of virtue has left Binzuru with an aspect of extreme senility and dotage, while the fact that he has bibs of red or white cotton around his neck, and "cuffs" of the same about his wrists give him an appearance which is little calculated to inspire professional confidence.

I watched many seek relief and comfort at this unusual out-patient's department. One pretty but shy maiden, having bowed before the much-worn ancient, passed her hand tenderly over his heart, and then over her own. I think she had a heart ache and that her trouble was lovesickness. If so, the kindly old wooden image may possibly have done her more good than could the mystified physician in the town. After her came along a wizened peasant from the country. He seemed to have travelled from afar, for there was a dazed look in his face. He led by the hand a boy, whom I supposed to be his grandson, and who was suffering from wide-spread ringworm of the scalp. It is probable that the learned in the village had wrought their best upon the lad's head, but without effect, for the malady is obstinate. The old man had evidently journeyed to Kyoto to seek the aid of the famous healer of Kiyomizu. He rubbed the bare wood on Binzuru's head vigorously, and then he rubbed the boy's head until he giggled. He repeated this ritual many times, and then left with great faith in his heart.

The next applicant was a worried woman bringing with her a bald-headed boy who was evidently mentally deficient. I think she hoped to convey to her son's brain some of that bright sense and that power of learning which dwelt beneath the brow of the patient

A RELIGIOUS PROCESSION AT KYOTO.

divinity. She rubbed the two heads—one after the other—with even more ardour than the peasant had displayed. The boy laughed uproariously, but the mother was very grave. Whether in the course of days a brighter intelligence dawned in the lad's dull eyes I know not; but I have little doubt that in its appointed time ringworm appeared upon his scalp. Women are patient; still there is trouble in the learning that the growth of a parasite outside the skull is no cure for a lack of activity within.

In the most remote nook of Kiyomizu-dera is an ancient timber shrine, drab and worn, with something of the look of a discarded wardrobe about it. It is sacred to the god who watches over lovers. There is a wooden grating in the front of this unpretending ark, and through it can be dimly seen the deity who has taken upon himself such lamentable responsibilities. One would expect him to be of amiable countenance, but the face that is visible in the dusk is that of a repulsive man with a grinning mouth and erect hair. To have listened for endless æons to the woes of the lovesick may possibly account for this sourness of visage.

The grating is thickly covered by little knots of white paper, which have been tied around every available bar of the wood. The maiden who is in search of a husband climbs up shyly to Kiyomizu, possibly after sundown. She there purchases a homily on white paper from the priest. This she rolls into an anguished cord, and, after praying to the dim man in the ark, and casting coins into his treasury, she proceeds to tie a knot around the grating with the thumb and little finger of one hand—a performance of some cunning. If her prayer be answered she shows her gratitude by hanging a little highly-coloured picture about the shrine, upon which is usually depicted a grateful woman kneeling at the feet of a heaven-sent husband.

I had once noticed in a country tea house a girl in a corner trying with great earnestness to tie a knot with only her thumb and little finger. It was not until I had seen the shrine at Kiyomizu that I understood the purpose of her endeavour.

Some way along the terrace is a poor little wooden shed in a corner against the bare hillside. In it are coarse shelves, one above the other, and on the topmost ledge is the bronze figure of a benevolent man with a bald head and a genial face. He is Jizo, the god who is kind to little children. Not only does he watch over them during life, but he cares for them after death and protects them from the hag Shozuka, who would rob the poor mites of their clothes when they are wandering in the other world. On the shelves below the image are many rude stone figures, which are archaic images of the kindly god himself. Around the necks of most of these are cotton bibs in red, in yellow and in white, while here and there on the shelves are children's toys, or a baby's cap. All these objects are offerings to Jizo, so that he may keep the dead children in mind.

This small shed of the benevolent old man, with nursery bibs about his neck, is the poorest building in Kiyomizu; and yet, from the bare earth to the shabby tiles, it is full to bursting with the love of mothers. All the gold of Japan weighed against this love would be as nothing. No resplendent shrine, no priceless emblem laden with costly stones, could represent all that intense, tragic, piteous affection with which tens of thousands of mothers have committed their babies to the care of Jizo under this mean threadbare roof.

The shed is against the damp rock of the mountain, the pine trees hang over it, the ferns have filled up gaps where the woodwork has fallen away. So it is that this poor worn shrine of dead children has for its real canopy the everlasting hills.

Inari—the goddess of rice—is one of the most popular of all the Shinto deities. Her emblem is a fox, and Fox Temples exist over the length and breadth of the land. This is the goddess of the peasant, for she makes his ricefields to flourish; the goddess of the housewife, for she fills her larder and replenishes her tubs of meal. In every kitchen is a small red shrine to Inari, and even in the modern hotel, with its electric light, its latest thing in English stoves and its French menu, there is sure to be found in the kitchen an altar of the Fox.

The great Inari temple at Kyoto is so placed that the worshipper is led up, step by step, from the valley until he finds himself in the wild untutored woods on the hillside. Many pilgrims tramp to this place. They are mostly of the poor, and many of them come

THE TEMPLE OF THE FOX.

hither by long roads. A prominent feature of this temple is the torii, a kind of gateway made of two upright pillars, across the tops of which stretch two horizontal beams. The uprights are, as a rule, painted a bright red and the beams a dull black. Many of the pilgrims bring little red torii with them as offerings to the good goddess.

Everywhere about the approaches of the temple are statues of foxes in stone, bronze, or wood. Some have in their mouths a key—the key of the celestial "godown" where the rice is stored, others hold a ball which is the world, others a roll of the sacred writings.

The way to the temple is by a wide stone path and many stairs, beneath innumerable torii, by many sheds for offerings, and countless lanterns and small shrines. The temple with its thatched roof, its timbers aglow with gilt and crimson, and its tassels of hemp, differs in no way from the ordinary Shinto sanctuary. Beyond the temple, and its cluster of dull buildings, paved paths make their way up the hill. They vanish into the silent wood, and thence creep upwards for more than a mile. These paths lead to sacred foxholes among the rocks and bracken, or to rustic shrines. They are almost roofed in by votive torii—pillars of vermilion with architraves of ebony—which are so closely placed as to make of the way a tunnel or roofed colonnade.

These thousands of torii in solid file wind through the wood like a slow-moving solemn procession of cowled monks in scarlet. This creeping cavalcade in brilliant red, passing among the awed pine trees and through the trembling multitude of ferns, is most wonderful to see. At the end of the strange path there is merely a tiny shrine among the moss and the boulders. It is over a foxhole, and is almost buried in toy torii in red, or by a caressing undergrowth of green.

There is a religious procession in connection with this temple which stirs the heart of Kyoto every spring time. Elaborate shrines, covered with Shinto emblems, are carried on poles through the streets by coolies dressed in white, who gather in their hundreds, and who show by their magnificent physique that Japan does not yet lack men for her armies. In the procession are uneasy officials, with strange head dresses, on horseback, innumerable bearers of umbrellas and lanterns, or of waving white trophies emblematical of rice. There are attendants in limpet-shaped hats, with necklaces of black and white squares, and solemn men who walk alone, but are dignified by some dangling badge of office.

Chion-in is a magnificent temple, whose immense two-storied gate is approached by an avenue between banks planted with cherry trees. Like other temples of its kind in Kyoto it is built upon the slope of a hill, and is on every side surrounded by pines. Near to it is a picturesque monastery with an ideal Japanese garden hidden among its sober buildings. Outside the monastery is a stone walk where are cherry trees, whose frail white blossoms stand up in sensitive contrast against the rust-brown roof.

Curious as it may appear, the most remarkable thing about Chion-in is neither the painted egret on its walls nor the gilt lotuses by its altar, neither its towering bronze lanterns nor its fountain with a dragon crawling out of it. The strange thing is a sound. It is the sound of a great bell which stands alone among the trees in a dip on the hillside. The bell is rightly called great, for it weighs seventy-four tons. It is of green bronze, and the wooden tower in which it swings raises its mighty mouth but a few feet from the ground.

In Europe a bell is struck by a metal hammer, and the hard crashing sound comes upon the ear like a concussion. The bell, too, is raised above the housetops, so that the clang of it scatters about the sky and reverberates away to the horizon. This temple bell is struck by a hanging ram of timber which strikes softly.

The sound which comes down from the pine woods above Chion-in is like the sound of no earthly bell. As heard at dawn, when the first streaks of light are creeping into the shuddering east, it is mysterious, thrilling, and solemn beyond all imagining. The sound comes out of the wood and rolls downward to the town. It is a deep, soft, melancholy note like that of a humming gong. It never rises skywards; it rumbles along the ground. It flows through the listener like water through sand. It permeates the body like a subtle tingling current. It sweeps through the living tissues like a Roentgen ray.

THE CHERRY TREE BY THE
MONASTERY WALK.

If it be the knell tolled for a departing spirit, the bell must be upon the other shore of the Great Gulf; and the sound that comes down from Chion-in is but the echo of it resounding across the void. It is so sad, so wandering, so desolate, that each slowly recurring boom comes like a sob.

XII.

A JAPANESE DINNER.

A Japanese dinner has been described so many times that there is little to be said about it that is not already well known. It is a dinner without tables and chairs, without knives, forks, spoons, or glasses, without bread or butter, potatoes or puddings. Thanks to the most kindly hospitality of the many Japanese gentlemen I met I had experience of both public and private dinners, and a grateful remembrance of all of them. A certain dinner of four will serve to illustrate to what state of nicety the art of eating has attained in the Far East.

The meal was served in a small, low room in a garden approached by stepping stones. Within, the walls were of brown or grey paper screens, while one side was open to the mimic landscape. A kakemono, showing a crow on a bamboo spray, hung from the wall. On the glistening yellow mats which made the floor were four kneeling-cushions. Dining on the floor to a European involves a certain degree of physical endurance, as well as an extended experience of the phenomena known as "pins and needles." There is a considerable difficulty in disposing of one's feet, which tend somehow continually to find their way among the bowls and dishes. The dining Japanese, on the other hand, appears to be a creature without legs. Before each of the cushions, on the occasion I have in mind, was placed a bronze charcoal stove, which also had a tendency to force itself as inconveniently upon the notice as did the European sock-covered feet.

The serving maids who entered noiselessly kneel before the guests and touch the floor with their foreheads. They serve each dish kneeling and with the most fascinating grace.

The first feature in the repast was tea—of the type known as "tea-ceremony tea." It is a pea-green mixture, thick, opaque and frothing, which is served in china bowls. It is made by whipping tea powder up with warm water. It possesses an agreeable taste suggestive of hay, while with it are brought sweet cakes on a wooden dish. Now before each diner is placed a small black lacquer table, about four inches high, on which is deposited a porcelain dish containing raw fish in neat segments, together with horseradish paste and a minute cup of soy. A fragment of the fish is picked up with chop-sticks, is dipped in the soy and then eaten. Those who express horror at the idea of eating raw fish will consume uncooked caviare with relish.

The course next in order is represented by a lacquer bowl, with a cover, containing rice, together with a like bowl of clear fish-soup, in which float shreds of lotus bulb. The soup is sipped as from a cup. During the meal saki—a wine made from rice—is taken. It is poured from a porcelain vase, and is drunk from minute bowls with a capacity akin to that of a liqueur glass.

Now on the table is placed a red lacquer box with a red lacquer lid. It contains eels roasted in oil. These also are eaten with chop-sticks. Following this appears another basin of clear soup made with lobster, and furnished with pieces of mushroom and sprigs of green. The remaining dishes consist of hot grilled fish in squares, served with sweet cakes, cold crab with ginger-flavoured vinegar, and finally (as a yielding to the Western appetite) fragments of roast teal with burdock, served with slices of raw apple and orange. At the end of all is a bowl of plain rice and clear Japanese tea. Everything is deposited upon the floor, or on the little lacquer stand, and as no dish is removed it is *en règle* to return to a particular course at any stage of the meal.

There is about the whole repast, from the beginning to the end, something of the little atmosphere of a doll's dinner party.

On a public occasion the later stages of the banquet are enlivened by geishas and dancing girls, whose brilliant costumes create in the room an effect as beautiful as a bank of flowers. In the last act of the dinner for four came the two little waiting maids, standing at the door of the house before the rickshaws, bowing their heads simultaneously to the ground, with their hands on their knees.

Japanese cooking would, I imagine, be not unfitly called exquisite. The food is neither greasy nor messy, nor in crude lumps, while every dish is pretty to look at. The serving of the food is a revelation, involving as it does a quaint and piquant ceremony. It may be claimed, moreover, that there is no method of taking food more refined or more delicate than that by means of chop-sticks. Civilisation in the West has as yet not advanced very far in connection with the circumstances of eating. While watching a number of Japanese gentlemen at dinner in the tea house it was impossible to avoid recalling the spectacle of a company of Germans —each with a yard square serviette tied about his neck—gorging noisily on a Rhine steamer. No contrast could well be more extreme.

The Japanese dinner is noiseless, but for the talking of those who gather on the floor. There is no clatter of knives and forks, nor of plates and dishes, nor does the floor tremble under the tread of perspiring waiters who bawl hotly in the ear such mysteries as, "thick or clear?"

Civilisation in the West has proposed but feeble attempts to mitigate the brutality of eating. If a boar's head be served up at a rubicund banquet it is ceremoniously brought in entire, and is made so realistic that there shall be no doubt but that the diner is about to eat the face of a recently living pig. On the more homely table the roasted hare appears in a ghastly guise—minus its fur certainly —but with ears and tail erect. It is hard to say what feature could be introduced to make it look more horrible or less suggestive of a creature which had been burnt alive. The leg of mutton, too, is dumped down as an obvious piece of a carcase; while the slab of blood-coloured beef makes no pretence of being other than a chunk of flesh cut from a cow.

There is no logical reason why the fact that man is a carnivorous animal should not be kept prominently before the eye; yet there are many functions appertaining to the animal man which we have, illogically, no need to be constantly reminded of. In the Japanese meal the circumstance that what is being eaten was once a live fish or a live bird is concealed prettily, and with commendable affectation.

The affairs of dining among Western folk have advanced but little since the days when the hunter or the backwoodsman killed his deer, skinned it, roasted it, and ate it before the fire, cutting off the flesh in strips. A good deal of the business of eating in the Occident is occupied with acts which rightly belong to the kitchen and the butcher's block. To the hungry is given a cooked fish; whereupon he proceeds to skin it and to remove the bones—the spine and the ribs. The Japanese are of opinion that this imitation of the methods of the nomad fisherman is obsolete, and that such incident of the meal might be anticipated in the scullery. A family essay to eat a turkey. The entire bird—which was possibly familiar as an individual during its lifetime—is placed proudly upon the table whole. The head of the family then rises in his might and, cleaving the bird with a knife, chops it up and hands fragments of limbs and trunk to those around. The cave man, when he dined *en famille*, did no less.

Japanese food is served up ready to eat, and there is about it no ostentatious display that man does not live by bread alone. Moreover, the native of Japan, when he dines, dispenses with the camp fire phenomena of a meal, with the relic of the hunting knife and of the fork with which flesh is fished out of a pot. A Japanese critic, if present at an enthusiastic harvest supper in England, would be justified in thinking that we eat surrounded with the bustle of a mêlée, use knives like forest rovers, and drink out of buckets—for the Japanese bucket is small.

XIII.

THE PALACE.

From time immemorial the government of Japan has been vested in an Emperor who was of heavenly descent, who could trace his origin to the sun, who was holy and inviolable. The present dynasty goes back to a time beyond the dawn of accepted history.

"The Sovereign Ruler was a personality deemed too sacred and apart for connection with affairs of general administration."* In stirring times he could take no active share in military movements, while in times of peace the mere details of civil government were beyond his ken. Thus it came about that, some time in the ninth century, a "Shogun" was appointed by the Emperor to relieve him of the burdens of military and civil administration. He became the Commander-in-Chief when war was abroad in the land, and the Governor-General when the islands were at peace. It is little to be wondered that the Shogun, although always acting in the name of the Emperor, rose to be a more and more independent power, that in due course the office was made hereditary, while the position assumed was practically that of the ruler of the country. As years went by, moreover, it is easy to understand that the actual influence of the Emperor became less and less; until he faded into what was little more than a reverenced name, a shadowy emblem.

In the twelfth century the establishment of the feudal system throughout Japan greatly strengthened the position of the Generalissimo. The Shogunate continued until the Restoration in 1867, and on October 17th in that memorable year the full supremacy of the Emperor was restored. He became again, as in ancient days, the ruler in fact as well as in name, and the Shogun vanished from out of Japanese affairs.

* "Japan by the Japanese," London, 1904, p. 500.

So it comes about that there are in Japan palaces of two kinds, the one of the Emperor, and the other of the Shogun. In Kyoto two such palaces exist within little distance of one another, and they serve to illustrate the characteristics of these two great powers in the country.

Nijo Castle became a palace of the Shogun more than three hundred years ago. It is still a place of great dignity and splendour. It is surrounded on all sides by a moat, full of lotus flowers, beyond which rises a massive wall made of great black stones. On the summit of the rampart is a grassy bank where are ranged savage-looking matsu trees. The moat is crossed here and there by a bridge leading to a gate in a huge two-storied tower. The tower is white, windowless, and silent.

Within this simple but impressive stronghold are wide courtyards and many ancient trees. The palace is approached by glorious wooden gates, roofed by a thatch of cedar bark. The timbers are a dead grey, the thatch a bronze green, but the whole crowning of the gate is made brilliant with gilded metal work and with wondrous carvings of birds, phœnixes, and peonies in high relief, as well as in vivid colours. The most sumptuous blaze of gilt is in the shadows under the eaves, while the most bounteous array of birds and flowers is just above the princely gateway.

The palace is a plain building as seen from the outside; but within is a cordon of solemn rooms which are magnificent in the extreme. The ceilings are coffered, and each sunken square is richly painted with flowers, crests and geometric designs. The wood of the walls is seaweed-brown, and on this sombre ground are depicted peacocks and eagles, maple boughs and finches. Everywhere are there exquisite lattice-work and worthy carvings in teak. The ramma—which comes in the place of the frieze—is of perforated cedar, alive with strange ducks and monster flowers, all radiant in brilliant colours. In the gaps between the gaudy blossoms and the birds, light streams into the rooms.

On the sliding screens in every chamber are paintings on a background of dull gold. Here a branch of a matsu tree, the size of the living stem, spreads across the wall, and there is a cloud of cherry blossom, or a branch of the maple afire with the tints of autumn.

In another place are herons fishing, or wild geese hurrying seawards across the sky, and often are to be seen imagined landscapes, fantastic mountains and magic lakes. Every room is framed—as it were—in black lacquer and gold bronze, while now and then the sweep of the wall is broken by a polished cupboard with gilt doors, or by a mysterious recess.

The outer walls are of white paper screens. If a slide in the corridor be drawn aside there is a view over a shut-in garden. The garden shows a lake with islands and bridges, but without water. The water is represented by white sand raked into ripples. Stepping stones lead down the beach to the water's brink, while a winding track of river-worn pebbles on a hillside makes believe to be a mountain torrent making for the pool.

A palace aims at embodying the grandest conception that the people of a country can form of a home or of a place to live in. The abode of the King must be the most superb dwelling that the imaginative can imagine, or that the cunning can construct. Everywhere in the world is this endeavour the same; this determination to raise the Sovereign to a position which shall be above all others. In the Kaffir village the largest and the best built kraal is the kraal of the chief. The most pretentious house in Burmah is the palace at Mandalay. The finest buildings in India have been the abodes of Kings; while throughout the Western world there is little need to seek the history of the loftiest castle, or the most stately château.

Here at the palace of Nijo has the will of the people been the same. The palace is a Japanese house made immense, made beautiful. Those who designed it and those who built it gave of their best. It was not finished until all conceptions of magnificence had been exhausted, and until that time was reached when no added fillet of gilt, no further painting nor carving of wood, could bring it nearer to the realisation of the most august dwelling in the land.

As the Shogun was the creature of the Emperor, it may be supposed that the Imperial Palace at Kyoto would present a degree of grandeur of which the glory of the castle of Nijo was a mere shadow. This, however, is not the case. The Shogun, although he was virtually the ruler of the country, was only a man. Recognition of his position required that his dwelling place should be the proudest that could be designed or erected for men. The Emperor was a divinity; his person was sacred; he was a presence, not an individual; he was the embodiment of a mighty principle, not a mere mortal. His abode, therefore, must accord with the conception of a temple, and more than that, a temple of the Shinto faith—the old faith of the country. The Shinto temple is secluded, quiet, unpretending; a sanctuary for meditation as well as for communion with the powers that rule the world.

The Imperial Palace is shut away within a plain drab wall. There is no pretence at a stronghold, for the person of the Emperor could never be assailed. Around him was Japan; that alone was defence sufficient. The palace gates are temple gates of plain, unpainted wood, without either carving or gilt, which are crowned by a village thatch. No gates could be less alike than those of the Shogun's palace and the Palace of the Emperor. The one may be worthy of a king, but the other is worthy of a god. Within the drab walls are the palace buildings—plain houses of one storey covered with the humble thatch—so that the royal residence is not unlike a hamlet in an enclosure, even though the roofs curve skywards as do the canopies of a shrine.

Within are long corridors of quite bare wood, with above a plain ceiling and below primrose mats. The light comes in through paper screens. These are the corridors of a monastery. The dingy throne room, with its dull roof and its unornamented timber pillars, is no longer in keeping with the spirit of the palace, since in it is a modern canopy of silk over a modern throne to meet those conditions which now attend the ceremonial of the court.

That part of the palace which is the most interesting is the Imperial Study, in which, it may be assumed, much of the day of the Emperor was, and still is, spent. Six rooms in all constitute this retreat, and they no doubt represent the ideal of such an apartment as is considered fitting for the Ruler of Japan. They are no more than the rooms that border on the temple close, ascetic and unpretending. On the walls, as well as on the sliding panels, are painted landscapes of sacred and historic association against a background of gold. The general colour of the walls is that of a gold-tinted autumn leaf. The wood around is severely plain, and is untouched by carving of any kind. On the floor are yellow mats edged with red, and the lights steals in through simple paper screens.

When one of these white shutters is drawn aside there is revealed the scene upon which it is considered appropriate that an Emperor's eyes should rest. The screen opens upon a convent garden so closed about with trees and banks that it may be a league from the abodes of men. There is a lake with, at one part of it, a shore at high tide. This is shown by a beach of pebbles crossed by large stepping stones which lead from the verandah before the Emperor's rooms. The tide has so risen that the lowest stones are already under water. In the lake is a green island with pine trees and granite lanterns on it, approached by old somnolent stone bridges. Beyond are hills crowned with maples; while from over the summit of one height a waterfall tumbles down through a ravine of rocks into the lake. There are glimpses, too, of a wistaria arbour, of a summer house, of a little copse. The garden is small, but it is as exquisite, as suggestive, as full of imagination as any garden in Japan could be.

This, then, is the abode worthy of an Emperor, a simple room looking out upon a garden, a corner in a monastery, a world-forgetting cloister, dainty, reposeful, lovable. It is a place for the recluse, the student, the meditative. Here on the verandah at sundown the sacred Ruler of Japan could stand and dream over the fortunes of his country, with always before him the inspiring parable of the Rising Tide.

XIV.

TWO INTERVIEWS.

When I was at Tokyo I had the honour of being presented to His Majesty the Emperor of Japan, and when at Washington—some weeks later—the like honour of being presented to Mr. Roosevelt, the President of the United States.

There is only a sea between the islands of Japan and the continent of America, but there could be no contrast of nations more extreme if the wide world parted them. On one side lies Japan, just emerged from feudalism, with its ancient civilisation, its leisured culture, its slumber of centuries, its elaborately developed country; on the other America, the newest of the great powers of the world, with its freedom from old prejudices, its pushing commercial activity, its intense energy, and its miles of yet undeveloped prairie and forest.

It was America who opened Japan to the world, who pierced the cordon which had made the island an isolated sanctuary upon the earth, within whose jealous circle no strange foot could step. It was an American sea captain who woke the Sleeping Princess, who blew such a blast before the cobwebbed castle that those within were constrained to come forth and listen. Commodore Perry then told them the surprising tale of modern progress, and let them know that America proposed to take part in their arousing, and would accept no refusal.

The Emperor of Japan was born in 1852, just one year before Commodore Perry anchored his "black ships" in Yedo Bay. He is the representative of the oldest dynasty in the world, a dynasty, which according to the words of a recent Imperial Decree, has existed "for over 2,500 years."* "The Sacred Throne," says the

* "Japan by the Japanese." London, 1904, p. 4.

Articles of the Constitution, "was established at the time when the heavens and the earth became separated. The Emperor is Heaven-descended, divine, and sacred; he is pre-eminent above all his subjects. He must be reverenced, and is inviolable."* Of the throne, the Emperor himself speaks as follows:—

"The Imperial Throne of Japan, enjoying the grace of Heaven, and everlasting from ages eternal in an unbroken line of succession, has been transmitted to Us through successive reigns."†

The present Emperor has not only seen the opening up of his wondrous country to the outer world, has not only witnessed changes which are beyond all reasonable imagining, but he himself has taken part in the abolition of the Shogunate (1868), and in the breaking up of the feudal system (1871). He has indeed watched a revolution in his country which has had no parallel in the history of the world. He still remains a divine being, who is regarded by his subjects with the most intense admiration and reverence, and who is obeyed with a loyalty which recalls the superb heroism of mediæval times.

Mr. Roosevelt was born in 1858, and commenced his life in the study of the law, partly at Columbia College and partly in his uncle's office. He soon abandoned the law for politics, and in but few years his sturdiness of purpose and his high principles made him a marked man. The success with which he held successive important offices in the state is well known, as are also his gallant services in the war with Spain. Finally recent events have shown that he has secured, in his position as President of the United States, the confidence of the nation to a degree which has never before been surpassed.

Between the Imperial Palace at Tokyo and the White House at Washington there is little in common.

In the very centre of the great bustling city of Tokyo is a secluded area some miles in circumference. It is surrounded by a steep bank and a moat, and somewhere within this circuit is the Palace in which the Emperor dwells. The moat is singularly impressive, and forms, indeed, the most beautiful feature of the

* "Japan by the Japanese." London, 1904, p. 33.
† Ibid., p. 610.

THE PALACE MOAT, TOKYO.

Royal City. The fosse is wide; its waters are deep and clear; its banks of grass are as vividly green and as smooth as an English lawn. On that side of the winding lake which borders on the town the bank is low and edged with Japanese willows. The Palace bank, on the other hand, is as high and as steep as the glacis of a fortress; only its covering of well-trimmed grass drapes it like velvet. On the summit of the precipitous slope is a wall, black with age, a primeval wall which may have been built when building began. On the verdant slope are a few ancient matsu trees. Some bend moodily over the moat. Others seem to be staggering down the incline towards the water, like scared demons, with wild, outstretched arms and eerie tresses. Within this barrier of pond and dell the ground is level with the summit of the crowning wall. It can be seen that it is covered with grass, and that many pines are standing on the height like sentinels.

The green-banked moat is the cordon around the King; the rim of the charmed circle; the bulwark against the world. What is beyond the bank and the wizened wall belongs to the mystery which shrouds the dynasty of Japan. To those in the city there is nothing to be seen across the girdle of the moat but a tree-covered heath—no roofs, no signs of a Palace. Among the turmoil of the great capital this is a hushed oasis; among the crowding houses this is a piece of the heart of the country; among a million homes this is the home of the Heaven-descended King.

The Emperor of Japan is a being alone, the living representative of the soul of the nation, and here at Tokyo the solemnity of this fact is taught. No environment of a monarch could be more dignified or more simple than the green still moat around a pine-covered land, which to the common world has remained always unknowable.

I was presented to the Emperor by His Excellency Sir Claude MacDonald, G.C.M.G. Passing across the moat we entered the mysterious country, which proved to be a gracious park with green lawns and many pine, matsu, and maple trees. It is encompassed by an inner moat with cyclopean walls of immense height and cliff-like steepness. The Palace is a simple building of one storey. The portal we entered by differed but little from the gateway of a village temple. At the door were footmen in European liveries trimmed with gold. They wore breeches with white silk stockings, but being very short they seemed to lack the most familiar quality of the Royal servant. The Lord Chamberlain and other officials were in uniforms which closely resembled those of the English Court. There was a fine Entrance Hall, but it was furnished in the Western manner with chairs and tables, carpets, and the orthodox fireplace and mantel-piece. The corridors, too, were carpeted, and it was impossible not to feel that nothing had been gained by the loss of the primrose-coloured Japanese mat. On one side were glass windows in the place of paper screens, and on the other a wall paper in lieu of exquisite bare wood.

The Waiting Room was large and lofty, with a prettily painted coffered ceiling. The floor was of parqueterie. The furniture was European and apparently German. Over the fireplace were a few exquisite Japanese curios, by the side of "ornaments for the mantel-piece" which had come from the far West. These latter could well have been spared. The most beautiful thing in the apartment was a gold lacquer cabinet. It put to shame whatever else was in the room, and especially some very strident electroliers which were possibly fresh from England.

The corridors which led to the Royal Apartments were simpler. There were still the Brussels carpet and the glazed windows, but the plain ceiling, showing the beauties of natural wood, had come back again. On the wall were gold panels in that ancient style which makes Nijo Castle magnificent, while near to the reception room was a plain gold screen which must have blushed for the carpet beneath its foot.

The room in which the Emperor stood, surrounded by the great officials of his household, was small, and lit only from the corridor. It was furnished after the Western style, and had the appearance of a small sitting room.

The Emperor was dressed in a dark military uniform very like to that of a French general. He is the 122nd member of his family, in unbroken line, who has ruled over Japan. His appearance is familiar through published photographs. His face remains immobile, and, if one may say so without disrespect, it is expressionless, impassive, and mask-like. As His Majesty does not speak English, his questions and my answers were interpreted by one of the Lords in Waiting. The etiquette of the Court requires that the conversation should be in so low a tone as to be practically whispered. The Emperor was good enough to ask about my journey and my impressions of Japan. He made enquiries as to the health of His Majesty the King of England, and asked me much as to my opinion of the Japanese military hospitals, medical field equipment, and the like.

Her Majesty the Empress received me in an adjacent room, in which she had already graciously received my wife and daughter. She was attended by her Lord Chamberlain and three Ladies-in-Waiting, who were all in European dress. The Empress, whose face is most vivacious and alert, also speaks no language but Japanese. The conversation I had the honour to hold with her took place through the medium of a Lady-in-Waiting, and was conducted in a whisper. These Royal apartments looked out upon a charming Japanese garden, but they lacked the dignity, the graciousness, and the elemental splendour of the Royal rooms in the Palace at Kyoto.

The old Japanese audience chamber is beautiful, as well as a realisation of perfect daintiness; but as soon as the garish glare of Western civilisation creeps into it the whole charm vanishes.

The Throne Room of the palace is decorated in black lacquer and gold. The walls are hung with claret-coloured curtains. The two gilded thrones are on a raised daïs. Behind them is a panel of pale green silk, upon which is embroidered the royal crest—the sixteen-petalled chrysanthemum. The canopy over the thrones is supported by sloping gilt poles crowned with ostrich plumes. The Audience Chamber is of red lacquer and gold. Pictures of flowers on silk fill the sunken panels in the ceiling, while brilliant silks cover the walls. Other public apartments follow more or less on the same lines, and everywhere the furniture and general arrangement of each room are European.

Washington is a picturesque and dignified city, which, when the improvements which are now in progress are completed, will be, with little doubt, one of the most stately capitals in the world.

The White House stands a little back from the road in Lafayette Square. In no way is it isolated or shut off from the city. It has the appearance of a gentleman's country house, a solid, simple building, with a long-settled air of quiet refinement about it. While it is exactly appropriate to the spirit of the American Republic, it is in a way a vivid embodiment of its principles. The mansion is by comparison very modern, for when the first President of the United States was elected, the present dynasty in Japan had already ruled that country for 2,449 years.

I was presented to Mr. Roosevelt by my friend, Professor J. William White, of Philadelphia, who had already made me agreeably acquainted with many of the charms of his great country. As Mr. Roosevelt burst into the room it was impossible not to feel that he who had written upon the Strenuous Life had written upon what he knew. Here was a man of intense vigour and activity, who looked in every inch of him what he is—a strong man. He met me without formality of any kind, but with a breezy heartiness. One could hardly fail to be electrified by his irrepressible energy. Those who know the President of the United States will agree that his face is neither expressionless nor habitually impassive. When Mr. Roosevelt smiles there can remain no doubt in the mind of any that he is smiling. It is the smile of a determined and brilliant man who has taken no uncertain position among the great influences of the time.

XV.

THE VILLAGE.

No mean idea of the features of the country in Japan can be gained among the villages and hamlets round about Yokohama. Along the coast towards the south lies a district very like to England. It is a land that changes restlessly from hill to dale, from wooded copse to wandering down, from wild yellow cliffs to sober barley fields. In many a place a drowsy coombe opens to the sea, and often the path that has led through a pine forest will drop into a Devonshire lane. Far inland is the superb mountain of Fuji, capped with snow; far out at sea is a liner with a pennon of smoke making for San Francisco.

The rickshaw road from Yokohama to the village of Sugita—famous for its plum blossoms—follows the sweep of a generous bay, keeping ever along the margin of the sea. The country is clad with verdure to the very edge of the beach. Tufts of bamboo hang over the fawn-coloured sand, and the sampan, drawn up so as to be beyond the touch of the creeping wave, may have its prow buried in a field of millet.

It is a wonderful sea road. On one side all is green; on the other all is blue. On the one hand are fields of maize and corn, of beans and rice, in which men in indigo jackets and tights, with white handkerchiefs on their heads, are eternally at work. They are the peasants who people the country of the old coloured prints. Beyond the fields are fir-covered hills and occasionally a bramble-draped precipice. On the side towards the Pacific is the beach, where men are busy with sampans, and where, here and there, are the picturesque, untidy belongings of boats, the ropes and spars, the brown sails and nets, the piles of old timber. Now and then there is to be seen a man building a wherry. His methods are so primitive, his carpentry so rude, while he himself is so elementary in dress, that he might be Robinson Crusoe fashioning that famous craft which has interested a world.

On occasion a tiny creek will cross the road, running under a wooden bridge. It soon loses itself among a tangle of ferns, or in a tunnel of overarching bamboo and inquisitive bushes. Far up the creek there is sure to be a boat. It may be very old, half filled with water and half buried in weeds. If so, it has crept up the creek to die. It may be hearty and trim, but injured in its struggle with the sea, and then the creek becomes its dock, and the shipwright works upon it standing in the water with his tools on the bank of grass.

On one side of the path is the smell of the sea and the seaweed, while, landwards, is a perfume blown from off fields full of flowering beans.

The village, when it is come upon, is very picturesque—a line of houses straggling along in the company of a brown, unsteady road. All the cottages have a soft velvet thatch, with commonly a crop of green lilies growing along the crest of the roof. The rest of the house is of weather-stained wood and paper, a construction as simple as the house a child draws on a slate. About it is a paling of bamboo, or a laurel hedge, while within is a garden such as the Japanese love, or a yard filled with the lumber of the fields and the lumber of the sea. Around every house and in every court are women, with bright handkerchiefs on their heads, dallying with children, or washing clothes, or damply active with dripping brooms and splashing buckets.

At some spot by the side of the street is the pet tree of the hamlet, a cherry tree as a rule, or possibly a maple. Then comes a bright red torii, flanked with stone lanterns, guarding a temple with whose paltry adornment the village priest is busy. There are humble village shops, left apparently to look after themselves, and unassuming tea houses, where a few gossips linger on the mats. There will probably be one great house in the village with a walled garden and tiled roof. It stands a little apart, for it is quite aristocratic, in spite of some piles of seaweed which are immodestly

A COUNTRY HOUSE.

near to its confines, and some red-brown nets which are actually drying on its camellia bushes.

The largest of the country houses, those lost among trees or those with heavy roofs curled up at the corners, are usually monasteries, or have been at some time connected with temples. Japanese farms are small, so small that the family can work them themselves unaided. The cultivated fields—marked as they are by precise trenches and rows—are as trim as gardens. Everything is "done by hand," and each plant is tended as an individual, not as a part of a crop. From the care expended upon a single onion, one might imagine that it would one day blossom into an orchid.

There are children everywhere in the village, crawling in the road, nodding asleep on their mother's shoulders, or playing in the creeks. There is the leisured, critical village dog, who is the same in every small settlement all the world over, and the old man of the place, who was once a daring sea fisherman, but who now shuffles about with a baby on his back.

It is well for the visitor to go on from Sugita to Kamakura. It was a populous city with a million inhabitants in the days of its glory. It was the capital of eastern Japan, moreover, and the scene of faction fights, of sackings and of burnings of a fine heroic type. Now it is a little seaside village grateful for the patronage of the holiday-maker from Yokohama.

Here in the open, in a quiet garden by the side of a Japanese pond, is the great Daibutsu—the colossal bronze figure of Buddha, which photographs have made as familiar as Fuji or the geisha. The ponderous deity looks dull and stupid, as well as infinitely bored. He seems to be squatting in a hollow of the ground and to have lost his lower limbs. The height of the image is nearly fifty feet. His sluggish eye measures four feet across, while his mouth, in width, is but little less. There are windows with shutters where his shoulder-blades should be, and within his chest is a temple with a wooden stair leading up to the windows.

This immense image is less ungracious than the Daibutsu at Nara, which claims to be three feet higher. The Buddha of Nara is in an enormous but dilapidated house, with no more pretence than a shed for a mammoth. The building, patched in places with corrugated iron, is shabby and mean-looking. Within, the Daibutsu is exhibited as a penny show, and is presented with no more reverence than that which surrounds the Fat Woman at a fair. There is a tawdry dust-covered altar before the image, with a background of European wall paper such as is used in servants' attics. In front of the altar are bunches of paper flowers six feet high, in flaring blue and red. The colour of the figure is bottle-green, and from head to foot it is powdered in dust. It presents a brutish, dropsical lump of a man, sitting apparently in a sponge bath, but in reality on a lotus. His eyes are closed, his eyelids are sodden, his cheeks bloated, his puffy hands are enormous and seemingly too heavy to lift. This repulsive creature of bronze suggests the model of a man suffering from the stupefying disease known as myxœdema. Those who go to Nara would do well to avoid the exhibition.

From Kamakura it is but a few pleasant miles to Enoshima—the Mont St. Michael of Japan. This little steep-cliffed island can be reached at low tide by crossing the sands, but when the tide is in flood it is cut off from the mainland, and then the only way to the place is along a wooden causeway, which is lamentably decrepit. The island is very green, for it is covered with trees and a dense undergrowth. Even the stones are green, for they are spread over with moss. A very trivial town clings to the one steep street which makes its way, step by step, from the yellow sands to the wood-crowned summit. There are tea houses without number in the street, for the island is sacred to Benten, the Goddess of Good Fortune, and is a favourite place of pilgrimage.

In the woods are many aimless paths which loiter all over this Elysian Isle like delighted idlers. Some of them are cut along the edge of the cliff, whence is a glimpse of a miniature harbour, a long way down, with the sampans of the island huddled in it, or of a sandy cove among black rocks where are many sea birds. Through the trunks of the trees can be seen, on one side, a grey, fern-encompassed temple hiding in the woods, and on the other the circles of widening waves streaming into the bay from the Pacific.

XVI.

NARA.

Nara lies at the foot of a range of low hills some twenty-six miles from Kyoto. It is a place of infinite leisure. For three score years and ten it was the capital of Japan, but that was as long as twelve centuries ago. Since then it has slumbered. It is a tidy, self-respecting little town, with a certain prim old-maidenly stiffness about it. It lives upon memories of the past, and could gossip delicately about a glory that was. Its ancient park and moss-grown terraces are as full of old-world legends as are the avenues and courts of Fontainebleau. In all its ways there is still the dignity of the Royal Borough, the consciousness of a never-to-be-forgotten past, when Imperial processions moved through its streets. The vase is broken and shattered—

> "But the scent of the roses will hang round it still."

A long, straight road leads through the town to the foot of a deeply wooded hill. Where the town ends, along this way, is an open common of miniature downs and miniature dells, all graciously green, and covered with cherry trees which were in full blossom when I visited the dowager city. Many who had come to see the flowers were picnicking under the trees, but with a certain solemnity appropriate to Nara the Highly Born.

Near by the common is a beautiful pool with green banks planted with cherry trees and pines and the sorrowful Japanese willow. One slope is crowned by the graceful Pagoda of Kobukuji, while on other sides of the pool are white-walled houses, with gardens about them, which were probably planned when the Emperor lived in the city. There is a certain melancholy about this exquisite lake, for it appears that, once upon a time, there was "a beautiful maiden at the Mikado's Court, who was wooed by all the courtiers, but rejected their offers of marriage because she was in love with the Mikado. The latter had pity on her for a while; but when he afterwards began to neglect her, she went secretly away by night and drowned herself in this pond."*

Between the cherry tree common and the lake is a venerable park belonging to the temple of Kasuga, which was founded here in A.D. 767. The shrine is far up the hillside among the trees. It is approached by a stately avenue of cryptomeria, which extends from the common to the foot of the hill. Here, where the solemn walk ends, stands a red torii against the blue-green of the wood. The way now becomes steeper and steeper, winding up by many terraces to the middle of the forest. Gigantic trees grow about the path and make it dark. The wood becomes at each step denser and wilder until there is seldom a splash of sunshine to be seen on the paved way.

On each side of the road are rows of stone lanterns, not in scores, nor in hundreds, but in thousands. They are of all heights and shapes as well as of all ages. They incline at many angles, for now and then they are tilted by ancient tree roots which are crawling out of the earth. They stand like a row of ghosts, shoulder to shoulder, and often in ranks three deep. Many are turned to bronze-green by a growth of moss. The path still climbs up through the shadows of the wood by crumbling walls and steps so old that they have become a part of the forest.

Plodding up this hushed ascent are pilgrims in white, with straw hats on their bowed heads and inscriptions on their chests. They carry each a staff and beads and a pilgrim bell. They mutter as they go. Men clad as these were climbing up to Kasuga when Chaucer's pilgrims were making their way to the shrine at Canterbury. As they were then so are they now, for nothing is changed. The way is a thousand years old, and for a thousand years pilgrims have crept up the hillside to the holy place.

The forest is full of sacred deer, who make a rustling among the bracken as if the place were haunted, or who patter over the stones in the wake of any pilgrim who seems likely to give them a

* Murray's "Handbook of Japan," London, 1891, p. 330.

NARA.

brought hither on their last march, just as the dead Kings of Egypt were carried ceremoniously forth into the silent desert.

Nikko is some ninety miles north of Tokyo, and stands about two thousand feet above the level of the sea. A village which has sprung up near by the sacred hill has changed a little the solitude of the place. It lies in a small, homely valley among the mountains, by the side of a torrent which rushes seawards through a gully of blue rocks. The near hills are covered with pine trees, but the far away heights are bare, and at the time of my visit—early in May—were deep in snow. The little town is no more than a mountain village in a mountain valley, just such a settlement as is found in a hundred crannies among the foot hills of Switzerland. The village creeps up to one bank of the torrent, while on the other is that steep hill among whose pines the tombs of the two Tokugawa are hidden.

Crossing the water at the end of the one long street of the place is the sacred bridge, which is the centre of Nikko. From the south the bridge is approached by an avenue of cryptomeria. This avenue—four miles in length—is straight and profoundly solemn. Self-absorbed and with determined purpose it passes across the level fields of rice and maize to the crossing of the holy bridge. It is a processional road, the road of the dead, as well as the path which would needs be followed by those long trailing retinues which attended upon the great who came to pay their homage to the unforgotten. The avenue is dark, funereal, and pitiless, yet most impressive. The way along it is narrow. On either side stand the tall cryptomeria trees in formal line, an unbroken rank of towering trunks, bare and erect as masts. The stem of each is a ruddy brown softened by the silver grey of lichen. The foliage of each is a soft sombre green which is almost blue. The boughs meet high above the road, and make of the way a rustling aisle. They shut out the sky, so that the causeway is dim; while about the topmost arches hangs a mist like the smoke of incense. There is no more solemn road than this, none perhaps so sad, for it is tuned only to the music of a funeral march.

The sacred bridge was washed away a few years ago, and has not yet been rebuilt. It was of vermilion coloured lacquer, orna-

XVII.

NIKKO.

The most famous dynasty of the Shogunate was that of the Tokugawa family. It was not only the most famous, but it was also the last. The dynasty was founded in 1603 by Ieyasu, who is spoken of "as one of the greatest generals and altogether the greatest ruler that Japan has ever produced." The Tokugawa princes were still in power when Commodore Perry came with his black ships to Yedo Bay. It was with a Shogun of this family that he treated; and when the Revolution broke out in 1867 the Shogun who was deposed, and who thus became the last of his race, could claim direct descent from the ever illustrious Ieyasu.

In 1616, when the great general lay a-dying, he ordered that his body should be buried among the mountains of Nikko in a spot he knew well and which he himself indicated. To Nikko, then, in the following year, his remains were brought. Thirty-five years later his grandson, Iemitsu, the third of the Tokugawa Shoguns, who was himself a scarcely less able ruler than the founder of the house, was buried near by to him. The mausolea of these two leaders of men still stand upon the hillside of Nikko, and to them is owing the unparalleled glory of the place.

What the Taj Mahal is to India, Nikko is to Japan. It is, in the first place, one of the most beautiful spots in the country, while the buildings which have gathered around the tombs of the two famous dictators are—according to their kind—without an equal in the East.

Nikko was chosen as a burying place because it was in the heart of the country, remote from towns, a lonely valley among the hills where any might rest in peace. Ieyasu and his grandson were that the real bond of affection was between a very old cherry tree and a faithful camellia. They were both in blossom, and the flowers of each—the white and the red—were mingled together as in an old-fashioned bouquet. The other four trees were mere philanderers. Those knots which were closest, those stems which were so interlocked that they had blended into one, belonged to the camellia and the cherry. Under the tree was a small red torii and a shrine to show that the place was sacred, while about the boughs which were in tightest embrace were tied many paper knots, as at Kiyomizu-dera.

It may be supposed that those who prayed here, and who left these memorials of their longings upon the altar of the ancient tree, followed a dream of life which was founded upon the idyll of the Camellia and the Cherry.

rice cake from his bag. At last the path opens upon a stone courtyard where are a cistern and an oratory. A few paces higher up the slope is the temple. It is a small and simple sanctuary, whose thatched roof is studded with moss. It is in the very bosom of the hill. The breathless pilgrim as he prostrates himself before the shrine can see around it nothing but the untrodden forest, with, perhaps, a stray deer moving through the undergrowth. Here, at the summit of the dreary steps, at the end of the dark avenue and beyond the phantom muster of stone lanterns, he has come to the very heart of things.

There are roads trodden by pilgrims which lead at the end to resplendent shrines rich with relics and overladen with precious offerings. This pilgrim's road at Nara leads to a quiet hollow in a wood and to a temple which is little more than a woodman's hut.

There are many other sanctuaries upon this hillside which are reached by desultory avenues among the trees, all marked by lines of lanterns, by worn stairs, by banks of moss. Some of these temples are brilliant with bronze lanterns, which hang under the wide eaves in many hundreds; others are brave with crimson paint or bright lacquer; others seem to have dropped entirely from out of the memory of men and to have faded—gate, pillar, and balcony—to the tint of ashes.

Near the main sanctuary and in a court of the temple buildings is a tree called "The Lovers' Tree." That it is very old is evident, for it is propped up with solicitous care. It is claimed that its extravagantly twisted trunk is composed of six trees, viz.: A camellia, a cherry tree, a plum tree, wild ivy, wistaria, and nandina or barberry. What strands make up the knot of intertwining boughs no man can say, for such is the fervour of this ecstatic embrace that the stems have in places become fused together as if by amorous heat. This picture of eternally clasped hands can scarcely find favour with any but a polygamous people. The tree might have been adopted as the emblem of the Agapemone, but if it be assumed to depict the anguish of the maiden with many suitors —the one Juliet of five Romeos—then her fate is assuredly no less terrible than that of Laocoön.

A closer examination of this burning bush made it apparent

NIKKO.

mented with plates of gilt bronze. It was a fragile bridge suited for a place of lawns and flowers, but here it crossed a rude torrent hissing along the chasm of a savage gorge, filled with sharp rocks and dead pine trees, which had been torn up by the flood. From the opposite bank there is again the stern avenue of cryptomeria which now winds up hill to the tombs of the two Shoguns.

The hill is steep, and is draped from its foot to its summit with trees, cryptomeria, firs and pines, a forest of dark, everlasting green. In places it is rough with immense outjutting rocks. In places it is smooth with the velvet of moss or the plumes of innumerable ferns, while from twenty points a little frightened stream hurries noisily down the slope. Far up on this gaunt hillside, and in the deepest part of the forest, are the mausolea. They are approached through courts crowded with fair buildings, brilliant with polished lacquer and gilt bronze, and laden with such ornament and such carving as befits a rare cabinet. This is the marvel of Nikko, that among the wilds of a rough, untended height should be found the daintiest and most exquisite buildings which the art and ingenuity of the country have ever produced.

The road to the mausoleum of Ieyasu is long and steep, but there is much by the way. The funereal avenue ends at a huge granite torii, four centuries old. By the side of it, and almost hidden by tall trees, is a five-storied pagoda. Against a background of bluish green there rise five black roofs, the underparts of which are in colour a fervid red. The end of each beam and each row of tiles is capped with gold. To each storey is a balcony with a shining balustrade of vermilion lacquer. The wall of each storey is of carved wood painted in faint reds, blues, and greens, in white and in gold, so that at a distance the colouring is that of lichen on a wall.

The ascent is by a series of terraces, approached by stone stairs and entered by resplendent gates. The buildings passed on the way are beyond remembering. As the climber looks up there is ever before him the same background of green pines, against which stand out black roofs shining like ebony and edged with gold, dazzling walls of scarlet lacquer, balustrades of grey stone, great bronze lanterns, with here and there a cherry tree in bloom.

The gate leading to the first terrace is weighed down with coloured carvings of fabulous beasts, of lions and peonies, of tigers and bamboos. Within are store-houses whose huge black beams are stamped by medallions and clasps of gold, a granite cistern under a canopy of winged dragons, and a gaudy building in lacquer and gilt for the holy scripts. Higher and higher the steps toil up, past torii of bronze, standard lanterns of iron, centuries old, brown candelabra and rusting bells.

On the upper terrace is the gate Yomeimon, the most beautiful gate of all. No part is free from wonders in graven wood. Its pillars are white, its roof dead black crested with gold. Strange beasts form the capitals of the columns as well as the supports of the small white and gold gallery. Scaly dragons with gaping red mouths crawl from under every eave, while gargoyle-like heads project from every shadow. The balustrade is in carved wood gently coloured, showing children at play; while beneath the balcony are Chinese sages and immortals, peonies and birds. Each white beam of the gate is clamped with yellow bronze.

In due course the main shrine is reached. It has beyond it and around it only the forest. The whole of the front of the shrine, as well as its gate, is a mass of gold—gold toned with mauve, lilac, faint blue, and fainter green—for the ornamentation is made up of an arabesque of peonies in gold relief surrounded by birds and flowers in natural tints. The decoration of the interior of the shrine is gorgeous beyond words. In panels of lavender, primrose, and forget-me-not blue are phœnixes, chrysanthemums, eagles, and lions wrought in lines of gold. The panels are framed by beams of black lacquer, whilst like beams, highly polished, traverse the low ceiling.

Beyond these brilliant buildings the visitor passes through a humble gate to mount up the hillside once again. The way is cut out of the rock of the mountain and climbs up into the forest. The stair of two hundred steps is plain and solitary. The buildings of lacquer and gold have vanished; the funereal avenue is far below. There is nothing now but the grey stairs and the brown earth. At the end, within a simple stone wall, is the tomb—a small pagoda of bronze. In front of it are a low stone table, green with moss, a bronze stork, and an incense burner. This is all. Here then, alone, on the wind-blown height, among the sturdy boulders and the murmuring pines, rests the man who is said to have been the greatest ruler of Japan.

Iemitsu's tomb is at some little distance, but it is upon the same hillside, and is approached by a like steep way, by like proud gates and gorgeous buildings. The main temple stands far up the mountain in a deep well or court quarried out of the wood-covered height. Enormous cryptomeria crowd down from the hilltop to the very edge of this sunken terrace. They so shut it in on all sides that the sky becomes a gap but little larger than the court itself. A lofty wall of rough masonry holds up the sides of this cutting in the cliff. Every stone in the great scarp is covered with gleaming moss. Among the pines about the summit of the wall are clusters of rhododendrons. The boughs hang down into the court so that the flowers are as patches of pink against the gold-green moss; while below, on the blue pebbles with which the terrace is strewn and on the bronze lanterns which stand therein, a shower or pink petals has fallen.

Still higher up the slope, in an absolute solitude among the pines, is a tomb of severest simplicity, where rests the grandson of the founder of the dynasty.

XVIII.

THE CHERRY FESTIVAL.

Among the many childlike qualities of the Japanese is a love of flowers. Flowers make the chief attraction of their holiday resorts, and of not a few of their places of pilgrimage. Often at railway stations are notices to be seen giving the distances to the Plum Blossoms of a village, or the Iris Pools of a monastery. The Japanese man or woman will trudge miles to see a favourite tree in bloom, which tree they have probably watched each springtime for years. During the first week of April thousands pour into Kyoto to admire the great cherry tree there and to make a temple-rambling holiday of the occasion. Every little tradesman has before him in his shop either a vase containing a single select flower, or, what is more usual, a dwarf tree of his own upbringing. If in due course a few blossoms break out upon the tree his delight is complete, and the street is envious of him.

I could not fail to notice at a certain fair the stall of a quack. He was a sinister-looking rogue, who sold nostrums to the ignorant. His booth was hung with appalling coloured diagrams of human viscera and of crude human dissections. On his table was a decayed spirometer (with an English maker's name on it), with which he essayed to test the lungs of the innocent. He had also an ancient dynamometer (of British origin) by means of which he demonstrated the muscular power of any who could be induced to think that they were failing. From the tellings of these dire instruments, as well as from the awful writings on the wall in the form of his lurid diagrams, he drew deductions which would make the strongest uneasy, but which led to the selling of his messes. He was, no doubt, a contemptible old scoundrel, who had learned his villainy in the West; but prominent upon his death-suggesting table was a white dish full of water, in which was a rock island with a dwarf pine on it. There were other rocks in the lake besides, as well as a toy tortoise. He evidently regarded his lake with great pride, and this atoned for much it was hard to forgive in him.

At Kyoto, at the time of the cherry blossom, the two chief attractions of the district are Arashi-Yama and the great cherry tree. Arashi-Yama is a steep hillside some few miles from the town. At the foot of the slope is a clear river sweeping over brown pebbles. Here long timber rafts, which have just descended the rapids, swing by, for Arashi-Yama is at the mouth of a gorge. A long grey wooden bridge crosses the stream within sound of the rushing water in the ravine, and from it is afforded a fine view of the hillside. It is a slope entirely covered by trees—mostly pines. From the sentinel firs along the sky line to the brink of the torrent is a bank of dark green tree tops, out of which masses of cherry blossom rise up as pale pink clouds.

This is the charm of Arashi-Yama, the badge of the pale flower on the escutcheon of weather-beaten pines. It looks as if a white wedding party of girls had become entangled among an army of dour veterans. As the cherry trees are planted in patches among the pines, it happens that wherever they stand there is on the harsh green a sudden gleam, like a puff of white smoke. On the flat beyond the river people are picnicking among the temporary tea houses which have been erected on the stretch of grass, and which are brilliant with hundreds of red paper lanterns.

The great cherry tree of Kyoto is near the outskirts of the town at the foot of the eastern hills. Here is an open space with gravelled roads, with an orchard of plum and cherry trees, a pond surrounded by Japanese willows, and certain stalls and tea houses which complete the conception of a public park in the eyes of the Japanese.

On one day, early in April, this park becomes a scene of astounding activity. Booths are erected everywhere, and a cohort of adventurous tea houses assails the usual quiet of the place. These latter consist of bamboo sheds about an enclosure in which are a number of benches covered with red blankets or mats. There are, moreover, orange stalls, cake stalls, restaurants on barrows, hawkers of every kind of ware, bow and arrow galleries, stages for wrestling matches, peep shows, and bands giving utterance to a desolating music.

At night the place is packed with holiday folk, so that the amused, good-tempered crowd can hardly move along. There is a subdued clatter of clogs, and an unrestrained chatter of tongues. Everywhere are paper lanterns swinging from poles, suspended on lines, or dimly seen among the feet of the crowd, where they serve to light trays on the bare earth on which are laid out china, toys, chopsticks, pipes, and endless other things for sale. The air, indeed, is full of lanterns, so that in the small clearing around the famous cherry tree there will not be less than ten thousand lights. It is to welcome the blossoming of this tree that the immense concourse of people have come together.

The tree is of extraordinary size, as well as some centuries old. It stands alone on the summit of a green mound by the pond. Its wide spreading boughs, weighed down by age, are supported by fifty timber props. On the lawn around the tree are braziers of blazing wood, aloft on iron poles. The eddies of smoke from these cressets and the flickering flames from the baskets cast a fantastic and unearthly light upon the overhanging flower-covered branches. Near by are arc electric lamps on immense standards, so that, what with the paper lanterns, the cressets, and the great lamps, the place is as light as at noon-day.

The spectral tree towers above all, a cloud of pink and white. Its branches bend earthwards, so that the great outspreading mass of flowers makes a pale cascade against the indigo sky. Standing above the glaring lights and the restless sea of a thousand upturned faces, the old tree looks like a phantom. Its vitality, moreover, is wonderful, for its blossoms never fail. One day it stands bare and leafless, by the next evening a pink glow has spread over it, and on the third day it has burst into bloom.

The crowd gazes up at it with admiring affection. To them it is the symbol of so much. As the poet Motoori exclaims, "If one should enquire of you as to the spirit of Japan, point to the cherry

CHERRY BLOSSOM.

blossom shining in the sun." The sleeping baby, nodding on its mother's shoulder, is wakened to look at it. The small boy is held aloft so that he can see the great soft dome of pink. The husband and wife come together because the blossoming of the tree marks the years of their lives, years which date from one springtime when they first made their way to Kyoto together.

Among the crowd is an old man who—oblivious of the press—keeps his eyes fixed upon the tree in speechless adoration. It may be that of late, year by year, he had felt that each springtime as it came would be the last on which he would see the flowering of the cherry tree he could remember from a boy. The majestic tree is a part of old Japan, of the old, cultured, world-forgetting country. It had budded and blossomed for centuries before the troublous and uneasy men from the West had broken in rudely upon its monastic calm. It was still an old tree when Japan was yet alone, dreaming out its own dream in a far away corner of the Pacific.

I should imagine the old man to have been about seventy-five. If so, he would have been twenty-four years of age when Commodore Perry landed upon the slumbering island with his importunate message. The old worshipper of the cherry tree must therefore have known the country as it was, before the coarse, inquisitive world burst in upon it. He must have watched, many a time, processions of Daimyos trail into the town, followed by retinues in strange dresses, and by marching men with bows and arrows, wearing fantastic helmets.

Since these heroic days, dignified by old ceremonies and by the picturesque costumes of a thousand years, he would have seen the quiet of the land depart, and its peace become troubled by uncouth inventions, which scattered the romance of Japan, as a Gatling gun would scatter a circle of dancing fairies. He would have seen the idyllic town encompassed with telegraph wires, cleft in twain by tramway lines, deafened by steam whistles, and blinded by flaring gas.

It almost surpasses belief that any one individual, in a lifetime by no means unduly extended, could have viewed with his own eyes changes such as these. Yet the old man who gazes at the cherry tree by the light of an arc electric lamp could remember the very

Japan that was depicted by Hokusai and Hiroshige, for in that Japan he lived.

The idea is uncanny and full of marvel. To conceive of it is to imagine—as an actual parallel—that a man of seventy-five, alive in London at the present moment, could remember the capital of England as it was in the days of Queen Elizabeth, could recall the narrow streets, the ruffles, the slashed doublets, and the clanking swords. Such a man, frock-coated and tall-hatted, a user of electric railways and of telephones, would yet have seen with his own eyes Raleigh on his way to the Tower, and would have talked with Drake when he landed at Deptford from the *Golden Hind*.

XIX.

THE PEOPLE OF THE COUNTRY.

To the stranger from the Occident the Japanese are a somewhat inscrutable folk, bristling with the unexpected, full of surprises and apparent contradictions. They take upon themselves with astonishing ease the outward and visible signs of Western civilisation. They would seem to be wholly transformed, and yet beneath the ingenious disguise there ever remains the man of the East with his strange beliefs, his mysticism, his unintelligible thoughts. This double existence, this feigning of Dr. Jekyll and Mr. Hyde, may well lead to anomalies which startle the unimaginative.

The Japanese appear to be easy-going and unbusinesslike, while those who have lived long with them speak of their hosts as "casual and sketchy," and as incapable of great intellectual effort. Yet these very people are conducting a war as no war has ever been carried on before. They are the most artistic people in the world, and yet their exports consist largely of porcelain and other goods which for vulgarity and poverty of design are utterly deplorable.

As has been many times said, the Japanese are acutely imitative; but to this must be added the further fact that they have improved whatever they have copied. From China they acquired a knowledge of lacquer-making, with the result that very soon they far surpassed their teachers in this exquisite industry. From Korea they learnt the art of porcelain-making, which they proceeded to develope to such heights that their masters must needs have stood aghast. From the Continent also came to them silk weaving, yet no country has brought this manufacture nearer to perfection than has Japan.

Long after the East had been exhausted the Islanders turned

their faces to the West to learn whatever was to be gathered there. With their astounding capacity for absorbing knowledge they soon acquired the much that was learnable, and now they are improving upon it, criticising it, remodelling it in the light of Eastern subtleness. In illustration of this I may allude to one branch of knowledge, that of surgery. When Japan was opened in 1853, surgery—as it is known in the West—had no existence. What was to be learned from China, Japan had learned, but it was little enough. Japanese surgery at the middle of the last century was that of mediæval times. When this inquisitive people turned Westwards they cultivated surgery at first mostly in England, and later in Germany and America.

So far as there is any character in modern surgery, that of Japan is German. It is, however, being improved upon in countless details. The Japanese surgeon is no longer a servile imitator. He is introducing into his methods the results of his own ingenuity. Many features which in Europe are of the latest suggestion have already been anticipated in Japan. There is every probability that the Japanese school of surgery will become a great school, for the native of Japan has qualities which are excellent in the making of a surgeon: he is not troubled by "nerves," he is infinitely patient, fastidiously clean, as well as most neat and dexterous with his hands. Morever, he has a love of ritual as well as of precision in ritual, and in the prosecution of antiseptic surgery this counts for much.

The Japanese are shrewdly observant, nimble of apprehension, receptive, and of large-minded and catholic views. It is said that they are neither logical nor profound. If this be true, they seem to have come to small ill from the lack of these qualities.

It is acknowledged by all that they are not original, and it is interesting to hear what a learned Japanese Professor, Inazo Nitobe, says upon this point. "It is true that in a sense we certainly possess imitativeness. What progressive nation has not possessed and made use of it? Just think of how little Greek culture has originated on Hellenic soil! It seems to me that the most original—that is the least imitative people—are the Chinese, and we see where their originality has led them. Imitation is educative, and education itself is, in the main, imitation. . . . We shudder to think what might have been our fate, in this cannibalistic age of nations, had we been always consistently original. Imitation has certainly been the means of our salvation."*

In this matter of imitation the Japanese, sitting at the feet of the Western world, have copied a few of our failings, while they have been busy imbibing our virtues. We have taught them—this people of infinite neatness and of exact and perfect finish—to be slovenly, and to turn out any kind of work, however bad, so long as it will sell. In any large porcelain depôt in Japan will be seen a few pieces of exquisite china together with a lamentable amount of coarse, gaudy, ignoble stuff which is beyond pity. The Japanese merchant will tell you that this flaring output is for the "art furnisher" in the West. With his natural politeness he will assure the American that these fearsome vases and urns are made for the London market, while he will inform the Londoner that they are made for New York.

One thing is certain—the great bulk of Japanese "art goods" are entirely unknown to the inhabitants of Japan, and find no place within their walls.

The Japanese have imitated us in the science and art of advertisement. An advertisement is intended to meet the eye, and the Japanese make their efforts in this direction so blatant and violent that the intention can never fail. Much of the fair country of England is marred by the hideous advertisements which shriek in fields and meadows, by comely villages, and by shrinking woods. In Japan they have intensified the vileness of this, and have crowded the country, through which the main railways run, with hoardings and placards which would make the most offensive field advertisement in England appear modest and pleasant. In England we are fortunately becoming advertisement-blind, but the most exhausted retina will still respond to the shocks of the bill-poster in Japan.

Recent events have demonstrated with dramatic emphasis the bravery of the people, their superb loyalty, their powers of self-sacrifice, and their heroic manliness. When the interests of their

* "Japan by the Japanese." London, 1904, p. 280.

country are concerned they move as one, and no Japanese soldier need be told that he is expected to be obedient, to be regardless of self, and to be "faithful unto death." All this he is, and more.

The native of Japan is not troubled by "nerves." He is not neurotic. Among the many things of his adoption is not included the fashionable disorder known as neurasthenia. He does not waste his time over "nerve storms," and he declines the fascination of a "rest cure." His men do not worry and fuss. His women do not fidget. If he misses the man of energy who is "a bundle of nerves," he also misses "the managing woman" and the lady of "the nervous breakdown."

As an instance of the solidity of the Japanese nervous system, I might mention the following circumstances. Through the kindness of the eminent surgeon, Professor Ito, I had an opportunity of visiting the chief civil hospital in Kyoto. This splendidly equipped institution is not only up-to-date from the standpoint of the Western world, but it also possesses features which Europe will no doubt copy when it is up-to-date from the standpoint of Japan.

To a bed here and there was affixed a red ball on a stick. Outside the door of the ward was a like-coloured disc, upon which was shown what number of beds in the ward were distinguished by the red ball. This insigne, I found, served to indicate that the occupant of the bed was so dangerously ill that he must neither be disturbed nor talked to. I wonder how this method would answer in England, and what would be the feelings of the sick man, full of doubts as to how his malady would end, when he saw, after the surgeon's visit, the red ball hoisted above his bed!

In the operating theatre a man was being anæsthetised prior to a serious abdominal operation. In the arena, strange to say, was another operating table, upon which was another man who had been "prepared" according to the ritual of antiseptic surgery. He was to undergo an operation identical with that which was soon in actual progress. It was explained to me that it was more convenient to prepare two patients at a time than one. The second man watched with interest the operation upon his ward companion, saw the abdomen opened and the viscera protrude. It was quite possible that the first man might die on the table, in sight of the patient who was waiting his turn. Knowing the extreme kindness of the Japanese to one another, and their consideration for one another's feelings, I asked if this ordeal was not an indifferent prelude to an operation, and if the second man was not likely to be upset. The surgeon's answer was, "Please feel his pulse!" I did. It was beating as quietly as if the man had been asleep.

The Japanese are light-hearted and pleasure-loving, amiable and generous, and above all things gentle. In the street are never to be heard the sounds of quarrelling men, nor of wrangling women. If current events are discussed they are debated quietly, without either brawling or hammering of fists. The children neither cry nor squabble, and never once in Japan did I see a child punished. There is no place in any part of the islands, nor in any phase of Japanese life, which could reproduce the features of an East London alley on a Saturday night. The sobriety of the people has no little to do with this.

The exquisite manners of the Japanese, their invariable courtesy and most gratifying politeness, have been rapturously described by all who have written upon the country, and it is worthy of note that this excellent good-breeding is apparent in all grades of society. It has been shown in the Occident that manners are not necessary to existence, and thus it is that they are being gradually abandoned. The manners of the courtier and of the lady of the minuet are being replaced by those of the chauffeur and the modiste, so that in a decade or two we may expect to be comfortably mannerless. In the meantime those who wish to understand the full charm of "pretty manners" must go to Japan.

Of the actual soul of the people the wayfarer will glean but little, and that little will be hard to understand. Lafcadio Hearn, of all students of this wondrous folk, seems to have come nearest to an appreciation of their sentiments and to a knowledge of their inmost thoughts.

There is much that is childlike in the Japanese, especially in their fancies and in their powers of "make believe." The world they have imagined around them is a child's world, their gardens a child's garden, and their pictures the outcome of one little budding idea.

They seem, moreover, to see a world that is preternaturally small and strangely near at hand, as if their minds were influenced by a kind of myopia, or fantastic shortsightedness. This is as well to be seen in their little carvings as in their mimic landscapes.

The men, judged from the standpoint of the Aryan, may be said to be plain, if not ugly. Their cropped hair and wrinkled foreheads do not add to their attractiveness. The costume of the country gives them a monastic appearance. The younger men may be undergraduates of some undiscriminating university, while the old men, with their ascetic faces, may be dons made wizen by study, or cathedral vergers who have meditated much among the tombs.

According to the European standard very few Japanese women could be considered pretty. Their heads appear too large for their bodies, their eyelids are often puffy, and their features coarse. They are, however, neat to a fault, dainty, graceful, and full of fascination. They have beautiful necks and hands, and exquisite voices. Bare legs ended by feet cased in white socks are features too strange to be at once admirable.

Owing to much wearing of clogs the Japanese woman walks awkwardly. She totters or stumbles along with little mincing steps and in a semi-paralytic manner. She walks a little as water birds walk on land, while the white sock with only a division for the great toe is curiously like a webbed foot.

The English girl is all curves, the Japanese girl is all angles. The sleeves of her kimono form great squares. Her obi, or sash, is tied in a stiff square bow behind, and follows rectangular lines in front. The opening in her jacket at the root of the neck is angular, so that from head to foot she is picturesquely geometric, save for her oval face. The lower part of her ceremonial dress tapers away so suddenly that she looks top-heavy, although the padded edge of her gown spreads out on the floor like the stand of a wine-glass.

These gentle women all appear to be pleased and contented, even if their faces are apt to be sometimes a little expressionless or a trifle moonish-looking.

The children are the best known of the inhabitants of Japan. They crowd everywhere in every part of the country. Their round, ruddy cheeks, brown lacquer, almond-shaped eyes, and circular mats of hair are familiar enough. They affect long dresses as soon as they can walk; the boys scuffling along like old men in gaudy dressing gowns and slippers, the girls waddling like stubby matrons with their waists under their arms. There is no "leggy" period in the growth of a Japanese girl. She begins as a bundle, and continues as a bundle until she blossoms forth into a kimono.

As soon as she can walk she has a lump of rag tied to her back to represent a doll, and whenever her sturdy legs can bear the weight the doll is replaced by a live baby of the smallest size. The woman without an infant on her back is comparatively uncommon among the denizens of the streets.

The children are wise-looking because they have seen so much. They are always swinging on somebody's back with their heads nodding over somebody's shoulder. Thus they become familiar with many industries, with house cleaning, with shopping, with worshipping at temples, and the elements of street gossip. They are not always carried by women either. I have seen an old man gardening with a baby on his back, and by the side of Biwa Lake I came upon two boys fishing, each with the head of a wise baby nodding sleepily over his shoulder.

XX.

SIGNS OF THE TIMES.

In the passage through the Inland Sea from Nagasaki to Kobe we came upon many transports on their way to the front. Their decks were lumbered with bald hoardings and packing-case-like erections, after the peculiar manner of transports, so that they were strangely like the untidy vessels that lurched into Cape Town Bay in 1899. Many hundreds of those who crowded the decks were taking their last look of Japan, for many were never to return. It was a pleasant scene to carry away in their memories—this glimpse of the picturesque coast of the Inland Sea.

Ashore there were signs on all sides of the progress of the war. Railway travelling was slow, uncomfortable, and uncertain, for the lines were of necessity occupied in transporting men and arms, stores and ammunition to the coast. There were evidences neither of confusion nor of hurry. In the large towns regiments were being mobilised, while from morning till night ranks of sturdy little men were being drilled on the many parade grounds. When the companies were disbanded for the day they strolled about the streets, or flocked around the humbler tea-houses. In physique they appeared to be splendid, while in the matter of cheerfulness they could not be surpassed. They behaved like a posse of school-boys out of school. They rehearsed items of drill in the street, drilled one another, pretended to engage in mortal combat, and filled not a few rickshaw coolies with panic by kneeling in the roadway as they advanced, and levelling rifles at them. They appeared to find soldiering a most excellent jest, which they appreciated with keenness and exuberant enjoyment. It is needless to say that there was an absence of that drunkenness which, in more countries than one, makes the surroundings of gallant men squalid and pitiable.

I saw many regiments entrained for the front. There was much enthusiasm in these leave-takings, much cheering, much waving of paper flags. It was a little curious to see the sweetheart pressing upon her hero a bunch of flowers in place of the whiskey bottle, which to many is inseparable from the ceremony of seeing soldiers off.

There was everywhere an absence of swagger and bravado. The enemy were spoken of neither in terms of hatred nor of contempt. The war, they said, was most regrettable; and I never once congratulated a Japanese acquaintance upon a victory when he did not reply by expressing regret that so many Russian lives had been lost. This might have been mere politeness, and possibly a little insincere; but, at least, it was not brutal.

The crowds which collected to celebrate a victory were curiously restrained. They moved through the streets in thousands, but their rejoicing was dignified. Save for the clatter of clogs or the shuffling of sandals, and an occasional cheer, they were almost silent. There was no rioting, no aimless yelling, no horse-play, no raucous buffoonery. The Japanese crowd has not yet learnt the savage cult of "mafficking." That they can rejoice without knocking off hats or fighting with sticks might be due to the fact that few wear hats and none carry sticks. If the manner in which a victory is celebrated can be regarded as a criterion of national taste, then the taste of the Japanese is much to be commended.

I gathered from those with whom I discussed the position that there was a general belief that the war could be maintained, as it had been begun, for at least two years, and that for that period there would be no lack in the matter of the sinews of war. I further deduced that when two years had passed the way might be a little less clear to see.

Owing to the kindness of the Minister for War and the Director General of the Army Medical Service, I was able to see the Medical Field Equipment, the Military Hospitals, as well as the general arrangements for the reception of the sick and wounded. I also became acquainted with the Japanese Red Cross Society. This business-like organisation is the most remarkable and efficient of its kind in the world. It not only undertakes to look after the sick and wounded, and so relieve the War Department at a critical moment of an enormous responsibility, but it concerns itself with the soldier's comfort from the beginning of the campaign to the end. It "mothers" him in a sensible manner, without either extravagance or hysteria, and makes him feel that all that is done is merely the endeavour of the country to show its appreciation of his services and its sympathy with his hardships. The society continues its work when the war is over, and does not depend for its maintenance upon a fitful and ecstatic outburst of sentiment which barely survives the crisis that evoked it. This is the noble feature of the Red Cross Society of Japan, that after the glamour of war has faded the soldier is not forgotten.

I will not add to the much that has been already written upon this unique organisation. In Miss McCaul's admirable book, "Under the Care of the Japanese War Office," will be found a detailed account of the Society, of its aims and intentions, and of the manner in which they are carried into effect.

The Japanese woman, when she has been suitably trained, makes a splendid nurse. Her neatness, quickness, and dexterity are marvellous to see. What her small hands can do with a pair of forceps only a prestidigitateur could mimic and only a life-long use of chopsticks could explain. She has that passion for cleanliness which is a feature of her race, she is quiet and gentle, she is perfect in discipline, and—last but not least—she has the exquisite soft voice which is common to all her countrywomen.

The army medical outfit, as supplied in the recent campaign, is most ingenious. It is simple, light, efficient, and economical. The panniers used in the British Service have the merit of being substantial and strong. The Japanese panniers are comparatively frail. When I commented upon this an army surgeon replied, "Please reflect that the science of medicine changes quickly; these cases are made for the war, not for posterity." The Japanese Army Medical System presents many features which might with advantage be imitated, as can be gathered from the following report by an American army surgeon, who has recently returned from the seat of war in Manchuria:—"Major Seaman found that the care of the sick and wounded occupied but a small share of the time of the medical officers. The solution of the greater problem of preventing disease by the careful supervision of the smallest details of subsistence, clothing, and shelter was their first and most important duty. Nothing was too small to escape their vigilance, nor too tedious to weary their patience, and everywhere, in the field with the scouts, or in the base hospitals at home, the one prevailing idea was *the prevention of disease.*

"The medical officer was to be found both in the front and in the rear. He was with the first screen of scouts, with his microscopes and chemicals, testing and labelling wells, so that the army which followed should drink no contaminated water. When scouts reached a town, he immediately made a thorough examination of the sanitary conditions, and if cases of contagious or infectious disease were found, he put a cordon around the quarter where they were. A medical officer accompanied foraging parties, and, with the commissariat officers, sampled the various foods, fruit, and vegetables sold by the natives before the arrival of the army. If the food were tainted or over-ripe, or if the water required boiling, notices to that effect were posted in suitable places. So strict was the discipline from commanding officer to rank and file that obedience to the orders of the medical officer was absolute.

"The medical officer also supervised the personal hygiene of the camp. He taught the men how to cook, how to bathe, how to cleanse the finger-nails so as to free them from bacteria, as well as how to live in general a healthy, vigorous life; and it was part of the soldier's routine to carry out these instructions in every particular. As a result of this system the medical officer was not obliged to treat cases of dysentery and fevers that follow the use of improper food and the neglect of sanitation. During six months of terrible fighting and exposure in a foreign country there was only a fraction of 1 per cent. of loss from *preventable disease.*"*

In the Boer War 13,250 soldiers died of disease. It may be safe to conclude that the greater proportion of these deaths were

* "British Medical Journal," November 12th, 1904, p. 13.

due to preventable disease. It is a little distressing to reflect how many lives might have been saved if the methods of the Japanese Medical Service had been adopted by the British Army.

Major Seaman may well remark that "the Japanese are the first people to recognise the true value of the Army Medical Corps."*

* "British Medical Journal, November 12th, 1904, p. 13.

Part VI

AMERICA

I.

THE SANDWICH ISLANDS.

THE journey of five thousand five hundred miles across the Pacific from Yokohama to San Francisco was delightful, because the weather was faultless and the Pacific pacific. As the ship was moving from east to west it was possible to see at night the Great Bear in the northern sky, and the Southern Cross in the south. During the week in which Honolulu was reached a day was doubled. It was a Monday; so that many experienced the novelty of a week of eight days with two Mondays in it.

The Sandwich Islands lie just within the circle of the tropics, in the centre of the great ocean, and two thousand miles from the nearest town. As they are approached they appear as a line of low bare hills presenting sharp peaks and ridges. The hills seem as if made up solely of crests and spines, so that the sky-line is jagged like the edge of a broken shell. The sides of the heights are of seal-skin brown. They slope seawards to a yellow-green flat. Then come white beaches with black rocks on them, the breaking sea, and the coral reef. The islands are of volcanic origin, and in many places the outlines of old craters are to be seen.

On nearer access the land becomes less bare, and the flats by the sea are seen to be wooded by many trees. On one such plain lies Honolulu, at the outlet of a verdant valley, with ever before its eyes the incoming lines of breakers, and ever ringing in its ears the roar of the surf.

The town itself is bright and pleasant. It is springing up under the eye of the American, and the native of the United States is an adept at rapid town making. There are tram-lines and parks, wide streets and Western shops, while everywhere fine buildings are bursting into existence. Many Chinese and Japanese find a home in the settlement, and their quarters in the town bear the characteristics of the two races, much chastened and modified by close association with a people of extreme modernness.

The outskirts of Honolulu are singularly beautiful. There is the lavish growth of the tropics without the too generous heat and too liberal fume of moisture in the air. All the villages and cottages have charming gardens with lawns as green as those about the homesteads in England. Here flourish cocoanut palms, royal palms, fan palms, the banyan tree, the mango, the guava, the bread fruit. The place is glorious with flowers and flowering shrubs, as well as with whole hedgerows of hibiscus in bloom. By the beach are noisy duck farms kept by the ingenious Chinese. Towards sundown one lean Chinaman with a long wand will be seen driving a flock of three hundred ducks home, from dabbling in the seaweed, to their inland quarters. He keeps them in a compact waddling patch with as much skill as a sheep dog "rounds up" sheep.

The climate is delightful all the year round, for the islands know only an eternal summer. The temperature ranges from 52° F. at the coldest, to 90° F. at the hottest, while the rainfall in Honolulu is only 40 inches in the year. The natives are rapidly becoming extinct or absorbed. They are tall, of handsome bearing, with beautiful, sad eyes. They look lazy and they are lazy. They are quite content with an idyllic life which is free from the fever of ambition and the weariness of work. Like many other elementary people they only wish to be left alone to doze their lives out. This joy has been denied them now for many a year. Their quiet bay has been invaded by the whirl of the screw and the slashing of the paddle-wheel. The waters are churned up with soot and coal dust, the grove of palm trees is filled with the mist of steam and the clang of anvils. In the stress of all this trouble they have either fled or died, for the visitation from the enlightened world has been to them as a visitation of the Black Death. They appear to be extremely fond of flowers, since flowers mark all their ceremonies and furnish their chief means of adornment and decoration. The men have adopted the costume of Europe as it is translated colonially. The women wear a school-girl type of straw hat and a long skirt which hangs sheer from their necks to their feet. There is no attempt to indicate a waist, and as most of the women are distressingly fat this is wise.

Everyone who lands at Honolulu is constrained to visit the Pali, six miles from the town. The range of hills at the back of Honolulu presents, on that side which is towards the city, a gentle slope seawards. On the other side the slope is replaced by a mighty cliff. The Pali is a gap on the jagged summit of these hills, at the spot where the slope is ended by the drop of the precipice. After a long toiling up-hill the road comes upon a crack on the skyline, between ashen crags—an abrupt mountain pass. Here the traveller finds himself at the brink of a sudden cliff, steep as a wall. At the foot of this lies the mysterious "back of the island," a great level country which sweeps away for miles and miles, and is bounded by the circle of the sea.

To right and left the immense black precipice extends—in front and far below is the immeasurable plain. The plain is green with every tint of green—apple-green, olive-green, the green of old bronze, the blue-green of old pines. There are little hills on the flat upon which one looks down as would a soaring bird in the sky. On the border of the plain is a glorious bay open to three thousand miles of sea. Its beach is a curve of dove-coloured sand which alone divides the green of the island from the blue of the deep. The sea is iris blue, so calm that masses of white cloud are reflected on its surface, so clear that there can be seen the streak of mauve which marks the submerged coral bank and the splash of amber where is a fathom-deep meadow of golden weed.

One great joy of Honolulu is the sea-bathing, for nothing can surpass it. Those who find delight in this rudimentary pursuit must go to the Sandwich Islands to understand it in perfection. It may be claimed that there is luxurious bathing on the Lido by Venice, or at Atlantic City, or on the coast between Cape Town and Durban. These places, as Mercutio said of his wound, "will serve," but they fail to approach such bathing as can be found in the cove which lies in the shelter of Diamond Head.

The day is hot and tiring, while the roads and the bare heights seem famished by drought. The sea is grey-green and glistening in the sun. The heated man plunges into it and swims out, with panting eagerness, towards the coral reef. The water is soft, silken, and caressing. His hands, as they move forward at each stroke, look already cooler under the ripples. The sea dashes upon the reef with a thundering roar as if a white-crested multitude were storming a long trench. Within the reef the high wave rolls shorewards. As it sweeps along, hurrying and hissing, the summer wind blows a mocking spray from its angry ridge. As it nears the swimmer it is curling to break, its walls stand up green, smooth, and polished, like a section of a great glass tube. Through it he can see the light in the sky. He dives into the rushing comber and comes up into the sun on the other side of it. It tears past him to the beach with imperious hauteur, leaving in its track a dazed waste of white foam which is whirled into circles by bewildered eddies. Then comes "the hurl and the crash" upon the sloping shore, and, after a moment of hush,

> "The scream of a madden'd beach dragg'd down by the wave."

If the swimmer turns seawards he can watch line after line of white horses "girth deep in hissing water," galloping in from the coral reef towards the shore. Beyond the surf on the reef are the untroubled sea and a black-hulled schooner sailing away to the uttermost island.

If the swimmer turn landwards there are the biscuit-coloured beach, a thicket of palms, with a brown thatched house in its shadows, and behind a line of purple hills which shimmer in the heat.

DIAMOND HEAD, HONOLULU.

II.

THE YOSEMITE VALLEY.

On nearing the "Golden Gate," which opens into the superbly beautiful harbour of San Francisco, those who were early on deck had an opportunity of witnessing a great sea fight. It was a combat, on a Titanic scale, between a sperm whale and an invisible bravo. Experienced mariners assured us that the whale who took part in this fearsome drama was forty feet in length, but whether this was based upon the sea-serpent-standard of measurement, or upon that of King Edgar, I know not. In the absence of marines they beguiled us with the attractive story of the fighting alliance between the thresher and the sword-fish; although it is probable that the aggressor in the present disturbance was that wild sea brigand, the Orca.

The battle was terrible to behold. The smooth ocean was convulsed at one spot into a circle of terror-stricken waves, as if it shuddered. In the centre of the arena was the harassed whale. At one time he would be invisible. Then a column of water would shoot into the air as if from a submarine mine that burst through the waters. Afterwards a huge square fabric would lift out of the sea, like the apparition of a sunken ship rising from the bottom. This was the tank-shaped head of the whale. The arena boiled like an acre-wide kettle. Out of the foam would climb a round, shining hillock—the back of the beast—as if an island had come up in search of the ship. Here was, indeed, to be seen a mountain that moved. Then, with an awful earthquake effect, the creature of many tons leapt from the sea like a minnow, so that its great tail was at one moment black against the sky, and was, at another, hacking a whirlpool out of the deep. Of the

Orca that wrought this evil nothing was seen, so that the writhing cachalot seemed to be wrestling with a ghost.

It was such a fight as might have taken place in antediluvian waters while yet the earth was without form. An ancient-looking mist hung over the waste, such as possibly exhaled from the cooling world; while above the haze was a rose-pink sky which might have been lit by the rays of a still unfamiliar sun.

Of San Francisco, of the amazing country of California—where must have grown both the bean and the story of "Jack and the Bean Stalk"—of the long journey across the continent, and of the many great and astounding cities which are encountered on the way, it is needless to write, for the story is already familiar by reason of much telling. It may be tempting to discourse of a city which has a score of Towers of Babel in its midst, all of which have been built and completed without confusion of tongues, and which, when viewed from Mars, must look like hairs on the back of a rolled-up caterpillar. But the tale of the city is already commonplace. It would be inviting to deal with the old world conceptions and insular prejudices with which America and the Americans are, even to the present day, regarded by the untravelled in Europe; but the occasion is hardly opportune, nor has the topic lacked consideration.

Among the many astonishing "sights" in the United States two might be selected for some brief notice, viz., the Yosemite Valley and the Grand Canyon of Arizona.

The distance from Raymond—where the railway ends—to the Yosemite Valley is seventy miles. This has to be travelled by road in a "stage" or open waggon drawn by four horses. Allowing for a halt for lunch, this drive occupies over twelve hours. It is a journey through seventy miles of wild forest land, along a road which is rough and reckless as well as enveloped in dust. It winds over hill and across valley, it climbs to the height of six thousand feet, but it is ever through the forest and ever the same. Hour after hour the "stage" rocks along through clouds of dust, until the aching traveller changes to the colour of the earth and his mind to the blank of infinite weariness. The monotony becomes oppressive. It is ever the pines and the rocks, the rocks and the pines, the firs and the dogwood, the dogwood and the firs. With the exception of the charming hamlet of Wawona and a few squatters' settlements by the way there are no signs of man. Here is a lumber camp on a hillside which has been laid waste by hatchet and fire, and there a house of rough logs with a post bag hanging from a tree for the driver to snatch at, or a soap box on a pole, into which he can drop a letter if he has one.

When any height is gained there is to be seen, as far as the eye can stretch across the immense expanse, nothing but hills and pines. The circle of the horizon is bounded by pines, and with pines every hill is draped from summit to base and for mile upon mile. The landscape has only the one feature of endless trees on endless hills. It is all in one colour—the dull green of pines. Along each side of the road, away from the clearings, are aisles of brown resinous trunks springing in unwearying thousands out of an unvarying undergrowth. Above is the green cloud of trees, below is the drab cloud of dust.

By the time that the last hill is climbed the traveller has become numbed by monotony; he is weary of the eternal swaying hour after hour, through a world of many ups and downs, but of one persistent sameness.

At the summit of the height is a bend in the road and a gap in the trees which serve to show that the track is skirting the edge of a sloping precipice. The spot is called "Inspiration Point." Those who step to the brink come upon a scene which is hard to forget. There is a sudden view down a long, winding valley, a sudden glimpse of an unexpected world, a sense of indescribable charm and of infinite relief. The whole landscape has changed. After the tiresomeness of hundreds of square miles of dingy pine trees, here is a silver-grey valley shut in by dazzling cliffs, on the floor of which are homely meadows skirted by woods and traversed by a river sweeping over bronzed stones. The valley is only seven miles in length, and about half a mile in width—a mere span when viewed from a height like this. What is remarkable is that its great walls close it in so jealously that the everlasting pine hills have all vanished. The glen is barricaded against the world as if it were an enchanted secret place, while at the end of the valley there would seem to be a pass leading into a new, unimagined country.

So far is this pearl-coloured gorge removed from the haunts of men that it remained undiscovered until 1851, when a small party of soldiers, in pursuit of Indians, came upon it suddenly.

The walls which encircle this pale valley rise sheer from its floor to the height of three-quarters of a mile. Nay more, there is at the end of the gorge an erect precipice which is nearly a mile in height, from the pool at its foot to the cap of snow which smooths its summit of bare stone. The glen is filled with an unearthly light. After the forest of dinginess it is as a place flooded by the moon. Above is a canopy of the bluest sky. The sky and the grey cliffs blend. The earth and the heavens meet, for the air in the valley is blue as if the sky had come down and filled it to the river's brink. There is a sense that on descending into the valley one would dip into an azure depth. After the forest shades the light in the valley is as the cold, silvery gleam at the mouth of a cavern.

The spot would seem to be the "heart of the hills," and such a "hiding place" as is spoken of in the Psalms of David. It would be a fitting scene for some great drama of the world. So apart is it that it affords no mean conception of the garden which was planted "eastward in Eden."

On one side of the gorge, on that wall which is in shadow, a white river drops down from a ledge into the valley—a fall of nine hundred feet. Whence it comes no one can tell, for it seems to gush forth, in a torrent thirty feet wide, from the black rock. Below it dives into a thicket of mist-shrouded firs. It may be that one of the four rivers of Eden entered the garden in this wise, and that this is the river named Pison, which "compasseth the whole land of Havilah, where there is bdellium and the onyx stone." By the narrow gap at the end of the gorge the first two wondering folk may have been driven out of the garden.

In the way through the valley there is always the contrast between the soft meadows of flowers and the stern, terrific walls which stand guard over them. One precipice, called El Capitan, rises perpendicularly to the height of nearly three-fourths of a

THE YOSEMITE VALLEY.

mile, a pearl-grey battlement, bare as an iceberg, with winter on its summit as a drift of snow, and with summer at its foot in the guise of opening ferns.

Into the glen project enormous bastions of rock, half a mile high, like buttresses of a rampart, or great capes along a coast of precipices. A quarter of a mile up the face of a bald cliff there may be a ledge—apparently an inch in width—on which are three old pine trees looking like blades of grass. There are ravines and chasms, immense slopes of pigeon-blue stones, slopes also where the green of the valley climbs up the height like moss, only the moss is a forest of ancient oaks. There are rocks with splinters, many hundreds of feet high, like cathedral spires, heights crowned by round spheres of granite like temple domes.

At the far end the valley closes mysteriously. It bends sharply behind a buttress and is lost to view. Here it is that the wall of the great fosse had a drop of nearly a mile, and here it is that the landscape is reduced to primeval elements—bare granite and blue sky.

On the floor of the valley, besides the water meadows and the great river, the flowers and the bracken, are rapids tearing through savage glens, islands that cling to the half-drowned stones of foaming streams, pathways in woods and Devonshire lanes, a tiny hamlet and the smoke of camps.

On every side waterfalls tumble over the brink of the great scarp into the gorge. The most wonderful of these is the Yosemite Fall, where a pale river, from thirty to forty feet wide, drops over a nude cliff. It appears to come from the heavens, for it takes its leap from the skyline. It falls vertically a quarter of a mile—a wild, howling column of frenzied water. It drops into a black pit from which rises ever a steam as from an infernal cauldron. There breaks from it a terrific roar which is startled by the crashing of iceblocks and by hollow, cracking sounds like the rattle of artillery in a cavern. To conceive of the magnitude of this white column, imagine the Avon falling from the top of the Eiffel Tower on to the pavement below. Then pile upon its summit another Eiffel Tower, but four hundred feet less than the first, and let the river leap from the higher pinnacle down into the roadway. In such wise some idea can be gained of this sheer torrent. This, however, is only one step of the fall. There are two others below, each of which is three times the height of Niagara, for the drop of the Yosemite from the rock ridge among the snows to the trees at the cliff's foot is but little less than half a mile.

On the way to this valley is the famous Grove of Big Trees. America is the country of great things, but among its gigantic products the "sequoia gigantea" of California is not the least marvellous. A tree twice the height and twice the diameter of the Colonne Vendôme is difficult to realise, but there are many scores of them. It is not their size, however, which is their most impressive feature. It is rather, as Mr. Muir points out, the fact that they are the oldest living things on the face of the earth. "The Big Tree cannot be said to attain anything like prime size and beauty before its fifteenth hundredth year, or, under favourable circumstances, become old before its three thousandth."* The world that lived when they came into being has wholly perished, and these sequoia alone remain.

It is in accord with the spirit of the times that these solitary survivors of the great past should be usefully employed as advertisements, and should be introduced to the modern world through the medium of a trade mark.

* "Our National Parks," by John Muir. Boston, 1903, p. 275.

IN THE BIG TREE GROVE, CALIFORNIA.

III.

THE SCENE OF THE END OF THE WORLD.

In Arizona is a flat, arid, man-deserted plateau which is so vast that it covers nearly 100,000 square miles. On the shrivelled surface of this uplifted waste is a chasm—a stupendous crack in the earth. It is 217 miles in length, some 12 miles wide, and its walls, which are nearly vertical, are a mile in depth. At the bottom of this fearful abyss runs the Colorado River. This same Colorado is "one of the great rivers of North America. Formed in Southern Utah by the confluence of the Green and Grand, it intersects the north-western corner of Arizona, and, becoming the eastern boundary of Nevada and California, flows southward until it reaches tidewater in the Gulf of California, Mexico. It drains a territory of 300,000 square miles, and, traced back to the rise of its principal source, is 2,000 miles long."*

This riverway is called the Grand Canyon of Arizona, and is claimed to provide "the most sublime spectacle of the Earth."

Among the many conceptions which have been formed of the circumstances which shall attend the end of the world is one which imagines that life shall gradually vanish from the face of the globe, grade by grade, the lower following the higher. Into the details of such an idea comes the supposition that the races of men would pass away, that the beasts of the field and the birds of the air would die in turn, and that a slower decay would fall upon the more gracious trees and flowers until the great world became a fruitless waste. On such a desert only the hardiest things that grow would linger, while, at the last, the dried-up earth itself would crack and crumble into nothingness. Any who incline to such a

* "The Titan of Chasms." Chicago, 1904, p. 3.

foretelling as this will find in the country of the Grand Canyon some realisation of what they have pictured in their fancies.

From a land of fields and prosperous villages, from a point not far distant from the vineyards and peach orchards of Los Angeles, the road crawls upwards on to the great table land. It is a miserable track, through a parched and dying country, which is grey with the burden of unnumbered years. The earth has the pallor of cinders, and is strewn everywhere with a harvest of lean stones. The sickly grass is sapless and harsh. The few bushes are blanched of all colour; their branches are spidery and emaciated, their leaves rustle like shreds of dried skin. There are mummified shrubs which have still a semblance of life, and still bare their sterile tendrils to the unheeding air.

The only trees are firs and pines, but they are dwarfed and stunted, or are bent and deformed by drought and horrid winds. Many have died, for the dead are standing dead in hundreds. Their bare boughs rattle in the passing gust, like bones in a gibbet, while the skeletons of those that have fallen are stretched in every shadow upon the stones. Only the sturdiest things that have life have survived—the fir, the pine, the sage bush, and the outcast of the desert.

It may be that at one time, on this drear plateau, there were orchards and cornfields, meadows and the abodes of men. The place is now desolate and abandoned. The shrunken earth is waterless. There are signs of neither bird nor beast, and upon the table land has fallen the first hush of an eternal silence.

The country, indeed, that is traversed on the way to the Grand Canyon may well be a realisation of the last struggle for life on the face of the earth. If the ending of the world be slow, there must needs be a time when the once luxuriant country will come to look as wan and pitiable as this.

At the end of many miles of this Golgotha the traveller finds himself at a moment on the brink of an incredible chasm. He comes upon it suddenly and without warning. The whole expanse before him is as level as the sea—a limitless stretch of earth and stones and struggling pine trees. There is no shelving edge; no slope to the ravine. The chasm is a Titanic crack in the earth, with edges as sharp and as abrupt as a crack in an earthenware urn.

The first view of this undreamed-of abyss conveys, with dramatic suddenness, only a sense of the awful and the stupendous. Here is an unsuspected, clean-cut breach in the earth, so immense that it is impossible to realise that to the pines on the opposite side is a flight of ten miles, or that the drop to the bottom of the trench is a mile sheer.

It would seem that the rent is fresh, that the world has burst asunder but yesterday, for trees come to the very edge of the gap, the face of the fracture is raw rock, and this jagged cape that stands out from the side must have fitted—a day ago—into the wedge-shaped bay on the other brink, ten miles across.

The sight of this portentous trough is so astounding, so sublime, that all sense of distance or of proportion is lost. Here is a spot where the planet is riven in twain. Here is the scene of a terrific world-ending catastrophe. One expects to hear rumblings far down in the depths, or to see smoke and tongues of flame shoot up from the gulf; but the chasm is silent as death, and through its channel there sweeps a clear, untroubled air.

The view is not such as can be gained from a mountain top; it is a down-looking into a mile-deep gash in the earth, a peering into a well or into a terrific trench many leagues wide.

It is useless to attempt any comparison of its proportions. Since the Canyon is in places twenty miles across, one may imagine that the English Channel, between Dover and Calais, had become dry, that its floor had sunken almost out of sight, and that those who looked into the trough, from the brink of Dover cliff, would gaze down a wall from 5,000 to 6,000 feet deep.

This great fissure in a forlorn land may well be one of the rents in the crust of the world which shall herald its final rupture into fragments.

The chasm is in vivid contrast to the drab level on either side of it, for it is a gulf of colour. Its walls and its floor are red—brick-red where the sunlight falls, claret-red in the shadows—a glowing channel of fervent tints, whose slopes and cuttings and piles of riven stone appear to be red hot.

It is no mere depth of wall and gulley. The floor of the Grand Canyon presents a gigantic sunken landscape, in which are rugged mountains, boding cliffs, fathomless ravines, and level plains. Hills of rock rise out of the abyss, peak after peak, and spire upon spire. There are prodigious coves and gulches. There are black pits miles in width, like counter-sunk mountains, and in such Titanic moulds Alps might have been cast.

The earth seems to have been cracked by fire, and these masses of rent and tumbled rock may have been plucked out of its depths by bursting heat and be still aglow.

Red is the prevailing colour of the Canyon, but it is not the only one. There is, in this underworld landscape, every tint of garnet, orange, and rose. There are the colours of the Alpenglow, the colours of the dawn; a cliff of Pompeian red, a plateau of brimstone yellow and copperas green, with a lavender shadow on it a mile in length. At one place is a blue-grey gorge, called Bright Angel Canyon, in which is a sapphire stream with an edge of emerald on either side of it.

The very bottom of the chasm can only be seen at rare spots. Elsewhere the remotest floor of the gorge is a ragged fissure in black rocks, where, far down in the sunless hollows of the sinister cleft, the mysterious river roars on its way.

On closer viewing of this ghostly landscape there is some suggestion of artificiality about it. The strata are horizontal, and the great torn masses of red rock look like colossal ruins of heaped-up brick with broken edges. The whole Canyon is a labyrinth of tumbled masonry. Here are, it would seem, the ruins of huge pyramids, ten miles square, rising from a slope made up of the dust of ages. Here are fractured battlements, roofless subterranean passages, cellars that would hold a city, great stairs with steps three hundred feet high, and level terraces on which an army could be marshalled.

There are wall sculptures of incredible proportions, curved mounds of stones, which might have borne aloft some fearsome amphitheatre, or which may mark the ruins of cirques and cloisters of a girth beyond the imagination of man. There are fragments of castles and of majestic temples, as well as towering masses of brick-like rock, which stand in rows as if they were the plinths and pediments of cloud-reaching pillars.

Viewed in this wise it would seem that the mighty Canyon presents an allegory of the Foundations of the World which have been laid bare as the great planet became rent and shaken ere it crumbled into space.

Far down, on a cliff side, are certain holes, such as sand-martins make in the wall of a quarry. They say that they belong to men of the Stone Age, and that they are many thousands of years old. On the other hand, they may be imagined to be the habitations of the very last human beings who eked out a vanishing life upon the surface of the earth.

Seven days across the sea and the dawn breaks upon the white cliffs of England, upon the still twinkling spark in the lighthouse on the Needles, upon the gentle downs above Freshwater, and the still slumbering village of Yarmouth, with its grey fort, its old red roofs, and its guardian company of homely trees.

Here is a land of kindly-tended fields and of hedges trim with the care of centuries, a country with all the graciousness of a pleasure garden and all the dignity of an ancient husbandry, a modest and comfortable country without the uneasy exuberance of the tropics, or the homelessness of the unbounded Indian plain.

Across an upland creeps a soft, white cloud of sheep, in place of the herd of lean kine who prowl the dust of the Great Peninsula; along the beach the languid palm has changed into the sturdy English oak; a bell rings out from an ivied tower, and the sound of the Buddhist temple gong is forgotten, while dancing over the sea, instead of the sampan, is a Portsmouth wherry.

"God gave all men all earth to love,
But since our hearts are small,
Ordained for each one spot should prove
Beloved over all."

THE END.

INDEX